Knowledge-Based Systems
for Multiple Environments

Knowledge-Based Systems
for Multiple Environments

L.J. Kohout, J. Anderson
and W. Bandler

*a*SHGATE

© L.J. Kohout, J. Anderson, W. Bandler 1992

All rights reserved. No part of this publication may be reproduced, stored in a retrieval system, or transmitted in any form or by any means, electronic, mechanical, photocopying, recording, or otherwise without the prior permission of the publisher.

Published by Ashgate
Ashgate Publishing Limited
Gower House
Croft Road
Aldershot
Hants
GU11 3HR
England

Ashgate Publishing Company
Old Post Road
Brookfield
Vermont 05036
USA

A CIP catalogue record for this book is available from the British Library and the US Library of Congress.

ISBN 1 85742 063 2

Printed in Great Britain by
Billing & Sons Ltd, Worcester

TABLE OF CONTENTS

PART I MULTIPLE ENVIRONMENTS AND MULTIPLE CONTEXTS IN KNOWLEDGE ENGINEERING

CHAPTER 1 3
Introducing Multi-environmental and Multi-Context Knowledge-Based Systems: A New Approach

1.1. Why Multiple Environments? 3
1.2. What is a Multi-environmental Knowledge-based System? 5
1.3. Multi-environments in Non-medical Knowledge Domain 7
1.4. What is Multi-context and Why Should It Be Introduced? 8
1.5. The Need for a Multi-environmental Design Approach 9
1.6. Three Essential Features of Multi-environmental Knowledge- ... 10
    based Systems: Acceptability, Reliability and Protectability
1.7. Multi-environmental Reliability of Knowledge 12
1.8. Testing Knowledge Structures: Their Multi-context Acceptability. ... 13
    and Multi-environmental Reliability
1.9. References 14

CHAPTER 2 17
What is a Multiple Environment and How Does It Affect The Function of a Knowledge-based System?

2.1. Introduction 17
2.2. Expert System Shells 18
2.3. Multi-environment Medical Aspects 21
2.4. Dissimilar Components of Medical Environments 23
2.5. The Main Aspects of the Multi-environmental Problem 25
2.6. References 27

CHAPTER 3 29
A Framework for Transfer of Expert Systems Between Environments

3.1. Systemic Orientations 29
3.2. Engineering and Technical Orientations 32
3.3. Transfer—A Key Problem of Multi-environmental Knowledge ... 33
    Engineering
3.4. Systematicity of Expert Systems 33
3.5. A Relational View of Expert Systems 34
3.6. Paradigmatic Aspects 35
3.7. Summary 36
3.8. References 36

v

CHAPTER 4 . . . . **39**
Impact of Multiple Environments on the Functioning of Medical and Other Knowledge-Based Systems

4.1. Introduction 40
4.2. Historical Perspectives in the Development of Multiple Medical Environments . . . 42
4.3. Shared Environments 45
4.4. Impact of Multiple Environments in Health Care 46
4.5. Support and Record Systems 47
4.6. Transfer of Constructs to Other Fields 48
4.7. Conclusions 50
4.8. REFERENCES 51

CHAPTER 5 . . . . **53**
Activity Structures: A Methodology for Design of Multi-environment and Multi-context Knowledge-based Systems

5.1. What are Activity Structures? 54
5.2. Activity Structures as a Tool for Analysis and Synthesis of Information Processing Machines . . . 55
5.3. Towards a Design of a Reliable, Correct, Robust and User-friendly Multi-Environmental Computing System . . . 61
5.4. Analysis and Evaluation of Information Processing Machines by Means of Activity Structures . . . 69
5.5. Knowledge Identification, Elicitation and Representation 72
5.6. Realisation of Substratum Structures by Means of Virtual Machines . . . 75
5.7. Functional Refinements of Activity Structures 77
5.8. General Systems Constructs in Activity Structures Approach 80
5.9. References 84

PART II METHODS OF KNOWLEDGE ELICITATION

CHAPTER 6 . . . . **91**
Knowledge Elicitation – An Exercise in Identification and Verification of Expert Knowledge

6.1. Introduction 92
6.2. Problems in Knowledge Elicitation 94
6.3. Expertise and the Expert 96
6.4. Expertise and Knowledge Elicitation 97
6.5. Methods of Knowledge Elicitation 98
6.6. Results of a Medical Case Study 100
6.7. Summary 102
6.8. References 102

CHAPTER 7 105
Knowledge Elicitation – The First Step Towards the Construction of Expert Systems: The outline of a Method

7.1. Introduction 106
7.2. Is the Human Expert an Essential Component? 106
7.3. An Overview of a Complete Construction Process 107
7.4. Analysis of Knowledge Structures 109
7.5. The Main Results of a Knowledge Elicitation Experiment 112
7.6. Knowledge Elicitation: The First Step Towards Construction of . . . 118
   Expert Systems
7.7. References 120

CHAPTER 8 123
Linking Argumentative Discourse with Formal Evaluation Procedures in Design

8.1. The Problem: The Proper Basis for Decisions 125
8.2. Preliminaries: procedural building blocks 127
8.3. Interface Points Between the Argumentative Process and . . . 146
   Evaluation
8.4. A Procedure for Decision-making Through Systematic . . . 152
   Argument Evaluation
8.5. Conclusion 155
8.6. References 161

CHAPTER 9 165
Problems of Knowledge Elicitation in Insurance

9.1. Introduction 165
9.2. Knowledge Elicitation 166
9.3. Concepts and Terminology in Insurance 166
9.4. Context in Insurance 167
9.5. Bounds to Contexts 168
9.6. Questioning Strategy 168
9.7. Conclusions 169
9.8. References 170

PART III DESIGN OF KNOWLEDGE-BASED SYSTEMS AND ROBOTS FOR MULTI-ENVIRONMENTAL SITUATIONS

CHAPTER 10 173
An Overview of Clinaid

10.1. Generic Specification of Medical Knowledge-based Decision . . . 174
   Support System Clinaid

    10.2. An Overview of Functions of Clinaid and Specification of Its Activities . . . 177

    10.3. The Role of Activity Structures in the Design of Clinaid 179

    10.4. The Global Description of the Activity Structure of Clinaid 181

    10.5. Multi-context Fuzzy Inference of Clinaid 190

    10.6. Formalization of Clinical Management Activities 195

    10.7. Time and Context in Decision Planning 197

    10.8. References 198

CHAPTER 11   203
Design of Questioning Strategies for Knowledge-based Systems

    11.1. Expert System Needs a Questioning Strategy 203

    11.2. The Basic Concepts of the Questioning Strategy 204

    11.3. Questioning Strategies in Fuzzy Knowledge-based Systems 205

    11.4. Realisation of a Questioning Strategy in Clinaid 206

    11.5. Effective Questioning Strategies for a Multi-environmental Situation . . . 208

    11.6. Conclusion 211

    11.7. References 213

CHAPTER 12   215
Concurrency in Clinaid

    12.1. Requirement for Concurrency 215

    12.2. Blackboards and Whiteboards 216

    12.3. Two Substratum Structures to Support Concurrency 218

    12.4. Functional Structures and Concurrency 223

    12.5. Summary 224

    12.6. References 225

CHAPTER 13   227
Distributed Architectures for Computer Aided Manufacturing (CAM) and Other Embedded Robotic Systems

    13.1. Introduction 228

    13.2. The Structure of the Reconfigurable Architectural Modules of a Multi-Environmental System Shell . . . 228

    13.3. Methods for Embedding Knowledge into the Empty Shells of Active Multi-Environmental Systems . . . 231

    13.4. Skeleton Knowledge Structures of a Knowledge-based System Employing Deep Knowledge . . . 234

    13.5. A Multi-environmental Robotic System 237

13.6. Basic Characteristics of Functional Environmental Activity Structures for Directing a Computer-assisted Manufacturing Process	238
13.7. References	240

CHAPTER 14 — 245
Towards a Design of a Real-time Adaptive Robot for Multiple Environments: Part I - Basic Design and the First Experiments

14.1. Introduction	246
14.2. A Blueprint for the Design of an Adaptive Real-time Mobile System for a Multi-environmental Situation	246
14.3. Initial Selection Criteria for the Robot Hardware	253
14.4. The First Set of Experiments	254
14.5. The Second Set of Experiments	258
14.6. Consequences of the Experiments for the Design Blueprint of a Multi-environmental Robot	259
14.7. Computer Simulation of Real Environments	260
14.8. Appendix	262
14.9. References	263

CHAPTER 15 — 267
The Design of the House as a System in Multi-environmental Space

15.1. Introduction	268
15.2. The Idea of the House	269
15.3. The "Aspatial Structure"	271
15.4. Environment and Meaning	273
15.5. Context and Meaning	274
15.6. Multi-environments	275
15.7. The Ensemble: Is Symbolic Design Possible?	276
15.8. References	278

PART IV METHOD FOR DESIGN VALIDATION OF MULTI-ENVIRONMENTAL KNOWLEDGE-BASED SYSTEMS

CHAPTER 16 — 283
The Use of Fuzzy Relational Products in Comparison and Verification of Correctness of Knowledge Structures

16.1. Introduction	284
16.2. Sources of Endocrine Medical Knowledge	284
16.3. TRISYS – The Automatic Processing Package	289
16.4. Semantic Meaning of Relational Products	290

16.5. Criteria for Selecting the Appropriate Implication Operators 296
16.6. The Comparison and Evaluation of the Endocrine Knowledge . . . 320
   Structures by Means of the Appropriate Implication Operators
16.7. Substratum Classification of Endocrine Knowledge Structures 328
16.8. ACKNOWLEDGMENT 329
16.9. References 332

CHAPTER 17 . . . . **335**
Development of the Support Tools and Methodology for Design and Validation of Multi-environmental Computer Architectures

17.1. The Role of Activity Structures in the Design and . . . 336
   Performance Evaluation of Multi-environmental Architectures
17.2. The Objectives of Our Approach 337
17.3. Possibilistic Design Process 339
17.4. A Tool for Possibilistic Design of Multi-environmental Well- . . . 341
   protected Computer Architectures
17.5. Describing the Activities of the Possibilistic Simulator by . . . 350
   Means of Activity Structures
17.6. References 353

PART V EPILOGUE

CHAPTER 18 . . . . **359**
Knowledge as a Confidential Marketable Commodity: Cultural Danger or Economic Blessing?

18.1. Introduction 360
18.2. Knowledge as a Marketable Commodity 361
18.3. Structure of the Knowledge-based System 364
18.4. The Distinction Between Surface Knowledge and Deep . . . 365
   Knowledge
18.5. The Distinction Between Basic and Purpose-oriented Knowledge . . . 366
18.6. Consequences of the Withdrawal of Knowledge From Open . . . 367
   Circulation
18.7. Knowledge Structures Within the Context of a Culture 371
18.8. Conclusion: The Need for Technological Artefacts Capable of . . . 374
   Adapting to the Dynamic Changes of the Environment
18.9. References 375
SUBJECT INDEX **379**

ABOUT THE EDITORS

Ladislav J. Kohout is Professor of Computer Science at Florida State University. The innovative methodology in his recent book, "Pespectives on Intelligent Systems: A Framework for Analysis and Design", has provided the unifying conceptual structure of the present volume. Professor Kohout is the U.S. editor of the *Journal of Intelligent Systems*. In 1988 Professor Kohout received an international prize from the Systems Research Foundation, 'Outstanding Scholarly Contribution Award,' for developing his Methodology of Activity Structures.

John Anderson is Professor Emeritus at Kings College School of Medicine and Dentistry in the University of London. He is Fellow of the British Computer Society (BCS), Fellow of the Royal Society of Medicine and Fellow of the Institute of Biology. Professor Anderson was founding editor of the International Journal *Medical Informatics – Informatique et Médecine* for many years. He is a Founding Member of AAMSI, an Americal Medical Systems Society and served for a number of years as the Chairman of the BCS specialist group on Medical Computing.

Wyllis Bandler is Professor of Computer Science at Florida State University, where he is a founding member of the *Institute for Cognitive Sciences* and the *Institute for Expert Systems and Robotics*. His research specializations include problems of Knowledge Representation and the Theory and Applications of Crisp and Fuzzy Relations, in particular Relational Methods for Knowledge-Based Systems. He is on the editorial board of the *International Journal of Approximate Reasoning*, and a Member of the Board of Directors of the *North-American Fuzzy Information Processing Society*.

LIST OF CONTRIBUTORS

John Anderson (editor)
King's College School of Medicine and Dentistry
University of London, England, U.K.

Wyllis Bandler (editor)
Department of Computer Science
and Institute for Cognitive Sciences
Florida State University Tallahassee, Florida 32306, U.S.A.

Ali Behrooz
Department of Computer Science
Middlesex Polytechnic (Hendon)
London, England, U.K.

Mohamed Ben-Ahmeida
Misurata Research Centre for Engineering Sciences
P.O. Box 668, Misurata, Libya
North Africa.

Farouk Dowlatshahi
Department of Electrical Engineering
Brunel University of West London
Uxbridge, Middx. England, U.K.

Song Gao
Department of Computer Science
Northern Jiaotong University
Beijing 1000 44, CHINA

Christopher C. Johnson
School of Computing Sciences
University of Technology Sydney
Broadway Campus
Broadway NSW, Australia

Hasan Kalantar
Department of Computer Science
Middlesex Polytechnic (Hendon)
London, England, U.K.

Ladislav J. Kohout (editor)
Department of Computer Science
and
Institute for Expert Systems and Robotics
Florida State University Tallahassee, Florida 32306, U.S.A.

Garry Marshall
GEC
Hirst Research Center
Wembley, Middx. HA2 OJL
England, U.K.

Vasco Mancini
Architecture and Environments
Colchester, Essex, England, U.K.
and
Department of Computer Science
Florida State University Tallahassee, Florida 32306, U.S.A.

Thorbjoern Mann
School of Architecture
Florida A & M University
Tallahassee, Florida, U.S.A.

Sabah M.A.M Mohamad
Computer Science Department
College of Science
Saddam University, P.O.Box 47077, Al Jadiryiah
Baghdad, Iraq

Chris Trayner
Department of Physics
University of Essex
Colchester, Essex, England, U.K.

Stephanie Weisbauer
Boltzmann Institute for Social Gerontology
University of Vienna
Vienna, Austria

PREFACE

This book identifies the problems facing the designer of multi-environmental knowledge-based systems, and explains the principles which must be followed to obtain successful results.

Systems based upon knowledge—whether they are computer systems or not—are increasingly called upon in the modern world to function in a variety of widely differing environments. Even the best present-day knowledge-based systems, however, display often fatal flaws when the environment in which they are used alters even slightly. The need for software deliberately constructed for multi-environmental use is being felt ever more widely, and will be increasingly demanded in fifth (and sixth) generation machines. Such systems must be able to perform satisfactorily over a wide band of varying environments, whether these arise because of the individual or cultural diversity of users or their changing circumstances, or because of the rapid progress of the technology upon which the knowledge of the system is based.

This volume is the first full-scale discussion of such systems, the requirements they must meet, and the methodology for designing and evaluating them. While primarily aimed at workers in Artificial Intelligence and Expert Systems, as well as the producers of other kinds of sophisticated software, the content of the book is of wider validity, just as the multi-environmental demands are of wider incidence. It will also be of great interest to:

Serious designers of software with a large and variable knowledge component.

Builders of systems for use in the Third World that would match carefully the local environmental, cultural and economic conditions of each particular developing country.

Planners, designers and prospective users of systems intended to withstand the effect of technology transfer.

Builders of computer design tools, and in general,

Designers of extended expert database systems or other ambitious knowledge-based systems.

The book can also be used as the second text in a number of courses in knowledge engineering, expert systems and applied AI. Not only departments of computer science and electrical engineering, but also other department such as psychology, business administration, and indeed those in any branch of science and engineering offering graduate courses and pursuing research in expert systems, need to have the know-how of what pitfalls to avoid when building an expert system using a commercially available shell. The methods of efficient knowledge elicitation, and techniques for the verification of elicited knowledge structures offered in our book are of crucial importance in this context.

The book divides into five parts:

1) Multiple Environments and Multiple Contexts in Knowledge Engineering,
2) Methods of Knowledge Elicitation,

3) Design of Knowledge-Based Systems and Robots for Multi-Environmental Situations,

4) Methods for Design Validation of Multi-Environmental Systems,

5) Epilogue on knowledge in present-day society.

The first part deals in some detail with the reasons why the multi-environmental approach is needed, and with some of the areas in which it is most called for. The second part goes more deeply than is usual into the crucial questions of determining the relevance of knowledge for a proposed system and methods for finding its essential structures. These are absolute prerequisites to the design of knowledge acquisition systems, which in our view cannot be general-purpose, but must be closely keyed to the appropriate domain and to the purpose of the ultimate system.

This leads naturally to the third part, which illustrates with successful examples the general principles for synthesis of actual systems able to distinguish contexts and therefore to perform specific functions in a variety of environments.

All such systems require careful validation, and the fourth part of the book discusses the special requirements which are needed for multi-environmental, multi-context systems. Emphasis is placed on the discovering of hidden differences in knowledge structures and on early checking of the dynamic match between the system architecture and the environments, prior to embarking on actual construction.

The fifth part, the epilogue, is a somewhat controversial consideration of economic aspects of knowledge in the contemporary world, especially of the cyclical effects of commercial confidentiality upon flexibility of knowledge and even upon its correctness.

Unlike most edited collections, this one began with a careful outline of the main subdivisions of its theme, after which the individual chapters were commissioned from a group of researchers of quite diversified background who had deeply explored their subjects. The participants in this group had a unique opportunity to work together on the development of the multi-environmental theme for several years. The present book is the result of their fruitful collaboration. In writing this book, each topic was covered in close connection with others, so as to form a coherent whole. Every section and chapter is preceeded by an editorial introduction clarifying its place in the scheme and summarising its contribution. Locating specific aspects and following cross-currents of the ideas is thus facilitated.

While primarily aimed at workers in Artificial Intelligence and Knowledge Engineering, as well as the producers of other kinds of sophisticated software, the content of the book is of wider validity, just as the multi-environmental demands are of wider incidence. We hope that our contribution will facilitate the efforts for a better match between technologies and natural as well as cultural environments, thus improving the overall quality of human life.

L.J. Kohout, J. Anderson and W. Bandler

Tallahassee, Florida, USA
and
London, England, UK

March, 1991

PART I

MULTIPLE ENVIRONMENTS AND MULTIPLE CONTEXTS IN KNOWLEDGE ENGINEERING

Editorial Comments:

For the first time we raise in detail the topic of multi-environmental systems. We have organised the structure of exploration so that the first section of the book clarifies when and why this approach is needed. After investigating in detail actual problems in the first 4 chapters, a unified framework and methodology is proposed.

PART 1

MULTIPLE ENVIRONMENTS AND MULTIPLE CONTEXTS IN WILDLIFE TOXICITY

CHAPTER 1

INTRODUCING MULTI-ENVIRONMENTAL AND MULTI-CONTEXT KNOWLEDGE-BASED SYSTEMS: A NEW APPROACH

M. BEN-AHMEIDA AND L.J. KOHOUT

Editorial Comment:

> Outlined here is the basic case for multi-environmental systems. This should be read first as it carries the basic motif for the book.

LIST OF CONTENTS

1.1 WHY MULTIPLE ENVIRONMENTS?
1.2 WHAT IS A MULTI-ENVIRONMENTAL KNOWLEDGE-BASED SYSTEM?
1.3 MULTI-ENVIRONMENTS IN NON-MEDICAL KNOWLEDGE DOMAIN
1.4 WHAT IS MULTI-CONTEXT AND WHY SHOULD IT BE INTRODUCED?
1.5 THE NEED FOR A MULTI-ENVIRONMENTAL DESIGN APPROACH
1.6 THREE ESSENTIAL FEATURES OF MULTI-ENVIRONMENTAL KNOWLEDGE
1.7 MULTI-ENVIRONMENTAL RELIABILITY OF KNOWLEDGE-BASED SYSTEMS
1.8 TESTING KNOWLEDGE STRUCTURES: Their Multi-Context and Acceptability and Multi-Environmental Reliability
1.9 REFERENCES

1.1. WHY MULTIPLE ENVIRONMENTS?

Within the artificial intelligence general framework, a new field called expert systems has appeared and attracted much interest over the last two decades. These computer programs have two fundamental characteristics that set them apart from conventional programming style. Firstly, an expert system is designed to perform a task usually requiring expertise of some domain, such as medical diagnosis, medical therapy, fault diagnosis. Secondly, the method applied to develop the system is to acquire and codify the knowledge used by human experts in a particular domain.

Knowledge-Based Systems for Multiple Environments

Although expert systems have became to play a role in practical applications and are receiving currently large publicity, their use is restricted to very narrow knowledge domains, where these have been very successful. Their successful application remains problematic in the areas

a) where the knowledge of the domain is changing rapidly

b) where the knowledge domain is complex, with multiplicity of contexts

c) when the system is likely to be transferred from one to another environment.

This is demonstrated particularly vividly in medicine. In the medical field, expert systems have received much attention from both, computer and medical specialists in the last few years. As a result, a considerable variety of medical expert systems has been developed for diagnosing and recommending treatment of diseases. Although many of such systems have been developed for a restricted medical domain, very few are used in a real medical environment. Horn et al. (1985) points out that

> ... the last two decades have seen the development of a large number of medical expert systems such as CASNET (Weiss and Kulikowski, 1979), INTERNIST (Pople and Mayers 1982), MYCIN (Shortliffe 1976). Most of these systems have been shown to perform at the level of their domain experts. Despite the impressive performance very few systems have appeared in "real world" applications.

This inadequacy of the current medical expert systems is caused by the fact that each of these systems has been developed for a restricted medical domain to match a specific medical environment and ignoring the multiplicity of contexts of the medical domain. Moreover, the same applies also to the expert systems dealing with other knowledge domains. The possibility of transferring medical systems to other medical environments is very limited. Medical environments, from one part of the country to another, and from one country to another, are different. These differences which prevent the transferability of such system to other medical environments in general and of medical environments in developing countries in particular, may be traced to several sources, some of which have to do with the nature of real life situations, others have to do with the accessibility and reliability of medical knowledge sources and with availability of computing facilities, as well as the incompatibility of the existing design methodologies to match the requirements of designing medical expert systems for a multi-environment situation. In order to deal adequately with these problems, we have to introduce multi-environments and multiple context into all the stages of construction of expert and knowledge-based systems.

1.2. WHAT IS A MULTI-ENVIRONMENTAL KNOWLEDGE-BASED SYSTEM?

What is understood by the term "multi-environmental situation" can be best demonstrated by an example from the medical domain. We shall see later, that the multi-environmental situation appears also in other domains, such as insurance underwriting, process control and robotics. But we shall discuss the medical example, which does not require specialist knowledge, first.

The term "medical environment" in our example covers the hospital users, such as consultants, physicians, nurses, technicians, patients and their activities. In the activity structure terminologies (see Chapter 5), this term includes participants, actions and properties of both.

In looking at the activity of the medical diagnosis and decision support using human experts, we can see that the expert specialist is helping a physician by means of his expertise to deal with a particular medical environment. When the medical expert is transferred to a new medical environment in another part of the country or another country, he has to capture the expertise of the other medical environment which is different from the expertise that the expert already has. Since expert performance can involve a combination of skill of rapidly recognising complex patterns in the environment, skill in interactive behaviour, skill in problem solving, and decision making skills, the characteristics of these skills may change with this transfer (Schvaneveldt et al., 1985).

This can be represented by the diagram of Figure 1.1. If the medical expert is transferred from medical environment (a) to (b), he has to capture the expertise of part (e) of the medical environment (b), where (d) is the overlap between both environments (the part of expertise which is similar in both (a) and (b). This overlap depends on the differences and similarities of the environments involved. For example, the overlap of expertise between two medical environments in England is much bigger than the overlap between a medical environment in England and in North Africa.

To make the so far rather vague notion of multi-environmental situation clear and more precise, we have to define what a multi-environment expert, and an multi-environment knowledge-based system are.

(i) **Definition:** A multi-environment expert is an expert with expertise of a particular knowledge domain who has the additional expertise of using his knowledge in more than one environment.
(ii) **Definition:** A multi-environment knowledge-based system is a knowledge-based system which is modifiable in such a way that it can be used in more than one environment.

In spite of the widespread interest in medical expert systems, very little has been written about the modifiability and multi-environmental usability of these systems. It will be seen later that in many situations, medical expert systems need to be designed to match more than one environment.

Referring to our Figure 1.1, if the medical expert system is to be used in two medical environments (a) and (b), the expertise of both environments has to be captured.

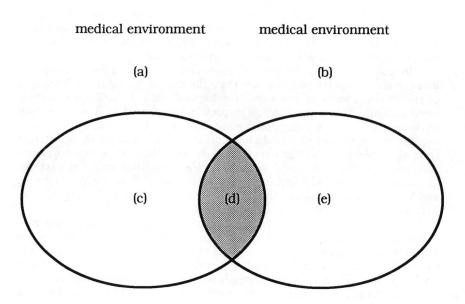

Figure 1.1. The overlap of two medical environments

1.3. MULTI-ENVIRONMENTS IN NON-MEDICAL KNOWLEDGE DOMAIN

The problem with transfer of a designed technological artefact from one to another environment also appears in Architecture. Below we provide a simple real live example from the architectural engineering field to point out the importance of capturing the knowledge about other environments in which the architect will design the buildings. The example follows:

Twenty five years ago or so, large buildings such as schools in some North African countries had been designed by western architect engineers who had never been in these countries, and knew very little about them. The buildings were inappropriate, and raised many problems with the necessity of expensive modification and readjustment. One example of many wrong features for instance, were the large glass windows which were completely unsuitable because of the high temperature increases during the day, and sunny days almost all year round.

It has been stated in this field that to design a building for more than one environment, architect engineers have to consider the following key points:

1) Acceptability of the building by different types of users.
2) Reliability of the building from the functional and the foundations point of view.
3) Protectability against misuse and undesirable activities.

We can see that the concepts of a structure and function (cf. Kohout, 1987) play important role here. The above is applicable also to the area of designing multi-environment medical expert systems, or indeed to the design of any multi-environment knowledge-based systems. An interesting comparison between the architect's approach to the design of building and the Activity Structures approach of Kohout, for designing knowledge-based systems was done by Mancini (1986). The following quotation points out the correspondence in his view, to the analogous terms in Kohout's approach:

> There is a correspondence between system architecture and aspatial structure. The identification of the structure of the system's function the functional structure, can be arrived at, in similar fashion through the activity structure. Conversely, the embodiment of the functional structure into a particular substratum structure, say the various modules of a set of computer programs, corresponds to the designing of the spatial structures in the built environment.

In a knowledge-based system for computer-aided manufacturing, each environment corresponds to a different industrial or manufacturing process to be controlled. In robotics, again, each modality of the robot's activity represents a separate environment and is also executed in a multiplicity of contexts.

KNOWLEDGE-BASED SYSTEMS FOR MULTIPLE ENVIRONMENTS

1.4. WHAT IS MULTI-CONTEXT AND WHY SHOULD IT BE INTRODUCED?

Multiple context is generated by those features of the knowledge structures *which cause* that not all knowledge and data are equally relevant under all circumstances. This, what can be called "locality of relevance" can be effected by the interaction of several environments, or by the complexity of the situation in which the knowledge is used.

Again, we shall discuss this looking at the medical domain. In current AI and expert systems literature and at the scientific conferences concerned with these, the medical domain is usually trivialised. It is reduced to matching symptoms and physical signs to diseases to obtain diagnosis. The systems reached similar diagnoses to those of experts and it was therefore concluded, that we have nothing to learn from the medical domain in knowledge engineering. Yet, the medical domain in its full complexity presents many adequate solutions to some knowledge engineering problems, and a large variety of challenging problems of considerable complexity and difficulty, from which expert systems designers and knowledge engineers can learn. For this reason, we start again with the discussion of the medical domain.

The process of clinical decision making is of considerable complexity. For example, medical diagnosis is the process by which the disease is identified. It is similar to the art of detection. First clue are the symptoms; which are usually pain or fever, a physical problem or general ill-health. Interviewing the patient is the way to find out about the problem in detail. After the patient symptoms are discussed, a good idea of the general nature of the problem may be identified to a fair degree. This will direct the questions towards what physical signs are noticed and then to the configuration of the diseases that seem most likely.

As the next step, new elements in addition to symptoms and signs are introduced. These are laboratory data, radiology findings etc. The new components that have to be taken into account involve not only the diagnostic system, but a physician, the hospital system and medical records. Basically, even with this addition, the diagnostic process is the same. The physician looks at other similar cases, and suggests diagnosis, but more information is available. Part of this information comes from patient's records such as medical history e.g. previous diseases, treatment, etc. Other information includes details of patient's conditions during hospitalisation such as blood pressure, laboratory tests, etc.

Medical scientists sometimes know exactly how a disease presents itself, and occasionally why the treatment for it works. Medical opinion about diseases is constantly changing and each change is the result of extensive research. Every patient has a different level of resistance to a disease according to the age, diet, heredity factors, culture, beliefs and previous illnesses. Because of these variations, it is very difficult to make any categorical statement about medicine and diseases.

The words 'possibly', 'sometimes', 'usually', 'occasionally', 'extremely', 'rarely', 'excessive', 'mild' and 'common' are often used by the patient describing his symptoms or by medical knowledge sources describing signs (see Chapter 16). This reflects in practice the fuzziness and uncertainty of information in medicine. This in turn leads to locality of inference and local relevance of terms (cf. Bellman and Zadeh, 1975; Kohout et al. 1987).

With all of these complicating factors it is perhaps surprising that physicians are ever able to make a diagnosis. Their ability to unravel the complexities and uncertainties of diseases is a skill learned through experience and many years of education and intensive training they undergo before qualification. This points out the importance of a medical consultant or expert with many years of experience in providing the essential help in the diagnosing process to physicians with lesser experience.

Examining the goals of the majority of current medical expert systems, we discover that these inadequately treat such a complex situation. They are usually involved in a narrow specialty field and a single context.

For example, AI/RHEUM medical expert system assists physician, in diagnosing connective tissue diseases of clinical rheumatology by applying formal diagnostic criteria obtained from experts in their particular speciality. The system uses patient symptoms, signs, and laboratory findings to provide assistance with several diseases.

Another example is MYCIN, one of the well-known medical expert systems which was developed at Stanford University in 1976. This system assists physicians in selecting suitable antimicrobial therapy for patients with bacterial infections. The system identifies the agent or at least the type of the agent causing the infection, It uses knowledge relating infecting organisms to patient history, symptoms, signs, and laboratory test results. Based on this identification, the system recommends drug treatment, apparently according to the procedures followed by the physicians experienced in infectious diseases therapy. The scope of other such systems can be seen in Table 1.1.

The Table 1.1 shows clearly the restricted medical domains and medical environments in which these systems are used. For example, Thyroid MODEL was designed to diagnose disorders of thyroid which is one of several organs of the endocrine body system.

In contrast to this, dealing with the full complexity of medical clinical decision making leads to inducing multiple contexts in the knowledge structures. This has been demonstrated elsewhere and is further discussed in Chapter 10 of this book.

1.5. THE NEED FOR A MULTI-ENVIRONMENTAL DESIGN APPROACH

As Hayes-Roth (1984), and Parker (1983) pointed out, the process of building an expert system may span several months and sometimes several years. Acquiring knowledge, a major task of developing this system is not performed all at once. Bobrow et al., (1986) stated that in the course of the expert system development, it is typical to expand and reformulate the knowledge base many times. One reason is that choosing the terminologies and ways of factoring the knowledge base is subject to so much experimentation.

Table 1.1. Summary of a few selected medical expert systems

Med.E.S.	DOMAIN	Devel. Place	State Reached
ANGY	Diag. the narrowing of coronary vessels	University of Pennsylvania	Demonstration prototype
CENTAUR	Diag. interpretation of pulmonary function	Stanford University	Research prototyping
Diagnoser	To identify heart disease	University of Minnesota	Research prototyping
GUIDON	Diagnose congenital heart dis. in children	Stanford University	Research prototyping
HEME	Diagnose hematologic disease	Cornell University	Field prototyping
MIDX	Diag. of the liver syndrome (cholesis)	Ohio State University	Research prototyping
Thyroid MODEL	Diagnose disorder of Thyroid	Rutgers University	Demonstration prototyping

In all these previous design approaches, rather typical of the whole expert systems field, the elicitation of knowledge is inadequately separated from the expert system engineering process. That the dynamics of knowledge elicitation is different from the dynamics of the evolution of the system being implemented was argued by Behrooz (1986). In the multi-environmental situation, this is complicated by the fact that even slight environmental changes lead to vast differences in the structure of the knowledge structures (cf. Chapter 16) of this volume).

Furthermore the multi-environmental knowledge-based system design places emphasis on the need to explore the fundamentals of the engineering design process by looking at the suitability of the existing design methodologies for building such system in multi-environment situation.

1.6. THREE ESSENTIAL FEATURES OF MULTI-ENVIRONMENTAL KNOWLEDGE-BASED SYSTEMS: ACCEPTABILITY, RELIABILITY AND PROTECTABILITY

In this section we shall define, and further discuss in greater detail, the three key factors by which multi-environmental knowledge-based systems should be evaluated, namely acceptability, reliability and protectability.

A knowledge-based system will match more than one environment only if some definite conditions of its transferability from one to another environment in the predetermined set of environments are satisfied. For this reason, the importance of the whole, and of each of the environments of the set cannot be overemphasised. The main design constraints predetermine whether and how the conditions of transferability can be fulfilled.

ACCEPTABILITY ultimately determines the users' satisfaction with the system in each environment. The following definition determines what acceptability is and how it can be measured.

Definition 1.6-1: *Acceptability within an environment*

1. Acceptability is defined as the degree of users' satisfaction with the system in a particular environment.
2. User satisfaction is qualitatively determined by the set of functional requirements.
3. The degree of users' satisfaction is quantitatively measured by the *degrees of containment* between the set of *intended* functional requirements and the set of *realised* functional requirements. These may be differently determined in each particular environment.

In practice, with multi-environmental knowledge based systems, a greater emphasis must be given to determining the nature of the activities that the system will supply. The system should communicate with the users of each environment in a way familiar and acceptable to them. The mechanism for acquainting the users of each environment with the facilities needed in that particular environment may differ from one environment to another.

The second important factor that determines the quality of a multi-environmental knowledge-based system is RELIABILITY. An unreliable system produces unacceptable errors which are originated by a diversity of sources. The error sources divide into two distinct categories, namely

a) Mistakes in the design.
b) Failures caused by the outer environment in regard to the other environments in the shell.

For example, part of the outer environment are climatic factors. In some African countries (cf. Ben-Ahmeida, 1987), these are characterised by a high temperature increase during the day, high absolute humidity, high percentage of dust in the air, etc. These determine the choice of the acceptable hardware for this particular environment, as well as the nature of the maintenance procedures of the system. Fluctuations in the voltage of the mains electricity supply is another important factor.

PROTECTABILITY is the third and final factor that has to be considered in the knowledge-based systems usability for multi-environment situations. By going back to our medical example, protectability means preventing access to classified information by unauthorised user accidentally or otherwise.

Generally all medical information is sensitive in any medical environment, but it is not equally sensitive in the same environment or from one environment to the other. All the intended users of each medical environment have the right to access the information but the authority is not the same.

This emphasises the need to distinguish the two major forms of accessibility as:

1- Access of classified information by classified groups of users.
2- Access of classified information by individual users.

In building knowledge-based systems for a multi-environment situation, protection aspects, therefore, have to be considered for the following reasons:

1- For each environment there are various desired levels of protection which vary from one environment to the other.
2- For each environment there are dynamic changing requirements of protection levels.

Referring to the medical environmental case study presented in Chapter 2 illustrates this. It has been shown that the distinctions between the medical, social, language and educational aspects of various medical environments are significant. In addition to the variation of these factors from one medical environment to the other, the dynamism of each factor in the intended medical environments has to be considered.

The above highlights the need for a total design methodology that can deal adequately with the protection aspects in addition to the other aspects of a multi-environment situation. **Activity Structures** provide such a methodology (cf. Kohout 1987, and Chapter 5 of this volume).

1.7. MULTI-ENVIRONMENTAL RELIABILITY OF KNOWLEDGE

In a knowledge-based system, knowledge is the fundamental part. This knowledge also ought to be reliable. That means, it must not contain errors and must be consistent. If this is not so, it may be caused either by mistakes in the design or failures caused by the outer environment. The latter may be caused either by an improper use of the knowledge base, or by the cultural or semantic mismatch between the users and the system knowledge in a particular environment. The inconsistency may be caused either by the mismatch of the system with the environment or by design mistakes, i.e. those caused by the faulty procedures during the knowledge elicitation process. This has substantial practical consequences, namely:

a) Knowledge must be represented as the domain expert meant it to be.
b) Users must get only what is relevant in a particular context and in a particular environment. This determines what we call usability and accessibility, respectively.

Our multi-environmental approach, however, is to adopt the activity structures terminologies by dealing with this knowledge reliability from both functional and substratum point of view before it is transferred to implementation stage. Here by the **substratum** point of view is meant the structure and the *interrelationships* of individual hardware and software modules. The **functional** point of view takes into account the *structural description of the behaviour* of these modules (Kohout 1987, and Chapter 5, section 5.2.2 of this volume).

Therefore, according to this distinction between the functional and substratum structures, the knowledge structures from the sources of the intended environments need to be compared, analysed, and evaluated. This evaluation should be done by examining the functional reliability aspects, as well as the factors that influence the technology (i.e. hardware), the substratum in which the knowledge is stored.

1.8. TESTING KNOWLEDGE STRUCTURES: THEIR MULTI-CONTEXT ACCEPTABILITY AND MULTI-ENVIRONMENTAL RELIABILITY

Medical knowledge is the essential major part involved in building a medical expert system. Hence, the medical knowledge from the sources of several medical environments needs to be analysed, compared, and evaluated before it is transferred to the system, in order to provide reliable and compatible medical knowledge structures for the construction of a multi-environmental medical expert system.

In order to be able to do this comparison and evaluation in the process of development of multi-environmental knowledge-based systems, we need suitable tools and techniques to perform the following:

1) Complexity analysis and syntax comparison of the knowledge structures from the selected sources.
2) Structural analysis and evaluation of the knowledge structures.
3) Utilization of suitable design methodology that can deal with the multi-environmental design problems.

Medical data need to be analysed in ways which present and illustrate dependencies and implications among its variables in order to select reliable medical diagnostic knowledge. Fuzzy logic provides mathematical techniques for analysing medical data allowing the revelation of dependences, hierachies and partial order in the data. Bandler and Kohout (1979) discussed the reasons for using fuzzy logic as a tool for the analysis of these types of data.

Fuzzy relational products (Bandler and Kohout 1986, 1988) together with the fast algorithms (Bander and Kohout 1982, 1988) for testing of relational properties, a tool developed by Bandler and Kohout (1979) is used to analyse and evaluate medical knowledge structures from different medical knowledge sources to point out and compare dependencies and hierarchies in their knowledge structures (Bandler and Kohout 1980b, 1986 and Chapter 16 of this volume). This methodology, which is based on the theory of fuzzy relations, provides a natural way of dealing with problems in which the source of the imprecision is the absence of sharply defined criteria of class membership rather than the presence of random variables (Bandler and Kohout 1980b).

By proposing a total design methodology approach (based on activity structures) which is compatible with the three points above, for designing multi-environment medical expert systems and using fast fuzzy relational algorithms to analyse their knowledge structures, we provide some means to deal with the problem of multi-environment knowledge-based systems analysis and construction.

1.9. REFERENCES

Bandler, W. and Kohout, L.J. (1979):
The use of new relational products in clinical modelling. In: Gaines, B.R. (ed.) *General Systems Research: A Science, a Methodology, a Technology* (Proc. 1979 North American Meeting of the Society for General Systems Research), SGSR, Louisville, Kentucky, U.S.A., 240–246.

Bandler, W. and Kohout, L.J. (1980a):
Semantics of implication operators and fuzzy relational products, International Journal of Man-Machine Studies, **12**, 89–116.

Bandler, W. and Kohout, L.J. (1980b):
Fuzzy relational products as a tool for analysis and synthesis of complex artificial and natural systems, in: Wang, P.P. and Chang, S.K. (eds.),*Fuzzy Sets: Theory and Applications to Policy Analysis and Information Systems*. Plenum Press, New York, 341–367.

Bandler, W. and Kohout, L.J. (1982):
Fast fuzzy relational algorithms. In: Ballester, A., Cardus, D. and Trillas, E. (eds.), *Proc. Second Internat. Conference on Mathematics at the Service of Man* (Las Palmas, Canary Islands, Spain, 28 June – 3 July 1982). Universidad Politechnica de las Palmas, 123–131.

Bandler, W. and Kohout, L.J. (1986):
A survey of fuzzy relational products in their applicability to medicine and clinical psychology. In: Kohout, L.J., and Bandler, W. (eds.) *Knowledge Representation in Medicine and Clinical Behavioural Science*, An Abacus Book, Gordon and Breach, London, 107–118.

Bandler, W. and Kohout, L.J. (1988):
Special properties, closures and interiors of crisp and fuzzy relations, *Fuzzy Sets and Systems*, **26**, 317–331.

Behrooz, A. (1986):
Meta Description of Experimental Identification of Medical Knowledge, Ph.D. Thesis, Department of Computer Science, Brunel University, U.K., August 1986.

Bellman, R. and Zadeh, L.,A. (1975):
Local and Fuzzy logics. In: Dunn, M. J. and Epstein, G. (eds.), *Modern Uses of Multiple-Valued Logic*. Reidel, Dordrecht, Holland, Boston, Mass. U.S.A., 105–165.

Ben-Ahmeida, M.,M. (1987):
A Study of the Design, Reliability and Knowledge Structures of a multi-environmental Medical Expert System, Ph.D Thesis, Department of Computer Science, Brunel University of West London, March 1987.

Bobrow, D. et al. (1986):
Expert systems: perils and promise, *Communications of ACM*, **29**, No.9.

Hayes-Roth, F. (1984):
The knowledge-based expert system: a tutorial. *Computer IEEE*, No. 9, 11–28; No. 10, October 1984, 263–273.

Horn, K.A., Compton, P., Lazarus, L. and Quinlan, J.R. (1985):
An expert system for the interpretation of thyroid assays in a clinical laboratory, *The Australian Computer Journal*, **17**, 7–11.

Kohout, L.J. (1987):
Activity structures: a general systems construct for design of technological artifacts, *Systems and Cybernetics: An International Journal*, **18**, 27–34.

Kohout, L.J.(1990):
A Perspective on Intelligent Systems: A Framework for Analysis and Design, Chapman and Hall, London; and Van Nostrand, New York.

Kohout, L.J., and Bandler, W., eds. (1986):
Knowledge Representation in Medicine and Clinical Behavioural Science, Abacus Books, Gordon and Breach, London.

Kohout, L.J., Behrooz, A., Anderson, J., Gao, S., Bandler, W. and Trayner, C. (1987):
Dynamics of localised inference and its embedding in activity structures based IKBS architectures. In: *Proc. of Second IFSA Congress*, International Fuzzy Systems Association, July 1987, 740–743.

Mancini, V. (1986):
An architect's view of system architecture. Paper presented at *Symposium on General Systems Constructs and Approximate Reasoning in Knowledge-Based Systems*, at the Third International Conference on Systems, Informatics and Cybernetics, Baden-Baden, West Germany, August 1986.

Parker, R. and Mokhoff, N. (1983):
An expert system for every office. *Computer Design*, Fall 1983, 37–46.

Pople, M. and Meyers (1982):
INTERNIST-1: An experimental computer based diagnostic consultant for general internal medicine. *The New England Journal of Medicine*, **301**, No.8, 468–476.

Schvaneveldt, R. W. et al. (1985):
Measuring the structure of expertise, *Int. J. of Man-Machine Studies*, **23**, 699–728.

Shortliffe, E.H. (1976):
Computer Medical Consultations: MYCIN, American Elsevier, New York.

Weiss, S. M., and C. A., Kulikowski (1979):
Expert: A system for developing consultation models. *Proceedings 6th Int. Joint Conf. on Artificial Intelligence*, 942–947.

CHAPTER 2

WHAT IS A MULTIPLE ENVIRONMENT AND HOW DOES IT AFFECT THE FUNCTION OF A KNOWLEDGE-BASED SYSTEM?

M. BEN-AHMEIDA AND L.J. KOHOUT

Editorial Comment:

> This shows concretely how multiple environments are interleaved in medical practice in a particular culture.

LIST OF CONTENTS
2.1 INTRODUCTION
2.2 EXPERT SYSTEM SHELLS
2.3 MULTI-ENVIRONMENT MEDICAL ASPECTS
    2.3.1 Hospital Staff Availability
    2.3.2 Patient Analysis
    2.3.3 Styles of Physician-Patient Interaction
2.4 DISSIMILAR COMPONENTS OF MEDICAL ENVIRONMENTS
    2.4.1 Language
    2.4.2 Culture
    2.4.3 Education and Beliefs
    2.4.4 Domestic Atmosphere
2.5 THE MAIN ASPECTS OF THE MULTI-ENVIRONMENTAL PROBLEM
2.6 REFERENCES

2.1. INTRODUCTION

In this chapter, we shall present a concrete example from one of the developing countries in North Africa in which we examine the essential aspects of a complex medical environment of a developing country. It will become obvious from our detailed discussion of this situation, that some particular features or characteristics of such an environment may prevent transferability of the current medical expert systems, which are designed without due attention to complex multi-cultural and multi-environmental situation, that occurs in such a complex medical environment.

Knowledge-Based Systems for Multiple Environments

This case study highlights the fact that medical environments vary from one country to another, or may vary even within the same country. In addition to possible differences in medical knowledge about diseases appearing between medical environments, some other differences may be caused, for example, by patient's life-style and by what we shall call the local domestic atmosphere. This may influence the appearance of symptoms and signs and therefore have an impact on the character of diseases. It will, also, influence the quality of patient-physician interaction because of impact on the perception of language, culture, patient's education and beliefs.

Not much is said in the current literature about the suitability of medical expert systems to operate in a multi-environment situation, indeed its existence is usually ignored. While tools have been developed which are called skeletal or shell systems such as EMYCIN (Van Melle et al., 1981), and Expert (Weiss et al., 1979), these systems which are thought to eliminate the necessity of rebuilding a medical expert system from scratch do need to take multi-environments into account.

Section 2.2, reviews some of the skeleton medical systems that are available and examines their usability in the multi-environment situation. The important aspects of medical multi-environments are demonstrated in section 2.3 by discussing in some detail a real medical environment. In section 2.4, the dissimilar components of medical environments are investigated. Section 2.5 presents the main aspects of the medical multi-environment problem and final discussion on the question whether or not the current medical expert system can be transferred to other medical environments.

2.2. EXPERT SYSTEM SHELLS

Skeleton or shell medical expert systems can provide help in building a new medical knowledge base. These shells do offer various facilities for defining data types and writing rules according to some specified sets of conventions; these must be related to an environment. This use of the shell in a different knowledge domain than that for which it was originally designed can be done because of the separation between the knowledge base and the inference engine (see Figure 2.1). This provides the possibility to detach the knowledge base of one domain and replace it with one for a different domain (Jackson, 1986; Miller 1986).

A number of systems have been built using various expert system shells. In medicine for example, PUFF expert system diagnosing respiratory ailments was developed, using those parts of MYCIN that were knowledge domain independent, such as the facilities supporting the rule based inference and the explanatory facilities. The domain specific rules of MYCIN were replaced by the rules pertinent to the diagnosis of respiratory diseases.

Generally, the designs of expert systems in various domains using the same supporting shell are based on the assumption that the dynamics of expert inference is environment and context independent, the difference between the various distinct knowledge domains being captured by the contents of the domain dependent rule base only. Moreover, in a shell it

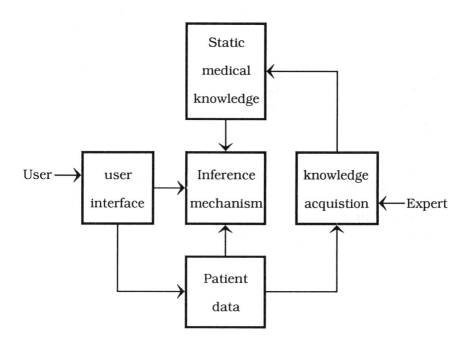

Figure 2.1. Architecture of the current medical expert system

is usually assumed that the process of substituting the rules by other rules for a different set of expert tasks is a relatively easy job in "real world" applications. Hayes-Roth (1984), however, highlights the difficulty of this process of substitution of the rules of one knowledge domain by the rules of another. He suggests that

> *Permitting the replacement of these rules by rules for a different task greatly simplifies the process of building an expert system for the second task, although in practice this process is rarely quite this simple.*

A few systems, however, have been built using these shells. The major advantage of using these shells is that the new system uses the available facilities of the original system. For instance, PUFF used the available facilities of MYCIN expert system, such as explanation features, etc. In a practical situation, however, it is doubtful whether these shells systems could be applied in any medical environment. Hayes-Roth (1984) points out the following problems which may arise in this context:

1. The old framework may be unsuitable to the new task. This is both the most likely and the most serious problem.
2. The control structure embodied in the inference engine may not sufficiently match the new expert's way of solving problems.
3. The old rule language may be not appropriate to the new task.
4. There may be task-specific knowledge hidden in the old system in unrecognised ways.

In addition to the above listed problems however, other problems appear. In medical multi-environment situations, the shell medical expert systems without specific domain knowledge, are very unlikely to be used for the following additional reasons:

1. The environment insensitive explanatory facilities are not adequate in a multi-environment situation, where the form and the contents of explanation crucially depends on the environment.
2. The shells are very expensive to buy in many medical environments, particularly in developing countries.
3. Most of these systems necessitate large computing facilities to run on. These facilities are not available in many medical environments of developing countries.

From what is said above it can be seen clearly that implementing medical expert systems using conventional shells that are currently available may not be the most appropriate way for building medical expert systems in a multi-environment situation at present. In the next section, we shall demonstrate the complexity of the multi-environment situation by examining the essential aspects of a real medical environment which have to be taken into account in building multi-environment medical expert systems. This will give the reader some appreciation of the difficulties that may occur.

2.3. MULTI-ENVIRONMENT MEDICAL ASPECTS

In this section we establish some important features of the multi-environmental problem of medical expert systems. This cannot be achieved in a concrete and easily understandable way without introducing a real example. We introduce an example that provides a good representation of the medical environments of developing countries that use the western medical system. If we want to introduce a completely different medical environment, the Chinese medical environment would be a good example, but the western medical framework does not fit the Chinese traditional medicine, and therefore we choose to present the concrete example from one of the North African countries. As an example of one of the developing countries, the Libyan medical environments are discussed here. It will be seen that this example demonstrates the features and characteristics of a multi-environment situation of considerable complexity.

Very few sources are available that adequately describe medical services in this country, therefore, most of our information has been collected by interviewing a number of local physicians with several years' experience, and from a direct experience with the health service. In this medical environment, all the hospitals and community Health Centres are supervised and supported completely by the Government. They are varying in size and in facilities according to population and geographical location. All patients, whatever their social class, their residencies, their nationalities, and whatever are the routes by which they have entered the hospital, are equivalent in receiving medical services in the same hospital.

Moreover, the facilities available, differ greatly from one hospital to another. Usually central hospitals in the cities are better equipped than other hospitals. Most of the equipment is imported from some industrial countries, such as West Germany, Italy, and the UK.

2.3.1. Hospital Staff Availability

The health service in Libya is staffed almost exclusively by foreign consultants, physicians and medical personnel. About 98% of the experts, 90% of the physicians, and 70% of the nurses are from foreign countries (Governmental Statistics, 1980). The majority of the foreign medical staff work as teams on the basis of one or two year contracts. Each team is from the same country and in many cases more than one team with members of different nationalities are working in the same hospital. Each team consists of consultants, physicians, nurses, and sometimes technicians. In addition to the foreign teams in the hospital, there are a number of local physicians, nurses and technicians as well as individual physicians from other Arab countries. The majority of local doctors were educated and trained in medical schools which were established recently in the local universities. The rest were educated in different foreign countries.

2.3.2. Patient Analysis

Although the majority of the patients are from a single homogeneous cultural group, the patients are different in their educational background, their health, beliefs and their customs. The largest group of patients are the rural and illiterate people. These persons share a value of traditional system, a set of experiences, behaviour patterns and a more conventional health and religious beliefs than other patients.

The other group is smaller than the previous group. It consists of the patients who may be described as having better level of education or professionals, whose patterns of thought and behaviour closely resemble each other. Beyond these groups, one can find a third group of patients who may be described as foreign experts, foreign labourers, visitors, and their dependents.

Although all sex and age groups are represented in the patient population, female patients tend to be more frequent than male patients in using the medical services, specifically those from rural and uneducated groups.

The first group seems to constitute a single class, about whom some generalisations could be made. They are fatalistic and poorly educated or illiterate. Their language is concrete and they seldom ask questions, preferring that other local staff provide them with the information. Usually, this type of patient tends to be older, very religious, and more patients of female sex are present in this group.

The other group of patients which may be classified as a distinct group, consists of urban and rural members, who are educated or partially educated. They ask more questions than the previous group and are more modern in their beliefs and their cultural traditions.

Both groups believe in the same religion and share certain characteristics. The majority have, and value, strong kinship ties. They value personal relationships and life co-operation. Female patients in both groups share also certain characteristics. The majority in both groups are poorly educated or illiterate, very conservative in dealing with male medical staff, and in many ways less able to communicate.

2.3.3. Styles of Physician-Patient Interaction

Roberts (1977) indicated a number of physician-patient and patient-physician interactive styles. The following describe physician-patient interactive styles where a *physician* is labelled as:

1. **Dominant** if, in his early contact with his patients, he tends to give orders, to take actions without first giving information, and to be unresponsive to patient's volunteered statements.
2. **Egalitarian** if, in his early contact with patients he tends to explain his actions and to ask for and respond to patient's statements.

The patient-physician *interactive* style can be classified into different types:

1. **Egalitarian**, if in his early contact with physician, he expected, and often demanded or negotiated for, as nearly equal share of information and decision making, as his situation allowed.

2. **Silent egalitarian** if, patient wants information but does not ask for it, and wants to share in decision making but does not make it known.

The majority of the patients belonging to the first group described in the previous section, behave in a subordinate manner in that they ask none or a very few questions. In the second group the majority of the male patients behave in egalitarian manner. The majority of female patients in this group behave in silent egalitarian manner.

Physician-patient communication is very extensively treated in the literature. Pendleton et al., (1983) reviewed extensive evidence which indicates that interaction between physician and patient needs to possess certain specific elements. Many of these elements may constitute necessary prerequisites for better diagnosis and effective treatment.

In view of the previous discussion, in the next section we will discuss the components of the medical environments which are not similar.

2.4. DISSIMILAR COMPONENTS OF MEDICAL ENVIRONMENTS

As we pointed out before, several components of a medical system are changeable from one medical environment to another. This needs to be taken into consideration when building a medical expert system for multi-environment situation. The following variable components were identified from the data collected about the selected medical environments.

2.4.1. Language

The majority of the patients are speaking the same language which is different from the language spoken by foreign medical staff. A short course in the local language is provided to new foreign medical staff including a few medical terms, which is hardly sufficient for basic communication with patients. As a result, only few words are acquired by the physician and nurses initially, to make it possible to communicate in a very poor way with most of the patients. Some patients of the second group try to communicate in the English language if the physician or nurse speaks this language. Few patients try to learn some words of the native language of the medical team and try to communicate with physician and nurses as adequately as they can. The size of the problem is bigger when a new medical team starts, and then the situation begins to improve with time and as experience in communication is acquired by both sides. The problem appears all over again when the old medical team finishes the contract and a new team takes its place. Many times the new medical team comes from a country different to that of the previous team. In this situation the language problem becomes more critical.

The following example is taken from one hospital in a city of about 250,000 population.
- Patients. Approximately 85% – speak Arabic.
- Local staff. Approximately 15% of the total staff speak Arabic, the rest other languages.

- One medical team consisting of approximately 35% of the total staff, are from Yugoslavia speaking a Yugoslavian language.
- Another medical team (approximately 35% of the total staff) from Romania speaks Romanian.
- The other nationalities (approximately 15% of total staff) – speak various languages but not Arabic.

2.4.2. Culture

Pendleton (1983) pointed out that, to communicate effectively with other people, it is not enough to know their language, one must also have a degree of familiarity with their culture. The most general statement of the (cross-culture) problem is that successful communication depends on the understanding of the cultures of interacting participants. The following extract from Bochner (1983) comments on this:

> ...*communication effectiveness decreases as the distance between the respective cultures of the participants increases.*

Davis (1978) suggested that in the medical field communication effectiveness depends on the physician becoming more sensitive to the frames of reference, linguistic usage, and life-styles of the patients.

In our selected medical environment, however, familiarity with its culture can be achieved by physician and other medical staff improving their communication style with patients, and by knowing more about the patient history and background. This depends on the ability and interest of the medical expert or physician to learn about the culture from his experience with patients. For example, some patients in this medical environment do not like to communicate some symptoms to the physician unless they get friendly reaction from him.

2.4.3. Education and Beliefs

In our selected medical environment (see section 2.3), the level of education is associated with age. The older age of the patient the more likely is the patient to be perceived by physicians as poorly educated, this is particularly apparent with female patients. The majority of those patients are illiterate and traditional in their religious beliefs. Their knowledge about medicine is very limited and very traditional. The causes of diseases in their thinking are related to mainly climatic conditions and diet. A large number of these patients believe that whatever the cause of disease is, disease is a test sent by God to test his worshippers.

In general, the majority of patients in these medical environments, if they agree to meet the physician, have great faith in them and great admiration for their knowledge and skill. Furthermore, they are co-operative within their understanding, and accepting what is suggested.

2.4.4. Domestic Atmosphere

In addition to the above three components, consultants transferred to another medical environment need to consider what we shall call the domestic atmosphere of that environment. By this we mean, the local diseases caused by the natural structure of the surrounding conditions, eating habits, and the influence of the climatic situation on the appearance of symptoms and signs. For example, patients in North Africa usually do not suffer exactly from the same diseases as patients in England. Even in the same country, for instance, patients of the northern part of the country do not suffer exactly the same diseases as patients in the southern part. The following specific examples are from North African medical environments.

- It is not easy to notice sweating symptoms because of high absolute humidity specifically in the southern part of the country.
- A low-fibre diet, as well as other eating habits need to be recognised by the foreign medical expert.
- In some areas of the country where drinking water is direct from springs or wells, it may cause diseases which are not usually recognised by foreign physicians.

From the above description we can extract four components of medical environment, that influence medical knowledge as depicted in Figure 2.2. All these environmental components considerably influence medical knowledge and hence must become part of the knowledge and expertise of the medical expert.

It is clear from the description presented in this chapter that the elements of each component vary from one medical environment to another. As a result of this, the medical knowledge structures from the sources of different environments may not be similar. This will be further investigated in Chapter 16.

2.5. THE MAIN ASPECTS OF THE MULTI-ENVIRONMENTAL PROBLEM

This section describes the aspects of the problem of developing a medical expert system for a multi-environment situation. These aspects can be identified as follows:

1) The nature of the available expert system architectures and their suitability for a multi-environmental situation.
2) The nature of the medical environment activities.
3) The classes and types of participants.
4) The technical constraints.

These aspects can be further described as follows.

a. **The architecture of the available medical expert system:**
According to the discussion in Chapters 1 and 2, it is quite clear that the expert system is unlike an ordinary data processing system such as payroll system or stock-control system. The expert system has specific requirements that make it more an information retrieval and processing system rather than a traditional type of computer system.

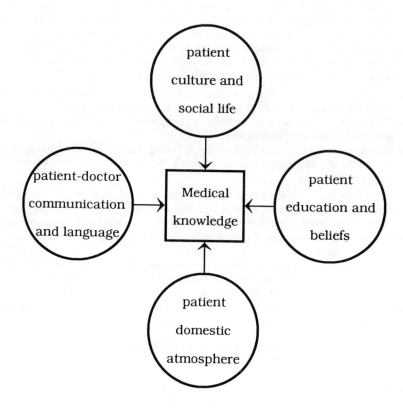

Figure 2.2. Multi-environmental components of medical knowledge

Essential to the notion of the medical expert system is, for example, that it must be capable of providing and maintaining the reliable consultations which the user needs at any time. Furthermore, it must be able to provide a secure protection structure. This structure must be modifiable to suit the user needs.

b. **The nature of the medical environment:**
As we explained previously, we need a methodology that is able to match the medical environment activities. The medical environment is characterised by the high interaction between the participants, and the essential interaction between medical diagnosis and the other clinical activities (Kohout et al., 1985; Kohout and Bandler 1986; cf. also Chapter 10 of this volume). Moreover, as medical information is incomplete and inexact and continuously changing, it is important to look for a design methodology that can deal with the dynamic aspects of the medical system and fuzzy structures in the actual design.

c. **Classes and types of participants:**
In view of the previous discussion, it is obvious that the diversity of the classes and types of participants have to be taken into account in the actual design of any medical expert system. It is not an ordinary conventional system which deals with specific class of users who are trained in how to use the system. Classes of the participants of medical expert systems are many, consultants, physicians, nurses, and in each class there are an experienced and an inexperienced type of users.

d. **The implementation of technical elements:**
As we pointed out in Chapter 1, the availability of the suitable substratum (technical elements) in the medical environments to implement the multi-environment medical expert system has to be considered in the design (cf. Kohout, 1990; cf. also Chapter 5 of this volume). These technical elements, such as the hardware technology, languages, knowledge representation schemes, etc. imply various restrictions on the design. This has been discussed elsewhere (Ben-Ahmeida 1987, Chapters 6 and 7).

From our case study, it has became obvious that the transfer of a medical expert system, or indeed any expert system, from one environment to another is by no means simple. This necessitates the development of a new methodology for dealing with multi-environmental situation the exposition of which is presented in this book.

2.6. REFERENCES

Ben-Ahmeida, M (1987):
A Study of the Design, Reliability and Knowledge Structures of a Multi-environmental Medical Expert System. Ph.D. Thesis, Department of Computer Science, Brunel University, U.K., March 1987.

Bochner, S. (1983):
Doctor—patients and their cultures. In: Pendleton and Hasler (1983).

Davis, A. (1978):
Relationships Between Doctors and Patients. Teakfield Ltd. Publisher, England.

Hayes-Roth, F. (1984):
The knowledge-based expert system, *IEEE Computer*, No. 9, p 11–28; No. 10, 263–273.

Jackson, P. (1986):
Introduction to Expert Systems. Addison-Wesley, Reading, Mass.

Kohout, L. J. (1990):
Perspectives on Intelligent Systems: A Framework For Analysis and Design, Chapman and Hall, London; and Van Nostrand, New York.

Kohout, L. J. et al (1985):
CLINAID: A Knowledge Based Clinical Decision Support System for Use in Medicine. In: Mitra, G. (ed.), *Computer Models for Decision Making*, North-Holland, Amsterdam, 133–146.

Kohout, L.J. and Bandler, W. (1986):
Knowledge Representation, Clinical Action and Expert Systems. In: Kohout, L.J. and Bandler, W. (1986a), 1–10.

Kohout, L.J. and Bandler, W., eds. (1986a):
Knowledge Representation in Medicine and Clinical Behavioural Science. An Abacus Book, Gordon and Breach, London

van Melle, W. et al. (1981):
The EMYCIN Manual. Technical Report, Department of Computer Science, Stanford University, U.S.A.

Miller, D. (1985):
Prototype expert system for design oriented problem solving. *The Australian Computer Journal*, vol. **17**, No. 1.

Pendleton, D. and Hasler, J. (1983):
Doctor-Patient Communication. Academic Press, London.

Roberts, C. M. (1977):
Doctor and Patient in a Teaching Hospital. D.C. Heath and Company

Weiss, S. M. and Kulikowski C. A. (1979):
Expert: A system for developing consultation models. *Proc. 6th Joint Conf. on Artificial Intelligence*, 942–947.

CHAPTER 3

A FRAMEWORK FOR TRANSFER OF EXPERT SYSTEMS BETWEEN ENVIRONMENTS

F. DOWLATSHAHI AND L.J. KOHOUT

Editorial Comment:

> Even for the transfer of conventional expert systems between different environments, a new extended framework of reference is explained.

LIST OF CONTENTS

3.1 SYSTEMIC ORIENTATIONS
3.2 ENGINEERING AND TECHNICAL ORIENTATIONS
3.3 TRANSFER–A KEY PROBLEM OF MULTI-ENVIRONMENTAL KNOWLEDGE ENGINEERING
3.4 SYSTEMATICITY OF EXPERT SYSTEMS
3.5 A RELATIONAL VIEW OF EXPERT SYSTEMS
3.6 PARADIGMATIC ASPECTS
3.7 SUMMARY
3.8 REFERENCES

3.1. SYSTEMIC ORIENTATIONS

The problem of the transfer of an expert system from one environment to another is a complex one; there exist many different levels and many different parts capable of consideration from many different points of view.

The position presently adopted is that the problem is best approached in *systemic* terms. Thus both the expert system and what is most inseparable from it, namely, Knowledge Engineering enterprise, are regarded as a system and an activity in a systemic context, respectively.

It is important at the outset to be clear as to what is transferred. We need then to specify (or allow for the discovery of) both *variables* as well as *stable* features that are in all transfers. The structure to be dealt with is of Gargantuan complexity, since we must consider the problem not in isolation but in terms of the enterprise as a whole.

KNOWLEDGE-BASED SYSTEMS FOR MULTIPLE ENVIRONMENTS

We thus need to construct a coherent set of ways of handling this particular form and this kind of mighty largeness and complexity. And we must distinguish between large and complex in a finite way, and large and complex in an infinite way.

Let us consider a situation, in which an expert system will be transferred from one environment to another. How will its functions be affected by this transfer?

Clearly, what is being transferred in a multi-environmental situation is the whole expert system structure, as well as the set of assumptions into which this structure is hidden. Every part of the structure may undergo change and thus affect every other part when a transfer occurs. An Expert System capable of transfer across all envisioned environments needs to be talked about in more general formal terms. These terms are *system*, *region*, *neighborhood* and *transfer*.

Postulate 3.1.-1: *region*
 a) The *region* is a composed entity that encompasses some components that are filtered out of the totality of a universe of discourse by some action or activity of *selection*.
 b) The selection is performed according to some *selection criteria* (such as relevance, competence or coherence).
 c) Given a region, it might be possible to construct or distinguish a sub-region within that given region.

Definition 3.1-2: *domain*

If the act of selection is guided by the criterion of *relevance* with respect to some conditions, we call this sub-region a *domain*.

Definition 3.1-3: *range*

If the criterion is *competence*, we call the sub-region a *range*.

The term 'region' is an extension and generalisation, of the notion of 'neighbourhood'. A notion derived from that of neighbourhood is 'environment.'

Given an object, we can construct a neighbourhood $N_{i,j}(Obj)$ composed of elements associated with that object, supposing that a region Reg_i and the association criteria $Assoc_j$ are also given. Formally, we have

Definition 3.1-4: *neighbourhood*

$$N_{i,j}(Obj) := \{E \in P(Elem) | Elem\} \sqsubseteq Reg_i \text{ and the predicate } Assoc_j$$
$$(Obj, Elem) \text{ is } \pi(TRUE).\}$$

where $x \sqsubseteq y$ reads x is a part of y, and $x \in Z$, x is an element of class Z, and $\pi(TRUE)$ is the degree of possibility of the predicate being true.

It is necessary to introduce the notion of 'region' because there is the hazard of confusing it with the notion of 'neighbourhood.' Once a neighbourhood is specified (in order that it may be talked about) a region is indicated. But to specify a region is to define neighbourhoods of another level which exist in another region. And this, clearly, continuing in this fashion, goes on ad infinitum. For this reason there is the possibility of becoming forgetful of the region in being preoccupied with neighbourhood.

There are several definitions of environment, but the most intuitive one in the context of the present book is the following. The entity called 'environment' encompasses according to *our* definition "some *coherent* and *relevant* components in interaction, which are filtered out of the totality of a region according to some criteria of relevance or competence."

In general what is transferred from one to another environment may be a particular or general sort of structure but the sort of requisite generality for transfer is not necessarily the same. The sort of generality intended here is that it should be of the same sort as General System Constructs (cf. Chapter 5).

The wish to regard systems from this systemic point of view stems in part from the desire not be laden with a certain sort of theoretical/practical labour in each and every case of a set of situations which have some commonality (Kohout 1986, Dowlatshahi 1986).

The most problematic of such transfers is the cultural one (cf. Chapter 1 of this volume) since the latter sort of environment is the most complex conceivable—that is, if by culture we mean that which human beings individually or collectively can create and/or participate in.

Any such transition is possible (given that it is desirable) just when some form of *invariance* and *change* is:

a) pre-defined or,
b) predictable.

In the first place we need systems which remain *general* but also capable of *specificity*. But, to these need be added the qualities of *change* and *invariance*. We thus arrive at a set of requirements which are General Systems Constructs whose features undergo change predictably or are pre-defined in transfer. This is formally equivalent to saying that their sense of generality is pre-defined.

What is interesting from a theoretical point of view about the defining characteristics of General Systems Constructs (generality and specificity) is that it 'places' them somewhere between the particular and the general. It is the *formulation* of how it subsists in the first place, that these apparently incompatible concepts of *generality* and *specificity* can be present in one and the same construct, which is in question, but not the simultaneous occurrence of these qualities.

It is thus not a contradiction to find that such qualities are frequently satisfied in *practice*. The *general* differential, e.g. a phenomenon such as oscillation is particularizable to some given case of oscillation, and this, generally speaking, is perfectly acceptable, not creating any problems or dilemmas. Within classical Pure Mathematics, this state of affairs is well defined via the notion of *variable, expression* and *constants*. These may be generalised to *change, structure* and *invariance* at the level of system. But these notions are not straightforward generalisations.

3.2. ENGINEERING AND TECHNICAL ORIENTATIONS

We shall define an expert system thus:

Definition 3.2-1:
Expert systems are technological, engineering devices which are designed to act *as* an expert, with respect only to the experts' relevant *expertise*.

The necessary functional components of which an Expert System is composed are:
1) Content System
2) Form System
3) Realisation System.

Content Systems:
This is a system of knowledge. As it captures the ways the relevant knowledge is organised, it is viewed by the Knowledge Engineers as *the* Knowledge System—either in the deep or superficial sense. It should be noted that any Knowledge System is prone to ambiguities of interpretation, as we have dealt with elsewhere (cf. Dowlatshahi and Kohout 1988).

The term *Deep Knowledge* is in the expert systems literature generally thought of as depicting the knowledge of laws, theories and models in the scientific sense. But the word 'deep' can suitably be applied to other kinds of knowledge which are not deep in the scientific sense. However, the (almost haphazard) classification in the literature of knowledge into Commonsense, Domain, Causal, World Knowledge does not help methodologically very much.

The distinction between knowledge and meta-knowledge is however very significant. Meta-knowledge is knowledge *about* knowledge, including the knowledge of what is relevant, significant, interesting etc. The knowledge *of* 'how' or 'what' is 'clearly' different and ought to be clearly distinguished.

Form System:
This pertains to the form of representation in which the knowledge is captured.

The Realisation System:
This is the system that pertains to the Information Processing Machine, the technological artifact in which the embedding of the relevant expertise is realised. It also pertains to all the aspects of its functioning.

The functional teleological triad thus described consisting of form, content and realisation is not complete. The modes of utilisation of it have to be added.

The knowledge engineer's task is to elicit knowledge from the expert regarding a certain domain, represent it in some computing medium. This cannot be done to full satisfaction unless the mode of utilisation of what is, or has been, elicited is unambiguously established. However, to these must be added a forth:

The Modes of Utilisation:
This are the modes in which the above system (i.e. the triad of functional components) is collectively utilised so that the net result is the expert system in its interaction with a single or multiple environment.

With respect to the interaction between expertise and deep knowledge, the following should be noted, in view of our above discussion:
a) this interaction is only via the expert;
b) such knowledge has no necessary connection with what it might be *used* for;
c) given a scientific law we may utilise it, so that technological products are in accordance with it;
d) knowledge of facts do not necessarily imply how they may be utilised. Thus: "this piece of metal is lead and its temperature is 100" taken as a fact about the piece of metal does not imply without a suitable context any mode of use or any particular use of it.

3.3. TRANSFER—A KEY PROBLEM OF MULTI-ENVIRONMENTAL KNOWLEDGE ENGINEERING

The task of Multi-Environmental expert system construction is inextricably bound up with the enterprise of Knowledge Engineering. Thus the multi-environmental expert system presupposes a discipline of Multi-Environmental Knowledge Engineering:

Such a discipline is different from Knowledge-Engineering-as-such, since characteristically, such a discipline is in the terminology of the present paper, concerned with invariance and change across boundaries. Thus its concern is not with this or that particular environment or a family of environments but also with the dynamics of *transition across* them. Logically this is a different task. Possible sources of variation are broadly speaking those of the Content System, Form System and Realisation System, which are the functional systemic constructs, that capture the multiplicity of terms as well as their dynamics.

3.4. SYSTEMATICITY OF EXPERT SYSTEMS

At the most general level we may take an expert system to be a *system*—to be taken formally to mean the way in which it is intended in System Theory. Once again, as in all System Theory, there is no absoluteness in determining exhaustively all the (possible) systems that there are. It is, however, desirable to determine the systems that exist *from a certain point of view*. Thus given our definition of an expert system, it follows that the question as to what is meant by the statement 'expert system being a system' may be answered in the following way:

An expert system is a technological system with a given architecture capable of replacing an expert to a suitable approximate degree in respect only of his knowledge.

Put in this way, questions such as adequacy, completeness and correctness (and so on) that so obviously arise in System Theory may be posed.

The *technological system* (as used in the statement above) is made up of the following kinds:
a) The Form, Content, Realisation and Utilisation Systems,
b) The Methodologically Oriented System (or equivalently, the Paradigmatic System).
c) The Meta-Meta...System (to be explained below).

This Meta-Meta...System consists essentially of the broad methodology according to which the *knowledge*, its *elicitation* from the expert, its representation, realisation in the machine and its utilisation are placed within an overall paradigm.

3.5. A RELATIONAL VIEW OF EXPERT SYSTEMS

As we said, at the most general level an expert system may be regarded as a system. This view may now more elaborately be put thus: An expert system is made up of a number of subsystems which in their modus operandi come to instantiate their systematicity. Modus operandi may be defined both intensionally and extensionally. Extensionally, in terms of an extended set of instantiated cases – distinguished temporally or by some other extensionalizing method. The intensional specification of Expert Systems remains a not yet formulated (let alone) research issue.

The relational point of view makes it possible to formally talk about expert systems from many different angles (cf. Chapter 10). We may take a system to be a set of 'components' and relations defined on them. The only caveat here is that such a conception is augmented by some suitable sense of 'wholeness,' 'cohesiveness,' 'unity' (and so on).

What this last paragraph suggests is that in transfer of an expert system from one to another environment – despite apparent indications to the contrary – changes may occur in respect of the qualitative aspects of systematicity ('wholeness,' 'cohesiveness,' etc.). Thus it may turn out that the system transferred may appear to be a system but which, in reality, it is not—or, not in the suitable or intended sense. This implies that systems and non-systems ought to be distinguished (Dowlatshahi 1987).

The relational view of expert systems can be explored with advantage for the purpose of checking the satisfactoriness of the completed artifact. Thus we define "the goodness of fit of an expert system" as the degree to which

user-machine relational structures
match
user-expert relational structures.

The goodness of fit is an important concept to employ in the evaluation of transfers across boundaries. It is of course the question of a particular set of environments and of a particular application what kind of measures and what kind fuzzy relations are used in each particular case.

3.6. PARADIGMATIC ASPECTS

The complexity of subject-matter that Knowledge Engineering involves implies that we have some kind of overall framework that can be used, so as to place the enterprise as a whole into some form of cohesiveness. This alone justifies cautious subscription to some framework. But for quite different order of reasons a framework that has the status of a paradigm is required: the enterprise of Knowledge Engineering is capable of realisation in many different ways and this poses a problem: which of these ways is true in the sense of correspondence with reality and coherence in the sense of logical consistency as well as systemic unity. This appeal is made to quite non-relative, independent criteria.

Thus it can be validly argued in these terms that an ill-conceived or disingenuous framework or, indeed no framework (!) would certainly, or most probably, lead to quite erroneous conclusions from a more global point of view, in spite of (defined in some sense) local plausibility.

The argument broadly runs thus: the Knowledge Engineer is in overall charge of the technological enterprise that begins with elicitation of knowledge from the expert to its realisation in the configured and constructed expert system.

Thus the knowledge engineer has the following difficult decision to face, namely to determine:

a) *the elicitation problem:* the very terms of what is to be elicited from the expert;
b) and how — *the communication with the expert problem;*
c) and within what *particular framework* — thus causing the indeterminacy of framework problem.

All these are to be decided by the Knowledge Engineer. This then is his *decision problem*. It is not by any means obvious at an *a priori* level what the basic terms ought to be or how the various decision problems are to be decided. Nor is it rational in this kind of context to simply act in apparent 'good' faith.

We may begin with what is indubitable in this enterprise, namely, the existence of two basic sorts of level – these are object and meta-levels. The level of *objects* and *participants* (object-level) and the level of the observer (the meta-level). Whatever is objectified comes to reside at the object-level of the framework.

The paradigmatic framework may be represented thus:

$$\langle \langle \text{Par},\ D(\text{Par}),\ D(\text{Obs}) \rangle,\ \text{Obs} \rangle$$

In this notation the set of observers (Obs) is at the meta-level to the participants (Par) as well as to the domain with which the participants are concerned D(Par), and the domain with which the observer is concerned D(Obs). D(Obs) would include the Observers and also all, some or none of their domains (Dowlatshahi 1987; cf. also Chapter 18 of this volume).

In the present context this Par could be the expert and knowledge engineer when the latter is participating. Obs would be the knowledge engineer when in the position of the observer. The D(Par) would be the domain of expertise (equated with knowledge of the domain). D(Obs) is the domain of the knowledge engineer.

The knowledge engineer's domain consists of the Form System, Content System (expert knowledge), and Realisation System. The basic terms of these systems, once determined, will need to be stated in terms compatible with those of the decision problems discussed in this section.

3.7. SUMMARY

We have argued here that the transfer of knowledge systems may be formulated quite generally in terms of notions of *region* and *environment*. A structure elsewhere introduced and called General System Construct (cf. Chapter 5) is then subjected to such transfer. The problem of transfer has been discussed in highly abstract terms so as to give it the requisite level of generality thus providing a link to General Systems field. [In general (Dowlatshahi 1987) and to General Systems Constructs in particular (Kohout 1977, 1978).]

3.8. REFERENCES

Dowlatshahi, F. (1986):
Participational and observational systemic-constructs and their relation to approximate reasoning. Presented by title at *Symposium on General Systems Constructs and Approximate Reasoning in Knowledge-Based Systems*. To appear in the *Proceedings of Third Internat. Conference on Systems Research, Informatics and Cybernetics*, Baden-Baden, West Germany, August 19-24, 1986.

Dowlatshahi, F. (1987):
METASYSTEMICS: A Many-Sorted Relational Theory of General Systems. Ph.D. Thesis, Department of Electrical engineeing and Electronics, Brunel University, England, June 1987.

Dowlatshahi, F. and Kohout, L.J. (1988):
Intentional possibilistic approach to dealing with incompletness, vagueness and uncertainty. *Fuzzy Sets and Systems*, vol.25, No.3., 277-295.

Klir, G., ed. (1978):
Applied General Systems Research: Recent Developments and Trends.
Plenum Press, New York, 1978.

Kohout, L.J. (1977):
Functional hierarchies in the brain. (An invited Major Contribution, presented at NATO Internat. Conference on Applied General Systems Research, Binghamton, N.Y., August 1977. Reprinted in: Klir, G. (1978), 531-544.

Kohout, L.J. (1978):
Methodological Foundations of the Study of Action. Ph.D. Thesis, Man-Machine Systems Laboratory, University of Essex, Colchester, England, January 1978.

Kohout, L.J. (1986):
Knowledge domains, systems constructs and approximation of Gestalt. An opening lecture for *Symposium on General Systems Constructs and Approximate Reasoning in Knowledge-Based Systems.* Third Internat. Conference on Systems Research, Informatics and Cybernetics, Baden-Baden, West Germany, August 19-24, 1986.

CHAPTER 4

IMPACT OF MULTIPLE ENVIRONMENTS ON THE FUNCTIONING OF MEDICAL AND OTHER KNOWLEDGE-BASED SYSTEMS

J. ANDERSON, M. BEN-AHMEIDA, L.J. KOHOUT AND W. BANDLER

Editorial Comment:

> An explanation is presented of how a multi-environment in one specialist field arises. It shows the historical links and the way interactions between multiple environments and various contexts evolve. This in turn impacts the Knowledged-Based System which has to be truly multi-environmental and multi-context. This prepares the reader for Chapter 10 which presents CLINAID as a special example of such an architecture.

LIST OF CONTENTS

4.1 INTRODUCTION

4.2 HISTORICAL PERSPECTIVES IN THE DEVELOPMENT OF MULTIPLE MEDICAL ENVIRONMENTS

4.3 SHARED ENVIRONMENTS

4.4 IMPACT OF MULTIPLE ENVIRONMENTS IN HEALTH CARE

4.5 SUPPORT AND RECORD SYSTEMS

4.6 TRANSFER OF CONSTRUCTS TO OTHER FIELDS

4.7 CONCLUSIONS

4.8 REFERENCES

KNOWLEDGE-BASED SYSTEMS FOR MULTIPLE ENVIRONMENTS

4.1. INTRODUCTION

In the medical field there has been for many years and at differing levels of practice, a *relationship* between the medical environment of such areas of practice and the function of the knowledge base of the doctor or doctors collectively in the provision of medical care. In practice, the functionality of the knowledge base is linked to the different clinical environments in which it is used. If the aim or the care objective of the doctor is to reach a diagnosis, then this diagnostic view or environment will condition the particular use of the knowledge base and this in turn will be reflected in the medical record of care given. If, however, the aim is to reach a prognosis as requested by the patient or the relatives , or to institute appropriate therapy, then the knowledge base will be used in different ways, to meet these differing objectives (Anderson 1970).

This often means that different elements of knowledge in the knowledge base may be selected or different aspects of these same elements used to match up with the clinical objective, so that clinical conclusions and decisions and the records of the patients reflect the clinical activity. In clinical medicine the major part of the initial data will come from the patient but how it is translated and used by the physician will depend on the objective perceived at that time and on the way in which it interacts with his knowledge base. Medicine is thus seen to encompass differing environments which are *conditioned* by the varying and different objectives taken up by the physician. This is not just a matter of retrieving appropriate data from a data base but rather how to match the objective to a knowledge structure to which the objective relates. When the clinician changes the objective, of course the environment changes and the knowledge used.

Other ways of viewing change in the knowledge environment relate to consideration of different activities of the patient in different environments. Here it is the patient who sets the objective in the interaction with the physical and natural surroundings. This environment is therefore mainly relevant to the patient and only indirectly physician related, for it reflects the interaction of the patient with the availability and use of natural resources in relation to his knowledge about them. This is reflected by the diversity of response to the need of the patient to feed, clothe, house and protect himself and to achieve appropriate social interaction. Naturally, such patient knowledge environments relate to the patient's own decision making, but indirectly to the decision making of the clinician. In this area personal knowledge of hygiene and, at a different level, of public health plays an important part in relation to clinical care.

Knowledge base systems are continuously evolving and developing due to man's inherent natural curiosity. This activity depends not only on being able to set and use objectives but in addition the ability to uncover new knowledge and be able to test it and use the experience. It is this last aspect that underpins the learning experience. Thus the use of knowledge in multiple environments is an essential part of medicine.

A variety of objectives may be used during learning in medicine and some are not necessarily oriented towards the goals of medical action.

Rather they may relate to the acquisition of knowledge for its own sake or reflect a perceived need to acquire scientific data and facts to satisfy an examiner or to pass an examination. Naturally the knowledge achieved in this way will relate to the objectives at the time the learning took place and the use of such knowledge would have to be changed by experience to relate it to a clinical goal. This appears to be an aspect of knowledge acquisition that sometimes escapes both student and teachers.

It is all the more important to recognise these changing objectives clearly when considering the exponential growth of scientific knowledge in medicine in the last century. Indeed the move towards specialisation was in part due to the recognition that no physician could know the whole of medicine and the ever increasing literature, nor could he be expected to use most of it effectively. There was also the expectation that the groups of doctors who specialised in a particular area of medicine could be more effective scientifically and clinically, if they concentrated their efforts. The process of deriving specialities not only included division into the major areas of medicine, surgery and psychiatry and separation of some of these areas by body systems, but also by patient age group such as the pediatrician and geriatrician specialists. Today further subspecialisation is being considered such as "organ" specialities, for example liver and heart diseases (Anderson 1981).

Because of the difficulties involved in seeing the whole from an assembly of some of its parts, it was thought that support of certain aspects of care could be created by encapsulating the abilities of an expert in a so called "expert" system, for giving both advice to those that used the expert system and if they wished it, the system could adopt a decision making stance. Usually such expert systems have only considered one particular aspect of medicine such as diagnosis or therapy of certain infectious diseases such as bacterial infections. These expert systems were small and particularly adapted to a well circumscribed environment chosen at the design stage. Thus they were oriented to one or at most a few environments.

It has been possible for nearly a century to view medicine as one of the international professions, with the shared goal of patient care and an international knowledge base. There are, of course, many and different Health Care Systems in the world but there is a *general sharing of common goals* between doctors everywhere. These shared goals of patient care apply not only to Western medicine and its look-alikes but to those who care for sick people generally, even if, as in China and India, there are tradition care systems which are different from and less sophisticated than the prevailing type of Western care. What brings this about has been the improvement in communication and knowledge, as well as shared goals for both individual patient care, general health and environmental care for communities of people at local and national level.

When considering disease, it is easy to forget the underlying systems for promoting health related to the environment, such as the provision of a clean water supply, the control of dangerous animals and pets including rodents, the improvement of food supply and distribution, hygiene and other environmental factors. Such systems are usually community based and these developments owe much to the public health system in England, the United Nations after World War I and the World Health Organisation after World War II. Both these bodies concentrated on establishing and promoting general health care systems and disease control.

The latest effort of the World Health Organisation is "Health for All" by the year 2000. They have not concentrated on medical knowledge systems or bases to achieve this but tried to raise the general standard of preventive medicine and personal care. The international medical profession as such, has played an important part in forming and implementing the goals that drive these two aspects of health care forward. Both at the international and national levels there are political and administrative aspects to these goals if care is to be managed appropriately in all nations.

Goals at this level often reflect the differing political, social and administrative elements that are present in national and local health care systems. Thus the international level differs from these other environments because of its integrative function and the *global* nature of its knowledge base. The knowledge base itself as well as being comprehensive needs to be coordinated *to reflect* the different environments and to be updated regularly so as to reflect "international health" as well as possible. It is also necessary to ensure that the whole is as correct as possible because the care subsystems will come to rely on it.

4.2. HISTORICAL PERSPECTIVES IN THE DEVELOPMENT OF MULTIPLE MEDICAL ENVIRONMENTS

When Hippocrates paved the way for the establishment of medicine as a separate discipline to religion he set prognosis as the major objective of medical effort. At that time there was a great deal of interest in predicting the future generally, and this was a major function of several religions and cults. However, he established that medicine was different in that, instead of viewing the entrails of animals etc. for predicting the future, it was able to use the circumstances of the patient, both symptoms and signs, as a guide to the outcome of illness. The possibility of having a diagnostic construct at this time was not available due to lack of appropriate knowledge.

However, it was necessary to support this activity with theory about the existing knowledge of the structure and function of the human body. This need was supplied by Galen who showed how the different elements of fire, air and water came into the structure and function of the largely animal bodies that he was able to describe. This logical union of theory and practical observation was so complete, comprehensive and compelling that it held sway for more than 1500 years. Thus the statement of appropriate goals to suit a comprehensive and well organised account depending on existing knowledge, was powerful and dealt with particular needs suited to the perceived medical environment as it then existed.

It was only during the Rennaissance that a challenge began to be made based on more advanced studies of human anatomy and following this of theories of human function. The first major medical challenge to theory was made by Sydenham in the 17th century, who in his endeavours to clarify fevers, developed the concept of the diagnosis of a disease. At the same time a general ferment was beginning and both existing medical facts and theories were being challenged.

However, the scientific movement did not get fully under way until the 18th and 19th centuries with the development of clinical medical tools such as the stethoscope and opthalmoscope and scientific medical tools such as the microscope and bacterial culture systems. It is the use of these tools that enabled the resolution of the structural and functional abnormalities at different levels in man and so increased the sophistication of diagnosis and prognosis.

Therapy of human illness in a general sense had been with us over the centuries but often therapy appeared to hinder recovery rather than promote it. It was because it was difficult to correlate clinical observations with the trial of a therapy and its outcome, that specific developments had to await the creation of the concept of a controlled clinical trial. Here a specific disease or clinical state was studied in relation to a new defined therapy, in comparison to either no therapy or the previous therapy, where all outcomes were noted. So it was that out of the druggist and pharmaceutical chemist activities at the turn of the present century that drug manufacturing factories were created and then the pharmaceutical firms and industry as we know it today, using clinical trials of different kinds.

Further a considerable number of more specific therapies such as physiotherapy, rehabilitation, psychotherapy, behavioural therapy, radiotherapy, etc. have been created with different technical and activity environments, under the supervision of the medical profession originally. Usually such therapies have not been as well and rigorously tested as drug therapy. This remains a challenge for the future. The achievement of such a therapeutic armamentarium has already been considerable covering behavioural as well as pharmacological change. As our perception of the cause and course of disease improves, so it is likely that therapy will evolve to meet the challenges of the new complexity.

The application of scientific techniques to the study of the abnormalities of human structure and function ushered in a new phase in pathology with the study of disease states and tissues during life and at death. The development of more sophisticated microscopy, such as ultraviolet and infrared as well as electron microscopy has increased the resolution and depth of the observations and led to the creation of histopathology, taking as its base cellular structure and function. Clinical biochemistry evolved to explain the functional change in disease and microbiology to explore the role of microorganisms including protozoa, bacteria and viruses in disease and the changes in tissue structure and function that they create.

On the clinical side these changes had impact. Because of increasing pathological knowledge, it was necessary to explore the mechanism and states of disease more and so the function of the investigation of the significant aspects of disease in patient care arose. Naturally, these investigations were undertaken in the clinical laboratories already alluded to. Therapy had to be tailored to patients and their diseases and monitored alongside this investigative activity1971 . With the development of detailed clinical records to encompass and record these changes in clinical procedures, the way lay open to the possibility of audit of the many aspects of these clinical functions. However, the physicians handwritten, individual patient medical record did appear to create a substantial barrier to any detailed analytical procedure.

In reviewing the knowledge base of medicine there is no doubt that it has grown exponentially over the past 50 years, fuelled by a scientific approach to the problems of health and disease and the encouragement of funded research especially at universities. The importance of original research in the gaining of higher university qualifications cannot be overlooked. This system of research supported by governmental and private grants has encouraged the emergence of an ever increasing medical literature. The universities have had a significant impact on medicine, in orienting students towards a scientific view of medicine and in encouraging practising physicians to have an interest in scientific research.

It is not surprising that during the past half century the medical knowledge base has been increasing exponentially, as has the number of medical journals and their publications, which emphasize the publication of research and its reporting to the medical profession at large (Reichertz and Anderson 1977). The significance of this increase in the knowledge base can be seen by the changes in Index Medicus and more recently, in the development of Medline and Medlars etc., which are computer based systems for accessing the titles of papers and their authors in the medical literature. This has been a development originating in the United States National Library of Medicine and is now supported by many countries on a contributing basis. This effort for providing appropriate reference access to a multiplicity of journals has highlighted the issue of the *maintenance and the updating of knowledge* and continuing education in the face of perpetual change. It is no longer the case that one doctor can know it all. Indeed, even if he attempted to do so, the rate of change would make it impossible. For this reason specialisation has been one of the methods the profession has used to deal with this problem.

There is a tendency to forget that the medical environment in patient care is now changing continually on a world basis. Patients all over the world are expecting higher and higher standards of care from scientific medicine. The appeal of the World Health Organisation for "Health for All by the year 2000" indicates that this is likely to be a patient decision as well as a professional responsibility. The global environment that now involves medicine will not go away but in itself will create new demands for change (Anderson 1977).

As has already been indicated local community and governmental support for different aspects of medicine and health care is already considerable in most parts of the world. This type of support will evolve and change. As part of this support governmental policies have supported medical education as a prerequisite for the provision of health care services. Also private funding has stimulated research into the problems of the education of other health care professionals in support of many ancillary services. However, the total knowledge base of medicine in all its aspects is still a challenge and becomes more so as multiple environments grow and expand. It *cannot* be regarded only as a literature retrieval problem.

4.3. SHARED ENVIRONMENTS

The climatic and geographical conditions of much of the land masses of the globe, materially provide for a complex series of differing physical environments. This is related to other variables which relate to the availability and usage of natural resources. The other major factor is the diversity of response in relation to the resources needed to feed, house, clothe and allow appropriate social interaction of people. The usage of important resources such as water, land, and food involve aspects of public as well as personal hygiene.

In addition to the natural environment, the political systems of the world vary greatly, both in respect of the complexity of their organisation and the scale of professional and individual participation. Thus the variations in political systems as well as the allocation of resources and the differing pathways chosen for development, all vary the health care environment. For example, some countries have an entirely state organised and funded health care system, while others have highly organised individual care run by professionals and funded by those needing care in the community. There are of course multiple, intermediate combinations possible, which vary according to the resources of different nations.

Social and cultural patterns influence the type of care given and accepted, taking into account the varying and different environmental factors. Social organisation may be as simple as that at family level or as complex as that of a state or nation. However, the medical profession does see its professional activity in part as the resultant of social forces. Naturally the medical profession itself does try to shape this interaction.

Individual variability because of genetic and environmental factors is so large that account of this has to be taken by health care professionals who provide clinical services. The medical profession indeed is interested in not only the individual aspects of care but the relationship of it to the political and social factors in the organisation of the health care system. Certainly most individuals accept the largely hidden benefits of public health until disease or a man made disaster strikes and the care infrastructure is no longer competent. Doctors do depend on multiple support factors and disrupting the organisation of care for example between family and hospital practice, reduces the effectiveness of the profession to provide as appropriate care as possible.

All of these environmental factors relate to how the community chooses to distribute its resources and the organisation chosen to do this. In the modern world this relates to financial systems which provide resources for health education, research and the ongoing provision of health care services. Naturally, any nation as a whole wants the highest standard of care possible, although the provider offering the cheapest tender may not be the best effector agent from every viewpoint. Thus the environments in medicine are subject to continuous change from all sides.

4.4. IMPACT OF MULTIPLE ENVIRONMENTS IN HEALTH CARE

Having established that there are multiple environments in health care supported by differing but linked knowledge bases, it is necessary to enquire how they are linked and relate, so that an appropriate information system can be designed. At this point too, it becomes necessary to look at *contexts* which differ in multiple environments and have different usage in an information system.

Contexts may be variable in any environment but each relates to a limited number of variables which have a range of response. Because of these local relationships it is possible to use context as a means of ensuring accuracy and reliability of an information system. The context situation also helps *protection mechanisms* to be inbuilt in many areas in information systems, so that the overall function is improved. This has particular relevance to expert systems.

Environments are, however, much larger and more independent entities which force an information system to cross a boundary and enter into a different knowledge base, which is usually in part related to the other knowledge bases. It is the recognition of these environmental boundaries and linkages that facilitates the provision of reliable transitions between the differing environments. Often, as we have already seen, this may relate to changes in goals in health care. If these changing environments are not carefully documented and supported, then the opportunity for significant errors, especially in expert systems, can arise. As these environments are a feature of medical advisory and decision support systems, to ignore their special features can have wide ranging effects. However, the human mind can easily take such changes into consideration and this is not a problem with literature interpretation.

The effect of multiple environments only becomes important with the increasing size of expert systems and where several different experts are involved. While such systems have been small and restricted to one environment this difficulty has not been apparent. Naturally such systems in the future will have to be designed to be responsive in differing environments and to be resilient in action. It is obvious also that such extensive systems cannot be the product or reflect only the views of a single expert and will have to take into account the existing literature. However, as expert systems have not been created with these goals in mind in relation to multiple environments, it is unlikely that the necessary clinical detail has so far been fully considered. New more comprehensive medical records will have to be designed for this purpose in the future.

The existence of multiple environmental variability affects expert decisions and this has been recognised in law by having more than one expert assist the court. This variability of experts does affect the knowledge base and so the advice that the system might give must reflect this new situation, in that such a system can only be as good as the common denominator of the advice received. The medico-legal complications that this problem raises for expert systems have not as yet been laid to rest. To the extent that multiple environments do affect the functioning of expert systems, there is no other way but to recognise the problem and ensure that such systems will be resilient in the face of varying knowledge support. Perhaps the time has come to avoid getting such systems to make clinical decisions for doctors but to aim to have them offer the necessary *advice for decision support.*

Because of this, the impact of a shared medical tradition in the Western world has not led to uniform patterns of practice and the organisation of care has been very different between the countries in Europe and the United States and Canada. Although their medical schools will follow a similar curriculum, the decisions in practice will vary because of differing environments, differing epidemology of disease related to differing climates and disease vectors. Patterns of human behaviour may depend on different life styles as well as genetic potential. Thus at the clinical level, the different emphasis on disease and its treatment will have to be recognised, so that more resilient expert systems can be designed. If such systems are to learn from an appropriate medical record knowledge base, then they will have to reflect this variability.

The need to establish these clinical goals and environments and the importance of having the necessary medical records linked to expert systems, may make it possible to adjust expert systems to clinical requirements. This will be achieved by such systems learning from recorded experience and by so doing adjust the basis for future decision-making. In this activity medical records become part of the knowledge base.

Individual doctors, because of their different interests and biases, may interact differently with expert systems and have *different scenarios* for gaining advice. Some may want more clinically oriented expertise while others will ask for more abstract theoretical advice related more to clinical principles than to ongoing clinical experience. This implies that they will be using multiple medical environments and the systems should be capable of adapting to users' styles.

4.5. SUPPORT AND RECORD SYSTEMS

There are considerable differences in the management of health care at the family doctor, health centre and hospital levels. Such organisational differences may reflect natural environmental factors or relate to the density of population and to transport facilities for seeking medical care. Differences in clinical expertise are likely to decrease with the advent of advisory systems, although specific skills will still be an important factor (Anderson 1982).

However, for the doctor problems remain with the use of expert systems even if the knowledge base is up to date and reliable. Accepting that the expert system may not always, because of lack of essential data or because of user error, be accurate in its decision making, the doctor will still have to decide when to accept the advice and the final responsibility rests with him.

It will be somewhat easier if the expert system uses medical record data in its knowledge base. It will also require, as has already been indicated, mechanisms for coordinating the record environment with that of the knowledge base and with the expert system logic. To a large extent this will depend on the ability of the doctor to create the most appropriate medical records to support such systems. This of course throws the responsibility back to the doctor. What is becoming apparent is that the introduction of expert systems requires a system change and will involve organisational as well as medical factors.

4.6. TRANSFER OF CONSTRUCTS TO OTHER FIELDS

When considering the transfer of previous concepts to another area involving multiple environments, the choice is broad and many professional organisations and businesses either of the manufacturing or service type of industry can benefit from the implementation of appropriate expert systems. Such systems can be built *around* the existing record system of the business for existing functions in both the financial and management activities. One of the major issues facing the development of expert systems has been that the existing systems and models are usually designed to deal with discrete and well circumscribed problems, yet in the world at large most activities involve multiple environments of various kinds. Finding a solution to the problem of multiple environments is necessary for developing the next generation of expert systems and increasing their usage.

The objectives for multiple environmental expert systems will be to recognise the interdependence of the environments and to be able to advise and to take decisions about the usual aspects of such systems. They should have the ability to be as useful as the expert in situations where the advice or decision making are usual and not very exceptional, including that the system should recognise when it is not competent to reach a decision because of special conditions. As such systems are still in the design and implementation phase, it is too early to expect them to show a great deal of expertise, for neither does a human expert develop without having ongoing recorded practical experience on which to base this expertise. Such systems will develop and increase in usefulness only when they have adequate practical experience and appropriate data to enable the stystem to update itself and to improve its reliability.

Two fields of activity have been chosen, one involving a *business* either in relation to the creation of an artifact and its sale and use by the public and the other, an example of a specialist service such as *banking*. Both these areas involve new theoretical constructs and there is a great deal of emphasis on profit and loss in the business as a whole and in relation to the operations it undertakes in producing a product. Thus the theoretical model for a business has its financial, production and management environments where advisory systems would be useful and practical. At present most businesses have an educational system to transfer the expertise to those who are either promoted or joining the organisation, so that the corporate expertise in the various environments is maintained, or hopefully increased. Expert systems by their explanatory stance offer more immediate help in relation to to decision taking than the educational system and can be designed to improve the knowledge of the user as well by reporting their logic and decision making pathway. This is the so-called explanatory aspect of expert system usage.

Within each of the *multiple environments in a business* there will be theoretical constructs to reflect practical reliability. In the financial area there will be appropriate financial planning and prediction based on the cost of input materials, the cost of transformation by providing effective labour and environmental conditions and the cost of the product for sale either to small or large groups of buyers, whether they be another manufacturer who would develop the product further or to the general public at large.

Production of the artifact involves knowledge of how to create the artifact in the most appropriate way and the transformations to be made to the starting materials to bring this about. Naturally quality control and organisational methodology to ensure maximum production at the most economic cost are part of the production environment. A lot of production control involves creating and managing the labour resource to deal with production. Also there is the necessity of creating the most effective and economic environment in which production can take place.

Management in general has the responsibility for maintaining the product quality and saleability at the optimum price so that the profit accruing to the organisation is maximised. A major function of management is planning as well as control and this requires the analysis of records relating to the product and all the processes and processors involved. Here information from the financial environment is used in both the control and planning processes. As management has responsibility for the quality of the product it must plan to keep the workforce well educated and skillful, especially in production and those involved in management. The success or failure of the business will to a large extent depend on the decisions made in production and management in the multi-environmental aspects of the endeavour.

The situation in banking as a business is different, as it emphasises that it is a service provider, mainly interested in providing financial services for its customers who are the general public and business organisations. The *multiple environments of banking*, having been static for a considerable period of time, are now about to increase due to an expanding interest in the type of finanical services that can be effectively provided.

The basic financial service to customers has been to offer savings, investment and credit facilities. It offers a variety of services to deal with money deposits and credit. It will have a facility for dealing with foreign exchange transactions as well as those in the currency of the country. In addition to offering loans to business, it also offers advisory services to improve business procedures, in part to ensure that loans will be repaid. More recently banks have gone into mortgages, buying and selling stocks and shares for their customers and offering advisory services about these matters. For all these additional services the bank charges the customer. The income from services is related to expenditure on personel and environments for these activities.

It keeps records both for the benefit of itself and for its customers dealing with both the financial transactions and the advisory systems. Expert advisory systems can support these differing environments in banking, as they have their requirements set by previous usage of the system and the requirement for appropriate records. Other data necessary for such multiple environments will be related to other fields. Naturally the financial and management aspects of running a business are also required and can benefit from expert systems.

What has been indicated is that similar relationships and transformations used in the production of an artifact or a service at a certain level of abstraction appear to be quite *similar*. Thus expert systems should relate to multi-environment activities to get relationships correct and reliable and in relation to the specialist nature of each environment and ensure that the knowledge base is in sufficient detail to enable it to support its expert domain.

As yet the interface between the educational aspects for maintaining and improving a business and the need to support decisions at all levels has not yet been realised. All too often the procrustean bed of rules has been assumed to meet the need. Indeed expert system shells have encouraged the user in the view that by answering questions he can pull himself up by his own bootstraps. While a simplistic approach can succeed in limited areas with well defined problems it does not provide a path for the solution of multiple environments in the world of real activity.

4.7. CONCLUSIONS

While it is fairly easy to account for knowledge base differences in medicine due to differing environments in general it is not easy to establish direct relationships with such changes. As data from adequate medical record analysis is also difficult to obtain there are problems in accepting such an arrangement. It has yet to be established how different the data used by different experts could be in reaching the same conclusion. As yet no expert has been checked in detail. As few expert systems have good protection mechanisms or are good at checking for errors without using the doctor who is using the system by recalling past actions on interrogation then doctors have to recognise the difficulty.

Our investigations in the literature suggest that diagnostic definitions do vary in the data considered and in the relations that are expressed. It would appear that this variability has to be accepted for much of it appears to be *due to* differing environments. This has important implications for new medical and other expert systems.

4.8. REFERENCES

Anderson .J. (1970):
Information processing of Medical Records, 3–13, ed. Anderson, J., and Forsythe, J.M., North Holland, Amsterdam.

Anderson J. (1981):
The Systematic Doctor, 159–170, in *BCS'81, Information Technology for the Eighties*, ed. Hammersley, P., Heyden and Son, London.

Reichertz P.L., Anderson J.(1977):
A Systems View of Health Care Organisation. Medical Computing, 87–98. Taylor & Francis, London.

Anderson J. (1977):
Information Systems in Hospitals. 115–156. *Information in Medicine*, ed. Reichertz, P.L. and Goos, G., Springer Verlag, Berlin.

Anderson J. (1982):
Medical Records as a Basis for Decision Making. 904–9, in *Medical Informatics Europe*, ed. O'Moore, R.R., Barber, B., Reichertz, P.L., and Roger, F. Springer Verlag, Berlin.

CHAPTER 5

ACTIVITY STRUCTURES: A METHODOLOGY FOR DESIGN OF MULTI-ENVIRONMENT AND MULTI-CONTEXT KNOWLEDGE-BASED SYSTEMS

L.J. KOHOUT

Editorial Comment:

> The methodology found to be most successfull in the design of multi-environment and multi-context systems was that of Activity Structures. A general systems conceptual outlook is combined with formal methods and techniques, using a possibilistic approach.

LIST OF CONTENTS
5.1 WHAT ARE ACTIVITY STRUCTURES?
5.2 ACTIVITY STRUCTURES AS A TOOL FOR ANALYSIS AND SYNTHESIS OF INFORMATION PROCESSING MACHINES
    5.2.1 Basic Notions
    5.2.2 Distinction Between Functional and Substratum Structures
    5.2.3 Constructing an Activity Structure
    5.2.4 Classification of Functional Structures of an IPM
5.3 TOWARDS A DESIGN OF RELIABLE, CORRECT, ROBUST AND USER-FRIENDLY MULTI-ENVIRONMENTAL SYSTEM
    5.3.1 Introduction
    5.3.2 Interaction of the System with its Environments
    5.3.3 A Meta-Theory of Activity Structures Based Design Process
    5.3.4 A Scenario of Knowledge Elicitation and Design Activities in a Multi-Environmental Situation
    5.3.5 Semiotics of Interaction: Communication, Conversation, Agreement
5.4 ANALYSIS AND EVALUATION OF INFORMATION PROCESSING MACHINES BY MEANS OF ACTIVITY STRUCTURES
    5.4.1 General Outline
    5.4.2 Comparative Evaluation of Implemented Knowledge-Based Systems by Means of Functional Structures

5.5 KNOWLEDGE IDENTIFICATION, ELICITATION AND REPRESENTATION
- 5.5.1 Introducing Knowledge Identification Processes
- 5.3.2 Postulates Defining Identification Activity Structures and Processes

5.6 REALISATION OF SUBSTRATUM STRUCTURES BY MEANS OF VIRTUAL MACHINES
- 5.6.1 Virtual Machines
- 5.6.2 Generalised Virtual Machines
- 5.6.3 VM-Process

5.7 FUNCTIONAL REFINEMENTS OF ACTIVITY STRUCTURES
- 5.7.1 Segmentation of System Behaviour
- 5.7.2 Task Descriptors
- 5.7.3 Concurrency of Processes and Tasks

5.8 GENERAL SYSTEMS CONSTRUCTS IN THE ACTIVITY STRUCTURES APPROACH
- 5.8.1 Systemic Aspects of Multi-Environments
- 5.8.2 General Systems Constructs
- 5.8.3 Activity Structures Viewed as a General Systems Based Possibilistic Theory of the Statics and Dynamics of Activities

5.9 REFERENCES

5.1. WHAT ARE ACTIVITY STRUCTURES?

The unification of the contents of a design description is achieved through the rather general methodological framework of Activity Structures – the conceptual and methodological tools for capturing the diverse features of adaptive activities in natural and artificial systems, and of their interaction with the environment.

The Activity Structures approach has found its applications in many fields concerned with the study, understanding, modelling and synthesis of action, such as brain sciences, (Kohout 1976a), medicine (Kohout 1978), psychology or social sciences (Kohout 1990). However, one of the most significant uses of Activity Structures is in design of technological artifacts (Kohout 1990; Anderson, et al., 1985; Kohout, et al., 1985, 1986).

An entirely new methodology for total (complete) design of information processing systems in general, and of expert systems in particular, has been developed using as its essential tools Activity Structures (Kohout 1978a, 1982, 1987, 1990). In this Chapter I shall present the fundamentals of Activity Structures that are indispensable for a thorough exploration of the multi-environmental issues.

The Activities Structures approach has three facets, which are mutually interlinked:

1) conceptual
2) methodological
3) formal and algorithmic.

In this chapter, the emphasis is placed mostly on (1) and (2) of the above. The formal side is covered in greater depth elsewhere. In particular our papers on the theory of general mathematical relations (Bandler and Kohout 1987, 1988) and their applications in information processing, place a particular emphasis on the use of our triangle and square products of relations in medical computing, information retrieval, knowledge engineering and computer architectures (Kohout and Bandler 1985).

5.2. ACTIVITY STRUCTURES AS A TOOL FOR ANALYSIS AND SYNTHESIS OF INFORMATION PROCESSING MACHINES

5.2.1. Basic Notions

Within the field of computer science and information technology, Activity Structures are used to provide new methodological foundations for the development of methods and tools for design of systems processing information. These systems I shall call *Information Processing Machines* (IPM). The term IPM is broader than a Computing System or a Computer. An IPM is a *organised* system composed of some parts that interact with its environment and it deals with the processing information. For example in my book "A Perspective on Intelligent Systems" I also discuss the dynamic changes in the structure of a business organisation. Computers or, indeed whole Computing Systems can be parts of an IPM (as defined here). Computing Systems can be classified by the **purpose** for which they serve, e.g., we have data base systems, information retrieval systems, expert systems, super-computer systems, clinical computing systems, etc. This a *classification by purpose* we shall extend to IPMs.

Activity Structures methodology is applied to analysis and synthesis of systems processing information, within a framework that can deal with the **total** system. The description provided by this framework captures a total activity structure which consists of IPMs, of their environments and also the mutual interactions and the dynamics of both.

In order to deal with the activities in an appropriate way, Activity Structures approach provides special classes of structures that can capture the **purposefullness** and **functionality** of activities of both the computing systems and their environments.

Further in this text, we shall examine more closely the structure of the activities of an Information Processing Machine (IPM) of which the multi-environmental knowledge-based computing systems are a special kind. As I have explained elsewhere (Kohout 1982, 1987), a computing system or indeed any IPM is viewed as an engineering artifact, **dynamically** interacting with its environment. The structures that come into the design and implementation of dynamic systems of this kind, and also for the analysis of their statics and dynamics, fall naturally into two distinct categories:
a) Information-handling structures
b) Constraint structures.

Although it is common in software design to concentrate solely on information handling structures in the initial design, thus neglecting the proper specification of undesirable activities, this may lead to designs that may not have even intrinsic potential for satisfying fully the intended design specification. By including the constraint structures, the Activity Structures methodology leads to more adequate designs, satisfying better stringent 'real life' requirements. The dynamics of protection of the system and user activities and of all the aspects of human-computer interaction in particular, can be treated more adequately by *functional constraint structures*. I shall outline their use in synthesis and analysis of an IPM in sections 5.3.3 and 5.4 of this chapter.

Any synthesis, and design is a kind of synthesis, presupposes a **method of construction**. Our method of construction is based on a *theory of possibility*(Kohout 1988a). What is meant by "construction" can best be elucidated by the following *prescriptive* meta-postulates:

Prescription 5.2.1-1: *Method of Construction*
a) Combine structures.
b) Impose further restrictions.
c) Repeat the activities consisting of (a) and (b) until these yield the desired construction.

The prescriptive meta-postulate 5.2.1-1 (Method of Construction) however raises immediately the following questions:

(i) What kind of structures are to be combined?
(ii) How (i.e. according to what criteria and rules) are these structures to be combined?
(iii) What kinds of restrictions are imposed while combining the structures?
(iv) How do we obtain the specifications of these restrictions?
(v) According to what specification criteria do we determine what is a desired construction?
(vi) By what means can we realise this desired construction?

These questions have been answered in the Activity Structures approach by introducing four broad categories of structures (cf. Kohout 1987; Kohout, Anderson, Bandler and Behrooz 1986):

1) Environmental Activity Structures ... EAS
2) Aim Environmental Activity Structures ... AEAS
3) Functional Activity Structures ... FAS
4) Substratum Structures ... SUB

These structures are classified into the above listed categories according to the purpose they have in the framework of the Activity Structures methodology, as shown in Table 5.1.

Another important feature of this approach is that it divides the activities of an Information Processing Machine into **primary** and **secondary** ones. The total relevant activity in the environment, which represents problem solving activities or expertise leading to the provision of a solution to a problem we are dealing with, will be called *the primary* activity.

Table 5.1. Teleological classification of activity structures

STRUCTURE CATEGORY	PURPOSE
EAS	To capture the essential activities of all relevant participants in the environment
AEAS	To determine what parts of EAS are to be selected to deal with a class of chosen problems
FAS	To capture the dynamics of the broad categories of the functions of the IPM
SUB	Physical realisation or description of the IPM (i.e., of its substructures and their interaction or interfaces)

Unfortunately once we construct, and start using, the IPM in a particular predetermined environment or a family of environments, the operation of the IPM artifact gives rise to new kinds of activities, concerned with the manipulation of the IPM by users contained and operating in each (and all) particular environment(s). These will be called *secondary* activities. Primary and secondary activities combined together give rise to the *Functional Activity Structures* (FAS) of an Information Processing Machine.

The use of Environmental Activity Structures (EAS) has an analogy in conventional software engineering design, in the so called process oriented design approach, which lays an emphasis on human-computer communication. Substratum structures on the other hand are paralleled by the so called object oriented design approach, which lays stress rather on the description of the actual software/hardware modules. The Functional Activity Structures (FAS) are my innovation, which I first introduced in connection with construction of knowledge based systems capturing deep knowledge (Kohout 1977), where I also also investigated the nature of **interconnection** of *FAS* and *SUB* and some of its formal algebraic properties. Care is needed in making proper conceptual distinctions, because some conventional software design methods also talk about functions, but these are usually functions of software modules or their parts, or elements of a functional specification of a system to be designed.

In contrast to this in my Activity Structures methodology, Functional Activity Structures form an indispensable core of the approach. It is the concept of **functional structure** (cf. e.g. Kohout 1986) that provides the essential conceptual *coupling between* the activities of the environment and the activities of an IPM.

5.2.2. Distinction Between Functional and Substratum Structures

The two qualitatively different structures of a system were distinguished in the Activity Structures classification table of the previous section. An interconnected collection of modules (hardware or software modules, brain centres, etc.) was called there *substratum structure* (cf. Kohout 1987, 1990). This structure is a description of physical (or virtual) parts of the system together with their interfaces.

When, however, we attempt to infer the structure of a system from its behaviour, the term *structure* used in this way has a **different** nature. The term "structure" in this second context means the structure of behaviour, not the structure created by interconnecting the components generating this behaviour.

In a biological context or in robotics, the activity of a system usually has the aim of changing the environment from an undesired to a desired state. These kind of systems are called **teleological** systems, since they are described teleologically. Thus we can say that teleological description is a description *that takes into account the purpose* of a system or of its behaviour.

If the goal-directedness or the purpose is selected as the criterion for the choice of the class of the model to which the behaviour of a system is to be approximated, then this defines a special structure of activity or of behaviour, called *functional structure* (Kohout 1978a, 1975). This structure of an activity is often called "function" in biological literature. For example, biologists speak of the function of respiration, or a locomotor function, describing the respiratory activity or locomotor activity, respectively. In the previous section one important class of functional structures has been introduced, namely Functional Activity structure (FAS) of an Information Processing Machine. In section 5.3 another important functional structure called *Functional Environmental Structure* (FEAS) will be introduced and used to capture the relevant features of an environment.

Reader is referred for a detailed exposition of other aspects of functional structures to (Kohout 1990). A useful foundational background and further reading on teleological functionalities is presented in (Kohout 1976b), which also touches upon their relevance to robotics and natural language representation.

It should be stressed that the main importance of a new Activity Structures methodology stems from the fact that functional and substratum structures are mutually **interdependent**. Couplings between these structures form an indispensable core of the whole approach to analysis and construction of complex artificial and natural systems (cf. Kohout 1990). In this respect, Activity Structures approach makes a sharp contrast to other approaches which do not make this essential distinction between functional and substratum structures.

Essential features of functional and substratum structures can be formally modelled by means of generalised topologies (Kohout 1975). In this formal approach, the couplings between the functional and the substratum structures take the form of so called Galois connections linking the closure spaces formally representing the former and the latter structures (cf. Kohout 1978).

5.2.3. Constructing an Activity Structure

5.2.3.1. Defining basic elements in the structure

We recall from (Kohout 1987) the following basic concepts of Activity Structures.

The ELEMENTS of three kinds appear in our framework. These are: OBJECTS, ACTIONS and PROPERTIES. Interacting objects we call PARTICIPANTS. Participants can be either *active* or *passive* elements. *Participants* can *communicate* or *act*. In **action**, we distinguish SUBJECTS which are active participants that act upon other participants. PARTICIPATING OBJECTS are the participants that are acted upon by subjects. ACTION is an element that relates two participants. In **communication** we have a SENDER and a RECEIVER of a message: both are active participants.

Activity Structures are the *system models* characterised by the criterion of *conceptual dynamics* and the criterion of *relevance* (Kohout 1990), stated below. These criteria are in fact intensional postulates, which allow us to decide if a particular structure is an Activity Structure acceptable within the framework.

Intensional postulate: *Criterion of conceptual dynamics*

Activity Structures are models that exemplify within a predefined conceptual framework three essential systemic aspects:
(i) the conceptual nature of actions,
(ii) the way the actions interact,
(iii) the action dynamics.

Intensional postulate: *Criterion of relevance*

Activity Structures are *simplified* models that omit the details of the modelled situation which are *irrelevant to the purpose* for which the model is built.

5.2.3.2. Algorithms for construction of Activity Structures

Models of systems capturing the *relevance of the given situation* can be constructed algorithmically, by applying the following steps (Bandler and Kohout 1983):

1. SELECT features judged to be significant, DISCARD the irrelevant ones (proper subset of the original).
2. REDUCE details by grouping similar cases together (partition of the data into equivalence classes or blocks)
3. REPRESENT the result of step 2 in a model (isomorphism).

The above algorithmic steps are related to the principle of relevance. This on its own is not sufficient to provide an Activity Structure, because these steps can also generate other types of **relevance models**.

So, Activity Structures are only those relevance models that satisfy in addition to the criterion of relevance also the criterion of conceptual dynamics.

Construction of an activity structure satisfying both criteria can be performed (amongst other ways) by obeying the appropriate *prescriptions* for their construction. This will be looked at in greater depth in section 5.3.2 of this chapter. As various kinds of functional structures are to be combined in constructing any global activity structure, we shall turn in the section that follows to the classification of functional structures.

5.2.4. Classification of Functional Structures of an IPM

We have seen above that the functionality of activities of an information processing machine can be captured by two categories of functional structures:

1. Information-Handling Structures (IHS)
2. Constraint Structures (CS)

These structures are further divided into the following six classes of functional structures (Kohout 1983, 1990) by which the functionality of behaviour of an IPM can be prescriptively specified.

Thus *Information Handling Structures* can be partitioned into

IHC: control structures
IHD: domain of relevance dependent knowledge structures
IHI: inferential structures.

Constraint Structures can be partitioned into

CP: protection constraint structures
CEM: environment-IPM interface and interaction constraints
CT: technology dependent implementation constraints.

IHS are concerned with computations, control and knowledge. Constraint structures embed the functional restrictions for the purpose of introducing protection against undesirable activities. The restrictions are imposed by the character of IPM-Environment interaction (including symbolic communication), and by the constraints introduced by the choice of a particular technology, i.e. hardware, firmware and software of the host computers over which the IPM structures are distributed.

The first category of functional structures of an IPM, i.e. the IHS-structures are implicitly used in the conventional expert and knowledge-based system design. Constraint structures are usually neglected. We shall see later why the explicit formulation and use of these structures is essential.

ACTIVITY STRUCTURES

In general, constraint functional structures limit and focus the class of possible functions of an IPM. The purpose of these constraint structures is to explicitly exclude those classes of behaviour of the system, which consist of undesirable activities. If we do not include in our functional structures of the IPM the imperative prescription of what are the undesirable activities, the class of behaviours of the IPM is greater that there exist more possibilities of producing undesirable side effects. This however may include the ways achieved via undesirable activities, which should clearly be avoided and therefore explicitly excluded. To ensure that they ar excluded in a proper way is the purpose of so called protection functional structures, which are a special kind of constraint structures.

The notion often useful in design is so called *leading concept*. Leading concept determines what is the result of the construction process. Each leading concept also raises a specific methodological problem, as can be seen from Table 5.2.

Table 5.2 Construction of activity structures and the methodological problems arising in this activity

LEADING CONCEPT:		PROBLEM RAISED:
combining	—	HOW?
structures	—	WHAT KIND OF structures?
restrictions	—	WHAT KIND OF restrictions? Where do these come from?
desired construction	—	According to what CRITERIA?

5.3. TOWARDS A DESIGN OF A RELIABLE, CORRECT, ROBUST AND USER-FRIENDLY MULTI-ENVIRONMENTAL COMPUTING SYSTEM

5.3.1. Introduction

A multi-environmental knowledge-based system (MKBS) is an engineering artifact that has to satisfy a number of *additional requirements*, enforced by the special constraints of each and every environment in which the MKBS operates.

The following are the fundamental requirements that ought to be satisfied by any multi-environmental knowledge-based computing system:

1) The right degree of generality of knowledge representation has to be chosen for the given class of problems in hand.

2) Good matching of the system to the users in each environment is required.
3) Protection against misuse or accidental mishandling of the knowledge-domain information is essential.
4) Attention has to be paid to the consequences of using a computing system and to the related ethical questions; this is particularly important for expert systems used in medicine such as patient monitoring systems, or systems that affect the behaviour or interrelation of various public institutions.
5) Standards ought to be elaborated, for representing professionally the domain knowledge. These shall be acceptable, and approved by the professions involved in the knowledge domains represented in the system if these systems are to serve public or affect the public at large.

All the points listed above are, in one or other way, linked with the activities of a professional user and the system designer, and to the other participants within the environments in which a knowledge-based computing system operates. The Activity Structures methodology takes special care about the structure of activities and provides tools for dealing with activities that are permitted and desirable as well as for protecting against undesirable activities. It is therefore particularly equipped for dealing with the problems of protection, which is crucial in multi-environmental and multi-context computing systems in particular.

5.3.2. Interaction of the System with its Environments

The **total structure** used in the design *is a functional description* in the teleological sense, which is generated by the following kinds of activities:

a) the activity of the information processing machine;
b) the activities of the environment in which the machine is used.

The activities (a) and (b) must appropriately co-operate and form together the *total dynamic activity structure* of the IPM in its environments.

An essential step in the total design of an information processing system is to *split* the total activity structure into two substructures:

a) An Environment Activity Structure, (EAS), with its proper part, a user activity structure;
b) An Information Processing Machine Activity Structure, (IPM-AS), characterising the behaviour of an information processing machine teleologically.

The two activity structures above have to be properly matched in their relevant aspects (Kohout 1987). Only if these two structures are appropriately and adequately matched, will the constructed artifact, i.e. the Information Processing Machine (IPM) function adequately in conjunction with its environments. Because the EAS embodies those relevant portions of the environmental tasks that will be delegated to the IPM for dealing with, it represents in fact the partial model of the activities of the IPM to be constructed.

Even a cursory look at the activities of any finished IPM shows that there is a big gap between the EAS and the corresponding IPM-AS. This distinction between EAS and the IPM-AS gives rise therefore to a considerable methodological problem as to what should be put into this gap.

The way that leads to the solution of this formidable design problem is the realisation that the **correct correspondence** is a *dynamic, conceptual* and *functional match* of the EAS and IPM-AS activity structures.

During the process of constructing a particular technological artifact, we can use the set of activity structures EAS, IPM-AS in two different ways. If we take the EAS as the initial structure and from it generate IPM-AS, we perform a synthesis of IPM-AS, one subsequence in the construction of an IPM. Which is subsequently completed by transforming the IPM-AS into the corresponding substratum structure SUB. Thus we have:

$$\text{EAS} \rightarrow \text{IPM-AS} \Longrightarrow \text{SUB}$$

If, on the other hand we start with SUBSTR of a realised IPM, from it then extract the corresponding IPM-AS, and then by embedding this into a particular environment EN_i we generate EAS_i, we perform an evaluative process, analysis of the constructed artifact. Thus chosen the set of environments $ENV_1, ENV_2, \ldots ENV_i, \ldots ENV_n$ we may have:

$$\text{SUBSTR} \Longrightarrow \text{IPM-AS} \rightarrow \text{EAS}_1$$
$$\text{SUBSTR} \Longrightarrow \text{IPM-AS} \rightarrow \text{EAS}_2$$
$$\cdot$$
$$\cdot$$
$$\text{SUBSTR} \Longrightarrow \text{IPM-AS} \rightarrow \text{EAS}_i$$
$$\cdot$$
$$\cdot$$
$$\text{SUBSTR} \Longrightarrow \text{IPM-AS} \rightarrow \text{EAS}_n$$

I shall discuss both, the analytic and synthetic construction processes in the sequel. Figs. 5.1 and 5.2 depict these two processes and show the way they can be used for evaluation of the design of an IPM.

5.3.3. A Meta-Theory of the Activity Structures Based Design Process

There are no easy shortcuts in the construction of systems for multi-environmental and multi-context situations. A full-fledged maxim of Activity Structures theory has to be used by the designer of the system to bridge the above mentioned gap between the EAS and IPM-AS. Namely, the construction sequence has to be based on an appropriate meta-sequence prescribing planning of a teleological activity (Kohout 1978a). This meta-sequence consists of:

1) Inspection and evaluation of the given situation.
2) Determining what the (activity) situation *must become* instead of what it is.

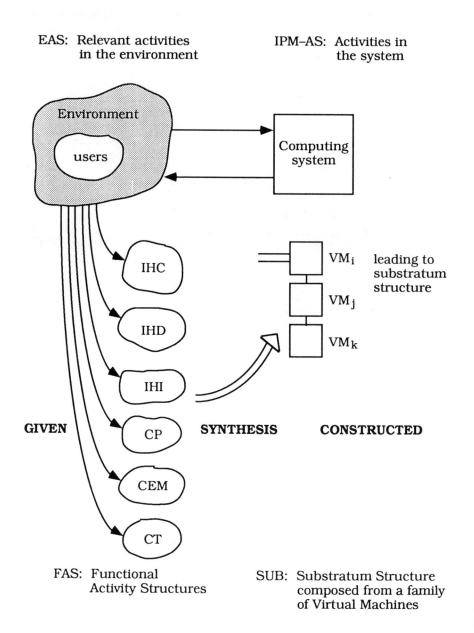

Figure 5.1. Synthesis of an IPM

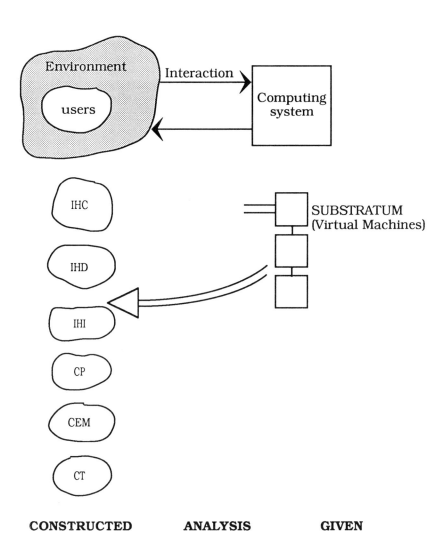

Figure 5.2. Analysis of an IPM

3) Determining what must be done.
4) Determining *how* it must be done and what are the available resources.

This meta-sequence can be particularised to the following meta-sequence, prescribing the aims that lead to generating the activities of the process of construction of a technological artifact (e.g. an IPM). Thus the construction process consists of:

1) Inspection and evaluation of the essential activities in the *initial* activity structure which depicts a situation of particular interest that forms the input which is to be entered into the design transformation.
2) Determining what the situation must become in order to eliminate or add some parts of the structure. Thus we have a *reductive* and/or *creative* transformation of the initial structure.
3) What must be done with the initial structure in order to transform it into the *final* structure.
4) How it must be done and what are the available means for the realisation of this transformation.

The complete design sequence that is generated by quadruple application of the above meta-prescription is pictured below.

$$\text{EAS} \longrightarrow \text{AEAS} \longrightarrow \text{FEAS} \Longrightarrow \text{FAS} \longrightarrow \text{SUB} \longrightarrow \text{IPM-AS}$$

In order to understand the significance of the whole design transformation one has to reflect upon the question what type of activities each successive structures captures and how each structure is to be used in the design process.

Thus EAS, AEAS and FEAS capture the activities of the environment. FEAS can be generated from AEAS by means of task descriptors (Kohout 1978a, b). The IPM activity structures are divided into FAS (Functional Activity Structures) and Substratum structures (SUB). FAS captures the dynamics of the six broad categories of the functions of the IPM (cf. section 5.2.4 above). SUB on the other hand represents the physical (or virtual) realisation or description of the IPM (i.e. of the IPM's substructures and their interfaces).

The construction sequence can be split into three broad subsequences of transformations:

1) Knowledge elicitation: EAS $\longrightarrow$ AEAS
2) Knowledge representation: AEAS $\longrightarrow$ FEAS
3) Design of IPM: FEAS $\longrightarrow$ FAS $\Longrightarrow$ SUB $\longrightarrow$ IPM-AS

Because the activities of knowledge elicitation (KE), knowledge representation (KR) and IPM design overlap, the three construction subsequences also interact. Thus we have the interaction of KE and KR via the activity structure AEAS, and the interaction of KR with design via FEAS. In order to have knowledge elicitation unbiased by the design process, we need to **separate** knowledge representation from both, the knowledge elicitation and the design processes. Behrooz (1986) demonstrated the importance of separating knowledge elicitation from the knowledge engineering (i.e. design) phase in expert system design, but even this separation is not observed in current knowledge engineering practice (cf. Buchanan et al. 1983).

As there is a whole section on knowledge elicitation in this volume, I shall proceed here with just a brief outline of the design subsequence of the Activity Structures based construction process. Some highlights of knowledge elicitation and analysis of IPM are however presented in sections 5.3.4 and 5.3.5 of this chapter, respectively.

The design subsequence FAS ⟶ SUB ⟶ IPM-AS of the total construction process is realised by applying the following prescriptions (Kohout 1983, 1990) iteratively:

1. Combine all the IH and C-structures of FAS into a new *potentiality* structure.
2. Resolve the conflicts arising by the application of (1) above; this will yield a functional *modification* or *refinement* of the potentiality structure, which is the *actual* specification structure.
3. Select a suitable substratum structure - generated by a set of software, firmware, hardware primitives or by their combination.
4. Combine with the actual functional structure from (2) above.
5. Resolve any arising conflicts.

5.3.4. A Scenario of Knowledge Elicitation and Design Activities in a Multi-environmental Situation

Let us assume that a customer commissions the design of a Knowledge-Based System, which will be used by groups of users, where each group may operate in one or more environments. The Knowledge-Based System performs, in interaction with the users, some activities that have a particular *purpose*, aiming at achieving certain goals, that may or may not differ in each particular environment. The system provides environment-dependent advice that helps the users to achieve their desired goals.

The designer has to supply a Knowledge-Based System that can provide *meaningful* and *correct* interaction in all the environments in which it is supposed to operate. In order to accomplish successfully the commissioned design, the designer needs a plentitude of information. The primary task of knowledge elicitation and representation is to extract the relevant knowledge of problem-solving and encapsulate it in Functional Environmental Structures that are used in the design process (compare section 5.3.3). A reliable Knowledge-Based System however, has to perform other tasks in addition to its primary problem-solving activity. For this reason, it must contain other structures apart from Knowledge Structures, or more generally, Information Handling Structures. This other information has also to be elicited and represented by carefully examining the activities of the users in each and every intended environment.

We have seen that this matter has became further complicated by the fact that creating a new technological artifact with which the user interacts, leads to the generation of new secondary activities of the users which are concerned with using and manipulating the technological artifact itself. We have seen that these secondary activities contribute partially to Functional Constraint Activity Structures. This is, however, a serious complication the of the whole construction process, for we do not know fully the secondary activities before the system is completely specified.

Knowledge-Based Systems for Multiple Environments

In Kohout (1990) I have argued that the activity scenario for identification of knowledge needed for the design of Knowledge-Based Systems (KBS) is more complex than is usually envisaged. Does the customer who commissions the KBS from the designer always coincide with the user of the system? If not then there will remain the problem of negotiating some or all the features of the problem domain with the user. That gives the rationale for distinguishing the following activities of the participants in the process of constructing a Knowledge-Based System or the Information Processing Machine:

(a) activities of the experts
- a1) in each environment
- a2) across environments;

(b) activities of the users
- b1) in each environment
- b2) across environments;

(c) activities of the knowledge-based system
- c1) in each environment
- c2) across environments;

(d) activities of the designer;
(e) activities of the customer, who is commissioning the system.

I can be seen from the above list of construction activities that the whole issue of the interaction of environments and participants reaches considerable complexity in a general multi-environmental situation.

In general, there is a need to describe the environments and situations, and to communicate these to all the participants of the construction process. It is also necessary to form, communicate and correctly interpret prescriptions and many sorts of additional requirements. This equally applies to the contract negotiation stage, the knowledge elicitation and representation stage, the design stage, and the stage of using and maintaining the technological artifact in question.

Owing to the considerable complexity of these issues, we cannot deal with them fully in this chapter, or elsewhere in this book. As the question of meaningful communication is the most crucial issue in the multiple environment situation, I shall deal with some basic concepts of semiotics of interaction in the next section.

5.3.5. Semiotics of Interaction: Communication, Conversation, Agreement

In order to guarantee an understandable communicative interaction between the expert, the user and the knowledge-based system, their languages must at least partially overlap.

More specifically, given two communicating participants P_1 and P_2 using a language $\mathcal{L}_1$ and $\mathcal{L}_2$ respectively, the shared parts of the two languages, say, $\mathcal{L}_{1s}$ and $\mathcal{L}_{2s}$ have to satisfy the following conditions:

1) There is a common vocabulary $\mathcal{V}_s$

2) there is a correspondence in the syntax of $\mathcal{L}_{1s}$ and $\mathcal{L}_{2s}$
3) there is a semantic agreement.

An exchange of sentences between two participants that satisfy the conditions (1) and (2) above, I have called *communication*. If the condition (3) above is also satisfied, then it is a *conversation*. Hence we have to take the language as a semantic system in which the *linguistic sign* and *communication* are two fundamental concepts, in order to be able to investigate whether or not is there semantic agreement (Kohout 1976b, 1986).

This in turn leads to problems of structural stability of language, and to the question of temporal (diachronic) changes, the fact the scholars of the Prague Linguistic Circle were aware of, and which played a crucial role in the development of their significant theories (cf. Kohout 1976b).

However, even semantic agreement between the shared segments of languages is not enough. The linguistic statements have to be interpreted within a certain contextual domain - the domain of expertise of the contracted knowledge-based system - and within this domain a *contextual agreement* has to be reached. *Apparent agreement* on context can turn out not to be real at all, because the individual participants have different views on the context. This misleading type of conversation will be called *phatic conversation*.

Phatic conversation during the contractual stage between the customer contracting a knowledge-based system and the designer of the system may lead to supply of a system useless to the customer. In the multi-environmental situation another problem arises. The suppliers of the technological artifacts may commission these to be constructed for their own environments, without real appreciation of the environments in which the users supplied with the artifacts operate. An example of this was already given in Chapter 1.

Phatic conversation between the *user* and the *knowledge-based system* is also dangerous—this may lead the user to making wrong decisions, believing that they are the correct ones, due to misinterpretation of the statements of the system. Built-in questionnaires on some subset of data, requiring operational definitions of some terms necessary for correct use of knowledge-based system, ought to be an essential feature of all knowledge-based systems, not only of the multi-environmental ones. This feature would facilitate the avoidance of phatic conversation and improve the chance of the system being used correctly.

5.4. ANALYSIS AND EVALUATION OF INFORMATION PROCESSING MACHINES BY MEANS OF ACTIVITY STRUCTURES

5.4.1. General Outline

The Activity Structures framework which provided directives for the design of Multi-environmental Knowledge-Based Systems and of other Information Processing Machines that was outlined in the previous section, is equally useful for the analysis and comparative evaluation of existing designs.

Knowledge-Based Systems for Multiple Environments

The essence of this analysis is to construct the descriptions of some Activity Structures from the existing (i.e. constructed) Substratum structure of a knowledge-based system, or more generally an Information Processing Machine. This can be done by constructing a description of the global IPM Activity Structure (IPM-AS) from which the descriptions of Information Handling Structures (IHS) and Constraint Structures (CS) are extracted that form the sextuple of Functional Activity Structures (FAS) listed in section 5.2.4. The substratum of an Information Processing Machine (IPM) and the associated IPM-AS can be described at many resolution levels. Fixing a particular resolution level for the analysis of the substratum determines a specific substratum description or an IPM-AS description. By characterising each IHS and CS of the Functional Activity Structures (FAS) adjoint to the obtained substratum description by means of a checklist of functional features, one can determine the degree of possibility of the localisation of each FAS in all the VM-modules of the substratum description. Thus I define the following prescription:

Prescription

a) Given a family of resolution levels of the substratum description, one resolution level is selected.
b) At this selected level, a substratum or IMP-AS description is constructed.
c) Each element of the description is evaluated with respect to its belonging to the set of features, where each set belongs to one of the 6 functional structures (cf. section 5.2.4).
d) An operator is defined, that assigns the grade of possibility for each substratum element indicating to what extent this element is adjoint to the elements of FAS.

Another alternative way is to extract the Functional Activity Structure from the implemented substratum directly, using a list of *evaluation directives*. This second alternative is particularly suitable for a comparative analysis and evaluation of a predetermined class of IPMs, say of expert systems or Knowledge-Based Systems, or various expert system shells (see section 5.4.2 below).

Care should be exercised in this analysis not to impose on the resulting functional structures those conceptual structures which are contained in the original design specification of the artifact being analysed, but to enter into the analysis only the structures that actually appear in the *implemented* design and its technical description. Only if this rule is strictly adhered to, can we compare the functional structures extracted from the existing implementation with those that are contained in the original functional specification, or even with those Environmental Activity Structures (EAS) from which these functional specifications were generated.

The comparison of the original functional specification with the functional structures extracted by the analysis of the corresponding substratum of a Knowledge-Based System may also help to reveal the existing design faults of the analysed system (such as a serious *semantic gap* or mismatch of these structures).

5.4.2. Comparative Evaluation of Implemented Knowledge-Based Systems by Means of the Functional Structures

The list that follows (Kohout 1982a), gives the *evaluation directives* that have been used successfully for the comparative analysis of a number of existing Expert Systems. Each of the six functional structures of the system to be analysed is examined from a number of points of view:

1. **IHC - control structures:** *evaluate*
   (a) General control structures.
   (b) The heuristics for the search that control the IHI- structure.
2. **IHD - domain of relevance dependent knowledge structures:** *evaluate*
   (a) How domain-specific is the IHD-structure?
   (b) Can a part of it be retained in an empty shell?
   (c) How was the IHD-structure obtained?
   (d) To which other Knowledge Domains is this structure. relevant?
   (e) What is the size of this structure?
3. **IHI - inferential structures:** *evaluate*
   (a) The object system of logic used.
   (b) The meta-system.
   (c) The heuristics of inferential strategies.

Note that:
(i) It is not always uniquely determined whether a heuristics or a strategy of inference should be included in the IHC or the IHI structure.
(ii) Particular attention should be paid to the types of logic used both as to the connectives and the rules of inference.
(iii) The use of fuzzy inference should be examined.

4. **CP - protection constraint structures:** *evaluate*
   (a) External protection against mishandling of information, and against incorrect manipulation of the system by the users.
5. **CI - environment-IPM interface and interaction constraints:** (concerned with human-computer interaction in this case) *evaluate*
   (a) User friendliness.
   (b) Available explanatory facilities.
   (c) Facilities for initial priming of inference.
6. **CT - technology dependent implementation constraints:** *evaluate*
   (a) Types of languages used.
   (b) Computer architecture.
   (c) Speed of response of the system.
   (d) Size of the memory.
   (e) Any other relevant parameters or characteristics determined by the technology used.

These directives have been used for the analysis of a number of expert systems at Brunel University. My framework of Information Handling and Constraint Structures has also been used for analysis of some expert systems at the Florida State University. The most notable contributions were analysis of Hearsay II by Zofia Roberts (1985); Casnet by Uta Ziegler (1985), Larry Hall (1985); Mycin by Elke Rundensteiner (1985); Internist by Jennifer Simms (1985).

5.5. KNOWLEDGE IDENTIFICATION, ELICITATION AND REPRESENTATION

5.5.1. Introducing Knowledge Identification Processes

In section 5.3.3 I argued that the complete design sequence consists of the following chain of transformations of the activity structures involved:

$$\text{EAS} \longrightarrow \text{AEAS} \longrightarrow \text{FEAS} \Longrightarrow \text{FAS} \longrightarrow \text{SUB} \longrightarrow \text{IPM-AS}$$

where the Environmental Activity Structure (EAS), Aim Environmental Activity Structure (AEAS) and Functional Environmental Activity Structure (FEAS) capture in various ways the activities of the environment. FEAS can be generated from EAS or AEAS by performing functional refinements (see sections 5.2.3 and 5.7).

We have also seen that the IPM activity structures are divided into Functional Activity Structures (FAS) and Substratum Structures (SUB). FAS of an Information Processing Machine (IPM), which are divided into Information Handling Structures (IHS) and Constraint Structures, capture jointly the dynamics of essential functions of an Information Processing Machine (IPM). We have seen that Substratum Structures (SUB) on the other hand represents the physical (or virtual) realisation or description of an Information Processing Machine (i.e. of its substructures and their mutual interconnections).

The construction sequence of an Information Processing Machine splits into three important subsequences:

1) Knowledge elicitation: EAS $\longrightarrow$ AEAS
2) Knowledge representation: AEAS $\longrightarrow$ FEAS
3) Design of IPM: FEAS $\longrightarrow$ FAS $\Longrightarrow$ SUB $\longrightarrow$ IPM-AS

In Knowledge Elicitation we gradually enlarge the EAS by a creative transformation which comes from a controlled dialogue of the knowledge elicitor with the domain experts, or by analysis of some texts containing the domain knowledge. We have seen that each step in the construction sequence is a transformation. Thus in the construction sequence depicted above, one starts with some knowledge of EAS involving the activities of the domain experts. Then the knowledge elicitor determines the elicitation aim. By applying the reduction rules (of section 5.2.3.2) we eliminate the parts of EAS that are irrelevant to this aim. The aim selection determines which parts of expert activities are to be relevant to the knowledge elicitor's interest and these are usually delegated to the knowledge-based system. Thus by performing this step one obtains the Aim Environmental Activity Structures (AEAS).

The sequences

Knowledge elicitation sequence: EAS ⟶ AEAS and Knowledge representation sequence: AEAS ⟶ FEAS usually mutually interact, as the Aim Activity Structures (AEAS) appear in both, the knowledge elicitation and knowledge representation processes. It should be noted that *context dependency* and *local relevance* are the most important characteristics of the concepts that capture the description of multiple environments. Thus we can say that general multi-environmental situation is characterised by

(i) strong interaction of knowledge elicitation and knowledge representation processes;
(ii) context dependency of concepts and modelling structures;
(iii) local relevance of concepts and modelling structures

For these reasons, we have to sometime consider the whole sequence

EAS ⟶ AEAS ⟶ FEAS

This sequence of forming Activity Structures I call *Knowledge Identification*. Thus we can see that Knowledge Identification consists of a process forming Activity Structures, involving both the creative and the reductive transformations of the activity structures participating in the sequence. In this case the transformations are effected by the processes of Knowledge Elicitation and Knowledge Representation that may mutually interact in the most general case.

Thus this most general case can be captured by what I call (Kohout 1990) *Knowledge Identification Activity Structures* (IAS). Formally, IAS can be viewed as a meta-structure, a fuzzy relation that is an element of the lattice of all fuzzy relations

$$\mathcal{F}\,(\text{TPART} \times \text{EAS} \times \text{AEAS} \times \text{FAS}),$$

where TPART is the represents elements that are participants of knowledge identification (e.g. expert, knowledge elicitor, knowledge engineer etc.). Thus we can see that Identification Activity Structures belong to the class of possibilistic systems as described in Kohout (1988a). It should be noted that identification system structures and processes were first formally introduced and methodologically developed in the fifties by the founder of Fuzzy sets theories, Lotfi Zadeh, in the context of control theories using continuous mathematics. Hence, for the concept of identification I am strongly indebted to Professor Zadeh.

5.5.2. Postulates Defining Identification Activity Structures and Processes

Without going into further formal details of Knowledge Identification Processes this section introduces a set of Knowledge Identification Postulates. These postulates emerged in connection with elicitation and representation of neurological and some other clinical knowledge in the context concerned with describing of and reasoning about neurological movement disorders and representation of some neurocomputational activities of the brain (Kohout 1975, 1976a, 1977).

5.5.2.1. Basic postulates of knowledge identification process

IP 1: *Teleological Functionality of Basic Process*
Each expert activity in an environment is teleological, i.e. performed for a particular purpose.

IP 2: *Local Functionality of Environmental Activity Structures*
Every Environmental Activity Structure (EAS) capturing some teleological activity is at least locally functional.

IP 3: *Employment of General Systems Constructs*

The description of knowledge by General Systems Constructs deals with conceptual and formal spaces of a variety of degrees of abstraction and generality; this induces a partial ordering on the family of local functional structures that are extracted by the knowledge identification process.

IP 4: *Semiotic and Dynamic Communication Constraints*
Each functional conceptual structure imposes specific constraints on the semiotics and dynamics of communication between the knowledge source and the knowledge extracting participant (knowledge extractor).

IP 5: *Identification Process as a Creative Transformation*
The set of coherent constraints imposed on the knowledge structure possessed by the knowledge extractor during the knowledge identification process creates additional symbolic or message contents (meaning); this is in addition to the contents implied by the initial semantic agreement needed for starting an interaction (e.g., communication or conversation) between the knowledge source and the knowledge extractor.

IP 6: *The necessity of minimal joint semantics*
The degrees of abstraction of individual substructures can be defined only in the case that there is a common initial or residual semantics shared by the whole functional family of descriptive structures.

For mathematical formal aspects and some methodological meta-formalisation, the reader is referred to (Kohout 1974b, 1976a, 1988a).

It is interesting to note that further experimental substantiation of the correctness of my Knowledge Identification Postulates has been provided by Behrooz (1986). A subset of conceptually equivalent but slightly differently formulated principles emerged from his experimental work in knowledge elicitation, concerned with the activities of investigation, diagnosis and decision making in general medicine. The assumptions and structures emerged dynamically by evolution through Behrooz's interaction with a clinical expert. This fact is particularly interesting, because Behrooz was not familiar with the above listed postulates, nor with the above quoted papers in which they first appeared. His important contribution therefore constitutes an independent experimental validation of my basic assumptions. In particular, the reemergence of IP3, IP4 and IP5 indicates that these are essential in the context of knowledge elicitation and representation concerning general diagnostics, repair and management activities in systems.

5.6. REALISATION OF SUBSTRATUM STRUCTURES BY MEANS OF VIRTUAL MACHINES

5.6.1. Virtual Machines

In the previous sections I described in some detail various aspects of structures of behaviour, such as Environmental Activity Structures (EAS), Aim Environmental Activity Structures (AEAS), Functional Environmental Structures (FEAS) and Functional Activity Structures (FAS). The last, FAS was defined as a functional structure that depicts and describes selectively certain aspects of behaviour of the substratum structure (SUB) of an Information Processing Machine (IPM). It has not been shown yet by what means a substratum structure of an IPM can be realised. In this section I describe one such abstract realisation.

The central motivation for introducing virtual machines is to have means for defining the objects (modules) that can describe any hardware, firmware or software units in a uniform and unified way. This is possible because hardware, firmware and software subsystems are treated as *logically equivalent* in the following sense:

a) any operation performed by software can, in principle, be *embedded* in firmware or hardware;
b) any instruction executed by the hardware can, in principle, be emulated in firmware or simulated by software.

In computer science an abstract notion of virtual machine is widely utilised. This notion, although widely applicable is not sufficient to satisfy all the requirements of Activity Structures methodology. For this reason I introduce a richer structure (Kohout, 1978a), which I call Generalised Virtual Machine (GVM). Conventional virtual machine (VM) is a special case of GVM.

A *Generalised Virtual Machine* (also an Efferent Object-Module) is a *structure* (object) composed of some *basic components* (atomic parts).

5.6.2. Generalised Virtual Machines

The Generalised Virtual Machine (GVM) has three communication interfaces: the *upper interface*, the *upper control interface* and the *lower interface*. The upper interface accepts texts in the main language $\mathcal{L}_i$, the upper control interface accepts texts in the upper control language $\mathcal{L}_{i_u}$ and the lower interface emits text in the lower interface language $\mathcal{L}_{i_e}$.

The condition enforcing *correct coupling* of VM's requires that the output language $\mathcal{L}_{k_e}$ of the target machine VM_k must be *acceptable* by the input of the host machine VM_j. In other words, the language $\mathcal{L}_{k_e}$ must be be a *sublanguage of* (i.e. it has to be contained in) the language $\mathcal{L}_j$ of the host VM.

A GVM_i accepts the text in the language $\mathcal{L}_i$ and *translates selected portions* of it it into the text in the language $\mathcal{L}_{i_e}$.

A GVM_i *executes* a portion of a text by the following algorithm:
1) it segments the text,
2) stores part of it in its inner state vector,
3) performs transformation and translation,
4) communicates with other modules (GVMs) to obtain necessary computations,
5) recomposes the result,
6) makes the result available through the upper interface.

As noted previously, conventional virtual machine is a special case of GVM because it has only the upper interface that accepts the language $\mathcal{L}_i$, and the lover interface that produces language $\mathcal{L}_{i_e}$. Thus we can see that the conventional virtual machine has no upper control interface. In this section, I shall consider only conventional virtual machines (VM's). For GVMs and their use I refer the reader to (Kohout, 1990, 1981), where construction of a multi-centre Expert System with deep knowledge and variable structure using GVMs is outlined.

To make the notion of virtual machine useful, we have to have at least a pair of machines, mutually interconnected. Thus let us consider a pair of *coupled* virtual machines VM_j and VM_k, where the coupling is done by interconnecting the lower interface of VM_k to the input of VM_j. With this type of coupling, the VM_k becomes the upper VM and VM_j the lower VM. The former is usually called the target machine and the latter the host machine. A given pair of virtual machines <Upper VM, Lover VM> is sufficient to define a translation from one machine of the pair to the other machine, of the texts (programs) that these machines execute. Well known computer science concepts 'compilation' and 'interpretation' represent special instances of such a translation.

5.6.3. VM-Process

In order to characterise the dynamics of behaviour of a virtual machine or a generalised virtual machine one has to introduce *Virtual Machine Process* (VM-Process).

A program is a text composed in the upper interface language. In order to capture the dynamics of the virtual machine behaviour and to show how the program can dynamically evolve one needs to couple with the dynamic changes of the state vector of the VM the sequence of program transformations that leads to its execution. This is done via the concept of a process.

Intuitively, we can picture the way the process is obtained by the following conceptual transformation sequence:

ALGORITHM

↓

PROGRAM + STATES OF THE VIRTUAL MACHINE

↓

PROCESS (what happens in the VM dynamically, when the program is executed)

One can see that a process is a dynamic entity consisting of the following parts:

a) the current state;
b) the transition: information as to what the next state is to be.

Any *realisation of a process in a virtual machine* consists of the following components:

1. Program,
2. indexing sequence (e.g. discrete time),
3. indication as to which portion of the program is to be executed next,
4. the state vector of the virtual machine.

The above sequence we shall abbreviate as VM-process. The collection of all states of a VM-process thus consists of the collection of the state vectors of its corresponding virtual machine, each state vector representing a particular state.

We have to be careful in using the term process. A VM- Process is a process characterising the dynamics of a virtual machine. Hence, if we choose a substratum realisation which is **different** from that of virtual machine we obtain a different type of process. In general, each distinct type of Substratum Structure (SUB) determines a different type of process.

The diversification of a process-type can be carried even further. Thus, it is possible to define other realisations of a dynamic process, e.g. a realisation in an Environmental Activity Structure (EAS) or in a Functional Activity Structure etc., but I shall not deal with this matter here. In our early work we called the VM-process "the dynamics of a participant" where a participant was realised as a collection of (what I call now) 'object modules' (cf. Kohout and Gaines, 1975, 1976). 'Process' as defined by Hoare is a different entity, it is related to what we called 'A trajectory of a model of activity' in the same early papers.

5.7. FUNCTIONAL REFINEMENTS OF ACTIVITY STRUCTURES

Method of functional refinements provides an important technique which is indispensable for more sophisticated uses of the Activity Structures Methodology.

5.7.1. Segmentation of System Behaviour

As noted above in section 5.2, the Functional Activity Structures are the *structures of behaviour* of a system, which **do not coincide with** *the structure of its substratum*, (i.e., with the structure of the software, firmware or software modules). From this it follows that the decomposition of the behaviour in terms of its subfunctions does not coincide with the decomposition into substructures of a physical structure which generated this behaviour. To determine how the functions are (or should be) distributed over a family of interacting substratum modules (e.g. virtual machines) is called *the problem of localisation of functions* (Kohout 1977, 1978a, 1990).

In an attempt to determine subfunctions of a functionally described behaviour, one has to deal with two related problems: (Kohout, 1978).
a) The problem of *segmentation* and of *identification of meaningful units* of behaviour.
b) The problem as to how to link the individual functional levels with the semantics of functional hierarchies.

Thus it becomes obvious that the problem of identification of basic units of behaviour (relevant to a particular purpose of the activity sequence) plays the crucial role in attempts to perform a functional decomposition of any activity structure. A useful device helping us to carry out successfully this aim are the so called *task descriptors*. Methods using task descriptors in analysis and synthesis of various types and instances of activity structures have been developed and applied.

5.7.2. Task Descriptors

An activity leading to achieving a prescribed aim or having a particular purpose, can be characterised by a task descriptor $\bar{T}$ (cf. Kohout, 1978a, b).

Definition: *task descriptor*

A task descriptor $\bar{T}$, associated with an activity α, performing a set of tasks T, is a partition of T into two disjoint subsets

$$\bar{T} = (T_p, T_f)$$

where T_p is the subset of permitted tasks and T_f the subset of forbidden tasks, of T.

Given a set of processes X, an Activity Structure can be represented by the corresponding task descriptors α (Kohout 1978a). This forms the basis for the synthesis of an Activity Structure from a given teleological dynamic description of an activity by means of dynamic processes and associated with them task descriptors.

Definition

If the *purpose* of an activity is to attain a certain goal z, and the activity has the *potentiality* for doing so, we say that this activity *aims* at achieving this particular goal.

Explanation

(i) In actuality, this activity may or may not attain this goal; this depends on some additional aggregate of conditions q. Aim therefore can be viewed as an ordered pair (activity, goal), or alternatively as a relative goal indexed by that activity.

(ii) An aggregate of conditions q when expressed in a logic, should be a syntactically well-formed formula. Generally, one can use a many-valued logic normal form (cf. Kohout 1978a, 1978b).

Definition

a) *Completion of an aim by an activity*:
We say that an activity α completes the aim (α, z) if it attains the goal z.

b) *Achieving a relative aim*

Given some aggregate of conditions q, we say that an activity α achieves its *relative* aim (α, q, z) if it attains the goal z under the effect of this aggregate of conditions.

The following postulate links tasks with the aims of activities (Kohout 1978a, 1978b).

Postulate: *completion of an aim*

An activity α *completes* its aim if all the associated tasks T_p are *accomplished*. It completes it *correctly* if none of the associated tasks T_f have been performed during this attempt at the realisation of the aim.

5.7.3. Concurrency of Processes and Tasks

An IPM is concerned with sharing information, having many sources producing and consuming information. This sharing can be *co-operative*, *competitive* or *mixed*, having both the former aspects.

More specifically, a task is performed by an IPM by enabling temporal activation of a community of processes that are in mutual interaction. These processes are representations of the activities that are needed to realise a given task. An activation pattern of the substratum structures adjoint to given functional structures can be described by *substratum activation diagrams* (cf. Kohout 1978a).

Interaction of processes which can be co-operative or competitive requires adherence of the participating processes to some prescriptive (imperative) rules of behaviour that would guarantee correct interaction.

Both, co-operative and competitive sharing require: 1) communication 2) co-ordination 3) adherence to some rules of behaviour that can guarantee correct interaction.

Concurrency is a mechanism for sharing. To describe or realise in some environment a concurrent form of behaviour of a family of processes, formal mechanisms for management of concurrency are required. These formal structures have the following functions in management of concurrent behaviours:

1) They simplify the management of concurrency in some substratum structure (i.e. in an IPM).
2) Permit an explicit formalization of the rules of behaviour.
3) Can function as a mechanism for enforcing the correct interaction.

Concurrency in utilisation of resources in a substratum is called *apparent*, if a family of concurrent possesses have to be scheduled in some temporal order to utilise this substratum. It is called *real concurrency* or *parallelism*, if the **substratum can provide** the sufficient resources to run the processes in real time. For example, so called multiprocessing is real concurrency, whilst multiprogramming may have only apparent concurrency.

Concurrent interaction of processes poses some problems that do not appear while concurrent mode of interaction is not utilised. Thus, process co-operation implies communication between interacting processes, which is performed by means of some messages of atomic character, or more complex message structures structured into texts. This requires that the communicating processes can deposit a message in some substratum and can also access the messages already deposited. This leads to the problems of simultaneous access to messages. If a part of a complex message deposited in the substratum is changed at the same time as when its modification occurs, this may lead to the distortion of the content of the message, which is sometimes called a time-dependent error.

Interacting processes share not only the information structures but also many different kinds of other resources. Both, co-operation and competition require some mechanism for resource allocation. In general, Control Functional Structures are the structures that were introduced to deal with these problems.

5.8. GENERAL SYSTEMS CONSTRUCTS IN ACTIVITY STRUCTURES APPROACH

We have seen that the Activity Structures approach requires elaboration of the three facets: conceptual, formal and methodological. In the next section I shall be concerned with the aspects that are relevant to multi-environmental situations.

5.8.1. Systemic Aspects of Multi-environments

The conceptual side of Activity Structures deals with concepts and the semantic rules for their combination. The concepts are characterised (i.e, epistemologically distinguished) by their abstract characteristics (Kohout 1986). These abstract characteristics can be used to provide the taxonomy of concept types. The rules for (dynamic) combination of concepts operate over some universe of objects, domains, systems, structures, etc.

Postulate: *concept characteristics*

Within the framework of Activity Structures, the following concept characteristics are distinguished:

a) their generality level,
b) the scope of their validity,
c) their meaning,
d) for what purpose the concepts are formed,
e) for what purpose and in what way the concepts are utilised.

The characteristics of the concepts given above are quite broad. For our use we need the formal definition of a suitable class of intensional constructs that would have the above characteristics and be also acceptable within the Activity Structures framework. Such acceptable concepts I shall call *systemic concepts*. In order to be able to define formally a systemic concept, we need to refine somehow the classification of Activity Structures elements of section 5.2.3.1. This is done by introducing the following definition.

Definition: *Taxonomy of elements*
 a) Elements of three kinds appear in Activity Structures: OBJECTS, INTERACTIONS, PROPERTIES.
 b) Objects and Interactions are called ENTITIES.
 c) Entities posses some Properties.
 d) Objects in interaction are called PARTICIPANTS.
 e) *Active* Entities are the entities that induce changes in elements or aggregates.
 f) *Active participants* are called SUBJECTS.

Definition: *Descriptive Universe*
A concrete selection of elements according to a family of some selection meta-criteria will be called a *descriptive universe*.

Remark:
An example of this can be found in Kohout (1988), where a physical, a conceptual and a semiotic universe are defined and their mutual interaction further explored. Forming systemic concepts over these three universae yields concepts describing the physical, conceptual and semiotic (e.g. language) objects, respectively.

Definition: *canonical systemic concept*
 a) A canonical systemic concept consists of the tuple <name, formal descriptor>.
 b) 'Name' (in this tuple) denotes an element, or an aggregate of elements, the systemic concept of which is to be characterised by the formal descriptor.
 c) 'Formal descriptor' is an expression formed in a Pinkava many-valued logic system.

Definition: *systemic concepts derived by inference*
Let us have a *valuation norm* of an inference process which is expressed by means of a two-valued or many-valued logical matrix, and the inferential (meta-) rules of that process. Then a *derived* systemic concept is the result of the application of these rules to a family consisting of canonical and/or derived systemic concepts.

It should be noted that the Pinkava normal forms are functionally complete, but not completely determined (partial) many-valued normal forms. Thus by completing the logical connectives entering the normal form, one can determine a particular many-valued logical system (cf. Pinkava 1988, Kohout 1974, 1978a, 1990). Functional completeness is essential, without it not all possible formal descriptors could be expressed. Partiality of the Pinkava connectives allows us to express uniformly a whole logical family of formal descriptors in a possibilistic way. It should be noted that particularly important are those derived systemic concepts that I shall call Galen-closed within a specific relevance domain (cf. Galen cca. 200 A.D.). These Galen-closed concepts yield valid logical inferences within that specific domain. The concepts that are not Galen-closed however, may not always yield a valid inference.

In the context of multi-environmental and multi-context systems, it is important to identify the concepts and their composites that are transferable across, and usable within, a multiplicity of environments and contexts. The concepts that are transferable *across environments* provide a **unification** of these environments. The concepts that are transferable *across various contexts* then perform by this virtue **integration** of various sources of knowledge within a common framework. An important type of concepts having these desired characteristics are General Systems Constructs (cf. Kohout 1986, Kohout and Gaines 1976).

5.8.2. General Systems Constructs

I assume that General Systems Constructs are *transdisciplinary, holistically* orientated and *integrative* (cf. Kohout and Pinkava 1980), and that they should interrelate with some important constructs or methods in non-general investigative areas or knowledge domains. Kohout and Gaines (1976) suggested that "it is an essential objective of General Systems Theory to develop constructs that are common to many diverse areas of knowledge yet also capable of deep theoretical development."

In order to satisfy the above quoted objective, it is essential to consider any systemic constructs jointly with their interpretations, in order to judge if these can satisfy the basic criteria of being General Systems Constructs. In particular, the constructs

(i) must not be vacuous or purely formal without a clearly stated interpretation or a family of mutually compatible interpretations;
(ii) their interpretations must be coherent, that is the possibilities encompassed by their formalism must not include the instances that have potential interpretations conflicting with the assumed semantics.

Constructs can acquire various degrees of generality. In our context it is essential to distinguish Systemic Constructs from General Systems Constructs. Thus we have the following definitions.

Postulate: *systemic constructs*

Systemic constructs are structures with the scope of validity spanning across more than one knowledge domain.

Definition: *general systems constructs*

are systemic constructs satisfying the following conditions:

a) They are concepts meaningful at more than one determinable level of generality;
b) have the identical meaning in all the knowledge domains in which they are valid at a particular level of generality;
c) are capable of generating some theory.

For atomic concepts, or a conceptual structure composed of atomic concepts and for other conceptual structures to qualify as a general systems construct, these have to satisfy the conditions as follows:

1) sufficient generality;
2) adequate specificity;
3) must be capable of diversification;

4) must have the property of semantic unification.

A GS-construct ought be sufficiently general in order to be widely applicable. If it does not possess the sufficient generality, it will not be transferable across contexts, environments, knowledge domains, scientific disciplines, etc. A GS-construct should also be sufficiently well defined, to allow a sufficient number of consequences to be derived from it. For example, a GS-construct valid within a whole scientific field has to generate in conjunction with other concepts substantial body of theory, which has also show its transferability to other fields. Without adequate specificity it will not have enough contents to express any significant information or portion of knowledge. To some extent, *generality* and *specificity* are the **competing** requirements, but under adequate conditions these can be reconciled and properly balanced.

Diversification property means, that if a GS-construct has relevance in a certain context, it will also have relevance in a multiplicity of other contexts. Without this property, together with specificity, its generality would be insignificant, or it may be empty.

Unification means that a GS-construct has relevance to certain *common purpose*, which coherently unifies a whole family of GS-constructs in some context, environment, knowledge domain, etc.

I have shown elsewhere (Kohout, 1986) that both, the systemic constructs and GS-Constructs can be classified according to their logical properties into the following categories:

1) Iso-constructs,
2) meta-constructs.

Iso-constructs have their scope of relevance defined within a particular domain of knowledge or a field of activity, whereas meta-constructs are relevant to statements that are valid at higher levels of abstraction or generality. An example of a iso-construct within the computer science is a data type, whereas less specific "abstract objects" as defined in computer language theories or in Expert systems domain can be either iso- or meta-.

5.8.3. Activity Structures Viewed as a General Systems Based Possibilistic Theory of the Statics and Dynamics of Activities

The Activity Structures methodology has proved successfull in transferring knowledge accross disciplines because of its General Systems base, utilizing the General Systems Constructs particularised to individual systemic constructs, when they were applied to particular specific disciplines.

The transdisciplinary power of the Activity Structures approach stems from the appropriate utilisation of the General Systems constructs within the Activity Structures framework. While effecting the transfer accross disciplines we proceed as follows: the Systemic Activity Structures constructs chosen from a particular *source* discipline or a field of activity are generalised in an appropriate way, then transferred, and *particularised* asgain within the *target* discipline or field.

In this section I provide the overview of basic elements of Activity Structures in a General Systems *setup*, which was originally concieved and developed as a possibilistic meta-theory of action (Kohout 1978a).

The components that were used in this theory had to capture all he essential features of a family of environments and contexts where the actions take place as well as of the teleological elements (called abstract organism) that effect the action and are affected by it. The concepts and definitions most essential to the material of the previous sections of this chapter, and indeed to the theme of this whole book, follow.

Definition: *Kinds of Teleological Functions*
Two different kinds of teleological function have to be distinguished (Kohout 1978a).
  a) *Substratum function*. This term denotes a construct characterising a particular property or a consistent family of properties of a substratum structure or of its substructure.
  b) *Function of an Activity*. Denotes a property or a family of properties of the activity of an object.

Definition: *Participants*
Participants are abstract elements of an Activity Structure that can take either a passive or active role in the dynamics of action.

Defintion: *Action*
An action is certain precisely specified piece of behaviour of participants.

Definition: *Acting on, Manipulation*
A subject *acts* on an object, and an object is *manipulated* by the subject if it effects any changes on the object or its behaviour.

Definition: *Aim*
Aim is an *a priori* specified (required) objective of a particular activity.

Definition: *Aim controllable by a group of subjects*
Aim controllable by a group of subjects X is an aim which can be achieved by a sequence of actions which must necessarily contain some actions exclusively performed by the group X.

5.9. REFERENCES

Anderson, J., Kohout, L.J., Bandler, W. and Trayner, C. (1985):
  A knowledge-based clinical decision support system using new techniques: CLINAID. In: *Proc. AAMSI Congeress 1985* (Amer. Assoc. for Medical Systems and Informatics, San Francisco, Calif., May 20–22); Levy, A.H. and Williams, B.T. (eds.), 187-192.

Bandler, W. and Kohout, L.J. (1982):
  Fast fuzzy relational algorithms. In: Ballester, A., Cardus, D. and Trillas, E. (eds.), *Proc. Second Internat. Conference on Mathematics at the Service of Man* (Las Palmas, Canary Islands, Spain, 28 June – 3 July 1982). Universidad Politechnica de las Palmas, 123-131.

Bandler, W. and Kohout, L.J. (1983):
Modelling for Computer Scientists. Course Notes, M.Sc. in Computing Systems, Dept. of Computer Science, Brunel University, U.K.

Bandler, W. and Kohout, L.J. (1986a):
On new types of homomorphisms and congruences for partial algebraic structures. *Internat. Journal of General Systems*, vol. **12**, 149–157.

Bandler, W. and Kohout, L.J. (1986b):
On the general theory of relational morphisms. *Internat. Journal of General Systems*, vol. **13**, 47–66.

Bandler, W. and Kohout, L.J. (1987):
Relations, Mathematical. In *International Encyclopaedia of Systems and Control*, Pergamon Press, Oxford.

Bandler, W. and Kohout, L.J. (1988):
Special properties, closures and interiors of crisp and fuzzy relations. *Fuzzy Sets and Systems*, **26**, 317–331.

Behrooz, A. (1986):
A Description of Experimental Identification of Medical Knowledge. Ph.D. Thesis, Dept. of Computer Science, Brunel University, U.K.

Buchanan, B.G. et.al. (1983):
Constructing an expert system. In: Hayes-Roth, F., Waterman, D. A. and Lenat, D. B. (eds.), *Building Expert Systems*, Addison-Wesley, Reading, Mass., 127–171.

Hall, L. (1985):
Analysis of CASNET by means of Activity Structures. CIS 5934 Report, Dept. of Computer Science, Florida State University, U.S.A.

Kohout, L.J. (1974a):
The Pinkava many-valued complete logic systems and their application in design of many-valued switching circuits. In: *Proc. 1974 Internat. Symposium on Multiple-valued Logic*, IEEE, New York (74CH0875-8C), 261–284.

Kohout, L.J. (1974b):
Algebraic models in computer-aided medical diagnosis. In: J. Anderson (ed.), *Proceedings of MEDINFO 74*, North Holland, Amsterdam, 575–579, addendum and list of typographical errors 1069–70.

Kohout, L.J. (1975):
A formal representation of functional hierarchies of movement in the brain and its relation to cybernetics. Second Conference on Recent Topics in Cybernetics, Cybernetic Society, London. Reprinted in Kohout (1990), Appendix 2.

Kohout, L.J. (1975a):
Generalised topologies and their relevance to general systems. *Internat. Journal of General Systems*, vol.2, 25–34.

Kohout, L.J. (1976a):
Representation of functional hierarchies of movement in the brain. *Internat. J. of Man-Machine Studies*, vol. **8**, 699–709.

Kohout, L.J. (1976b):
On functional structures. Presented as a companion paper to Kohout (1977) at NATO Internat. Conf. on Applied General Systems Research, Binghamton, August 1977. (Revised version reprinted in Kohout and Bandler (1986), 69–94).

Kohout, L.J. (1977):
Functional hierarchies in the brain. An invited paper for NATO Internat. Conf. on Applied General Systems Research (Binghamton, N.Y., U.S.A, 15–19 August, 1977).

Kohout, L.J. (1978):
The functional hierarchies of the brain, In Klir, G. (ed.), *Applied General System Research: Recent Development and Trends*. Plenum Press, New York, 531–544.

Kohout, L.J. (1978a):
Methodological Foundations of the Study of Action. Ph.D. Thesis, University of Essex, England, U.K., January 1978.

Kohout, L.J. (1978b):
Analysis of computer protection structures by means of multi-valued logics. In: *Proc. of Eight Internat. Symposium on Multiple-valued Logic*, IEEE, New York, 260–268.

Kohout, L.J. (1981):
Control of movement and protection structures. *Internat. Journal of Man-Machine Studies*, vol. **14**, 397–422.

Kohout, L.J. (1982):
Lecture notes on Activity Structures. Workshop of Man-Computer Studies Group, Brunel University, U.K.

Kohout, L.J. (1982a):
Directives for analysis of expert systems by means of Activity Structures. Technical Memorandum, Man-Computer Studies Group, Dept. of Computer Science, Brunel University, U.K., November 1982.

Kohout, L.J. (1983):
A Perspective on Intelligent Systems. Preprint, Man-Computer Studies Group, Brunel University, U.K., January 1983.

Kohout, L.J. (1986):
On functional structures of behaviour. In: Kohout, L.J. and Bandler. W. (1986).

Kohout, L.J. (1986a):
Knowledge domains, systems constructs and approximation of Gestalt. Opening presentation of Symposium on General Systems Constructs and Approximate Reasoning in Knowledge-Based Systems, 3rd Internat. Conference on Systems Research, Informatics and Cybernetics (August 19–24, 1986, Baden-Baden, West Germany).

Kohout, L.J.(1987):
Activity structures: a general systems construct for design of technological artifacts. *System and Cybernetics: An International Journal*, vol. **18**, 27–34.

Kohout, L.J. (1988):
Theories of possibility: Meta-axiomatics and semantics. An invited article for a special isuue on Interpretations of Grades of Membership. *Fuzzy Sets and Systems*, vol. **25**, No.3 (March), 357–367.

Kohout, L.J.(1990):
A Perspective on Intelligent Systems: A Framework for Analysis and Design. Chapman and Hall, London, and Van Nostrand, New York.

Kohout, L.J., Anderson, J., Bandler, W., Behrooz, A. (1986): Formalization of clinical management activities for a knowledge-based clinical system. *AAMSI Congress Proceedings*, American Association for Medical Systems and Informatics, Washington, D.C., 1986, 348–352.

Kohout, L.J. and Bandler, W. (1985):
Relational-product architectures for information processing. *Information Science*, vol. **37**, 25–37.

Kohout, L.J., and Bandler, W., eds. (1986):
Knowledge Representation in Medicine and Clinical Behavioural Science, An Abacus Book, Gordon and Breach, London.

Kohout, L.J. and Bandler, W. (1986a):
Knowledge representation, clinical action and expert systems. In: Kohout, L.J., and Bandler, W., eds. (1986)

Kohout, L.J., Bandler, W., Anderson, J. and Trayner, C. (1985):
Knowledge-based decision support system for use in medicine. In: Mitra, G. (ed.), *Computer Models for Decision Making*, North-Holland, Amsterdam, 133–146.

Kohout, L.J. and Gaines, B.R. (1975):
The logic of protection. *Lecture Notes in Computer Science*, vol. **34**, Springer Verlag, Berlin, 736–751.

Kohout, L.J. and Gaines, B.R. (1976):
Protection as a general systems problem. *Internat. Journal of General Systems*, vol. **3**, 3–23.

Kohout, L.J., Keravnou, E., Bandler, W., Trayner, C. and Anderson, J. (1984):
Construction of an expert therapy advisor as a special case of general system protection design. In Trappl, R. (ed.), *Cybernatics and Systems Research 2*, North-Holland, Amesterdam, 97–104.

Kohout, L.J. and Pinkava, V. (1980):
The algebraic structure of the Spencer-Brown and Varela calculus. *Internat. Journal of General Systems*, vol. **6**, 155–171.

Pinkava, V. (1988):
Introduction to Logic for Systems Modelling. An Abacus Book, Gorodon and Breach, London and New York.

Roberts, Z. (1985):
Formal structures on an expert system - Hearsay II. CIS 5934 Report, Dept. of Computer Science, Florida State University, U.S.A.

Rundensteiner, E. (1985):
 Analysis of MYCIN by means of Activity Structures. CIS 5934 Report, Dept. of Computer Science, Florida State University, U.S.A.

Simms, J. (1985):
 The functional structures of INTERNIST I. CIS 4934 Report, Dept. of Computer Science, Florida State University, U.S.A.

Zadeh, L.A. (1956):
 On the identification problem. IRE Transactions on Circuit Theory, vol. **CT-3**, December 1956, 277–281.

Ziegler, U. (1985):
 Expert system CASNET in terms of Activity Structures. CIS 5934 Report, Dept. of Computer Science, Florida State University, U.S.A.

PART II

METHODS OF KNOWLEDGE ELICITATION

Editorial Comments:

Knowledge elicitation has not had much prominence to date. Because of challanges of multi-environment and multi-context systems the need for a more appropriate and explicit foundation is made. The next 4 chapters introduce various aspects of this problem and present some working solutions. This is first part of the 9 stage realization process of multi-environmental knowledge based systems.

CHAPTER 6

KNOWLEDGE ELICITATION – AN EXERCISE IN IDENTIFICATION AND VERIFICATION OF EXPERT KNOWLEDGE

J. Anderson, A. Behrooz and L.J. Kohout

Editorial Comment:

> A new pragmatic view of knowledge elicitation is suggested. Some of the implications of this view are addressed, including the separation of knowledge elicitation from the knowledge engineering design process. How this is carried out is illustrated generally, then in a specific field namely in medicine.

LIST OF CONTENTS

6.1. INTRODUCTION
6.2. PROBLEMS IN KNOWLEDGE ELICITATION
6.3. EXPERTISE AND THE EXPERT
6.4. EXPERTISE AND KNOWLEDGE ELICITATION
6.5. METHODS OF KNOWLEDGE ELICITATION
    6.5.1 Learning Vocabulary and Concepts
    6.5.2. Formalisation of the Expert's Knowledge
    6.5.3. Translating Expertise into Informatic Models
    6.5.4. Protection Aspects
6.6. RESULTS OF A MEDICAL CASE STUDY
    6.6.1. Concepts and Data
    6.6.2. Formalisation
    6.6.3. Modelling
    6.6.4. Interaction
    6.6.5. Conclusions
6.7. SUMMARY
6.8. REFERENCES

Knowledge-Based Systems for Multiple Environments

6.1. INTRODUCTION

The development of new concepts in the field of artificial intelligence in the past decade has seen a change from the ideas developed to deal with the difficulties found in the creation of general problem solvers to those that are of use in the implementation of expert systems in limited areas in the fields of industry, business, finance and medicine. Such expert systems are used both for decision support and to give advice to those involved in the use of such an artifact. The creation of such systems initially involves the use of a knowledge engineer whose function is to put the expertise of the expert on a machine and make it available to users of it.

In the main the knowledge engineer has tended to consider the preparation of knowledge for machine usage to be the most difficult and important activity. Several strategies for the representation of the expertise of the expert have been developed from past work with proven problem solving techniques. It is recognised that this is a difficult area where there are as yet few important concepts and such problems seem at first sight to be rather intractable.

Because of these difficulties less attention has been paid to knowledge elicitation from the expert. Indeed in many of the important developments in the field of expert systems in industry, business, finance and medicine during the past decade, the subject expert has been an integral member of the team and was often familiar with the problems of machine representation and implementation. For him the expertise required by a knowledge elicitor was only an integral part of the process for formalising specialist knowledge in ways that were seen to be appropriate for implementation on a machine by a knowledge engineer.

But as the field of knowledge engineering is becoming recognised and is expanding, the knowledge engineer has tended to become a computer and information expert rather than a knowledge elicitor who becomes expert in the subject matter under consideration and in the other aspects of creating a knowledge based system from a particular domain of knowledge. This has meant that the knowledge engineer has tended to concentrate more and more on the areas he was usually familiar with namely knowledge representation and the implementation of an expert system on a machine. Inevitably this implied that knowledge elicitation was not regarded as an important process.

It is important when creating expert systems to have a view of knowledge elicitation from an expert which is **not coloured** by the necessity for machine implementation. If this process of knowledge elicitation is not well done, then the total knowledge which is available from the expert is not gained because it is either not understood by the knowledge engineer or it goes unrecognised as it appears to be too intractable to represent on a machine using present techniques. If the process of knowledge elicitation can be freed from such restrictions then the knowledge elicitor can concentrate on documenting the experts knowledge in more fruitful ways and with less bias than in the past.

It is likely that the processes of knowledge elicitation will be better documented when this is accepted. The problems that the more extensive presentation of the knowledge and expertise will bring, must encourage the process of clarification of that which has still to be achieved. The knowledge that has been *gained but cannot be transformed* for machine implementation becomes clear and the way is open to develop new approaches. It is evident that new strategies for knowledge elicitation will become necessary and the motivation to search for their resolution will be created. If such refinements are ignored then a lot of the expertise of the expert will remain with him and the field of knowledge based systems will progress more slowly.

There are several **key areas** in the activities known as knowledge elicitation that are critical. The first major issue is that the knowledge elicitor has to have some basic knowledge and experience in the field of expertise before he can usefully consult the expert. If this is not done and the expert is tolerant he will have to teach the knowledge engineer the basics of the area chosen for study, so that a meaningful dialogue can take place later. If the expert regards this initial activity as a waste of time then the knowledge elicitor will have to find an alternative way to reach the necessary basic level of knowledge in that field. Only then the knowledge elicitor can begin to *appreciate* and *understand* what the expert is saying during the knowledge elicitation process.

Thus for the process of knowledge elicitation to begin it is suggested that basic learning activities are essential for the knowledge elicitor. Such learning must encompass a knowledge of the established goals in the field of expertise and an acquaintance with its records and procedures for obtaining knowledge. In any field it is necessary to have an **understanding** *of basic concepts, data structures and their meaning.* Inevitably in any learning process the problems with vocabulary and terminology are significant. It is necessary to restrict the vocabulary to that needed by a young student studying the domain for the first time and not to try to acquire a familiarity with tens of thousands of terms and their meaning in a short space of time. Previous knowledge in the field under study is useful in that it gives a firmer base at the beginning. It is important to recognise also that constructive and appropriate attitudes to the difficulties can be helpful.

There is a need to recognise that time and learning effort on the part of the knowledge elicitor make the task of encapsulating the expertise of the expert easier. As a rule the expert cannot deliver all his expertise at once and must gradually work towards more sophisticated levels as the knowledge elicitor becomes more familiar with the knowledge base. The knowledge elicitor requires a good working knowledge of *logics* and *formal modes* of representing knowledge. Armed with these tools he can begin to translate the expertise presented to him. It is helpful to use audio recordings of each session with the expert. This makes recapitulation easier in difficult areas and makes the expert more aware of the difficulties. It supports the learning of the elicitor as well as the creation of written appropriate minutes of each session. In this way the expert can also find out how to build on the previous knowledge gained so that there can be a better transfer of expertise.

6.2. PROBLEMS IN KNOWLEDGE ELICITATION

a) **Vocabulary**. The knowledge elicitor must have some basic knowledge of any field he wishes to explore before proceeding to attempt to elicit knowledge from an expert in that area. This means that the knowledge engineer has to be familiar with and understand the meaning of the basic concepts involved in the area of expertise and the definitions of the terms used in these particular situations. To do this he should become familiar with the *theory* and elementary *models* involved in such a body of knowledge, so that he gets a clear idea of the goals of these activities.

b) **Goals**. Often the activities studied may have several goals indicating that he has to relate to different environments with some differences of vocabulary and procedures. For example in business there is the need to relate product lives to stock but also to the cost, selling price and profit. Similarly in medicine there will not only be diagnostic activity to be considered but prognostic and therapy activities in addition to investigation and the costs of care delivery. In most fields where expert systems are likely to be developed there are likely to be several goals and consequently *multiple environments* which need to be recognised and defined.

c) **Decision Making**. Thus the processes of decision making and advice creation are dependant on an extensive knowledge base and a knowledge of the problems that require solution either frequently or occasionally. Being aware of the goals and sub-goals involved in problem solving is essential if the appropriate knowledge is to be organised for this purpose. This is all the more important if results from multiple environments have to be reconciled. The necessary formalisation of the expertise may be difficult, especially if the presence of multiple environments is not recognised. The recognition of the breadth as well as the depth of knowledge needed for problem solving depends critically on the perceptions of the knowledge elicitor. Inevitably there will be some difficulties in agreeing these parameters with the expert but other problems arise when the importance of context is recognised. Here there is a need to recognise *the significance of data protection* as well as the main problem requiring solution. In the end some of these problems can only be solved by appropriate experiments. This in itself is a powerful stimulus to encourage learning and increase expertise.

d) **Systematics**. The knowledge elicitor has to have some expertise in the field of logics so that he can clearly interpret the logic and apparent intentions of the expert. However, without an adequate vocabulary and knowledge of the subject this can be arduous. The logic relating to different goals or environments in industry, business and medicine will mean that *different logics* will be used *to reflect the different contexts* which are involved. Thus the logics involved will not only reflect the goals and objectives relating to differing environments but also the the more numerous and discrete contexts.

In these situations the ability of the knowledge engineer to model both the process and the particular logics involved is vital. Modelling becomes important as a powerful technique to convey to the expert how he is being understood. It then allows him to bring into congruence his own models with those of the knowledge elicitor. Modelling knowledge so as to bring out the differing representations is a difficult but essential task. Here clarity of thought and familiarity with the precise meaning of terms in particular contexts is necessary. Perhaps the most fruitful aspect of the interaction of the expert and the knowledge elicitor is the way they match and resolve their differing models reflecting their own perceptions.

e) **Skills**. Learning and teaching, the particular skills required by the expert and the knowledge elicitor are becoming clearer. The need is for an aptitude to learn new subjects and areas of activity. Initially, the requirement is to have a basic fundamental insight into any new area of exploration so that there can be meaningful communication. Rarely the expert may become the mentor of the knowledge elicitor and in return the elicitor may help the expert to deepen his knowledge by reflecting the problems perceived. Thus elements of learning and teaching are involved in the elicitation process. The better these two participants are at these activities and the more open their participation, the greater will be the transfer of expertise and a significant reduction in the time taken to achieve it.

f) **Communication**. It is difficult for an expert to communicate effectively with a knowledge elicitor at all levels. It thus becomes very time consuming to ensure total communication and understanding of a limited area of knowledge. Whether the expert has the knowledge and familiarity relating to the problems to be solved and is able to communicate well may decide the outcome of a project. *Good communication involves* being competent at handling the data and processes used and having the necessary motivation to find and create solutions. Without acceptable motivation in both parties to drive the knowledge elicitation activity towards appropriate solutions they will be slow to arrive. Sometimes a battle of wits may take place, when the expert does not want to reveal his expertise as he feels he may not be able to back up his claims or there is a risk of loss of credibility. To some extent the knowledge elicitor should be familiar with such a reaction and be able to convince the expert of his importance and the usefulness of the results. The knowledge engineer has to remember that his role in the communication is to *clarify and establish* the expertise of the expert by motivating the expert to transfer all that he knows.

g) **Process of Formalisation**. The process of formalising the expertise of the expert is difficult and involves transforming it to make the logical nature of the knowledge clear. Gradually this knowledge has to be further transformed so that it is possible to represent it on a machine. However, the first process of formalisation is fraught with as many problems as the final one of machine representation. It is very easy to ignore knowledge which at a particulat time seems to be difficult to formalise in a familiar way. Furthermore the effects of multiple environments may create difficulties when the activities perceived are not clearly defined. Some help is usually obtained from an examination of the *particular contexts* involved by some of the data. Further review with the expert may reveal additional information which could at least help in a partial resolution of the problem while further possibilities await exploration. Often the expert may not be fully aware of the problem and the knowledge engineer has to direct his attention to these aspects so that clarification can precede resolution.

h) **Aspects of Knowledge**. It is important that the knowledge elicitor be alert to the problem of having multiple environments presented as if they did not further complicate the process of resolution. The *boundaries* of an expert system *have to be clearly drawn* so that what is internal to the problem and what is external can be clearly recognised. Here it is the duty of the elicitor to keep track of this problem and alert the expert when he sees difficulties. A similar problem arises in relation to close but different contexts. Here the elicitor must clarify with the expert the nature and content of the contexts so that the correct handling of the differences ensues. It may also be thought necessary by the elicitor to take steps to ensure that protective measures are taken in particular contexts to prevent errors arising.

6.3. EXPERTISE AND THE EXPERT

a) **Concepts and Knowledge**. The expert will be well experienced in his chosen field of knowledge and is familiar with the solutions to the common problems that he has encountered. Hopefully he is engaged in maintaining the base of his knowledge and also by research and experiment is increasing the level and sophistication of his expertise. This should imply that there is between the maintenance of knowledge and the quest for new knowledge by research and experiment, a *dynamic balance* making possible differing solutions to the problems of yesterday. To achieve this the expert is continually changing his concepts as a response to the dynamic changes in his knowledge base. Thus it is quite possible for the elicitor to feel that the expert may be inconsistent by comparing different statements about a problem over a period of time. It is obvious that the expert cannot be suspended in time and difficulties arising because of this must be resolved by good communication. The increase of knowledge in such scientific areas as medicine and industry is rapid and may well during the course of a project involve updating of some concepts. Naturally it is disturbing if it upsets the process of formalisation. It has to be recognised in medicine that what was perceived as general medicine at the turn of the century, by the end of the Second World War had been divided into a score or more specialities both by body system and by age. Today sub-specialities are being recognised, owing to the very large increase in our knowledge and the inability of the physician to maintain an extensive knowledge base. The situation appears to be little different in regard to industry and business.

b) **Goals and Decisions**. The expert has to be continually updating his goals in response to increasing knowledge. Just as these goals are changing so is the nature of the decisions needed to solve the problems encountered. These difficulties will apply to expert systems in a similar manner and part of the pressure for expert systems is made *in the mistaken idea* that this approach would produce similar results without so much effort. What has to be realised is that the expert is as essential for maintaining expert systems as he is in keeping up to date to be able to advise others at a personal level. The dynamic aspects of knowledge and expertise ensure that the challenges will not disappear.

6.4. EXPERTISE AND KNOWLEDGE ELICITATION

a) **Learning**. The knowledge elicitor has to be able to go into different fields of knowledge at short notice and be able to master the elementary concepts and vocabulary. This type of learning is probably best done by reading appropriate texts and other books, and if necessary the help of a teacher in that subject can be useful, especially in testing the achievements of the elicitor. It is probably uneconomic to use an expert for this purpose and many experts would not agree to it, as they may feel that it is a waste of their time and effort. Usually the knowledge elicitor is thrown back on his own resources and has to derive the necessary concepts and knowledge from books. It is helpful if the elicitor already has some elementary knowledge in the field upon which to build. It is important not to take the process too far for he may develop views that may be in conflict with those of the expert and time will be spent in revising them.

The importance of developing a defined vocabulary and some facility in manipulating it, cannot be overstated. It is essential to have this in order to explore the problems of different contexts. However, he should adopt a dynamic attitude to change recognising that the expert will have differing views. This is basic to the initiation of a successful dialogue with the expert. During the interaction with the expert he must be keenly aware of the need to see that the new concepts and knowledge gained update his original efforts. This type of interaction with the expert does mean that he will at times be in the role of a teacher as well as a learner.

b) **Communication**. Skills in communication are unlikely to change so much but every attempt should be made to improve communication with experts. This will be an important factor in regard to the quality of information obtained and the time taken to do it. Communication at all times needs to be appropriate and relevant, and these features can be supported by the motivation of the elicitor. It is helpful to create a firm basic structure at the beginning of the dialogue and to build further structures on this. The soundness of the knowledge base will certainly depend on good communication.

6.5. METHODS OF KNOWLEDGE ELICITATION

6.5.1. Learning Vocabulary and Concepts

It is fundamental at the start of a project to be clear about the general aims and concepts established by those initiating the project. These will guide the elicitor towards recognising the basic concepts and the necessary vocabulary to support this. Any attempt to build a greater superstructure without firm foundations is likely to lead to frustration. In relation to vocabulary it is necessary to establish the relationships of the elements of knowledge very clearly and their particular context.

Although this activity may seem to be difficult at the start, it is necessary to be organised and formal about the essential aspects of knowledge elicitation. Once the basic pattern is recognised by the expert he may well be able to encourage this process. Motivation is an important feature in learning and having good structures will promote it, thus establishing what in essence develops into a system for knowledge elicitation between the expert and the elicitor facilitates the transfer of expertise. Such systems are unique and rather informal being based on the interaction of the two participants.

6.5.2. Formalisation of the Expert's Knowledge

Once the elicitor has established the basic elements of knowledge and their relationships it becomes possible to clarify the differing contexts. At this time it will be necessary to determine the limits of a particular context as well as its content. It is helpful at this time to give thought to protection measures and how common mistakes in context can be recognised and dealt with. The activity structures methodology of Kohout will assist greatly in this endeavour. At this level the elicitor will be dependant on the expert for definitions and the knowledge about a particular context.

The next problem in formalisation is to relate the specific contexts to larger knowledge structures. At this time the logical nature of the knowlege base must be clear. It will be necessary to recognise crisp and vague knowledge and reach the appropriate representations. Often the expert may assume that because he reaches the right or perceived correct conclusion that the logic he has used is correct. However, there are subtle and differing views which can change contexts and give the expert the idea that the logic is correct. Laying bare and clarifying the views is an important function of the elicitor and a key aspect of formalisation.

6.5.3. Translating Expertise into Informatic Models

The knowledge elicitor will not achieve the desired result of representing the experts expertise in a single act of formalisation and modelling. As his knowledge grows due to the interaction with the expert so his ability to represent the expertise by modelling increases. With repeated transformations the move towards the possibility of machine representation proceeds. The major difficulty about formalisation and modelling is that the process tends to cause loss of information with transformation. This may be due to ill-defined concepts being ignored or a different meaning attributed to them from that of the expert. Also fuzzy values and relationships tend to give rise to errors of interpretation. At present with the level of knowledge elicitation that is usual there is a considerable loss of information, especially if considerations of machine implementation are given prominence too early.

The knowledge elicitor has to view the model building process as flexible and iterative, responding to the needs of different environmental requirements. When the models are changed to capture more closely the expertise, the changes have to be understood and agreed by both participants. Naturally the process of formalisation changes the boundaries and limits of concepts and has its repercussions on the knowledge base. It is not surprising therefore if loss of information does occur. Also in relation to expert systems, if the logical and formal bounds of processes are not clearly specified and verifiable, then the system is insecure. This problem has to be dealt with at the time of modelling the system and not left to the user to do it at the time of use of the expert system. Indeed an expert system by its very nature should be more expert than the user.

6.5.4. Protection Aspects

Protection and data security are not usually seen as important in the creation of knowledge based systems. Yet knowing the frequency of bugs in standard software, one would have thought that the problem would have received more attention. Because the whole nature of the system changes when modelling expertise is attempted, there is a danger in ignoring this aspect. This important view of expert systems in relation to data protection has received little attention, yet is crucially dependant on the process of knowledge elicitation. If the concept of protection of the system is not recognised at every stage of knowledge elicitation then such systems will be prone to error and will not live up to users' expectations.

Errors of course arise and the methods for handling them at different levels in the system are vital. It is not possible to expect the user to detect errors at the time when the system is requested to display the logic and the rules so that the user may see how a conclusion was reached. While it is agreed that expert systems should not be black boxes and that the function of explanation is useful, it is not part of the protection and security system.

The activity structures methodology of Kohout has taken this issue fully into account at the analysis and design stage. Recognising that systems are error prone and that errors are easy to propagate it is necessary to have error checking procedures at every stage in the development. Major areas where this is done occur in the knowledge base especially in ensuring that the relations of knowledge elements are clearly established and these relations followed. The use of context is a powerful tool for detecting errors early before they project into the higher structures. It is not an adequate approach to report these and leave it to the user to get resolution. But the system has to be resilient and deal with them appropriately.

For these reasons the process of knowledge elicitation is both critical and exciting. The knowledge elicitor and the expert can help the system development by giving emphasis to common errors and devise ways of overcoming them. A powerful strategy is to give the system the capability to ask questions of the user when errors arise, so that he can more fully define a context or clarify a logical process. In this way the system can by further definition avoid propagating errors. So far such systems are just being developed. No doubt other useful ways will be devised to make systems more secure.

6.6. RESULTS OF A MEDICAL CASE STUDY

At the begining of the medical study the knowledge elicitor was only interested in the diagnostic area and saw this as the major part of the project. However, as the expert discussed the various aspects of diagnosis and the intermediary stages before a final diagnosis could be reached, it became clear that other activities such as prognosis were necessary, so that relatives and the patient could be aware of possible outcomes. Therapy had to be started before a final diagnosis was available on many occasions, based on an intermediary diagnosis such as a syndrome, or a general diagnostic level, before investigations had revealed the final diagnosis. Thus clarifying the goals will often reveal the multiple environments involved.

6.6.1. Concepts and Data

At the begining of the project the knowledge engineer felt it necessary to acquire a basic medical knowledge in the area of interest in order to avoid the expert being involved in basic training. He found that this was best done using a variety of elementary textbooks and comparing their concepts and basic vocabulary. It was at that time necessary to consider basic medical theory in relation to diagnosis, prognosis and therapy. He found this more difficult, as it was far from easy to find an appropriate account. It was necessary to consult the expert and obtain guidance.

The elicitor then began his sessions with the expert. As new material was introduced he found it necessary to refer back to textbooks. When these were in conflict with the expert after comment he accepted the experts view. As the elicitation process evolved he found cross-referencing basic material essential in order to ensure consistency of the knowledge base and the logics.

He also recognised that as his learning progressed that it was necessary to modify and expand some concepts and their relationship to the knowledge base. It was apparent that the expert did not introduce all the complications and detail at once but tended to indicate the complexity gradually at a pace that appeared to him to match the progress of the interaction. This was evident at the reviews of the formalisation process and during the evolution of the various models. At times this tended to exasperate the knowledge elicitor but overall was helpful in ensuring the integrity of the knowledge base.

6.6.2. Formalisation

The first attempts were the checking of basic concepts and the definition of knowledge elements. At this time the need for error checking was apparent, as at times there were misunderstandings. These were useful in that they could give rise to errors in the system and changes had to be made to prevent such conflicts. Once the basic knowledge base structures were in place, the establishing of contexts gave rise to other difficulties. Here it was necessary to be specific about content and boundaries and how these related to the knowledge base. Here again out of the contradictions developed a possible system for ensuring the integrity of the knowledge base and the relevant logics.

As the project progressed, the necessity of reconciling the multiple environments arose. Here again misinterpretations were explored fully to establish consistent views. This became all the more important when ideas of parallel processing were introduced. During these processes the activity structures methodology of Kohout was very helpful both to the expert and to the knowledge elicitor. It created the necessary background when exploring the knowledge system.

6.6.3. Modelling

Alongside the effort at formalisation and really part of it was the procedure of modelling. Words are not always easily used to describe new and complex functions and models succeed rather better. This does not mean that description was abandoned but that the two methods of representation were used together, one supporting the other. Models were produced from the early stages and grew more complex as developments occurred. Keeping track of them was an important exercise as well as recognising their subtleties.

As refinement proceeded, it was important to reconsider the detail and ensure that there were no inconsistancies. Here having a strong structure was a great help. Also concepts of protection and security were always there and reinforced the need to be consistent and logical. By the end of the project the volume of the representations was considerable, due to the differing transformations towards implementation. Keeping track of these transformations created organisational problems and a tight file structure was instituted.

6.6.4. Interaction

The outcome of the project was not clear at the begining of the project and its time scale equally vague. Both the expert and the knowledge elicitor expected that the duration would be less but failed to take into account the primitive nature of the tools available. For both it proved to be a fascinating experience and journey into largely unknown territory and held the benefits of clarification of concepts and preconceived ideas. The detail required proved to be far more extensive than anticipated and indicated the complex nature of activies which are in daily usage. Nevertheless it helped to establish the way for future developments.

6.6.5. Conclusions

The importance of knowledge elicitation in its own right has been established as a key area in knowledge engineering. The interaction of the expert and the knowledge elicitor proved to be fruitful and revealed a new way to build expert systems with more reliability and to embrace new methodologies. Emphasis was given to the detailed specification of the knowledge base and the development of differing logics ranging from crisp to multivalued and fuzzy logics to express the range of activities. Formalisation and modelling were two important methods aiding both development and interpretation. The introduction of ideas of protection and reliability early in the analytical and design stages greatly eased the burden of trying to create these activities at a much later stage. The use of the activity structures methodology was found to be very helpful. The outcome has been to introduce some new ways of creating expert systems that may be more effective and reliable.

6.7. SUMMARY

A new approach to knowledge elicitation from an expert has been explored. The detail of this complex interaction has been discussed with a view to introducing it to the field. The needs of both participants have been explored to reveal the interaction and the requirements. The roles of the expert and the elicitor reveal the need for humility in the face of complexity. New ways of creating expert systems have been developed.

6.8. REFERENCES

Anderson, J., Kohout L.J., Bandler W., and Trayner C., (1985):
A Knowledge based Clinical Decision Support System using new Techniques, CLINAID; *Proc AAMSI 4th Intern. Congress*, 1985, pp 187–92.

Behrooz, A. (1987):
Meta Description of Experimental Identification of Medical Knowledge. PhD Thesis. (Dept. of Computer Science) Brunel University, Uxbridge, Middx.

Behrooz, A. and Kohout, L.J. (1987):
Experimental Identification and Formalisation of Knowledge Structures Representing Uncertainty. In *Proc. of the 7th International Congress on Cybernetics and Systems*, Imperial College, London, September 1987.

Kohout, L. J. (1987):
Activity Structures. A General System Construct for Design of Technical Artifacts, *Cybernetics System J.*, **18**, 27–34.

Kohout, L. J. and Gaines, B.R. (1976):
Protection as a General System Problem. *Intern. Systems J.*, **3**, 1–21.

Kohout, L. J. and Bandler, W. (1986):
Knowledge Representation in Medicine and Clinical Behavioural Science, pp 5–7, An Abacus Book, Gordon and Breach Science Publishers, London and New York.

CHAPTER 7

KNOWLEDGE ELICITATION – THE FIRST STEP TOWARDS THE CONSTRUCTION OF EXPERT SYSTEMS: THE OUTLINE OF A METHOD

A. Behrooz, L.J. Kohout and J. Anderson

Editorial Comment:

> The new partition of the field into Knowledge Elicitation and Knowledge Engineering results in bringing out the roles and mutual interactions of the Expert, Knowledge Elicitor and Knowledge Engineer in a more explicit way. The time dependency of the dynamic of the interaction raises new challenges.

LIST OF CONTENTS

7.1 INTRODUCTION
7.2 IS THE HUMAN EXPERT AN ESSENTIAL COMPONENT?
7.3 AN OVERVIEW OF THE COMPLETE CONSTRUCTION PROCESS
    7.3.1 Two Types of Approach Towards Eliciting Knowledge
7.4 ANALYSIS OF KNOWLEDGE STRUCTURES
    7.4.1 Binary Approach
7.5 THE MAIN RESULTS OF A KNOWLEDGE ELICITATION EXPERIMENT
    7.5.1 An Overview
    7.5.2 Medical Record Formalisation
    7.5.3 Clinician-Patient Interaction
    7.5.4 Diagnostic Process
7.6 KNOWLEDGE ELICITATION: THE FIRST STEP TOWARDS CONSTRUCTION OF EXPERT SYSTEMS
7.7 REFERENCES

Knowledge-Based Systems for Multiple Environments

7.1. INTRODUCTION

The present chapter is not about what can be elicited, but rather about how the necessary information can be elicited systematically, using a well-structured method of knowledge elicitation. We have attempted to explain here how the knowledge needed for the construction of a Knowledge-Based System could be materialised in the first instance, with as few *a priori* assumptions about its representation as possible.

Behrooz (1986) describes the dynamic evolution of a knowledge structure, and the knowledge elicitation activity, in an interactive experiment by means of a controlled dialogue between a knowledge elicitor and an expert.

Knowledge elicitation, when the elicitor is unfamiliar with the domain of knowledge, is similar to the case of compiling a Pascal program with a Cobol compiler. In the latter case, one ends up with some messages of incompetence, and advice to the user to act accordingly, and perhaps more intelligently. The knowledge elicitor would behave almost similarly during th first steps, but eventually it becomes clear that no excuse is acceptable; better to get it right, and build up a new complete compiler.

7.2. IS THE HUMAN EXPERT AN ESSENTIAL COMPONENT?

The answer to this question is both yes and no, depending on some parameters. Yes, it is possible to establish a sufficient result without help from a human expert, if certain factors are met. These are:

1. The knowledge elicitor must be familiar with the domain, in order to link all the elicited knowledge from different textbooks and databases.
2. The domain of knowledge must be limited and small, so that a single person can deal with the task.
3. The elicitor naturally needs a longer time so that he can read all the textbooks, and examine the data extracted from the stored records/databases, if any exist.

We should, however, bear in mind that the formalised knowledge so gained should be examined and tested by a second authority, otherwise it would have doubtful scientific value.

We believe that it will produce better results if the knowledge is elicited by interacting with the human expert. The expert at any given time can correct the results, and speed up the process of elicitation.

It is, however, a less demanding task if a computer is able to use the textbooks as a sufficient source of knowledge. This will introduce its own problems. Take an example from the medical field: there is no common understanding of characteristics of a disorder among the experts. The discrepancy of information in different medical sources has been discussed by Ben Ahmeida, et al., in Chapter 16 of this volume. They analysed over 100 symptoms and signs of disorders in endocrine body systems, as indicated in two medical textbooks CMIT (Finkel et al., 1980) and (Williams 1974).

It was shown that there are some symptoms and signs that have not been mentioned in either book and even *if the same diseases and symptoms/signs are selected* from both sources, the intrinsic relational structure of this interrelationship may be *different* from another source.

Further to the above-mentioned difficulties, there is also another major problem yet to be solved: that is, to understand a textbook written in a natural language. To this end, the system must have a way (program) to understand the sentences, text ambiguities, etc. (Schank, 1975; Weizenbaum, 1984, De Bono, 1983).

In addition to these problems, the system that acquires knowledge from the textbook, or even from a human user, must have the capability to communicate in order to achieve a dialogue understanding (Bobrow, et al., 1977). In some instances, the control of dialogue is with the user and sometimes with the program; i.e., mixed initiative (Carbonell, 1970, 1980). Rich (1984) has examined the rest of the problems with dialogue understanding and its relevant implications (Cohen, 1979; Kaplan, 1981).

7.3. AN OVERVIEW OF A COMPLETE CONSTRUCTION PROCESS

To capture completely the process of designing an expert system one generally needs to consider three phases; namely, *familiarisation* with the problem, knowledge *elicitation*, and *knowledge engineering*.

The **familiarisation phase** occurs when the task is first encountered, its very immediate problems are recognised and the early models of it are constructed. Within this phase, the desired field of interest is selected and the purpose is clearly established.

The **second phase**, knowledge elicitation, is a combination of three interrelated sub-phases. These are identification of concepts and components, formulation of the relationships between concepts and components, and, validation.

The **final phase**, knowledge engineering, consists of three activities: knowledge representation; selection of a suitable language and of suitable hardware; constructing the expert system and testing its performance.

The present work concentrates on the first and second phases. To this end, the knowledge elicitor tries to establish how an expert performs a task, given a limited amount of relevant information. This includes another objective, i.e., to examine whether the elicited knowledge can be formulated and to decide what difficulties arise formally in this activity of formalisation.

The **first sub-phase** generally involves *discussing observations* with the expert in the sessions, to begin familiarisation with the task. During this sub-phase, a massive amount of information is put together, basically by questioning the expert about his expertise, session after session.

In these sessions there is a mutual educational process. The expert becomes aware of the knowledge of the elicitor and tries to improve that knowledge as he answers the questions. The elicitor has to accept an educational as well as a questioning role.

Each session can be considered as having a **motivating factor** as well as a goal. A motivating factor is the element that throughout the interviews *causes changes in approach* towards the case, the reasons for a question, and reaching out towards a conclusion. There is no other way to come to any conclusion unless the process of the interaction is seen from and through this aspect (Behrooz and Kohout, 1987b,c,d).

The **second sub-phase** of knowledge *elicitation* then emerges. Every result the elicitor understands, whether it is correct or not, is formally represented in the elicitor's model and tested by the expert. The expert can then intervene to accept, amend or reject the formulation.

Finally, the **third sub-phase** of *validation* is both important and critical. During this phase all the previously obtained information reviewed is tested against the knowledge from other knowledge sources.

The same question may be put to the expert once again to check whether the same result can be obtained. Often inconsistencies may be discovered, as the expert may simplify or change the view of a problem as part of what he sees as the educational process of the knowledge elicitor. Elaborated concepts are often reached in a stepwise manner. Also, the expert and elicitor may have different views, owing to different reasoning patterns.

All the inconsistencies discovered must be resolved and corrected. This may require both the knowledge elicitor and the expert to loop back to reconsider the first sub-phase of knowledge identification.

7.3.1. Two Types of Approach Towards Eliciting Knowledge

Behrooz (1986) pointed out that there may be two ways for the elicitor to approach the domain. One way is to obtain as many facts about the concepts and components in the domain as possible, and then try to understand the reason for any existing relationship or any activity. He called this 'facts to reason'. On the other hand, there is a second way of approaching the problem of elicitation called 'reason to facts', and he chose this approach for his experimental work (Behrooz 1987a,d).

He began the interaction with the expert with a general and a somehow vague question, for two reasons:

a) He had no choice because he was a non-medical elicitor, and therefore he could not start with a domain-specific question.

b) Importantly, this allowed the expert to choose his own way of explanation, rather than being dictated to by a total stranger to his domain.

The crucial question to the expert is "How do you do it?" This question enables the expert to form his own *strategy* and therefore he knows what he would want to talk about next. The only things that would stop his plan to proceed are the knowledge elicitor's *in-between-questions*.

Knowledge elicitation can be seen as an activity based on *two types of general questions* posed to the expert. These are:

a) **How/Why** *do you take that particular step?* This would produce an *answer*. The elicitor will then analyse the context and hence the second question will arise.

b) **What** *is the meaning of that word/terminology used in the previous answer?* This will introduce the terms, concepts and unfamiliar relationships to the elicitor, as well as providing a *new answer*, to which either of the question types could again be applied.

The expert's explanation might never end, if the knowledge elicitor did not once in a while stop the expert, in order to get answers to some more questions. Each context considered contained several points that needed to be clarified. From this clarification a new set of questions and a new context would evolve.

The advantage about 'reason to facts' that we recognised is that when the elicitor identifies all the reasons that the expert has for doing certain activities, it is then easier to fit all the facts together, even those that may be extracted from textbooks.

For instance, when we know how to diagnose a disease, then it is easy to find the name of a disease and all the relevant symptoms and signs. But if we get the facts first, such as what symptoms and signs belong to which disease, we would still need the expert to explain how to link them.

7.4. ANALYSIS OF KNOWLEDGE STRUCTURES

The very first thing that a knowledge elicitor should realise is that knowledge is a complex entity with a complex multi-level structure. Each level of the knowledge structure is more complex than its previous level, but they all follow the same properties with some minor differences. The knowledge structure consists of two **constructing constraints**, namely, the *components* and the *relationships* between the two components.

Each contributing element (component) may itself possess a complex structure, or it may have the most primitive structure, i.e., no other elements constructing it. Further to this, we have to realise that interaction between two elements, e.g., expert and elicitor, has a structure of its own, with certain level of complexity, depending upon the complexity of the elements and the reason for the existence of that interaction (see Behrooz 1986, chapter 6).

In order to analyse an interaction, however, one must examine:

a) The contributing elements.
b) The existing relationships.
c) The structure as an element in a relationship with other structures.

It is also argued that there are several types of relationships. This should be noted when analysing a structure. Further to this, two types of goals for an interaction are introduced, i.e., the *goal of the contributing elements* (internal goal), and the *interaction goal* (external goal).

Having recognised knowledge as a multi-level complex structure, we have proposed a four-level investigational approach (Behrooz 1986; Behrooz and Kohout, 1987c,d), consisting of the following steps:

1. To recognise and analyse the contributing **elements** in that interaction.

2. To recognise and analyse the **structures** to which these two elements belong, and to recognise and analyse every interaction with those structures, involving the two contributing elements.
3. To move one level higher and recognise and analyse the **meta-structure** to which the two recognised structures possessing the two contributing elements belong. To examine all the relationships, directly or indirectly, from the contributing elements to any structure in these meta-structures. To recognise and analyse any relationships between the structures in those meta-structures.
4. The **meta-meta-structure level**, in which we **substitute** *structures* for *elements*, and *meta-* for *structure*, and start the process again from level-1 but at a higher degree of complexity (i.e., level 2).

7.4.1. Binary Approach

To sum up the above argument, we proposed in the previous section that the logical approach towards the analysis of structures is a binary one. The reason for this is when we want to analyse a structure/element, we actually have a reason for our analysis. The reason could be because we want to understand an interaction/activity in which that structure/element is active. In other words, we are actually analysing an interaction between two elements at that given moment.

Consider Figure 7.1 representing structure-Z, in which there are some interactions between its elements. Now we want to analyse interaction AM. To this end, we may find it necessary to analyse the rest of interactions in structure-Z, e.g., AN, CM, ND, etc. But it will be essential to analyse both A and M, and all their internal interactions.

Element A may have a structure consisting of several elements that interact with one another, e.g., PT, QT, etc. So the element M may consist of its internal interactions, which should also be examined.

In other words, no matter how complex is the structure of the contributing elements in an interaction, we should always take two elements that interact at any given time. When that one is analysed, the next two elements, e.g., CM, AN, BK, etc., should be analysed. Now, it is possible that one element interacts with several other elements at the same time, which will not change anything, for at the split second that we consider one of the element's interactions, we involve only two elements.

For instance, consider element A interactions with element M at the same time it interacts with N. It is possible that interaction AN is the reason for the existence of an interaction AM (see Behrooz 1986, chapter 6). This does not, however, change the fact that the analysis is about the interaction AM at that particular time.

	K	N	M	
		V	V	A
	V			B
			V	C
		V		D

STRUCTURE – Z

	S	T	
	V	V	P
		V	Q

ELEMENT – A

Figure 7.1. Elements of knowledge and their substructures

7.5. THE MAIN RESULTS OF A KNOWLEDGE ELICITATION EXPERIMENT

7.5.1. An Overview

We have concluded an experiment in medical knowledge elicitation of three year's duration at King's College Medical and Dental School (Behrooz 1985, 1986).

This experimental work has produced two different and distinct types of results, namely:
- a) A methodological approach towards the problem of knowledge elicitation. In this approach we consider knowledge elicitation as an interaction between two elements with some internal and external goals (Behrooz 1986, chapter 6).
- b) A more specific domain result has also been obtained, namely, the clinician's activities were explored when interacting with a patient. Several other aspects related to domain of medicine were examined, such as:
  - b1) How can a medical record be formalised for general use.
  - b2) How the process of clinician-patient interaction evolved, and identification of the contributing elements in that process.
  - b3) How a clinician diagnoses a disorder, beginning with a working or provisional diagnosis. After further refinement the diagnosis becomes more specific and the final diagnosis is reached. There may be more than one diagnosis for each patient.

7.5.2. Medical Record Formalisation

From a thorough examination of some computerised medical records, and the analysis of experts' explanations throughout our interactions, it emerged that a medical record has an implicit logical pattern of formation.

Most clinicians prefer to write down the patient's medical record the way they feel is the best. The formalisation that was proposed (Behrooz 1986, chapter 7) would not only help an intelligent knowledge-based system to access information with less complexity, but also a human user can employ the technique to advantage when writing down the medical record manually.

It is actually the expansion of the computerised record shown in Behrooz (1986, chapter 3). It is divided into several sections as the expert thought necessary, but this partitioning may be confusing for a young clinician or a non-medical user. For instance, the original medical record indicates present history, but does not say what kind of information to hold in that section, in what order and for what purpose. The content is a list of symptoms and other data with their essential properties. The advantages of this extended form can be recognised, if it is compared with the original medical record.

It emerged from this work that the **logical structure of a medical record** is a *very important part of the formulation* of this *domain knowledge*. This is also the case for the other domains, such as insurance underwriting or business organisation.

7.5.3. Clinical-Patient Interaction

The knowledge contained in records interrelates with the knowledge obtained by patient-clinician interaction. In order to understand what steps a clinician-patient process of interaction consists of, the knowledge elicitor had to undergo a three-stage process. These stages are:

1. Non-human expert involvement stage, i.e., using textbooks.
2. Intermediate stage, i.e., when the expert influences elicitor's understanding and formalisation.
3. Standardisation stage, i.e., the final version of the knowledge elicitor's understanding and the results that are accepted.

The main result of this process shows that the clinician-patient interaction consists of three main processes:

a) data collection and interrogation process;
b) patient management process;
c) decision-making process related to medical goals.

7.5.4. Diagnostic Process

When the clinician obtains at least some information concerning the investigated patient, then another concurrent process called the diagnostic process is started by the clinician.

The other result of our experimental work is an understanding of this process, which is concerned with the clinician's activity in order to diagnose the patient's disorder. Formalising its intrinsic features revealed an interesting multi-level structure.

A clinician undertakes a six-level diagnostic process. At each level, the clinician should handle more data and with the help of this data should make some kind of decision about the type and the reasons for the patient's disorder.

1. Symptom and sign level.
2. Syndrome level.
3. Body system level.
4. General disease level.
5. Specific disease level.
6. Aetiology of disease level.

Several substantial points can be made about these levels, namely:

a) The syndrome level is used explicitly as an essential component in making a diagnosis. Although it has been around for years, and most clinicians have looked for syndromes, still it has not usually been used in a significant way in any computerised diagnostic system, as an essential step in the diagnostic process.
b) It distinguishes distinctly the difference between the general level, such as lower respiratory tract infection, and diseases at the aetiological level, such as pneumococcal bronchopneumonia.

c) It introduces the very important aspect in clinical diagnosis, i.e., aetiology. To acknowledge the cause of disorder is as an important parameter as establishing the final clinical state of the patient. It is as essential as the physician tries to remove the cause by therapy.

It should be borne in mind that the above levels have always existed and been used by all the clinicians. All that the knowledge elicitor has done is to point them out, and try to formalise them in an easier form for the general use. This is one of the main functions of an elicitor. In other words, when the elicitor gets the existing knowledge and formalises it, he should not change anything in the existing rules and facts, even if the changes seem to be more logical. This is *the main difference between the system analyst and the knowledge elicitor*: the former analyses the system and suggests some changes, whereas the latter analyses the knowledge structure to formalise the identified components and concepts relating to one another.

7.5.4.1.   Diagnosing a disease

It has already been explained in a previous section how a clinician logically approaches the diagnosis of a disease. Looking at the same problem from the activity structure applicability point of view, we understand the reasons behind the expert's approach.

Consider Figure 7.2 which is an interaction between a patient and a disease. That is, the patient is known to be ill. The clinician's goal is to understand what disease the patient suffers from, what caused it, and what treatment to suggest.

What the clinician actually will first look for is any interaction between the patient and disease. This interaction could be considered as former (antecedent), which has brought about a 'consequent' interaction (i.e., signs and symptoms. These can be seen as consequent to some previous interactions.). For instance, a cough and high temperature may help to lead the clinician towards the right diagnosis.

On the other hand, to reach the aetiology of the disease the clinician enters a second diagnostic cycle (syndrome level).

7.5.4.2.   Knowledge elicitation — a general approach

The knowledge elicitation activity, like any other interaction, is between two elements, i.e., elicitor and expert (Figure 7.3). The external goal of this interaction is to understand the dynamism of another interaction, i.e., expert knowledge. This interaction between two participants in the process of knowledge elicitation can be represented by a model with certain properties and relationships. Unlike the description in Kohout (1978, 1990), where some theoretical assumptions are made *a priori*, the model here is presented in the form in which it was empirically observed and experienced by the knowledge elicitor. From this experimental material, a knowledge structure was identified and formalised. The conclusions arrived at were therefore concrete and representable (Behrooz, 1986).

Before the process of knowledge elicitation starts, certain aspects involved in this process must be acknowledged *a priori* by both the participants, in order to make possible **any communication** between them.

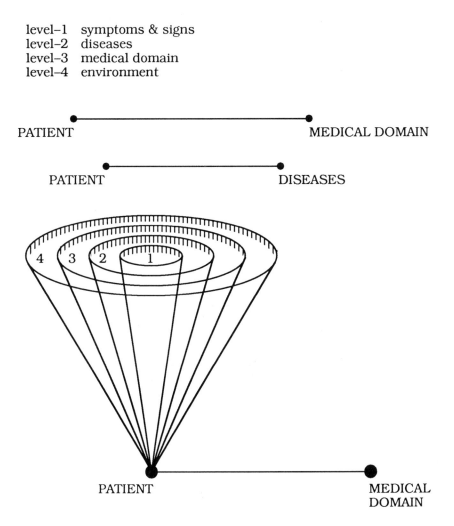

Figure 7.2. The patient-disease relation and its reflection in the medical knowledge domain

KNOWLEDGE-BASED SYSTEMS FOR MULTIPLE ENVIRONMENTS

level–1   To investigate interactions within
           the 'reasoning' and 'facts' of DOMAIN

level–2   To investigate interactions within
           the 'reasoning' and 'facts' of META Domain (MEDICINE)

level–3   To consider 'HUMAN KNOWLEDGE' :

level–4   To consider knowledge 'TO BE DISCOVERED'
           'TO BE RECOGNISED', 'TO BE ACCEPTED'

KNOWLEDGE ELICITOR   HUMAN EXPERT   KNOWLEDGE

                 FACTS   REASONING

                      INTERACTION-D1
RESPIRATORY DISEASES   SYMPTIOMS/SINGS/ETC...

                      INTERACTION-R1
REASONING–1   CONDITIONS/CASES

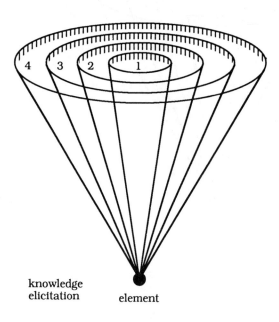

Figure 7.3. The levels of interaction of expert knowledge to be identified by the knowledge elicitor

Furthermore, activity entering into the Activity Structures model needs to be approached from three independent angles. It is essential to:
a) examine each contributing element of the structure independently;
b) examine the relationship between the elements independently;
c) examine the interaction as a whole structure.

In other words, we have to understand the goals of each individual element of the structure, to recognise the type of relationship the two interacting elements have, and to establish the goal of the interaction, i.e., the reason for the existence of such an activity.

It can be seen that each contributing element of an interaction has its own structure, with its several internal interactions. So, if we take the element 'knowledge' (Figure 7.3), we see that it has two major elements that mainly interact, i.e., facts of domain and reasoning knowledge. Now, if this process continues, we get to the interaction between, say, respiratory diseases and signs and symptoms, and/or reasoning-1 of diagnostic process to some conditional properties (interaction-D1 and interaction-R1 respectively).

The process of elicitation of the first atoms of knowledge starts at the level depicted in the inner circle of Figure 7.3. That is, *the first understanding* about the interaction-D1 and interaction-R1 *taking place*, say, in the respiratory system, and the next interaction in the reasoning knowledge (i.e., R2), **followed** by *the next interaction in facts* of domain (i.e., D2), and so on.

It is, however, necessary to know more about the other 'structures' within a meta-structure, e.g., cardiovascular, gastrointestinal body systems, and their internal and external relationships, in order to be able to elicit complete knowledge on a specific domain. At the same time, reviewing the *reasoning* aspect may make it necessary to know more about 'reasoning', and 'knowledge' from a philosophical point of view, for instance. It may be necessary to know how the present system's philosophies work, and this leads to the second circle.

To be more precise about the context of *knowledge elicitation*, one might find it necessary to enter the higher level (third circle). This presents concepts 'human knowledge', 'man's understanding', 'neuropsychology', 'pattern recognition', 'conceptual dependencies', 'intelligence', etc. The interactions within each meta-meta-structure should also be examined.

Therefore, the basic task of the elicitation is to *know which level is to be considered next* and to establish what types of relationships are being investigated. For instance, in the first circle, the elicitor may find out that some of the interactions in this structure are dependent upon the occurrence of some other interactions in the second circle. So, he will eventually look for those interactions, and will not be wondering about several sub-structures in the first circle unnecessarily, but will move directly to the right environment.

7.5.4.3. How to retrieve knowledge in a structured way

If we consider the retrieval of information from a knowledge structure as an activity, we would see that the interaction involved in this retrieval between the user and the system (say, an expert system) has a particular specificity.

Each element has its own internal goal; the user's goal is to satisfy the environmental requirements, and the system's goal is to activate the internal systems. both, however, have a common external goal, i.e., to get the right results.

Now, if we observe an expert system's activity, we see that part of its internal interaction is within the inferential system-knowledge base (Figure 7.4). The knowledge base could be imagined as a multi-story building with several structures used in each story. The inferential system first interacts with a section of the first floor (level); if that section does not satisfy the system's requirement, then a bigger section within the first level is approached. Now, if this level does not provide enough knowledge, then the inferential system finds it necessary to enter into meta-structure, and so on.

Each *interaction is a consequence* of some other interactions and **depends** on *several other elements and interactions*. We could, for instance, consider the user-system as the former interaction and expect several consequent interactions to be activated as soon as the former is activated.

These brief structural designs of parts of a system naturally have to be looked into in detail, which is beyond the scope of the present work and will be done elsewhere. We can, however, generalise that every investigation of an interaction must examine both contributing elements (each element may have a complex structure), the relationship between the contributing elements (establishing their types), and finally look at the interaction as a single structure within another interaction (an element of a super-structure).

7.6. KNOWLEDGE ELICITATION:THE FIRST STEP TOWARDS CONSTRUCTION OF EXPERT SYSTEMS

It is therefore possible to conclude that knowledge elicitation is the most essential and the first step for constructing an expert system.

It is a complicated process which involves a minimum of two human participants – the domain expert and the knowledge elicitor – who interact having a common goal, i.e., to make knowledge elicitation possible (in other words, to identify everything and anything in that domain and to formalise the elicited knowledge for general use). Using such a method, a knowledge engineer should be capable of representing it in a computer system.

It should be emphasised that all the work involved in elicitation must be explicitly discussed, so that a general formalisation is eventually agreed.

The present chapter is only an initial step in the development of a systematic method for knowledge elicitation, and naturally it does not deal with all the aspects in this field. Further work should extend the important issues raised and implicitly suggested by the context. For example:

1. Can questioning be systematically formalised? What Behrooz (1986) achieved was an experimental investigation where questions were not pre-designed, but were created as the expert explained various aspects of the medical domain. However, if such questions can be formalised in such a systematic manner that they can be asked by an intelligent computer, then there would be less need for elicitors.

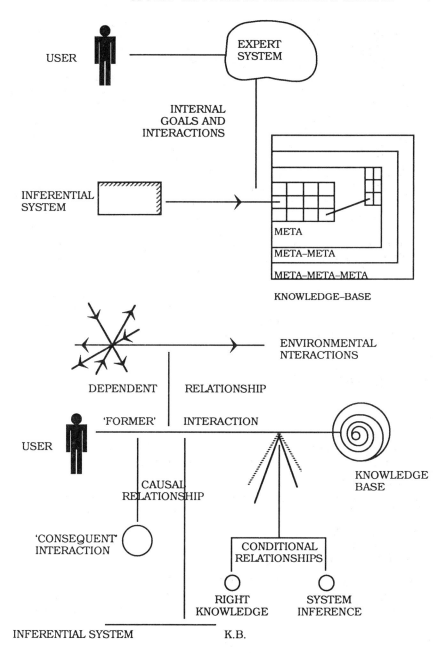

Figure 7.4. Interactions of an active expert system

2. Can the discussed elicitation process be employed as a component in an expert system? Now, using the system proposed here for eliciting knowledge, could it be possible to deploy the same technique in order to enable a computer to acquire this knowledge?
3. Starting from the discussion of section 7.4, is it possible to construct a 'real' autonomous expert system? The main aim of constructing expert systems at present is to come closer to such a 'real' expert system.

    But will it be possible to replace a human expert by an autonomous expert system? Would this be really desirable? If yes, then why? If not, why not? What is the main ingredient that makes this task nearly impossible? Is it because 'man' cannot formalise his own domain? Or perhaps because man has no competent tools. Or perhaps because there is no 'real' human expert in order to help a non-existing 'real' elicitor to formalise a non-established and ever-growing 'real' knowledge. Perhaps we need the system to be 'intelligent'. But what is intelligence? Who can judge the intelligent machine? The machine lacks the necessary ingredients that a psychologist may look for. On the other hand, is it essential to have an 'intelligent' system, if the expert system functions as it is expected, with the maximum accuracy?

Well, our answer to all these questions is that one cannot say unless one has tried, however imperfect the results obtained. In order to explore this avenue, the method proposed here may be essential. The reader who is interested in further detail of our method will find this in our new book (Behrooz, Anderson and Kohout, 1991).

7.7. REFERENCES

Behrooz, A., Anderson, J. and Kohout, L.J. (1984):
Knowledge elicitation sessions: tapes and transcripts. Kings College School of Medicine, London and Brunel University, U.K.

Behrooz, A. (1986):
Meta Description of Experimental Identification of Medical Knowledge, Ph.D. Thesis, Dept. of Computer Science, Brunel University, U.K.

Behrooz, A., Anderson, J. and Kohout, L.J. (1991):
Knowledge Elicitation, the First Step in the Construction of a Knowledge-Based System. Forthcoming.

Behrooz, A., Kohout, L.J., and Anderson, J. (1987a):
Identifying the Expertise of Expert. In *AAMSI congress Proceedings*, American Association for Medical Systems and Informatics, Washington D.C.

Behrooz, A. and Kohout, L.J. (1987b):
Experimental identification and formalisation of knowledge structures representing uncertainty. In: *Proceedings of the 7th International Congress on Cybernetics and Systems*, Imperial College, London, U.K.

Behrooz, A. and Kohout, L.J. (1987c):
Systemic Aspects of Knowledge Elicitation, *Symp. on Systems Research, Informatics and Cybernetics*, (Baden-Baden, West Germany, August 1987).

Behrooz, A. and Kohout, L.J. (1987d):
Experts Knowledge Elicitation for Risk Minimization Domain. *Proc. ESIB 87*, Expert Systems in business, Learned Information, Medford NJ & Oxford U.K.

Bobrow, D.G., Kaplan, R.M., Kay, M., Norman, D.A., Thompson, H. and Winogard, T. (1977):
Gus, a frame-driven dialog system, *Artificial Intelligence*, **8**.

Carbonell, J.R. (1970):
An AI approach to computer-aided instruction, *IEEE Transactions on Man-Machine Systems*, **11**, 190–202.

Carbonell, J.G. (1980):
Politics: an experiment in subjective understanding and integrated reasoning. In: *Computer Understanding: Five Programs Plus Miniatures*, Schank, R.C. and Riesbeck, C.K. (eds), Lawrence Erlbaum Associates, Hillsdale, N.J.

Cohen, P.R. and Perrault, C.R. (1979):
Elements of a Plan-based Theory of Speech Acts, *Cognitive Science*, **3**.

De Bono, E. (1983):
The mechanism of mind, Penguin Books Ltd., U.K.

Finkel, A.S., Gordon, B.L., Baker, M.R. and Fanta, C.M., eds. (1980):
Current Medical Information and Technology (CMIT), American Medical Association, 5th edition, Chicago.

Kaplan, S.J. (1981):
Appropriate responses to inappropriate questions. *Elements of Discourse Understanding*, Joshi, A.K., Webber, B.L. and Eag, I.A. (eds), Cambridge Univ. Press, Cambridge.

Kohout, L.J. (1978):
Methodological Foundation of the Study of Action, Ph.D. Thesis, Man Machine Systems Laboratory, Dept. of Electrical Engineering Science, Univ. of Essex, U.K., January 1978.

Kohout, L.J., Anderson, J., Bandler, W. and Behrooz, A. (1986):
Formalisation of clinical management activities for knowledge-based clinical systems. In Levy, A.H. and Williams, B.T., (eds.) *Proceedings of AAMSI Congress*, American Association for Medical Systems and Informatics, Washington, D.C.

Kohout, L.J. (1987):
Activity structures as a tool for design of technological artifacts. *Systems and Cybernetics: An International Journal*, **18(1)**, 27–34.

Kohout, L.J. (1990) *A Perspective on Intelligent Systems: A Framework for Analysis and Design*, Chapman and Hall, London and Van Nostrand Reinhold International, New York.

Rich, E. (1984):
Artificial Intelligence, McGraw-Hill International, New York.

Schank, R.C. (1975):
Conceptual Information Processing, North-Holland, Amsterdam.

Weizenbaum, J. (1984):
Computer Power and Human Reason, Penguin Books, New York.

Williams, R.H. (1974):
Textbook of Endocrinology, 5th edition, W.B. Saunders Co., London.

CHAPTER 8

LINKING ARGUMENTATIVE DISCOURSE WITH FORMAL EVALUATION PROCEDURES IN DESIGN

T. MANN

Editorial Comment:

> Design and planning decision-making in a "political" context, based on voting, tends to be relatively unsystematic in its use and evaluation of the information provided in the process, as compared for example to various formal evaluation and objectification procedures developed in the design methods literature.

LIST OF CONTENTS

8.1 THE PROBLEM: THE PROPER BASIS FOR DECISIONS
    8.1.1 Introduction
    8.1.2 Towards Procedures for Design and Planning Decision-Making through Systematic Argument Assessment
    8.1.3. The Connection of the Argumentative Process with other Design Activities
8.2. PRELIMINARIES. PROCEDURAL BUILDING BLOCKS
    8.2.1. The Design Process and its Constituent Components
    8.2.2. Evaluation System
    8.2.3. The Argumentative Process in Design
    8.2.4. Assessment of Argument Merit
    8.2.5. Decision-Making
    8.2.6. Other Components of the Design Process
8.3. INTERFACE POINTS BETWEEN THE ARGUMENTATIVE PROCESS AND EVALUATION
    8.3.1. Assumptions Regarding the Design Situation
    8.3.2. Matching Deontic Statements from Arguments Against the Evaluation Aspect Tree
    8.3.3. Generating Arguments from Evaluation Aspects, and Vice Versa
    8.3.4. Matching Weights of Relative Importance Assigned to Deontics with Evaluation Aspects
    8.3.5. Modifying Evaluation Scores as a Function of Argument Plausibility

8.4. A PROCEDURE FOR DECISION-MAKING THROUGH SYSTEMATIC ARGUMENT EVALUATION

8.4.1. Choice of Complexity Level

8.4.2. The Design Situation

8.4.3. The Procedure

8.5. CONCLUSION

8.5.1. Possible Applications

8.5.2. Remaining Problems and Unanswered Questions

8.5.3. Suggestions for Further Work

8.5.4. Summary

8.6. REFERENCES

This study explores ways of analyzing and utilizing the information offered in the course of such design processes – introduced in the form of arguments for or against design proposals – by making various connections between formal evaluation procedures and the process of decision-making according to the argumentative model of design.

This is done within the outline of a larger picture of the design activity to design proposed in the literature, in which certain recurring small scale procedural components or steps can be indentified. These are called "procedural building blocks." It further argues that even when approaches are perceived as different and incompatible, connections can be made between these components that would result in information from one approach being made available to another, for a more in-depth analysis. These building blocks can be used in a combinatorial fashion to compose new procedures, in response to particular requirements of each new design situation and project, and thus provide users with a greater variety of procedural options.

The study explores the potential connections between a selected set of design process aspects: – argumentation, evaluation, and decision-making – and proposes a procedure for design decision-making in an argumentative context using systematic argument assessment. A simplified and an extended version of the procedure are offered, responding to different requirements for procedural simplicity vs. in-depth analysis.

Possible areas of application of the underlying concepts in practical planning, and in information systems supporting planning and design processes are discussed, and suggestions for further research are offered.

8. ARGUMENTATIVE DISCOURSE AND FORMAL EVALUATION

8.1. THE PROBLEM: THE PROPER BASIS FOR DECISIONS

8.1.1. Introduction

Debate and discussion as well as formal systematic evaluation procedures have been recommended, among others, as appropriate vehicles for preparing design and planning decisions.

Formal evaluation procedures have been the subject of considerable work aiming at making the task of evaluation more systematic, explicit, transparent and objectified (Grant 1972; 1974; 1976; 1982; Helmer 1966; Hill 1968; Hoefler, Kandel, Kohlsdorf & Musso 1972; Joedicke 1976; Jones 1970; Kaufmann 1968; Miller 1970; Musso & Rittel 1969; Musso 1974; Rittel 1970; Ward & Grant 1970, to name only a few).

By contrast, not much attention has been given, at least in the design methods literature, to similar efforts for the output of discussions and debates. That is, to help decision-makers arrive at decisions based on some systematic, explicit assessment of the kind of information produced and exchanged in such forms of planning deliberation. (There are a few exceptions: for example Dehlinger/Protzen 1972, Mann 1972, 1973, 1977, 1980; Nagel 1971). The reason may be that argumentation is assumed to be part of more political decision-making processes in which negotiation, parliamentary procedure rules, the exercise of power, and above all, voting, are accepted almost without question as the proper vehicles by which decisions are reached.

Of course, logic and rhetoric have a more than 2000-year history of argument analysis. However, most of these efforts appear curiously inapplicable to the kinds of arguments dominating the design discourse. Only very reluctantly, it seems, did logicians become involved in many-valued logic and in the analysis of arguments that deal with normative, deontic statements (involving "OUGHT" rather than "IS" assertions). Even there, they seemed caught in the kind of thinking that dominated binary logic – notably Aristotle's "tertium non datur" (there is no in-between true and false). This prevented an examination of the merit of arguments based on how people *feel* about them (their degree of belief or conviction concerning some assertion) rather than on the theoretical truth that a statement about reality must be either true or false, regardless of how certain or uncertain we feel about it. Whatever the reasons, the kind of argument that occurs in design discourse does not readily lend itself to the type of analysis offered by formal logic. From a logical point of view, most design arguments are formally inconclusive, if indeed they can be brought into a form to which its methods of analysis apply at all.

The phenomenon of degrees of certainty has, of course, not gone entirely unrecognized. On the contrary, it has led to a considerable body of work under the heading of *probability*. Again, however, the concept of probability does not cover what we mean by saying that a design proposal ought to be implemented, and what we mean, for example, by saying that an argument carries more weight than another. A more promising approach may be the concept of "fuzzy sets" as suggested by Zadeh (1965).

Voting, finally, and the effect of such things as voting coalitions or of the sequence in which proposals are presented for a vote, have been investigated, for example by Buchanan and Tullock (1962). This kind of analysis, though, does not even consider the issue of concern here, i.e., the merit of arguments. The very approach of the analysis is an acknowledgement of the fact that voting does not guarantee that arguments will be presented, heard or studied much less assessed for their merit, prior to a vote – no matter how much we invoke the parliamentarian principle that voting is a decision rule in whose outcome we will agree to abide after having presented our side and duly listened to all other sides of an issue... The "political reality" is that many voters are assumed to have made up their minds ahead of time – because of political affiliation, ideology, propaganda, advertising, or political image-building and deals behind the scenes etc. – before even engaging in a debate. This seems to have discouraged any serious efforts at analyzing the force or merit of arguments and the role it might play in this process.

8.1.2. Towards Procedures for Design and Planning Decision-Making through Systematic Argument Assessment

Wherever design or planning decisions of some significance must be made and an argumentative/ discursive mode for treating the problem is adopted, decision-makers currently face a procedural gap if they also wish to base their decision on systematic evaluation. There is no systematic and yet practicable technique available to assist them in analyzing and evaluating arguments and in objectifying[1] how the decision becomes a function of such an assessment. The only recourse is to voting.

Part of the following study aims at contributing to the development of workable procedures of systematic argument assessment for such decision purposes. Regardless of the possible value of systematic analysis (and its outcomes) itself: this effort would be worthwhile if such a procedure serves no other purpose in practice than to induce those involved in a decision to actually examine the various arguments for and against a proposal more closely. It must be emphasized that making design decisions entirely and exclusively a function of such systematic analytical techniques is *not* the aim of this investigation. The procedures should be seen as means for *assisting* human decision-makers in preparing for decisions – not as algorithmic vehicles for producing the decision itself.

It may be, because of considerations of "political reality" such as the one mentioned above, that methods based on systematic and explicit argument assessment as the basis for decision-making will be applicable only to projects and decisions that are not affected by such political considerations beforehand – i.e., where the participants do not enter a discussion with their minds already irrevocably made up. But already this should be reason enough to investigate methods for more systematic

---

[1] "Objectification," to avoid confusion, is understood here as the process of explaining one's basis of judgment to the point of showing how some (subjective) evaluative judgment depends on some objective feature or measure of the thing evaluated.

analysis of the "force" or "merit" or "weight" (to use some colloquial terms) of arguments brought forward during a design discussion.

8.1.3. The Connection of the Argumentative Process with other Design Activities

The speculations presented in the following pursue a second major aim. The procedures (e.g., concerning argument assessment) to be sketched out below should be seen in the context of a general attitude concerning design methodology and paradigms such as the argumentative model of design which stresses the legitimacy of many *different* frames of reference and approaches rather than the predominant acceptance of one such model.

The design process is seen not as one well-specified sequence of steps and activities, either descriptively or normatively. Rather, the suggested picture is one of many different attitudes, activities, techniques, procedures that are and can legitimately be combined in many different ways. The focus of design methodology work should be on the interface points between the various elements of the design process. Efforts should be made to facilitate the connections between approaches, making the output of one phase, approach or form of analysis available and useful to other ways of dealing with the problem.

The following suggestions, then, should be seen both as some first examples of such interfacing efforts, and as an attempt to enhance design and planning decision-making through argumentative processes (debate, discussion, deliberation of pro's and con's of design proposals) by drawing on input from formal objectification techniques such as the Rittel-Musso procedure – and vice versa.

Figures 8.1a–e show a somewhat schematic view of some main groups of activities encountered in design, and how each one can become both the starting point and the organizing principle for the others.

Figure 8.2 presents a somewhat more detailed (but still selective and incomplete) picture of the various components or "building blocks" of design processes.

8.2. PRELIMINARIES: PROCEDURAL BUILDING BLOCKS

8.2.1. The Design Process and its Constituent Components

It may be necessary to elaborate somewhat upon the notions introduced in the last section above. In the literature of what Rittel (1972) calls the "first generation" design methods and systems approach, it was customary to distinguish various types of activities within the design process, and then to take these as the basis for specifying a well-ordered sequence of steps according to which design should be done. Rittel has argued that such a sequence is not very meaningful and that the actual process is a much more fine-grain, unsystematically alternating sequence of, for example, variety-generating and variety-reduction activities.

Knowledge-Based Systems for Multiple Environments

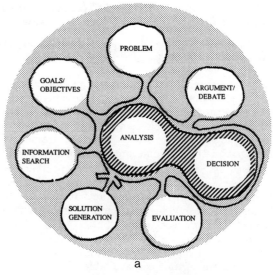

a

ONE VIEW OF THE POLITICAL PROCESS

A PROPOSED SOLUTION (BILL) IS THE STARTING POINT;
THE MAIN ANALYSIS WORK IS FOCUSED ON THE POSSIBLE
COALITION CONSTELLATIONS FOR ACHIEVING A DECISION
ARGUMENTATION IS A TOOL IN THE PROCESS BUT NOT A
DETERMINANT

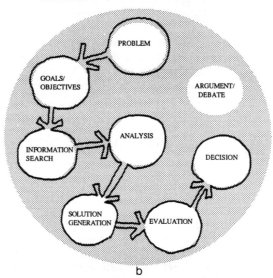

b

A STANDARD "FIRST GENERATION" SYSTEMATIC PROCEDURE SEQUENCE

THE ANALYSIS IS DETERMINED BY THE KIND AND
STRUCTURE OF THE INFORMATION GATHERED

Figure 8.1. Schematic views of activities encountered in design

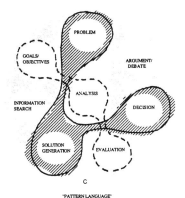

c

"PATTERN LANGUAGE"

THE WORK IN THE ACTUAL DESIGN SITUATION IS CONCERNED ONLY WITH COMBINING PRE-SELECTED SOLUTION COMPONENTS (PATTERNS) INTO A WHOLE SOLUTION. EVALUATION, ANALYSIS PLAY NO ROLE. THE DECISION FOLLOWS DIRECTLY FROM THE GENERATED SOLUTION

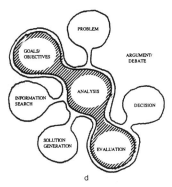

d

GOALS, OBJECTIVES, AND SYSTEMATIC EVALUATION FORM THE BACKBONE AND STARTING POINT OF ANALYSIS

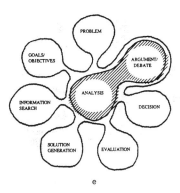

e

THE PROCESS ORGANIZED ACCORDING TO THE ARGUMENTATIVE MODEL OF DESIGN

Figure 8.1. Schematic views of activities encountered in design(Cont.)

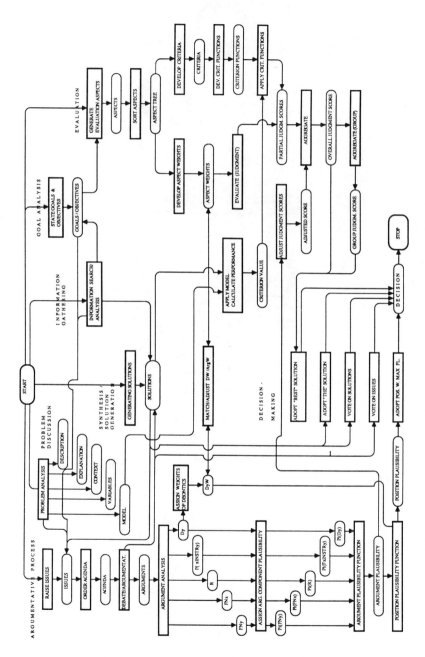

Figure 8.2. Various components of design processes and their interactions

Nevertheless, the distinctions can and have been made, are not entirely without basis, and have become the starting points for the development of many procedural aids and techniques. And they can be useful for the discussion of problems in design as long as certain key points are remembered:

- Almost any such phase or activity type can be a legitimate starting point for the design effort.
  (Most often, such activities as "stating the problem" or "clarifying objective" are placed at the beginning of the process, to arrive at a "solution" at the end. It is important to see that if someone sets out with a solution proposal, this constitutes an equally valid starting point.)
- The subsequent efforts should not be forced into a procedural "straitjacket," especially not with regard to the sequential ordering of activities.
- No assumptions regarding superior effectiveness of one approach (sequence) over another should be made. At least, such assumptions should not be allowed to predetermine the actual procedure.
- Instead, the role of design methodology should be that of making participants in design processes aware of all the procedural options and aids available to them, supporting participants in their use.
- Specifically, efforts should be made to facilitate transitions between different phases and techniques, so as to enhance the work in one phase or way of doing things, with results of other phases or other ways of looking at the problem.

To facilitate the discussion of some specific examples of procedural building blocks and their relations, certain conventions or common assumptions regarding format and vocabulary will be useful. They should be considered as convenient references to procedures and techniques proposed elsewhere and not in any way as claims of absolute or exclusive validity.

8.2.2. Evaluation System

First, it will be assumed that there is or can be, somewhere in the problem-solving effort, an "evaluation system" in the sense of Musso and Rittel (69), with the following features:

- There is a set of evaluation aspects, subaspects and sub-sub- aspects etc. that expresses the concerns of participants regarding the problem, and according to which they might evaluate proposed solutions.
- The aspect set can be ordered into a tree-like structure; it will therefore be referred to as the "aspect tree."
- The evaluators can specify, at least for some aspects or subaspects, measures of performance or "criteria" that permit objective measurement of the extent to which a given solution satisfies a specific aspect. For example, for the aspect "economy of solution" (costliness) the measure "total initial project cost, in U.S. dollars" might be specified. Or for the aspect "spaciousness" (of rooms) one might use the measure "total net assignable floor area" in square feet.

- The evaluators can specify a judgment scale (for example a grading scale such as the one used in schools, ranging from the score "A" (for "best" or "excellent") through "F" (for "Failing or unsatisfactory") or a numerical scale ranging from 100 (best) to zero (worst) or +3 (could not be better) to −3 (could not be worse).
- The evaluators are able to specify weights of relative importance of aspects and subaspects, etc.; with the usual condition that on each level of the hierarchy of aspects of the tree, $0 \leq w_i \leq 1.0$ and $\Sigma w_i = 1.0$. (Ref. the Churchman-Ackoff Approximate Measure of Value, a technique to obtain and validate such assignments of weights of relative importance; Churchman-Ackoff-Arnoff 1957.)
- The decision-makers can specify (for those aspects where measures of performance or criteria are established) how the judgment score will depend on the value of the performance measure achieved by a given solution; this dependency can be expressed in a graph or a mathematical formula and is called a criterion function (CF).
- It can be specified how a set of partial judgments x_{ij} (on a lower level of the tree) will collectively determine (be aggregated into) the respectively next higher level judgment, and ultimately how all partial judgments determine the overall individual judgment Xj for a given solution j. These rules are called "aggregation functions" (AF)
- A group of decision-makers can specify how it will determine, from a set of individual overall judgments concerning a specific solution, the overall "group judgment." If such a rule is specified, it will be called a "Group aggregation function" (GAF).

Figure 8.3 shows a sequence of steps for such an evaluation process.

8.2.3. The Argumentative Process in Design

Secondly, it will be assumed that the design or planning discourse is organized and carried out in such a way as to facilitate the identification of various issues, positions, and arguments. Following Kunz and Rittel (1970; Rittel 1980), distinctions are made between "factual" issues (F-issues), "deontic issues" (D-issues), "instrumental issues" (I-issues) and "explanatory issues" (E-issues). Issues are controversial questions concerning which various parties and participants in the discussion adopt different positions. They then seek to support these positions and weaken opposing positions by offering arguments as well as answers (for certain types of questions, depending on their wording).

Most important here are the deontic issues. All or most design problems can be expressed as one or several such issues: "Should x be the case?" (be adopted for implementation, etc.) In this form, there are three positions that can be adopted: "Yes" (x ought to be); "No" (x ought not to be) and "Inadequate question" (the issue as given does not address the problem in an appropriate way; it should be replaced by another question: the "real issue"...).

Furthermore, there is or should be a procedure or mechanism for examining the merit of the arguments brought forward. The aim of any procedure of argument analysis is that of eventually producing some form

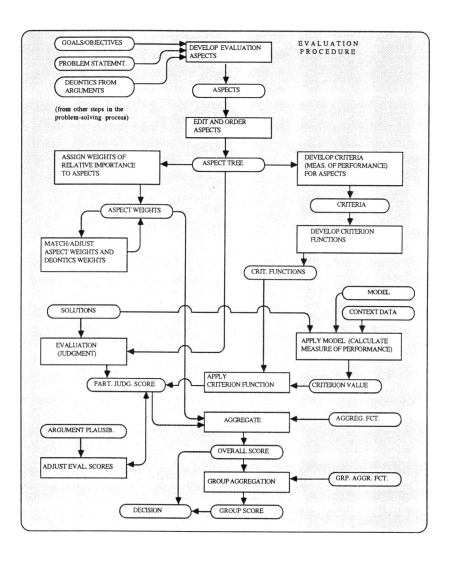

Figure 8.3. Evaluation procedure

of judgment regarding these three positions of an issue: what is the degree of support lent to the positions by the arguments brought up in their favor?

Such a procedure should of course be applicable both to the arguments for and against the positions of what may be called the "main issue" (the deontic issue to be decided upon as the outcome of the debate), and to the arguments of "successor issues." The latter term refers to issues that arise because premises of main issue arguments are challenged and that must be resolved before an assessment and decision regarding the main issue can be carried out.

The outline of one form of such a procedure is described in the following section. For the sake of simplicity, the procedure will be concerned only with "main issue" arguments. The reason for this is that the arguments for such deontic issues can all be expressed in a common format (see below). Successor issues may be deontic, factual, and explanatory. Thus, the arguments for these must be expected to exhibit the full range of argument forms or patterns (both formally valid, fallacious, and inconclusive) discussed in the literature of logic and rhetoric. Since argument assessment must include an assessment of the validity and appropriateness of the argument form (inference rule) this would introduce a considerable amount of complexity into the procedure. For a first step, in order to gain experience with the approach on an experimental basis, this level of detail is not considered necessary.

Figure 8.4 shows the sequence of steps involved in a typical "traditional" issue treatment, assuming decisions are eventually taken by vote.

Figure 8.5 suggests a sequence of steps involving systematic argument evaluation, following Mann (1977).

8.2.4. Assessment of Argument Merit

8.2.4.1. Notation

For the coherent discussion of such procedures as the ones envisaged here, a common format or notation for the analysis of arguments must be adopted. Logic has developed a number of different notation conventions for different types of statements and arguments – for example, the propositional calculus, the predicate calculus, syllogistic, set theory, relational calculus, deontic logic and other modal calculi. In view of the vast body of work done in the field of logic, and the overwhelming acceptance of these conventions, the suggestion of a common format for all argument forms occurring in design discussions might seem somewhat preposterous. However, it will be seen that the differences between the above calculi are not so important as the basic, generally "instrumental" relationship[1] between a design proposal

---

[1] The reference to "instrumental" here actually lumps together a number of relationship types that can be used in design arguments - for example: the causal relationship, class-inclusion, equivalence, the property of being appropriate to, supportive of, to name but a few.

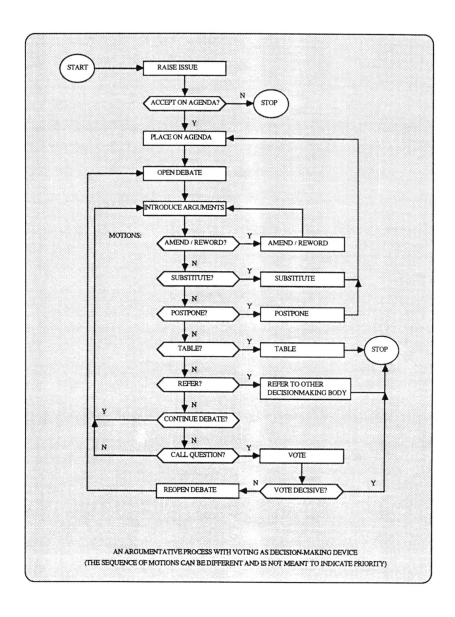

Figure 8.4. An argumentative process with voting as decision-making device

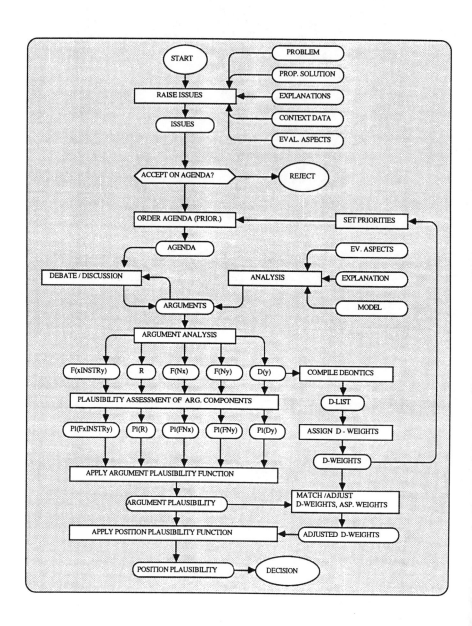

Figure 8.5. Procedure for decision-making with systematic argument assessment

and the reason offered in its support. Focusing on this feature, the following notation can be proposed as a first approximation.

Most design arguments can be transcribed into something like the following "standard design argument" pattern:

(1) x should be (done, implemented, the case ...) because
(2) (if x is implemented), x will lead to (cause ...) y; and
(3) y is desirable (should be the case; aimed for ...)

Here, (1) is equivalent to the conclusion, which is the position to be supported by the argument; (2) and (3) are the "factual instrumental premise" and the "deontic premise," respectively.

For (1) as well as (3), which are both deontic statements, the following notation is proposed: 'x' and 'y' are variables for descriptions of states of affairs (to be achieved) or descriptions of design proposals.

Such expressions as 'x' can be the subject both of factual and deontic claims. That is, they can be part of statements like: "x is the case" (factual claim), and "x ought to be the case" (deontic claim). These types of claims will be denoted by:

Fx (factual) and Dx (deontic).

In premises such as (2), there is also a factual claim being made. But the important aspect is the instrumental relationship established between 'x' and 'y', without which the argument would be useless.

There are of course many types of relationships that can be used in arguments. They range from the connectives of formal logic to all kinds of substantial assertions – set-inclusion, part-whole relationship, producer-product relationship, cause-effect relation, claims of compatibility and incompatibility, appropriateness to a stipulated image, etc.

In design argumentation, many relationships can be substituted by the general form "is instrumental to" without losing or distorting the essence of the claim. It is proposed to denote this as follows: 'x INSTR y'. Thus, the instrumental premise can be expressed as:

$$(2') F(x \text{ INSTR } y).$$

The entire argument can now be stated in the condensed notation as:

(1') Dx because   (2') $F(x \text{ INSTR } y)$
&
(3') Dy.

This three-part sequence constitutes what may be called the 'argument pattern' or inference rule R for the argument. This pattern is the basis of most arguments in design and planning, policy-making etc. and will be called the "Standard Design Argument."

The negation of claims can be handled much as in formal logic: by simply prefixing an appropriate negation operator such as 'N' to the premises in question. As usual, questions arise with regard to the proper interpretation of differences between, e.g., "NFx" and "FNx," "NDx" and "DNx," and similar expressions. There is no need to elaborate upon these questions here; it may be noted that the notation permits making the required distinctions if necessary.

Another, more serious problem is that of quantifiers. Two possible approaches can be seen here. The first is to omit all quantifiers as well as qualifying expressions (such as "probably" etc.) from the formal notation of arguments to be evaluated. The formal notation will now represent the most sweeping, basic claim that can be made about the matter in question. The evaluator would then, guided to some extent by the quantifiers and qualifiers supplied by the proponent of the argument, try to arrive at a judgment score for the statement appropriate to the statement as originally expressed. The second approach would be to introduce quantifiers much like the corresponding formal logic calculi, in which case each new combination of statements and quantifier constitutes a new inference rule.

The problem seems to be more critical at the level of arguments about successor issues than for main issue arguments. For the time being, it will be assumed that the first approach is acceptable.

It may sometimes be necessary to introduce additional statements into an argument (over and above those actually stated by a proponent) in order to account for various possible interpretations by evaluators. There are several types of such statements. One type concerns the actual state of affairs relative to the proposed design solution or course of action x, or to the goal y. I may agree that y is desirable and that x will help bring y about, but still oppose implementation of x if either x is already the case, or if y is already the case. Statements referring to such assumptions are of course rarely if ever explicitly supplied in a design argument. But they do make a significant difference in the assessment. For this reason, the formal notation of R should perhaps always include these statements.

Another difficult question deals with the assumed conditions or situation in which the instrumental relation in the factual-instrumental premise will actually hold. Reservations about the argument may be rooted in the assessment of these conditions. While it is of course impossible to introduce a statement specifying such conditions in an argument that did not mention them, it may be useful to suggest it as an "empty" variable for locating possible disagreement which should then lead to clarification in a successor issue.

Consequently, a more complete rendering of the whole inference pattern might look like this:

(1") $D(x)$ because   (2") $F(x \text{ INSTR } y)$
                                  given
                          (2a) $F(c)$ (conditions c)
                          &
                          (3") $D(y)$
                          &
                          (4") $F(Nx)$
                          &
                          (5") $F(Ny)$.

8.2.4.2. Evaluation of Argument Components

A number of different characterizations or types of predicates can be considered for the evaluation of argument components (premises and inference rule). A range of such candidates is discussed in Mann (1977). It is proposed, however, to evaluate all components in terms of one attribute only: "Plausibility." Judgments about the plausibility of premises can be expressed on a scale ranging from $+1$ to -1. The interpretation of these judgements can vary with the type of statement, e.g., as follows:

The plausibility score of '$+1$' stands for "couldn't be more plausible," "virtually certain" (i.e., the interpretation for factual statements could be that of probability); also, for deontic premises: "entirely desirable" ("I am in total agreement that y should be pursued"). Conversely, '-1' stands for "couldn't be more implausible," "virtually certainly NOT true;" "entirely unlikely, improbable;" "entirely undesirable." The intermediate score of zero is interpreted as "Don't know" or "can't make up my mind."

It should be noted here that a "high" (i.e., close to $+1$) plausibility score for a deontic premise is not to be confused with the importance of the goal or objective to which it refers. It might be interpreted (anticipating somewhat the discussion to follow) as the estimate of the plausibility of the "yes" position of a successor issue questioning the statement as it would be assessed given a lot of strong arguments in its favor and few weak or inconclusive arguments against it. Thus, I may be quite convinced that some deontic proposition is a good idea, that little if anythings speaks against it, yet it may not be that important compared to other objectives. The plausibility score expresses only, as it were, the balance between pro's and con's. Weights of relative importance will be discussed below.

The assessment of the inference rule R should strictly speaking consist of two separate evaluations. One would concern the trustworthiness or plausibility of the inference rule itself. (For arguments which conform to the patterns of formal logic we would say 'validity'.) The other would pertain to the question of how applicable the argument pattern is to the case at hand. For simplicity, it is suggested to merge these considerations into just one evaluation.

8.2.4.3. Argument plausibility

The next task consists of establishing a model of how the plausibility assessments of the various argument components (premises and inference rule) influence the overall plausibility of the entire argument. Another way of stating this task is that some "argument plausibility function" should be developed which expresses how argument plausibility depends on the plausibility of the premises and inference rule. For argument patterns that are considered valid in formal logic calculi (such as the patterns called Modus Ponens and Modus Tollens, to name only two examples), those calculi provide the values of plausibility (interpreted as truth- values) for the extremes of our plausibility scale. It remains to find suitable functions for the interpolation between these extreme values.

As discussed in Mann (1977), this is a rather complex task for various combinations of negative plausibility assessments; the surfaces of the functions are not necessarily smooth. Separate functions may have to be developed for each region of positive/negative plausibility values. However, as long as plausibility assessments for all premises including the inference rule are on the positive side (between zero and +1), two kinds of functions can be used which have good intuitive interpretation:

(6a) $AP1 = MIN\,[pl(\text{component } i)]$ for all n components, or:
$AP1 = MIN\,[pl\,(\text{premise } 1),\, pl\,(\text{premise } 2), \ldots (\text{premise } n),\, pl\,(R)]$.

(The plausibility of the overall argument is equivalent to the plausibility value of the least plausible premise in the argument).

(6b) $AP2 = PROD\,[pl\,(\text{component } i)]$ for all n components, or:
$AP2 = pl\,(\text{premise } 1) * pl(\text{premise } 2) * \ldots (\text{premise } n) * pl\,(R)$.

(The argument plausibility is equal to the product of the plausibilities of each of the components.)

For the "Standard Design Argument" as presented above, (SDA for short) the argument plausibility functions would be, correspondingly:

(7a) $AP1(SDA) = MIN[\,pl(F(x\text{ INSTR }y\,/\,c)),\, pl(F(c),\, pl(D(y),\, pl(F(Nx),\, pl(F(Ny),\, pl(R(SDA)]$

and

(7b) $AP2(SDA) = pl(Fx\text{ INSTR }y\,/\,c)) * pl(F(c)) * pl(D(y) * pl(F(Nx)) * pl(F(Ny)) * pl(R(SDA))$.

See figure 8.6 for a graphic representation of the argument plausibility function (where the premises regarding Fx and Fy are omitted). A complete discussion of the rationale and derivation of the functions is presented in Mann (1977).

8.2.4.4. Position plausibility

Given a set of arguments for and against a design proposal (the YES position of the corresponding issue), the next question is to specify how some measure of plausibility of this position (or of the position and its counterposition) can be obtained from the plausibility assessments of the individual arguments.

There are many considerations that might play a role in the determination of such a measure. For example, it might be influenced not only by the degree of plausibility of each argument, and be the relative importance of the deontics contained in the arguments, but also by relationships such as the logical consistency among the premises used in the set of proposed arguments.[1]

---

[1] Other candidates are the similarity or dissimilarity between the arguments proposed in support of a given position, the "degree of deliberation," that is, the care and thoroughness that went into establishing the plausibility measure for each argument or the degree of deliberative position plausibility *gain* as a result of the discussion. This involves a comparison between some initial offhand judgment, and the final deliberated position plausibility judgment. (Mann 1977). The latter is related to Popper's recommendation concerning the "degree of corroboration" of a scientific hypothesis as

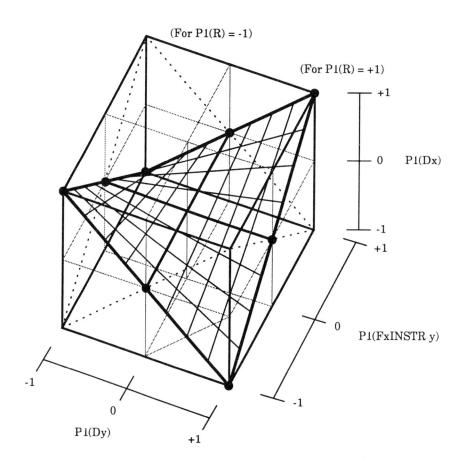

Figure 8.6. Argument plausibility function

corroborated only to the extent it has withstood our most determined efforts – tests –

As a first approximation, such relationships will be considered potential successor issue arguments. After discussion and resolution, these will influence the plausibility assessment of the corresponding premise. They will therefore not be addressed in the position plausibility function itself.

Argument weight

As the first step, each argument plausibility value will be modified by the degree of importance of its deontic premise: an argument referring to a very important goal or objective should "carry more weight" than one concerned with a perhaps valid but not very important objective.

The deontic premises correspond, roughly, to the evaluation aspects on the "evaluation aspect tree" mentioned above in section 8.2.2. If this correspondence could be made reasonably close (so that the aspect tree contains all deontics used in arguments, and vice versa – all evaluation aspects for which an instrumental connection to the design proposal can be established, have been used to construct an argument – then the weights of relative importance assigned to the evaluation aspects can be used directly as weights of relative importance of the deontic premises. A function for argument weight can then be suggested as follows:

$$(8) \quad ARGW_i = w(y,i) * ARGPL_i$$

(The argument weight of argument i is equal to its argument plausibility multiplied by the weight of relative importance of the evaluation aspect corresponding to the deontic y used in its deontic premise.)

Position plausibility function

Assuming that the issue has been reasonably thoroughly discussed (so that all relevant arguments that could be constructed based on the knowledge of the participants actually have been raised and deliberated, i.e., including examining premises and debating successor issues) and that the conditions of transitivity and additivity hold for the deontics, then a possible first approximation of a position plausibility function might be:

$$(9) \quad POSPL = \sum_{i=1,2...}^{n} (ARGW_i)$$

---

to disprove (refute) it. (Popper 1972). This recommendation could be rephrased for the problem of argument assessment as follows: "We are entitled to tentatively accept a position (of an issue) to the extent that it has survived our best efforts to find powerful arguments AGAINST the position, and our best efforts to discredit the arguments in its favor." That is, we should assign position plausibility not only on the basis of the arguments supporting it, but more importantly as a function of the extent to which we have tried to find flaws with these arguments, and how well they have stood up against these efforts. The importance of this recommendation can hardly be overemphasized. Recurring reminders of this principle should be built into all planning procedures as a standard feature. However, it is difficult to specify a position plausibility function that would fully satisfy this standard. To develop such a function in accordance with the spirit of Popper's recommendation should be considered as one of the prime tasks in the program of research in design methodology.

(The position plausibility of a position POS of an issue is equal to the sum of argument weights $AW(i)$ of all n arguments brought forward both in its support as well as in support of the counterposition – which is assumed to be simply the negation of POS.) Note that this measure cannot be used for establishing the plausibility of the "Inadequate Question" position since typically, the "arguments" supporting this position tend to be proposals for other issues that should be discussed instead. (One suggestion for research to be done as a next step would be to examine the logical status of arguments for the "Inadequate Question" position and their premises relative to the arguments for the Yes/No positions.)

One procedural consequence of adopting such a measure involves the alternating mutual adjustments between the evaluation aspect set and the argument set: before assigning weights of relative importance in the aspect tree, the argument set should be scanned for deontics that have no corresponding counterpart in the aspect tree, and the missing aspects added. Similarly, "potential" arguments that can be constructed from the deontics contained in the evaluation aspects must be added to the argument set before the position plausibility can be determined.

8.2.4.5. Procedure

A procedure for systematic argument assessment as proposed in Mann (1977) is shown in figure 8.7.

8.2.5. Decision-Making

Though not of primary importance in the context discussed here, a few comments must be devoted to the process of decision- making about a design or planning problem. The problem of arriving at a solution to which the decision-makers will be committed for implementation has been treated somewhat unevenly in the literature. There seems to be a tendency to neglect some decision- making modes that are widely used, and an emphasis on approaches that are more suited for the systematic deliberations of well-intentioned teams of advisors charged with making a recommendation to the actual decision-makers.

Voting

Decisions can be reached by vote, either voting on the issue being debated (where an issue refers to some feature or property of the eventual solution) or by voting on adoption or rejection of a "complete" solution proposal.

The question of how such solutions have been arrived at (in a context of decision-making bodies using voting) must be left to be discussed elsewhere. The voting process can play a role in this, either by building up the solution bit by bit (or, as in a party platform in a political convention, plank by plank), or in the process of changing a proposed solution, amendment by amendment, until it is acceptable to a voting majority.

Knowledge-Based Systems for Multiple Environments

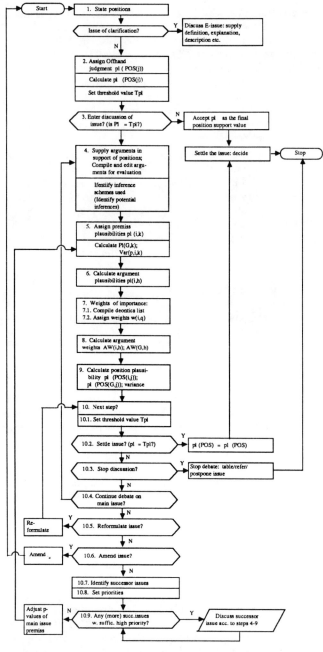

Figure 8.7. An argument assessment procedure (Mann 1977) *The (only) solution*

Voting, of course, requires for its effectiveness an institutional context which defines the group entitled to participate in the voting procedure. Where such a context is lacking the issue of right to participate (vote) becomes a controversy of its own, tied to or separate from the main planning issue but always to the detriment of the latter.

Another form of reaching a decision that is not widely discussed in the design methods literature as a decision-making process is that of adopting "THE" solution that has been developed during the design process. This is done either in an intuitive or otherwise unaccounted-for manner, or by means of applying certain pre-established rules which in themselves had to be accepted or never questioned. In such cases, there will be no concern with having to select one of a number of alternative courses of action or solutions, simply because the "right" process has procuded only one solution which therefore also must be "right." This notion, and approaches based on it, seem to be very attractive to designers, – perhaps for the reason that it preserves some of the mystique of creativity better than other systematic methods. An example of a major approach in this category is Alexander's Pattern Language. (Alexander et al, 1977)

Systematic evaluation procedures

Making the design decision a function of the outcome of some more or less formalized evaluation procedure seems to be the most widely accepted concept for systematic approaches to design – in the literature, not necessarily in practice. A set of alternative solutions is developed and subjected to the procedure which results in a judgment score or some other measure of performance (such as a benefit/cost ratio) for each solution. The solution achieving the highest score or performance measure will then be the one recommended for adoption. Of course, the outcome of such a process can then become the basis of further work aiming at solution modification, improvement, political negotiation, and so on.

8.2.6. Other Components of the Design Process

As has already been pointed out, the purpose of this study is to explore some of the interface points between the procedural blocks that can be roughly allocated to two main areas (argumentation and formal evaluation) – and not to cover all such components in a comprehensive fashion. For this reason, only an overview of the other major groups of such procedural areas of concern will be attempted here.

From the initiation of a design process onwards, attention may be focused on any of the following:

- "problem exploration" or "analysis";
- establishing and clarifying goals and objectives;
- developing solution ideas;
- gathering information
- analyzing information;
- systemic modelling and simulation;
- negotiation;
- argumentative process (discussion, debate);
- developing and applying an evaluation system.

The process may remain entirely dominated by one of these modes, (or a combination), or it may shift focus as it progresses. At some point it will then move towards a decision-making phase, reach a decision, or revert to one of the other modes.

This list might strike the reader as nothing more than a compilation of the traditional "phases" of the design process, without any organized picture of feedback loops. This is indeed true; the difference is that no claim to "natural" or "best" or "most efficient," "most time-saving," etc., sequence is made. Any path through these modes of problem treatment is considered possible and legitimate. The task of methodology is seen as that of providing assistance in carrying out the necessary steps for each mode, and most importantly, to facilitate the transition between them.

8.3. INTERFACE POINTS BETWEEN THE ARGUMENTATIVE PROCESS AND EVALUATION

In the following, some points or activity blocks are examined at which the argumentative process and its outcomes connect with formal evaluation procedures.

8.3.1. Assumptions Regarding the Design Situation

Some assumptions must be made regarding the overall design situation – not as normative provisions or even recommendations, but merely as a basis for the following discussion.

Thus, it shall be assumed here that a design process has been carried on, for example in order to produce a solution to some problem P; at least one solution S has been proposed and discussed, producing a set of arguments (ARGLIST) from which in turn a set of deontic statements has been extracted and compiled into a list (DLIST).

Furthermore, an evaluation system has been established which consists (among other things) of a set or list of evaluation aspects (ASPLIST) against which proposed solutions can be evaluated. These aspects have been ordered, (at least tentatively), into a tree-like structure of aspects, subaspects, sub-sub-aspects and so forth (ASPTREE), to which weights of relative importance ASPW can or have been assigned, for example, using the Churchman-Ackoff Measure of Approximate Value. (Ackoff 1961, p. 87)

8.3.2. Matching Deontic Statements from Arguments against the Evaluation Aspect Tree

The proposed activity block of matching DLIST and ASPTREE is based on the assumption that there is a correspondence between evaluation aspects and the deontic premises of design arguments. Therefore, DLIST and ASPTREE can be used as (partial) mutual checks for completeness. More specifically: if a deontic Dy has been used in an argument about a proposed solution, the question might be raised to the decisionmakers whether a corresponding evaluation aspect should not also be included in the aspect tree. And conversely, any evaluation aspect in the tree can be seen as a potential deontic premise for an argument for or against some of the solution proposals.

The matching process is likely to run into the question of semantics, i.e., of the equivalence of deontics and aspects if these are worded differently. This is not the place to try to resolve such questions in any definitive way; only to point out that they are likely to arise, and to offer a general scheme for the transformation.

Deontic premises can, in general, be reworded into something like the following form: "y ought to be" or "it is desirable to achieve y" where 'y' can be understood as a feature or property of a solution, a consequence of implementing it, a (partial) description of the situation characterized by the resolution (or absence) of the problem P; a goal, objective, or principle. For example, a proposed design detail of a building may have been advocated with the argument that "it will reduce the solar heat gain" of the building (as compared to a solution without that feature, or competing details). The complete deontic premise can be stated as "it is desirable to reduce the solar heat gain."

Evaluation aspects generally can be stated or reworded as follows: "the extent to which a proposed solution will achieve y" or "the goodness/appropriateness of a solution with respect to the achievement of y." Thus, the deontic in the preceding paragraph can be expressed as the evaluation aspect "the appropriateness of a solution with respect to reduction of solar heat gain," or "the extent to which a solution achieves reduction of solar heat gain."

In this way, both sets, DLIST and ASPTREE, can be tested for relative completeness (containing all deontics viz. aspects of concern to somebody involved with the problem). All deontics for which there is no corresponding aspect in ASPTREE should be transformed into appropriately worded aspects which then can be given their appropriate position within the tree. Conversely, all aspects for which there is no corresponding deontic statement in DLIST should be transcribed into deontic statements and included in DLIST.

8.3.3. Generating Arguments from Evaluation Aspects, and Vice Versa

Inclusion of such a "new" deontic Dy in DLIST is the first step towards completing the argument set in the discourse about design solutions that have been proposed with respect to problem P. For all such proposals it might be postulated that a new argument should be formed and offered to the decision-makers for evaluation: "position x (proposal x) should be adopted because x is instrumental to achieve y, and y is desirable." (Or, as the case may be, "proposal x should not be adopted because x is instrumental to the undesirable consequence y."

Here, the instrumental premise (which may be modified as appropriate to the nature of the concepts involved) is speculative. It may have to be investigated or researched to some extent before anyone can be expected to assess its plausibility. This would mean that it must be raised as a (factual-instrumental) successor issue ("Is x instrumental to y?") and discussed / evaluated before returning to the main issue argument to which it belongs.

It may be asked why it should be necessary to generate such "hypothetical" arguments when during the discourse, nobody considered it necessary or worthwhile to suggest such an argument. The answer depends on the extent to which systematic argument assessment will be made the basis for the eventual decision. If the decision is to be based on the outcome of an evaluation procedure, and the argumentative part of the process is only used to complete the aspect tree, completing the argument set is of course not necessary. If the decision is to be made on the basis of the merit of arguments, the comprehensiveness of the arguments becomes more critical.

There is another reason. Experience with argumentative processes and evaluation procedures suggests that there will be considerable differences between the concerns expressed in the arguments and in the aspect trees of evaluation systems. The latter tend to focus more on "stock" concerns tend to be more general and more concerned with the hierarchy of aspects.

By comparison, the concerns expressed in arguments are much less systematic and well-structured. Where reference to quantitative matters is needed, it is more difficult to make convincing arguments. They must be constructed by means of comparisons (between different solutions) and even then often turn out somewhat clumsy. If the situation is that of an actual verbal debate, where argument and rebuttal as well as the sequence in which arguments are introduced, are significant determinants of the following voting outcome, participants will refrain from being too comprehensive and number-minded for fear of losing the attention of the audience. Thus, many a potentially helpful and in itself worthwhile argument will not be made in such a setting. In addition, the set of concerns tends to be more specific, fine-grain, personalized, in short somewhat "richer" and colorful than the aspects of an evaluation aspect tree. (Such a comparison remains to be done in a systematic fashion, however; the above remarks are based on general impressions accumulated in a nonsystematic manner over a period of time, and have not been tested rigorously).

For these reasons, it seems rather worthwhile to provide some additional comprehensiveness checks into a design decision- making process, at least when the problem at hand is sufficiently serious and consequential.

The conversion of deontic statements into an evaluation aspect is comparatively simple and follows the explanation in section 8.3.2. Such new aspects will then have to be built into the aspect tree; this may cause some reorganization work.

8.3.4. Matching Weights of Relative Importance Assigned to Deontics and Evaluation Aspects

When the components DLIST (and the added potential arguments generated with the deontics gleaned from the aspect tree) and ASPTREE have been established and mutually complemented, the next step in the systematic assessment process – both in the argument evaluation and in the evaluation procedure – is the assignment of weights of relative importance.

This task will be rather difficult to achieve in DLIST if the deontics are not well ordered and structured into some hierarchy. It is therefore suggested that the weight assignment be done in the aspect tree (after having made sure that it contains all aspects corresponding to the deontic premises in all arguments that must be assessed.) This process can then follow some well-established technique such as the Churchman-Ackoff Approximate Measure of Value (Ackoff 1961), using pairwise comparison, ranking, assignment of numerical values to correspond to preferences of paired aspects, and normalization.

When the weights have been established within the aspect tree, they must be multiplied out so as to form only one level of weights that together add up to 1.0. For example, assume the following very simple tree and weight assignment:

Aspect A	Weight: 0.6	Subaspect A1	Weight	0.20
		Subaspect A2		0.40
		Subaspect A3		0.40
Aspect B	Weight: 0.4	Subaspect B1		0.50
		Subaspect B2		0.50

(In this assignment, the weights add up to 1.0 at each level of the tree; this ensures that during aggregation, intermediate scores will be on the same scale as the original judgment scale on which the first partial judgments are made.) For use in the argument evaluation, the subaspect weights must be multiplied out as follows:

Subaspect A1	Weight	0.12
Subaspect A2		0.24
Subaspect A3		0.24
Subaspect B1		0.20
Subaspect B2		0.20

Now, the weights of the subaspects can be assigned directly to the corresponding deontics in DLIST.

At this point, it can be seen that a further adjustment of the argument set (as it will be formalized and presented for the systematic assessment), will be necessary in order to avoid "counting arguments twice." For the kind of aggregation assumed in section 8.2, only those arguments should be included whose deontics are situated at the most detailed level of the corresponding aspect tree. If, therefore, some arguments contain deontics referring to subaspects, while others refer to aspects located on the same branches by "higher" in the (inverted) tree, the arguments containing those more general deontics should be replaced with a set of arguments based on the total number of aspects in the lower level. To use the above example: if the original argument set contained an argument referring to aspect A, and one referring to subaspect A3, the first argument should be split into two representing aspects A1 and A2 so that all three resulting arguments would together represent the three subaspects A1, A2, and A3, and use the corresponding weights.

Not all "unresolved" questions that can be raised in connection with weighting can be discussed here. For example, see Mann (1980) for some problems arising from the occurrence of general (e.g., moral or ethical) principles in the argument deontics.

8.3.5. Modifying Evaluation Scores as a Function of Argument Plausibility

When a (set of) proposed solution(s) to a problem has been evaluated by an individual or a group, a judgment score for each aspect (and for each solution) will have been produced in the process. As explained above, each such score either represents as offhand judgment, or is based on a criterion function.

In the latter case, it then represents another set of judgments: the estimate of the value of the measure of performance (criterion) that a given solution will achieve, and then the correlation of that performance measure with a goodness judgement score. It is important to see that even where the value of the measure of performance is the result of calculations in, e.g., a mathematical model, it is still an estimate or judgment.

However, the aggregation functions of the evaluation system discussed so far (in section 8.2.2) treat each score as if the respective assessments were all a matter of certainty. In reality, we may feel quite confident that some solution will achieve a given predicted performance level on one criterion (say, spaciousness as measured by square feet of a floor plan) but not so sure that it will achieve the predicted level of performance on another variable (e.g., degrees of user satisfaction).

Such considerations are, of course, nothing other than plausibility assessments of the instrumental premise that "solution S will achieve performance level c." This realization, in turn, strongly suggests that if such plausibility assessments have been carried out somewhere in the process, then their results (i.e., the plausibility values) should be used in some way to qualify or modify the goodness/badness scores produced by the evaluation procedure.

Some difficulties arise here with respect to the proper interpretation of negative plausibility assessments of the instrumental premise, For example, a plausibility score of, say, -0.6 might mean that the evaluator believes strongly but not with complete conviction one of the following:

(a) "x is NOT instrumental to achieve y" (not effective):
(b) "x is instrumental to achieve NOT-y" (i.e., counterproductive)
(c) "NOT-x will produce y"'
(d) "NOT-x will be instrumental to NOT-y –but not necessarily that x will be instrumental to y" (For example: in the absence of other measures, refraining from a blood transfusion will cause an accident victim's death – but just a transfusion will not be enough to save the victim's life ...)

With regard to a criterion function, such a negative plausibility assessment could be interpreted as follows:

(e) "While the performance value claimed by the argument or evaluation is in a region of c associated with positive goodness/badness scores (i.e., "good") the actual performance achieved will be in a region of c associated with negative judgment scores ("bad"). See Figure 8.8 below.

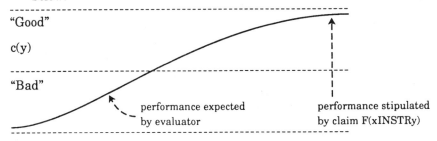

Figure 8.8

(f) or the actual performance criterion value achieved by the given solution will be "too far" away from the stipulated or desirable performance to be acceptable ("not good enough")

A rigorous resolution of these questions would require a separate analysis of all relationship types and all combinations of possible interpretations, and the corresponding goodness score adjustment functions defined separately (region by region or quadrant by quadrant) for each such combination.

To simplify matters, a procedural rule might be introduced to the effect that whenever there exist differences of opinion concerning the plausibility of a proposed instrumental relationship wide enough to result in negative plausibility scores by some participants, the respective premise should be discussed as a successor issue. This discussion should be carried out thoroghly enough to result in either withdrawal of the claim (if all participants join in the negative plausibility assessment) or in plausibility scores by all participants that are at least on the positive side of the scale.

If all the plausibility scores pl(F(xINSTRy)) are within the range of 0 to +1, one might then consider a simple reduction of the goodness judgment score 'js' roughly equivalent to the plausibility level of the instrumental premise – for example:

(10) js(adjusted) = js(unadjusted) * pl(F(xINSTRy))

(Judgment/plausibility adjustment function JPAF).

8.4. A PROCEDURE FOR DECISION-MAKING THROUGH SYSTEMATIC ARGUMENT EVALUATION

8.4.1. Choice of Complexity Level

The preceding discussion may have left the impression that application of these concepts for practical decision-making would become too cumbersome and complicated to be both feasible and worth the effort. This is not necessarily so. In the following, a simplified approach will be presented which will show that adoption of some of the ideas can be achieved with only a modest investment in added complexity. Conversely, simplified application can achieve the intended results to a significant extent at the expense of only moderate loss of rigor.

The procedure will be presented in two versions – one extremely simplified, the other with a few added features of successive rounds of circulation of results, discussion and adjustment (such as those provided in the Delphi Method – Helmer 1966), feedback, and matching against results of other procedures and techniques. The simpler version is outlined in the main paragraphs below; indented paragraphs are added to describe the more elaborate version.

8.4.2. The Design Situation

The assumptions regarding the decision-making situation can be taken much as sketched out in section 8.3.2. In response to some problem, various proposals (either partial provisions for solutions, or complete plan "packages" are prepared and put forward for discussion. The decision is to be made on the basis of systematic analysis and evaluation of the arguments brought up during the design discourse (which includes both actual discussion and debate and other ways of generating and submitting arguments).

8.4.3. The Procedure

A. A design proposal is put forward, and arguments for and against supplied by anyone concerned or interested. To avoid spending much time in meetings, this can be done by circulating folders with separate sheets for each position. Arguments are simply listed in consecutive order and numbered as they are contributed. Each participant should be given the opportunity to react to all arguments brought up including counterarguments against his/her own. For this reason, the complete list of arguments must be circulated as often as needed to ensure that no arguments remain "unanswered."

    A.1. An evaluation aspect tree ASPTREE is developed, for the purpose of evaluating any proposed solution to the problem at hand (in a "top-down" fashion).

B. The arguments submitted are analyzed to identify the deontic statements contained in their deontic premises. These are compiled into DLIST, a comprehensive list of deontics.

B.1. As outlined in section 8.3.2. above, a DLIST / ASPTREE MATCH is performed to identify deontics contained in ASPTREE but not in DLIST; these are added to DLIST; deontics from DLIST not contained in ASPTREE are added to the tree.
C. DLIST is edited and reworded so as to eliminate redundancies and overlap.
   C.1. The edited version should be recirculated to the participants to obtain everyone's consent to the wording: Each participant should agree that his/her arguments are adequately expressed in the revised wording.
D. The deontics in DLIST are then entered onto a form as shown in figure 8.9. The instrumental premise is summarized in the heading, and the deontics of each argument simply added underneath. The list is flanked by columns for entering numerical values: One will contain a person's assessment of the plausibility of the instrumental premise, the other the weight of relative importance of the respective deontic.

The plausibility values should be interpreted as:

- -1: the claim is totally implausible (i.e., the evaluator is convinced that the opposite is true)
- +/- 0: "don't know";
- +1: totally plausible (the evaluator is entirely convinced that the claim is true, appropriate etc.)

E. The deontics in DLIST are assigned weights of relative importance.
   E.1. DLIST is scanned for deontics not in ASPTREE; these are added to the tree.
   E.2. Weights of relative importance are assigned to the aspects in ASPTREE. These are multiplied out (as described in section 8.3.2).
   E.3. An AspW/DW MATCH is carried out: weights of deontics in DLIST are adjusted to match the weights of corresponding aspects in ASPTREE.
F. Plausibility values are assigned to the instrumental premises in column 1 of the form.
   F.1. If evaluators are not sure about how to assess this, the instrumental premise may be raised as a successor issue and discussed or otherwise "settled" before returning to the evaluation.
   F.2. In addition to the weights of relative importance, another column for a plausibility assessment of the deontic premise may be introduced. This will allow the evaluator to express disagreement with a given deontic (by assigning a negative pl-value) while also stating how important avoidance of the given goal is to him or her. Without this column, such an attitude can only be expressed by adding a negative sign to w.
   F.3. After a first round of such assignments, it may be decided to take up deontic premises as successor issues and discuss these before returning to a revision of the plausibility assessment.

ISSUE:	"Should proposal x be adopted ?"		
POSITION:	YES (NO / INADEQUATE QUESTION on separate sheets)		
	ARGUMENTS:		
Plausibility of claim "x is instrumental to achieve goal y" - 1 < pl < + 1	"x should be adopted because x is instrumental to (causes, contributes to) goal y" List deontics y	Weight of relative importance of goal y 0 < w < 1.0	(interim result: "argument weight" = pl * w
....	....	....	....
....	....	....	....
....	....	....	....
....	....	....	....
....			
....			
....	....	....	....
....	....	....	....
		POSITION PLAUSIBILITY	==========

Figure 8.9. Form for listing the deontics of DLIST

G. "Argument weights" are calculated for each person, by applying the "argument weight function" AWF to each line (e.g., by multiplying pl(F(xINSTRy)) with w(Dy) for each argument. Or – see F.2 – by multiplying pl (F(xINSTRy) with pl (Dy)).
H. "Position Plausibility" POSPL is calculated by applying POSPLF to the interim results in column 3.
I. The appropriate statistics concerning, e.g., the distribution of POSPL and argument weights over the set of participants are now prepared and displayed to the group in some suitable fashion. The discussion of these results will then determine the next step. For example, the group might now proceed by either

- voting (in the traditional fashion)
- using the POSPL outcomes in lieu of votes: e.g., if a person's POSPL value is positive, his/her vote is taken to be "YES", if negative: "NO"; if zero: "Abstain";
- preparing some form of aggregated group measure of POSPL, for example a mean group GPOSPL, and the result presented to the group for final decision-making.

Proposal revisions and modifications, amendments, logrolling etc. may come into play at this stage, as the traditional tools of parliamentary decision-making.

See figures 8.10 and 8.11, respectively, for flow diagrams of the "simple" and "extended" versions of the procedure.

8.5. CONCLUSION

8.5.1. Possible Applications

The intentions behind this study were to explore connection points between various facets of the design process that mostly had been treated as separate phases or even as separate paradigms of design decision-making, and to show how such connections could become helpful in constructing procedural building blocks for design and planning. At the same time, this effort was to serve as an exemplification of the underlying view of the design activity as one permitting many different starting points, ways of viewing the problem, procedural approaches and sequences. The specific examples also tried to close what the author considers current gaps in the inventory of tools for design and planning decision-makers.

By and large, these objectives have been met. The two areas of argumentative/ discursive treatment of design issues, and of formal evaluation procedures, have been examined for possible connection points. In the process, the procedural elements or building blocks for these areas have been identified, interface points have been defined, and possibilities shown for mutual enhancement utilizing results produced in one area as input for the other. A procedure that was felt to be somewhat of a missing link between decision-making based on voting (the traditional tool of parliamentary procedure and related approaches) and formal evaluation systems was described, in two versions of differing elaborateness.

Knowledge-Based Systems for Multiple Environments

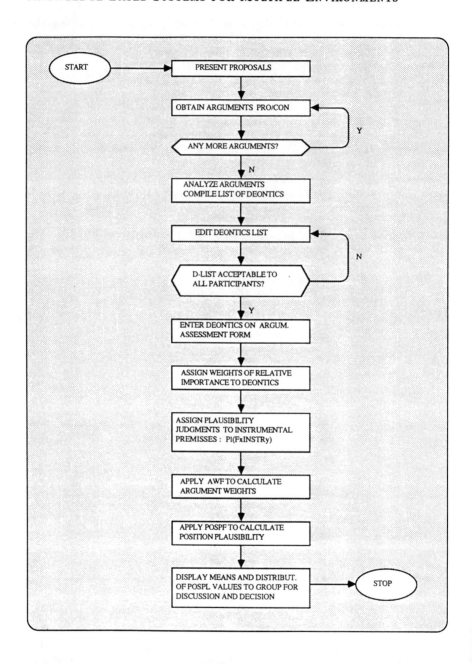

Figure 8.10. The simplified procedure for group decision-making by argument assessment

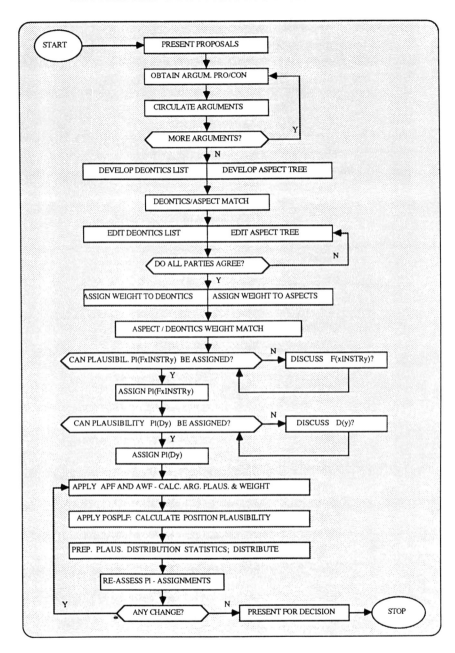

Figure 8.11. The extended procedure for group decision-making by argument assessment

Knowledge-Based Systems for Multiple Environments

This is not to say that the effort has been exhaustive, nor that the outcomes have removed all questions and controversy. Quite the contrary: a number of unresolved problems have been encountered. These will be summarized briefly, together with a quick outlook on further work that should be done. The relevance of both will be more clearly seen if placed in a context of possible applications, which therefore will be examined first.

Practical planning process

The straightforward use of the concepts outlined above as design and planning decision-making procedures is only one such application possibility. With appropriate adaptation, the proposed tools could be seen as vehicles for both user and citizen participation in planning projects, and for more general user needs/attitudes research. The information gained in this way might help to cut down some of the redundancy that often troubles such efforts (considerable work and expense being spent in each new project in generating basic, well-known information all over again). It can utilize existing knowledge together with new data while getting at the much more interesting issues of how people feel about the questions involved. Because it can be more detailed, the information can serve to pinpoint more accurately where conflicts are located and e.g., whether they arise from differences on values as opposed to differences relative to factual knowledge (or the lack of it).

Planning support information systems

The formalization introduced in the treatment of the argument analysis also opens up a quite different field of opportunity. This is the development of information systems and computer programs that could support planning efforts in a more active mode. For example, the various lists of components of arguments might be compiled by computer, making is possible to search and manipulate them automatically. Given the premises of arguments introduced by human participants, new implications and the resulting arguments could then be generated and presented to the human decision-maker for assessment. Of course, the tasks of calculating the various argument and position plausibilities would be prime candidates for treatment by computer. Such programs could also help users quickly assess the impact of newly introduced information, by rapidly scanning the entire stored knowledge base and forming implications and arguments from the new data.

It may be interesting to note that while the kind of program that is suggested here would have many of the features of an artificial intelligence or expert system, it would be different from most efforts in that field in one significant respect. The ideal AI system aims at supporting human decision-making by reducing the effects of human frailties such as poor memory and faulty reasoning. It will try to make only logically tenable, consistent, and "valid" inferences, based on as factually correct data as can be found, and on tested valid inference rules.

By contrast, the kind of system that would seem to emerge from the concepts outlined above is not only very different in its tolerance of contradiction and inconclusiveness. It also makes it clear that the pursuit of correctness and consistency in data base and inferences is futile, even (for the purposes addressed here) counterproductive. Contradictory beliefs are the *essence* of the problems designers worry about. Contradictions can (and should) be pointed out – but not as human thinking falling short of some impersonal "truth" distilled from "correct data" by the infallible machine, but as one person's knowledge being at odds with that of another.

This very difference makes it appear rather important to develop planning support systems based on these concepts.

8.5.2. Remaining Problems and Unanswered Questions

One of the foremost open questions pertaining to practical application is that of testing some of the proposed procedures so as to gain sufficient experience with their use to permit implementation in projects of significant size and consequence. This points to a dilemma: what would be an adequate project size for such testing? The discrepancy between the relatively greater required effort in detailed procedure and documentation and the significance of ends might cause some problems here. Large guns are not adequately tested by shooting at mosquitoes.

Some small-scale tests have been carried out in classroom settings under less than ideal conditions.[1] Their results are encouraging but of course not very conclusive. It is important that more such experiments be carried out within the context of actual planning projects.

The same question applies to the computerized support of such processes. Thus far, no actual programs have been developed for this purpose; again, this shortcoming should be addressed before more far-reaching conclusions can be drawn.

Some nagging technical and theoretical questions remain to be solved in more satisfactory ways. The most important of these is the development of the position plausibility function which at its current stage must be considered a very crude approximation only.

This (the issue of the position plausibility function) is related to another general question – the treatment of the always large body of background knowledge. It is against this body of knowledge and associated beliefs, attitudes, preferences, that humans evaluate new items of information. Seen by itself or only in the context of statements actually stated explicitly during a planning discourse, a piece of information may appear irrelevant. Seen against certain facets of background knowledge, it may gain vital and crucial importance. It would seem necessary to begin to build up large data bases about cases "similar" to a project to be supported, over extended periods

---

[1] For example, a number of students were asked to first contribute arguments for and against a simple design issue related to the design of a new building for a School of Architecture, and then to evaluate these arguments according to a version of the simplified procedure presented in section 8.4.3. Prior to this, an initial vote showed a clear majority in favor of one position. As a result of the argument assessment, this attitude was reversed, as indicated both by the position plausibility measures and a final simple Yes/No vote.

of time, in order to give computer programs adequate models of human evaluative powers.

Other unresolved issues have been discussed before, such as the question of weighting with regard to deontics which are not purpose-oriented (that is, pertaining to the narrow set of purposes associated with a specific planning case) but belong to more general sets of e.g., moral, ethical, political principles. (Mann 1980). Can or should these be assigned weights within an aspect tree for a specific problem, without also first listing, ordering, and then weighting all other such principles people might hold in life? This of course would open up the discourse to issues vastly beyond the scope of the case at hand.

Apart from the resolution of question such as these (which may or may not be possible) the philosophical implications of their existence remain to be fully discussed. No doubt, one general response both to the effort to raise such questions and to features such as the apparent complexity of resulting procedures will be to dismiss the entire discussion as "too theoretical and/or impractical," calling for simpler, more "realistic" and straightforward approaches, or even reverting to approaches resting entirely on non-explicit and intuitive judgment that remain unaccountable by intent.

It must be pointed out that such reactions will of course not resolve the problems or make them disappear, only hide them from view.

8.5.3.   Suggestions for Further Work

The discussion of the open questions in itself provides a good indication of areas that would benefit from further work.

Application tests

Most urgently, it would seem necessary to conduct a number of actual application experiments of various procedures. These could be partial procedures – it would not be necessary to cover the entire decision-making process in order to gain useful insights. The aim would be both at working out the specifics of particular application tasks (format, required level of formalization of rules, documentation provisions, and the like) and at comparing the effect of different procedural combinations and sequences on the overall outcome and effectiveness of the process.

Inventory and analysis of argument patterns in design and planning discourse

Both results of test applications of the kind proposed above, and suitably detailed, focused documentation of planning processes in general could provide the data for a comprehensive inventory of argument patterns used in design and planning discussions, as well as for the patterns of distribution of their use and effectiveness.

Scrutiny of interface points between other areas of the design process

The work of exploring the connection or interface points between various facets of the design process that was begun in this study with the relationship between argumentation and formal evaluation, should be continued for other areas as well. There seem ot be some gaps in the design methods literature that might be prime candidates for such work. One of these is the role of evaluation processes in design approaches that aim not at producing and then choosing from among a set of alternative solutions, but at using a set of rules to build up *one* solution which is adopted as "guaranteed" by virtue of having been generated according to the rules. This kind of work could proceed relatively independently from the other areas of investigation suggested here.

Development of computer programs for planning support systems

The aspect of (perceived) procedural complexity which will no doubt continue to present real or imagined obstacles to imlementation, lends some urgency to the task of computer programs that would help in the documentation, retrieval, and analysis functions of the support systems that should be provided for planning decision-making projects of some scale and significance.

There are many other aspects involved in the ideas presented in the preceding study which would benefit from closer scrutiny. These brief suggestions must suffice to highlight some of the main points.

8.5.4. Summary

The discussion in the above has touched on a considerable number of issues. For most of these, it would be premature to attempt to draw any definitive conclusions. While some progress has been made in exploring the concept of "procedural building blocks," linking these for two different areas of design and in actually specifyingprocedural provisions and incidental requirements such as plausibility functions etc., the main conclusion seems to be that this field of investigation is still rather unexplored and that further work would be worthwhile in view of the wide range of application possibilities.

8.6. REFERENCES

Ackoff, R. L. (1961):
Scientific Method, Wiley, New York

Alexander, Christopher, et al., (1977):
A Pattern Language, Oxford University Press

Buchanan, J. M. and G. Tullock (1962):
The Calculus of Consent, University of Michigan

Churchman, C. W. R. L. Ackoff and E. L. Arnoff (1957):
Introduction to Operations Research, Wiley, New York

Dehlinger, Hans and J. P. Protzen (1972):
Debate and Argumentation in Planning: An Inquiry into Appropriate Rules and Procedures, Working paper No. 178, Institute of Urban and Regional Development, College of Environmental Design, University of California, Berkeley.

Grant, Donald P. (1972):
Combining Proximity Criteria With Nature-of-the-Spot Criteria in Space Planning Problems, *Proceedings, Ninth Annual Design Automation Workshop*, Dallas, Texas, 1972; Association for Computing Machinery and IEEE, New York.

—— (1974):
The Problem of Weighting, *DMG-DRS Journal: Design Research and Methods*, Vol. **8**, No. 3.

—— (1976):
How to Use an Alpha-Beta Model for Decision-making with Multiple Objective, *Design Methods and Theories*, Vol. **10**, No. 4.

—— (1982):
Design by Objectives, (Multiple Objective Design Analysis and Evaluation in Architectural, Environmental, and Product Design), The Design Methods Group, San Luis Obispo, CA.

Helmer, Olaf (1966):
Social Technology, Basic Books, New York.

Hill, M.)1968):
A Goals Achievement Matrix for Evaluating Alternative Plans, *Journal of the American Institute of Planners*, Vol. **34**, No. 1.

Hoefler, H., L. Kandel, G. Kohlsdorf and A. Musso (1972):
Gesamtschule Nuernberg-Langwasser: Entscheidungsvorbereitung Fuer Den Bauwettbewerb. Institut fuer Grundlagen der Modernen Architektur, Arbeitsberichte zur Planungsmethodik No. 5. Stuttgart.

Joedicke, J. (1969):
Zur Formalisierung des Planungsprozesses, in A. Bottling, et al., *Bewertungsprobleme in der Bauplanung*, Arbeitsberichte zur Planungsmethodik No. 1, Institut fuer Grundlagen der Modernen Architektur, Stuttgart.

Jones, Christopher J. (1970):
Design Methods – Seeds of Human Futures; Wiley-Interscience, New York/London/Sydney/Toronto,

Kaufman, Arnold (1968):
The Science of Decision-Making: An Introduction to Praxeology, World University Library, McGraw-Hill, New York.

Nagel, Albrecht (1971):
The Argumentation Matrix as a Selected Tool of the Science of Political Decision-Making for Citizens and Groups of Citizens; in *Kommunikation*, Vol. **VII**, No. 1.

Mann, Thorbjoern (1971):
Notes On Combining IBIS – Supported Planning Debate with Formal Objectification Procedures, working paper (unpubl.) University of California, Berkeley.

—— (1973) Argument Assessment and Design Decisions, paper presented at the Third International Conference of the Design Methods Group and the Design Research Society, London.

—— (1977):
Argument for Design Decisions, dissertation, University of California.

—— (1980):
Some Limitations of the Argumentative Model of Design, in *Design Methods and Theories*, Vol. 14, No. 1.

Miller, William R. (1970):
A Technique for Making Non-economic Evaluations, *Proceedings, Fifth Annual Urban Symposium of the Association for Computing Machinery*, Association for Computing Machinery, New York.

Musso, Arne (1974):
Ueber die Bewertung von Angeboten im Bauwesen, in: *Fertigteilbau und Industrialisiertes Bauen*, Vol. 10, No. 5.

Musso, A. and H. Rittel (1969):
Ueber das Messen der Guete von Gebaeuden, in: *Inst. fuer Grundlagen der Modernen Architektur*, (eds.): Arbeitsberichte zur Planungsmethodik No. 1, Stuttgart.

Rittel, Horst (1970):
Der Entwurfsprozess als iterativer Vorgang der Varietaetserzeugung und Varietaetseinschraenkung, in: *Entwurfsmethoden in der Bauplanung*, Arbeitsberichte zur Planungsmethodik, No. 4. Institut fuer Grundlagen der Modernen Architektur, Stuttgart.

Vitruvius Pollio, Marcus (1960):
The Ten Books on Architecture, (transl.: M. H. Morgan) Dover, New York. (Orig. publ. by Harvard University Press, 1915).

Ward, Wesley and D. P. Grant (1970):
A Computer-Aided Space Allocation Technique, in *Proceedings, Kentucky Workshop on Computer Applications to Environmental Design*, Lexington, KY. University of Kentucky.

Zadeh, L. A. (1965):
Fuzzy Sets, in: *Information and Control*, No. 8.

CHAPTER 9

PROBLEMS OF KNOWLEDGE ELICITATION IN INSURANCE

L.J. KOHOUT, A. BEHROOZ AND J. ANDERSON

Editorial Comment:

>Outlined here are the first steps in knowledge elicitation in a multi environmental system in insurance. This gives consideration to the concepts, contexts and limits involved. It reviews the role of questions to the expert.

LIST OF CONTENTS

9.1 INTRODUCTION
9.2 KNOWLEDGE ELICITATION
9.3 CONCEPTS AND TERMINOLOGY IN INSURANCE
9.4 CONTEXT IN INSURANCE
9.5 BOUNDS TO CONTEXTS
9.6 QUESTIONING STRATEGY
9.7 CONCLUSIONS
9.8 REFERENCES

9.1. INTRODUCTION

Knowledge engineering should be concerned with the construction of knowledge-based systems that would be capable of operating correctly and efficiently in a multi-environmental situation. This requires more refined and sophisticated methods than the relatively simple and well established methods for the construction of rule-based expert systems.

Important knowledge domains, which have essentially a multi-content and multi-environmental character are those of business decision making and finance. This chapter is concerned with the application of our new knowledge elicitation methodology to the domain of insurance underwriting. Insurance underwriting, which is similar to clinical decision making, is concerned with making decisions under risk conditions and uncertainty. The information on which this decision making is based in such situations comes from, and is utilised in, a multiplicity of diverse contexts. As many important insurance contracts with high risks are concerned with world wide business, transport and communication systems, it can be clearly seen that the multi-environmental approach based on **Activity Structures** is indispensible in this knowledge domain.

Because the business activities of even small firms and the economies of small nations are influenced by the events happening world-wide, involving a multiplicity of environments, conventional knowledge engineering methods are not fully adequate in the insurance underwriting domain.

9.2. KNOWLEDGE ELICITATION

We have shown in Chapter 6 that our knowledge elicitation consists of the familiarisation phase, and the knowledge elicitation phase, which are followed by a knowledge engineering phase. In both the knowledge familiarisation and elicitiation phases an adequate *method for formulating and phrasing* **questions** plays a crucial role. Questions are formulated by the knowledge elicitor and the answers to these, obtained by direct interaction with the expert, as well as from the expert literature, form the basic material from which the domain knowledge is extracted and formalised. For formalisation, an adequate formal structure, called here the *Formalisation Structure* (FMS) must be available. Into this FMS the relevant domain knowledge is embedded by the knowledge elicitor.

9.3. CONCEPTS AND TERMINOLOGY IN INSURANCE

Insurance is about risks, their circumstances and measurement. In the process of familiarisation the main concepts in insurance become clear from consultation of the expert literature. In many texts the law of large numbers receives prominence because this concept is fundamental to the work of insurers. If they can collect together large numbers of similar exposure units, then there is the possibility the actual losses or damage occuring during a particular exposure in time will approach those that can be anticipated.

Usually insurers like to use a pool of identical or homogeneous exposure units but this is not possible in detail as the individuals involved, in the case of car drivers, are not of the same age, sex or duration of experience. Slight differences between the exposure units can be accepted, provided that such units are independent or separate from each other. Risks are not seen as independent, for example, if thousands of houses in a particular area are insured against the risk of an earthquake rather than considering the risk to thousands of homes scattered across a particular country where it is independent.

Another concept relates to nature of risk where the future cannot be entirely controlled or anticipated. Nevertheless, the possible alternatives may be able to be listed based on past experience, although the precise future may not be known. The chances of these possible alternatives occurring may also be estimated, using numerical or other descriptions.

There are various classifications of risk reflecting different ways of looking at the problem. Risks categorised by an effect on groups of people or society in general, say in relation to the weather or the economy are beyond the influence of the individual and are regarded as fundamental risks. Others, which can arise from individual decisions, are particular risks and people have to live with their consequences. Still other risks are categorised by a range of alternatives and may involve pure or speculative risks. When future alternatives or chances are not known, then the situation is categorised as uncertainty and is important to insurers. What we have been illustrating is the importance of not only concepts but the necessity of having a **precise vocabulary**, which the knowledge elicitor can use and understand in his dealings with the expert. These are essential features of the process of familiarisation. Naturally such concepts will be checked with the expert and used by him and the knowledge elicitor in the process of knowledge elicitation.

Another important concept in underwriting is that of reinsurance. This is a special form of insurance where an insurance company, or a Lloyds syndicate, can transfer to another insurer, usually known as the reinsurer, a part of or all of its liabilities in regard to claims arising from the contracts of insurance that it has written. This allows the insurance company, usually known as the reinsured or ceding company or the direct insurer, to protect itself against the risk that it could be faced with claims so large as to decrease its profitability seriously or make it insolvent. Naturally this service has premiums which have to be taken into consideration.

Apart from underwriting, a typical insurance company works in other environments. As a business it must achieve financial control which requires corporate planning, accounts procedures and investment. It must pay regard to marketing to ensure sales of its insurance services by advertising and other means, have a personnel department and undertake research and development. All *these different environments involve particular contexts* with which the knowledge elicitor must become familiar by consulting the literature and the expert. Not only has the elicitor to recognise the important facts but the many relationships that exist between them, so that they may be viewed as **related wholes** and not as just many small parts.

9.4. CONTEXT IN INSURANCE

There are many important contexts in insurance, which span marine insurance with its liabilities for the ship and cargo, damage to third parties and other ships and for other problems such as oil pollution. Aviation insurance deals with insurance of aeroplanes, cargo, passengers and freight as well as liabilities to non-passenger third parties and airport owners and operators. Other transportation insurance involves commercial and private motor vehicles. Property insurance against a wide variety of perils, including fire and theft and liabilities for third party damage or injury is another important context. There are many others.

Each context has its own special facts and a host of different relationships, some of which are particular to it and others of a more general nature which can relate to the business as a whole. Naturally the financial aspects of a particular type of insurance, such as premiums, have a local as well as a general importance. The assessment of the value of liability is important for every transaction as well as for the business as a whole, so that its overall exposure is known. In this connection the relationship of liability to loss should be determined.

The knowledge elicitor therefore has to pursue all detail, whether he recognises its importance at the time or only later, so that contexts can be fully understood for formal representation.

9.5. BOUNDS TO CONTEXTS

As has already been shown each context has its own detailed and formal description of its elements and their relationships. What is not so well realised is the importance of making clear **the limits of a context**, its boundaries and what is not included but often thought to be related. Only by paying attention to these features will it be possible *to provide protection* against errors and wrong conclusions by an expert system. So far protection and security of expert systems have received little attention, because their importance in the phases of familiarisation and knowledge elicitation has not been sufficiently emphasized.

Experts are not usually familiar with such a formal construct but usually intuitively take care of protection and security by being careful about definitions and by using the knowledge that comes from a wide practical experience of what is likely to go wrong. It is often difficult to get experts to volunteer such information, and careful questioning is needed to bring it out.

9.6. QUESTIONING STRATEGY

A mathematician or a philosophical logician is rightly concerned about logical and semantic paradoxes. These make logical inference and judgements inconsistent and in some situations nonsensical. A practising human expert on the other hand justly leaves out such considerations. The reason for doing so is the expert's implicit and often subconscious skill in determining the right context in which the reasoning and all of the relevant judgements are done.

When the knowledge elicitor attempts to capture a part of the experts knowledge in an expert system, we have to carefully clarify the contexts in which the elicited knowledge is valid and the contexts outside its validity, in which it may be dangerous to rely on the judgements that the expert system generates, as it may be built using this knowledge.

This has an important consequence for the questioning strategy that the knowledge elicitor uses in the interaction with human experts during the knowledge elicitation process. The questions asked must be of two kinds:

a) Those that are specific enough to identify the concepts and the strategies of inference in the contexts where these are valid and correctly used by an expert.
b) Those that are broad enough so that they can reveal the contexts in which the concepts and strategies of inference break down.

The second kind of question is the one that sometimes *triggers a curious response* from the busy expert, willing to participate in the knowledge elicitation process: "*You are wasting my time, everyone knows that this is true*", or alternatively, "*Everyone knows that this is nonsense, go and read this and that textbook and when you have done it come back and see me again !*" However, the knowledge elicitor must not be discouraged by such responses and must patiently now and then **incorporate** questions of the **second** category at the right moment in the dialogue.

Our experiences of knowledge elicitation in the medical field gives some clues, indicating what underlying psychological process may cause such a reaction. A junior doctor with little experience (say a house officer) taken aback by the possible shift of context by a question of the second kind, may not be able to give the right answer, and may feel that their expertise is being questioned. An experienced consultant, particularly an expert of worldwide renown, may say, "*Oh that is a deep question, you see. I have to be careful and have a further check on this and that, before I make any judgement on the patient in such a situation.*" Or the expert may possibly say, "*Well I have to think about this one! I can't tell you just now!*"

9.7. CONCLUSIONS

The fact that the *knowledge of every expert is valid* **just in some definite family of contents** has deep consequences for both the design and the use of expert systems. Such a family of contexts has to be explicitly identified and safeguards ought to be incorporated into the expert system, so that the not-so-expert user consulting the expert system can be warned about the limited validity of the expert system's statements in each particular dialogue situation. Each expert, when solving a problem similar to the expert system, may have a *different view*, which is reconciled with the other expert's view during an informed discussion. Current conventional expert systems, unfortunately, do not provide such safeguards. From the viewpoint of the expert systems use, we believe that the expert system should not replace the expert but serve as a sophisticated tool. The safeguards warning about the validity of the expert or the knowledge based system's advice should be incorporated into the design. The system should be capable of saying that it does not know the right answer to the problem.

An expert system is like a tool, a magnifying glass, or binoculars – it sharply presents the relevant advice or support, if competently aimed in the right direction. Thus, we believe we should have expert systems with sharply defined **limits** of their *competence* in the hands of competent experts. Competent expert systems (whatever that may mean in reality) cannot be in the hands of those who have no detailed knowledge of the field and the idea that they can be used by everyone should be relegated to the domain of science fiction.

We hope that the logical structures outlined in this paper will help to achieve this end. It is clear that expert and knowledge based systems have an imporatnt role to play in finance and insurance, but these must be firmly controlled by the financial experts and insurers who are using them.

9.8. REFERENCES

Dickenson G.C.A. and Steele J.T. (1981):
Principles and Practice of Insurance, Chartered Insurance Institute Texts, No. 010, London.

Carter R.L. (1980):
Economics and Insurance, P.H. publishers, 2nd edition, Stockport.

Diacon S.R. and Carter R.L. (1984):
Success in Insurance, in *Success Studybooks*, Tudor A.T. (ed.), John Murray, London.

PART III

DESIGN OF KNOWLEDGE-BASED SYSTEMS AND ROBOTS FOR MULTI-ENVIRONMENTAL SITUATIONS

Editorial Comments:

The methodology of Multi-Environmental Knowledge Elicitation yields the knowledge structures which have specific multi-environmental features, which are reflected in turn in the design and implementation of Knowledge Based Systems.

Part III, after presenting an example of Multi-Environmental Multi-Context Knowledge Based System CLINAID, *discusses important features of Multi-Environmental Architectures.*

CHAPTER 10

AN OVERVIEW OF CLINAID

L.J. KOHOUT, J. ANDERSON, W. BANDLER, S. GAO AND C. TRAYNER

Editorial Comment:

CLINAID is presented as a Multi-environmental Multi-context Architecture in which the specific features are classified by considering how the designer has interpreted challenges.

LIST OF CONTENTS

10.1 GENERIC SPECIFICATION OF MEDICAL KNOWLEDGE-BASED DECISION SUPPORT SYSTEM CLINAID
10.2 AN OVERVIEW OF FUNCTIONS OF CLINAID AND SPECIFICATION OF ITS ACTIVITIES
    10.2.1 Specification of Activities of the Diagnostic Unit
    10.2.2 Specification of Activities of Treatment Recommendation Unit
    10.2.3 The Purpose of the Patient Clinical Record Unit
    10.2.4 Specification of Activities of the Co-ordinator and Planning Unit
10.3 THE ROLE OF ACTIVITY STRUCTURES IN THE DESIGN OF CLINAID
    10.3.1 Functional and Substratum Structures – the Basic Distinction
    10.3.2 Interaction of the System with its Environments
10.4 THE GLOBAL DESRIPTION OF THE ACTIVITY STRUCTURE OF CLINAID
    10.4.1 EAS of Clinical Activities
    10.4.2 The IPM-Activity Structure of Diagnostic Unit in Interaction with its Environment
10.5 MULTI-CONTEXT FUZZY INFERENCE OF CLINAID
    10.5.1 Diagnostic Knowledge Structures with a Multiplicity of Contexts
    10.5.2 The Dynamics of Expert Knowledge: Modes and Strategies of Inference
    10.5.3 Building Substrata Structures of CLINAID by Means of Fuzzy Relational Architectures
10.6 FORMALIZATION OF CLINICAL MANAGEMENT ACTIVITIES
    10.6.1 Introduction
    10.6.2 Definition of Semantic Descriptor Structures for Patient Management
10.7 TIME AND CONTEXT IN DECISION PLANNING
    10.7.1 Planning in CLINAID Viewed as a Time and Context Dependent Inferential Process

10.7.2 Formalization of the Planning Process by Means of Fuzzy Relations – Specification of Semantic Descriptors

10.8 REFERENCES

10.1. GENERIC SPECIFICATION OF MEDICAL KNOWLEDGE-BASED DECISION SUPPORT SYSTEM CLINAID

Although there exist a number of successful medical expert systems within a narrow specialist domain which are capable of operating in an experimental or laboratory medical environment, there is a long way to go toward the completion of a comprehensive knowledge based system that would be widely accepted in medical clinics and hospitals. Kohout and Bandler (1982, 1986a) stressed that a clinical expert system is an engineering artifact which has to satisfy a number of other requirements in addition to providing its primary functions. This is so because of the special constraints imposed on the system by the medical environments in which this system operates.

We need to pay a great deal of attention to evaluating carefully the medical environments in which an expert system will be placed. It should be realised that any medical expert system will, wittingly or unwittingly, be placed in the situation that is in its essence a multi-environmental one. This is so because all the information concerning the patients comes from more then one environment. Thus, in a typical hospital situation, we have an administrative, clinical, laboratory, social and other environments. It is the *integration* into these environments that is overwhelmingly important. The lack of integration, or rather fixed, rigid integration is usually the cause of failure in realising any flexible and responsive computerisation of medical institution. In a way, the problems are similar to those encountered in computer aided manufacturing or complex business.

At the beginning of history of expert systems, a large number of successful expert systems originated, or were motivated by, the work on medical expert systems. A typical example is PROSPECTOR, which was heavily influenced by MYCIN. At present, the fashion prevails, in particular in the industry, to regard everything concerned with medical or clinical decision making as well understood, simple, almost trivial. Therefore most of the new techniques and architectures for knowledge based systems originating from the medical A.I. research are often ignored by the expert systems community.

The cause of this rather paradoxical view is the fact that the complexity of medical decision making is not well appreciated by the A.I. and expert system community. It is usually assumed that the medical decision making consists only of medical diagnosis, which in turn is understood to be the identification of a disease. And this is supposed to consist of simply matching patient's symptoms and all other indicators with the list of symptoms and indicators for a subset of all known diseases and finding the best match! Yet, real live medical decision making involves mostly decisions under risk, uncertainty and often in emergencies when the time factor is crucial. We can see from some chapters of this volume, that similar circumstances may also occur for example in insurance underwriting and computer assisted manufacturing.

We have shown (Kohout, Anderson, Bandler and Behrooz 1986) that medical diagnosis includes many other activities including planning! Planning itself is regarded to be a difficult topic of research in expert systems area, yet medical decision making is viewed by the non-medical expert system community to be relatively simple, well understood problem.

The clinician not only determines the diagnosis of a patient, but also makes a large number of other decisions, including the administrative ones. Trying to deal with that multitude of many diverse and often conflicting requirements, we have developed our generic CLINAID multi-environmental and multi-context knowledge-based system architecture.

In a series of papers, we have described the conceptual structures as well as the basic architecture of CLINAID. Its architecture is aimed at supporting not only diagnosis but also other types of clinical activity and decision in diverse hospital environments. In general, CLINAID generic architecture is aimed at support of knowledge-based decision making with risk and under uncertainty. Such a system has to operate in a multi-environmental situation and make *decisions* within a *multiplicity of contexts*.

The basic architecture consists of the co-operating units (cf. Kohout, Bandler, Anderson and Trayner 1985) that are called the Basic Shell Substratum (Fig. 10.1):

1. Diagnostic Unit
2. Treatment Recommendation Unit
3. Patient Clinical Record Unit
4. Co-ordination and Planning Unit.

The first demonstration of a CLINAID diagnostic unit as given by Trayner (1983). A recent addition to the CLINAID architecture is an adaptive learning unit (Gao, 1986), which will be monitoring the changes in the nature of the diagnostic and other clinical data, the rate of misdiagnosis of the system, due to the changes of the nature of the environments, and other factors. Another recent addition is the design blueprint for DEXTERON, a real-time fuzzy expert system with deep knowledge for assessment of movement performance of neurological patients by means of classification of the dynamic features of their handwriting (Kohout and Kallala, 1986). We have shown that the system is extendible to real-time monitoring / classification of dynamic characteristic of mobile objects, such as robots (Kohout, Kallala and Bandler, 1986).

The Activity Structures approach (Kohout 1987, 1990; chapter 5 of this volume) the design methodology that provided the necessary framework for construction of CLINAID generic knowledge-based system architectures.

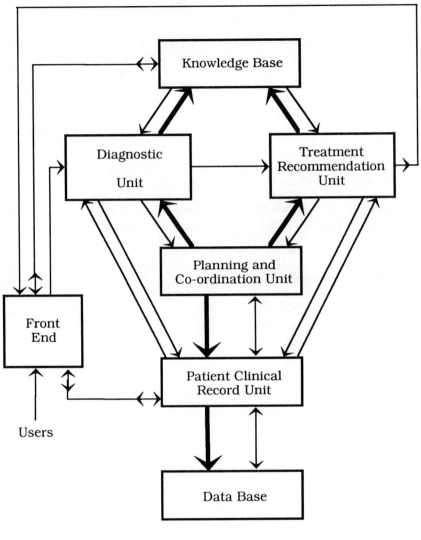

Figure 10.1. The basic configuration of CLINAID

10.2. AN OVERVIEW OF FUNCTIONS OF CLINAID AND SPECIFICATION OF ITS ACTIVITIES

This section summarises the major features of the environmental activities structures based specification of the functions of CLINAID.

The CLINAID architecture (Anderson, Kohout, Bandler and Trayner 1985; Kohout, Bandler, Anderson and Trayner 1985) consists of four main co-operating units which are connected to each other by appropriately matched interfaces. The whole configuration of CLINAID, including the data and control flow interaction between the units is shown in Figure 10.1. A more detailed specification of activities of the individual CLINAID units is given below.

10.2.1. Specification of Activities of the Diagnostic Unit

The purpose of the unit is to assist in the diagnosis of diseases that are within its purview. During this activity it accepts the information required in a dynamic manner. It is not connected to the patient but relies on requests to the user (clinician) for further information so long as it lacks sufficient information to recommend a working diagnosis. As it acquires more and more information, it restricts the set of the most likely diseases to fewer and fewer. During this activity, the unit is in potential communication with the treatment recommendation unit. This is in order to deal with possible emergencies if necessary, before the working diagnosis is reached. Finally the unit either proffers a conclusion for the user's consideration or, if it still lacks sufficient evidence, an indication is given that the unit is unable to reach a final diagnostic conclusion. If a conclusion is reached then this conclusion is communicated to the Treatment Recommendation Unit.

During the inference process, the Diagnostic Unit requires the experts' knowledge and experience which is obtained from the Knowledge Base. Sometimes this unit also requires use of the patient's medical record when it works towards diagnosis. All the signs, symptoms, the results of physical examinations, laboratory tests and the conclusion are communicated to the Patient Clinical Record Unit. It depends on the context and circumstances, when this communication occurs. Patients records are updated dynamically as the clinical process proceeds, and this in some situations requires concurrency (cf. Kohout, Anderson, Bandler and Behrooz 1986; also Chapter 12 of this volume).

10.2.2. Specification of Activities of Treatment Recommendation Unit

The purpose of the second unit is to advise about treatment, taking into the account the working diagnosis and the possible adverse effects (cf. Kohout, Keravnou, Bandler, Trayner and Anderson 1984) of each member of the family of prima facie treatments appropriate for each individual patient. This unit accepts the conclusion of the Diagnostic Unit as its input data. It also sends a request for the pharmacological drug history to the patient record unit. In order to make a treatment recommendation, it needs the experts' knowledge from Knowledge Base and the past history of the patient. Therefore it also must establish communication with the Patient Clinical

Record Unit in order to request and accept the record of the patient. After it fulfils this task, it will send the patient's medical record (which includes the given treatment recommendation) to the Patient Clinical Record Unit. The treatment recommendation is also sent to the user.

10.2.3. The Purpose of the Patient Clinical Record Unit

It is essential to incorporate a clinical record keeping unit that keeps track of all the data concerning the patient. This is essential for several reasons. First, the recommendation of treatment requires the knowledge of prior and current therapies and drugs in order to avoid adverse cross-interactions. Second, prognosis of the patient's state requires both present and past histories. Third, the advantage of the record keeping and retrieval unit is that it removes a considerable amount of time-consuming drudgery from the clinician's workload, as it provides the output of clearly printed notes, to be approved and signed by the clinician and left on file.

The patient clinical record functions as a communication and data processing unit. CLINAID has a data base in which the medical records of all patients are stored. The Patient Clinical Record Unit arranges the data base and provides a connection between the Diagnostic Unit and the treatment Recommendation Unit. It bridges the gap between these two units and the data base.

10.2.4. Specification of Activities of the Co-ordinator and Planning Unit

The fourth unit provides the overall control of the clinical management activities (cf. section 10.6) as well as all the necessary auxiliary matching functions such as generating and unifying the communication protocols. In addition it has to contain the log of the co-ordinating process to facilitate monitoring and auditing the operation of the whole system. Auditing is only one of a whole range of criteria that a clinical system ought to satisfy (cf. Kohout, Bandler, Anderson and Trayner 1985).

We have seen that each of these four units fulfils a certain global task. The global tasks co-operate concurrently and for this purpose the units are connected to each other by appropriately matched data and control flow interfaces which are structured within an additional unit called "whiteboard." It should be noted that each unit of CLINAID may consist of a number of centres and thus form itself a multi-centre fuzzy knowledge-based system.

10.3. THE ROLE OF ACTIVITY STRUCTURES IN THE DESIGN OF CLINAID

10.3.1. Functional and Substratum Structures – the Basic Distinction

The specification of activities of CLINAID given in the previous section characterised well the overall *required* activity and the aims of our system. This specification resulted from a careful scrutiny of the clinical activities that were placed in the appropriate environments. In order to do this systematically we have applied the Activity Structures methodology.

Activity Structures based methodology is a new methodology devised to be used for the total design of information processing systems in general, and of expert system in particular. It has been developed by Kohout (1987, 1990) using as its essential foundation the General Systems based theory of Activity Structures (Kohout 1974b, 1975, 1976a, 1977, 1978a). Chapter 5 of this book provides the reader with a brief overview of the Activity Structures based approach. Here we briefly recapitulate just the most important principles that were used in CLINAID construction. In the sections that follow we shall use these to capture the statics and dynamics of CLINAID structures.

It is explained in Chapter 5, that two qualitatively different structures of a system are distinguished in the Activity Structures methodology: structures of behaviour and structures of substrata.

An interconnected collection of modules (hardware or software modules, brain centres, etc.) is called *substratum structure*. This denotes the physical (or virtual) parts of the system together with their interfaces.

On the other hand, if we attempt to infer the structure from the behaviour of a system, this structure has a different nature. The term "structure" in this second context means the structure of behaviour. If in addition, the goal-directedness or the purpose is selected as the criterion for the choice of the class of the model to which the behaviour of a system is to be approximated, then this leads to a special structure of activity or of behaviour, called a *functional structure* (Kohout 1976a, 1978a, 1986, 1990).

To deal with the physical or virtual composition of the system and with its behaviour is not sufficient. The system in operation interacts with the user environments, the composition and the dynamics of behaviour of which has also to be taken into account. In order to deal with all these components in an appropriate way, Activity Structures approach provides special classes of structures that can capture the purposefullness and functionality of activities of both: the computing system and its multiple environment.

10.3.2. Interaction of the System with its Environments

The total Activity Structure used in the design is a functional description in the teleological sense, which is generated by the following kinds of activities (Kohout, 1987):
 a) by the activity of the information processing machine and
 b) by the activities of the environment in which the machine is used.

The activities (a) and (b) must appropriately co-operate and form together the total dynamic activity structure of the IPM in its environments.

An essential step in the total design of an information processing system is to split the total activity structure into two substructures:

a) An Environment Activity Structure, (EAS), with its proper part, a user activity structure;
b) An Information Processing Machine Activity Structure, (IPM-AS), characterising the behaviour of an information processing machine teleologically.

The two activity structures above have to be properly matched in their relevant aspects (Kohout 1982). Even a cursory look at the activities of any finished IPM shows that there is a big gap between the EAS and the corresponding IPM-AS. The distinction between EAS and the IPM-AS raises therefore a considerable methodological problem – what should be put into this gap.

The way that leads to the solution of this formidable design problem is the realisation that the correct correspondence is a *dynamic, conceptual, and functional match* of the EAS and IPM-AS activity structures.

There are no easy shortcuts in the design of systems for multi-environmental and multi-context situations. In the construction process we start with some knowledge of EAS involving the activities of the domain experts. In this chapter we take the EAS for granted. How this can be obtained by knowledge elicitation is described in Chapters 6, 7 and 8 of this book.

The next step is to determine the aims of the problem to be solved. In our particular case it will be the aims of clinical activities relevant to the overall patient management. By applying the reduction rules, we eliminate the parts of EAS that are irrelevant to this aim. The aim basically determines which parts of expert activities are to be delegated to the knowledge-based system. Thus by performing this step we obtain the AEAS (Aim Environmental Activity Structures – cf. Kohout, Anderson, Bandler and Behrooz, 1986; and Chapter 5 of this volume).

The construction process continues with questioning as to what the system must do, and for what purpose. This leads to determining the tasks (Kohout 1978a,b) of those individual activities that have appeared in the EAS. It is essential to scrutinise at this stage not only the required but also the undesirable activities in order to incorporate suitable protection against the latter at the early stages of design. The essential tool used in this pursuit are the so called *task descriptors* (cf. Kohout 1978a,b, 1990; for the definition see Chapter 5 of this volume). At the end of this stage we end up with Functional Environmental Activity Structures (FEAS).

The complete design sequence that was described in detail in Chapter 5 is pictured bellow.

$$EAS \longrightarrow AEAS \longrightarrow FEAS \Longrightarrow FAS \longrightarrow SUB$$

We have learned in Chapter 5 that EAS, AEAS and FEAS capture the activities of the environment. The IPM activity structures were divided into FAS (Functional Activity Structures) and substratum structures (SUB). We have also learned that the FAS captured the dynamics of the six broad categories of the functions of the IPM. SUB on the other hand captured the physical (or virtual) realisation or description of the IPM (i.e. of its substructures and their interfaces)

10.4. THE GLOBAL DESCRIPTION OF THE ACTIVITY STRUCTURE OF CLINAID

10.4.1. EAS of Clinical Activities

Using the general design sequence described in the previous section the activity structures of CLINAID were produced. To explain in a greater detail how this was done we shall start from a simplified picture of activity of a clinician during the diagnostic process. Then we shall discuss the analogous activities of CLINAID. In later sections of this chapter, we present a more refined picture of clinician's decision making activity, including also its other aspects, such as patient management (Kohout, Anderson, Bandler and Behrooz 1986).

The activity structure of CLINAID mirrors clinician's activity. In a simplified form, a clinician's activity is depicted in Fig. 10.2 (cf. Kohout, Bandler, Anderson and Trayner 1985; Kohout and Bandler 1983, 1986a). At least the following four components characterise the clinicians' activity while treating a patient:

1) Observation.
2) Conceptual classification and filtration of relevant observational data for (3).
3) Decision.
4) Clinical action.

All these basic components interact strongly with one another. For this reason the characteristics and the concrete contents of the knowledge representation structure will be strongly affected by every one of them. It is essential for the design of a usable system to recognise this and provide for its implementation.

Taken from the epistemological point of view the activities (1) - (4) above represent a systemic construct. By horizontal and vertical interleaving of these and other systemic systemic constructs the overall EAS is composed. The horizontal interleaving represents concurrent interaction and the vertical nesting represents various levels of meta-desccription (cf. Chapter 5).

An application of the vertical systemic composition produces the activity structure of *immediate clinician's activity*. In this case, two activity structures (EAS) of the above described type are nested to represent the clinician's short time activity, the time of which is in minutes or hours. The purpose of the inner one is to iteratively perform the classification leading to the immediate working diagnosis. The outer one is concerned with monitoring the patient's state and taking appropriate emergency actions, based on the clinical observation of the patient's clinical state. Part of the patient's clinical state is working diagnosis, iteratively produced by the inner loop. We shall not describe in detail the full EAS here (cf.

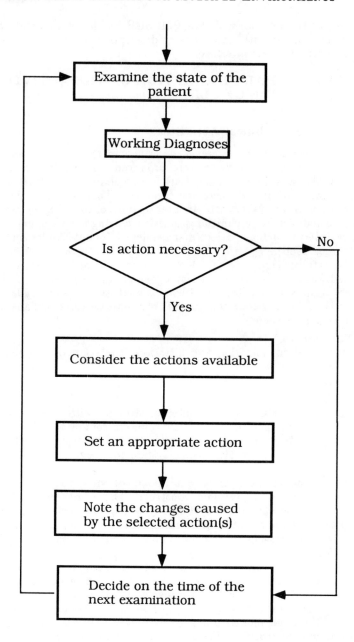

Figure 10.2. EAS of immediate activity of a clinician

Anderson, Bandler and Kohout 1982, Behrooz, Anderson and Kohout 1982-85, Behrooz 1986). The EAS representing the immediate activity of a clinician is depicted in Fig. 10.2.

By the three step modelling process (cf. Chapter 5) the Aim Environmental Activity Structure (AEAS) is produced.

At the most global level, the aim sequence of the clinician's activities consist of:

OBSERVATION AND INVESTIGATION ⟶ DECISION ⟶ ACTION.

The purpose of the observation and investigation is to obtain, what we shall call FINDINGS. The findings are *compared* with MEDICAL FACTS and THEORIES. The comparison provides GROUNDS for decision making. The purpose of the decision making activity is to generate further HYPOTHESES, decide on clinical ACTIONS as well as to decide what are the relevant facts concerning the patient to be recorded in appropriately structured PROTOCOLS for the future use.

Table 10.1 Global Inferential Activity Structure of CLINAID

INFERENTIAL ACTION:	Resulting SUGGESTION: ACTION or PROTOCOL	Participating: CLINAID units:
	patient management actions	DIAG + TRREC
FINDINGS @ FACTS and THEORIES	working diagnoses	DIAG
	investigations	DIAG
	patient clinical state	DIAG + TRREC + PCR
	patient prognosis	TRREC + PCR

@ ... denotes the operation of comparison of knowledge structures

Participating SUBSTRATUM units of CLINAID:

DIAG ... Diagnostic Unit
TRREC ...Treatment Recommendation Unit
PCR ...Patient Clinical Record Unit

The previously described activity scenario is the one to be put into the Knowledge Based Decision Support System in order to provide the essential activities of the Knowledge-Based System. We have learned in the previous section on the Activity Structures methodology that this scenario is called Aim Environmental Activity Structure (AEAS). The AEAS is embedded into the Knowledge Based System and forms an essential part of its overall activity structure (IPM-AS). The resulting activity structure, which broadly describes CLINAID's activities is given in Table 10.1 (cf. Kohout, Behrooz, Anderson, Gao, Trayner and Bandler 1987).

Table 10.1 gives the overall general activity schema concerned with the functioning and mutual co-operation of the three main units of CLINAID. In the next section we shall present in greater detail the activity structures that lead to the construction of the diagnostic unit of CLINAID.

10.4.2. The IPM-Activity Structure of Diagnostic Unit in Interaction with its Environment

As discussed above, the first essential stage in the design of an information processing machine is the construction of an IPM activity structure. However, in order to get this we have to already possess the corresponding environmental-activity structure. Following the activity of the actual process of diagnosis, we generated the EAS of the Diagnostic Unit as presented in Fig. 10.3.

In the case of CLINAID, there exists a close match between some parts of EAS and IPM-AS as can be seen from Fig. 10.4 which presents the IPM-AS of the Diagnostic Unit.

The dynamics of interaction of a body system of CLINAID with one of its environments is depicted in Fig. 10.5. This figure displays the Activity Graph of the dynamics of a body system. The graph consists of four hyper-processes (i.e. tasks) that mutually interact. The arcs labelled ! represent the outcome of the activities of the hyper-processes. Those marked ? represent a query (e.g. request for some information or question, etc.).

Table 10.2 specifies the types and the semantic meaning of the inputs and outputs of the hyper-processes. It should be noted that the hyper-process HP-1 represents the activity of the clinician, whereas HP-2, HP-3 and HP-4 represent the hyper-processes that belong to the CLINAID IPM-AS. The aim of HP-2 is to identify the possible body-systems affected by the ailment of the diagnosed patient, whereas HP-3 and HP-4 identify the relevant syndromes and the working diagnosis, respectively. Fig. 10.5 also displays the messages exchanged between the diagnostic unit and other units of CLINAID.

The corresponding substratum structure of one body system is depicted in Fig. 10.6. It shows the hierarchical decomposition of the individual substratum modules of an applicative implementation in which only the pure functional features of Lisp programming language were used (cf. Gao 1986). Each substratum module of a higher level calls during its processing activities for the services of the modules of the lover levels. This Lisp implementation is convenient for further development of the system by prototyping, although the first implementation by Trayner (in a non-applicative Pascal-type language) was more efficient computationally.

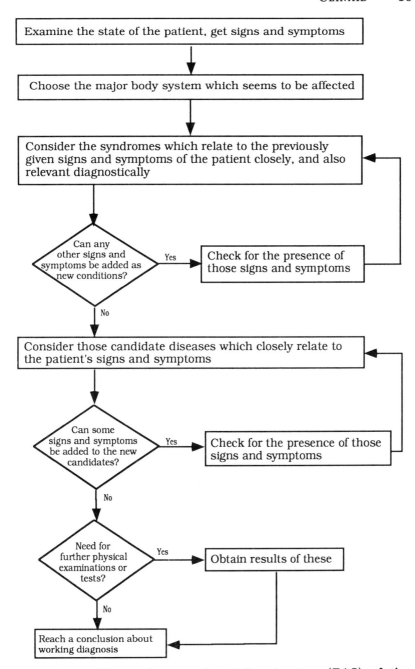

Figure 10.3. The environmental activity structure (EAS) of the diagnostic process

Knowledge-Based Systems for Multiple Environments

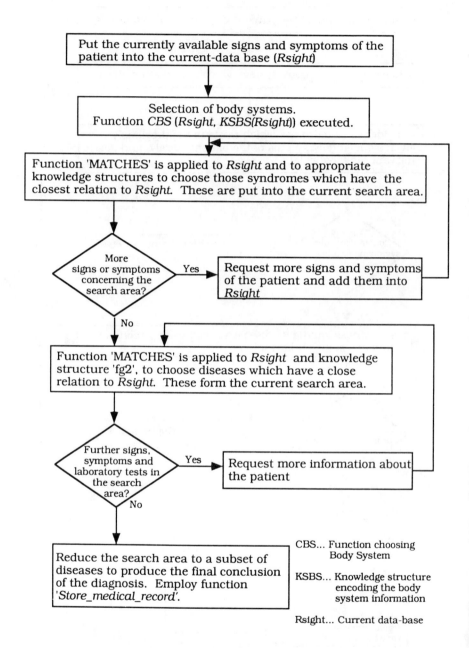

Figure 10.4. IPM activity structure of the diagnostic unit

Table 10.2 Summary of main hyperprocesses of a diagnostic unit of CLINAID

PURPOSE	Hyper-Process Identifier	INPUT	OUTPUT
Relevance filtering performed by the user of CLINAID	HP–1	Suggestions or questions presented by CLINAID	Data; assertions or rejections of the suggestions presented by CLINAID
Identification of body systems	HP–2	Initial or asserted data from the clinician-user	candidate to body systems
Selection of syndromes in a body system	HP–3	Initial or asserted data relevant to the selected body system(s); filetered out from input and outputs of HP1 and HP2	Diagnostically relevant syndromes
Forming the working diagnosis	HP–4	Diagnostically relevant syndromes; additional asserted signs and symptoms	A family of diseases forming "working diagnosis"

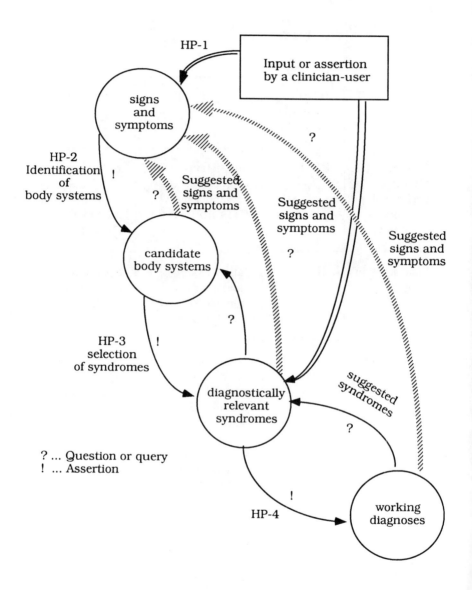

Figure 10.5. Activity graph of the dynamics of a body system of CLINAID

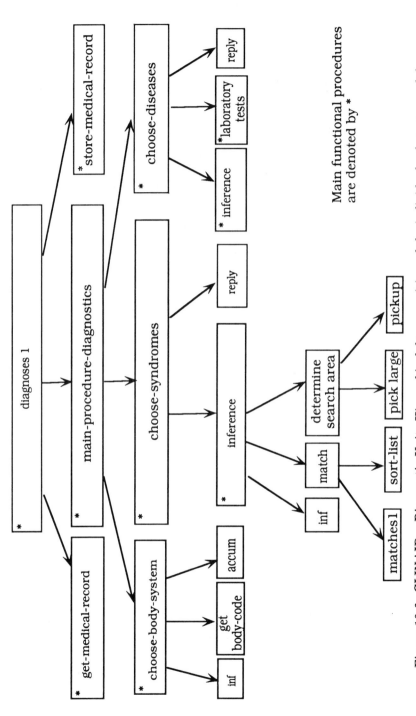

Figure 10.6. CLINAID – Diagnostic Unit: Hierarchical decomposition of the individual substrata modules as used in pure LISP functional implementation of CLINAID

KNOWLEDGE-BASED SYSTEMS FOR MULTIPLE ENVIRONMENTS

10.5. MULTI-CONTEXT FUZZY INFERENCE OF CLINAID

10.5.1. Diagnostic Knowledge Structures with a Multiplicity of Contexts

Extant medical expert systems just dealt with a limited context, the largest domain of knowledge being just a single medical field, e.g. Internal Medicine in CADUCEUS. The restrictions are not, however, due to the size of the field, although this is commonly believed. The problem of most existing expert systems goes deeper than that, being in its essence *conceptual*: their knowledge bases and inference engines cannot mix easily the knowledge from several fields. Only HEARSAY dealt with this problem – by introducing a multi-centre architecture.

As CLINAID attempts to be a comprehensive medical consultation system, its knowledge base has to contain a large amount of medical expert knowledge. Just take the diagnostic unit. Here, CLINAID deals with a number of body systems, where each body system belongs to a different branch of medicine. The average size of the knowledge structure of a body system of a comprehensive medical system indicates that the problems of efficiency and correctness of inference are not insignificant:

Signs/symptoms per body system ... 200-400 approximately
Diseases per body system ... 100-400 approximately
The total number of body systems ... 11

Seven of the body systems listed in the CLINAID specification (Kohout, Bandler, Anderson and Trayner, 1985) formed a part of the following list:

Cardiovascular
Respiratory
Central Nervous System
Muscular and Peripheral Nervous System
Renal
Endocrine
Blood and Reticulo-endothelial
Reproductive
Skeletal
Gastrointestinal
Psychological

A comparison with INTERNIST / CADUCEUS shows that in CLINAID we are faced with a formidable problem. INTERNIST deals only with internal medicine and contains several hundred diseases. In its size this corresponds to one body system of CLINAID. We are considering eleven body systems in the specification of our design (see above). The complexity of assembling the diagnostic knowledge structures to satisfy the specification is considerable. In particular the problem of compatibility and correctness of the diagnostic knowledge from different sources.

It is essential to verify the diagnostic knowledge, despite of the currently prevailing common belief of the expert system community that it is sufficient to fill the knowledge bases either by empirical rules given by the experts or by the information collected from the medical journals and diagnostic textbooks. We had to develop new methods of comparison of diagnostic knowledge structures using fuzzy triangle relational products of Bandler and Kohout (1986). Application of these methods to the investigation of reliability of diagnostic knowledge in the endocrine body system is described in detail by Ben-Ahmeida, Kohout and Bandler (cf. Chapter 16 of this volume).

10.5.2. The Dynamics of Expert Knowledge: Modes and Strategies of Inference

Any Activity Structure is characterised by its conceptual *semantics* and *dynamics* (Kohout 1982, 1987). The AEAS concerned with diagnostic knowledge is particularised in both its parts as follows:

1. Semantic Descriptor Structure captures the semantic definitions of all relevant diagnostic concepts.
2. Dynamic Descriptor Structure captures the clinician's inferential strategy and logic.

(cf. Anderson, Bandler and Kohout 1982; Behrooz, Anderson and Kohout 1982-1985; Kohout, Anderson, Bandler and Trayner 1985, Kohout, Anderson, Bandler and Behrooz 1986).

In section 10.5.1, we have briefly listed the types of static structures – the structures that contain the diagnostic semantic descriptors of the elements of the body systems (such as signs, symptoms, syndromes, diseases etc.). These static structures define descriptively or operationally (e.g. syntactically) the meaning of the concepts involved in EAS. This section is concerned with the dynamics of inference in AEAS. In the actual design of the system, this dynamic component transforms into the FAS of the IPM; partly into Inferential IHS partly into Control IHS functional structures. The former static part transforms mainly into Domain-dependent Knowledge IHS. If the dynamic component of AEAS in addition captures the specification of undesirable dynamics, this contributes to generating the Protection Constraint functional structure in the actual design transformation (Kohout 1990).

The experience shows that the dynamic paths of inference in diagnosis will be different if performed by an inexperienced medical student (despite of her/his textbook knowledge) from that performed by an experienced clinician.

Superficially, it would seem that the relation between signs, symptoms and illnesses suffices for performing an adequate diagnostic inference. However, the investigation of the logical structure of the medical knowledge shows that this is not the case. This leads to the following problems, that classical rule-based systems or Prolog systems using logic without types, cannot deal with correctly in all situations. Namely, we have:

1. *Problem of INCOMPLETENESS:* Not all signs and symptoms characterising the disease are always observable or present.

2. *Problem of LOCALITY OF INFERENCE:* Not all signs and symptoms are relevant in a particular given diagnostic context.
3. *Problem OF COMPLEXITY OF INFERENCE:* The complexity of exhaustive matching of all disease descriptors and indicators (e.g. signs, symptoms, tests, etc.) may be forbidingly high.

The simultaneous presence of problems (1) and (2) in some diagnostic contexts leads to what we might call "dead ends" or "blind alleys" of diagnostic inference. An interesting example is quoted (Anderson, Bandler and Kohout 1982):

> *I have just taken the students over a patient with a very obvious carcinoma of the stomach who had vomited and bled. There is a certain syndrome that links his metabolic state, anaemia and everything together.*
>
> *They (the students) just see it as a list of sequences and they are searching through textbook images. They cannot group these things together and ask more pertinent questions. If you do, it makes a lot more sense, a lot more quickly.*

The expert thus has shown how and why he uses certain higher order primitives. It transpires that an experienced clinician introduces new elements, namely, syndromes, into the diagnostic pathway. More detailed investigation of diagnostic inference shows that these additional concepts vastly reduce the complexity of the inferential task, as well as increasing its reliability. Without using these constructs (i.e. syndromes) the inference might not reach the final conclusion because of the combinatorial explosion of the inference task, so that the path has to be abandoned (problem 3 above). The expert's explanation just quoted showed that the inference may reach a wrong conclusion which is caused by the confusion of the context.

The expert continues his explanation of how the diagnostic inference may end in a 'blind alley' by ignoring a proper context of relevance:

> *He (the patient) is starving to death, he is very seriously ill, he is an old man and you wouldn't expect to find bowel signs. Well, they (the students) found no bowel signs, but they go to a surgical list for absent bowel signs and they are quite lost. The answer is, he is not eating anything so you wouldn't expect his guts to be churning around.*

We can see, that in this context, the bowel signs were not diagnostically relevant. We must, however, be careful and not exclude the substructures that are relevant in one context and irrelevant in another, from the knowledge base of a multi-environmental knowledge-based system. This would cause what we call "context-dependent incorrectness of logical inference" (cf. Kohout, Behrooz, Anderson, Gao, Trayner and Bandler, 1987). A formal characterisation of this phenomenon of local inference can also be given by means of a category of abstract logics (Kohout 1978a).

Generally, if the multiplicity of contexts is ignored in the design of knowledge structures dealing with locality of inference, the resulting expert system may exhibit unpredictable 'lapses of correctness of inference'. Namely, in the wrong context, it will simply reach a wrong conclusion, which unfortunately cannot be easily detected, as the 'red herring theory' eliminates the context at the design stage. To deal with this problem adequately, it is necessary to introduce multiple contexts into the inference of knowledge-based systems. In CLINAID, we deal with this problem by partitioning the IHI structures into multiple-body systems as well as using syndromes for diagnostic inference. In terms of functional activity structures, IHI *focuses* its activity into a particular area of locality, according to the context, which is *semantically* controlled by the *syndromes*. Once the inference is focused into one, or several body systems, then within each body system, the context is controlled by introducing an appropriate questioning strategy (Gao, Kohout, Anderson and Bandler 1987; Kohout, Gao and Kalantar in Chapter 11 of this volume) in which syndromes play an essential role.

What we have been describing is a static and dynamic characterisation of the logic and semantics of an EAS which enables the system to move from ignorance to adequate knowledge. In doing so, the system dynamically passes through various intermediate states. In these dynamic states, it has only partial information and strategies of inference generate partial conclusions. The dynamics of the AEAS are such that several partial conclusions can be kept under consideration until further diagnostic activity can distinguish between them. As more than one possibility is being considered at once, the system implements a simple form of parallel processing.

The other refinements of a particular inferential strategy are enforced by the time-dependency of symptoms. Strictly speaking, modification of the strengths of any sign or symptom changes with the progression of the illness or improves with treatment. To capture the dynamics of change, the time domain ought to be introduced. As a special case of this phenomenon, we note that different symptoms in the same illness have different time-ordering of their onset in different patients, although they characterise a particular illness. This has impact in patient management and characterisation of the clinical state, which is dealt with elsewhere.

Different time-orderings of symptoms in the same illness have also impact on the formal structures of diagnostic inference, which model the intrinsic structure of this phenomenon. Thus the diagnostic paths that are *not* time-dependent can be modelled algebraically in most cases by the Diagnostic Systems of the 1st Type, but those that are time dependent, by the systems of the 2nd Type (Kohout 1974b). The specifications of undesirable dynamics is a necessary part of the AEAS, if the control of the system has to be ensured. This specification does contribute *protection constraints* (Kohout 1987) in the actual design transformation. It is necessary to check for errors of inference and 'blind alleys' so as to resist a combinatorial explosion. While it is essential to build into the system protective features, they prove advantageous if they ensure as much correctness as possible and also prevent excessive computation in the pursuit of very unlikely diagnostic possibilities.

10.5.3. Building Substrata Structures of CLINAID by Means of Fuzzy Relational Architectures

In the previous section, the dynamics of inference, locality and multiplicity of context and the strategies of inference were discussed from the point of view of environmental and functional activity structures. In this section we shall turn our attention to the problems of embedding these structures into appropriate substrata structures.

There are two problems with adapting existing techniques used in the expert systems field, that we encountered. Namely:

i) large number of signs, symptoms and diseases are used in CLINAID
ii) each body system deals with a different medical field.

The first problem will be in the future resolved by adequate AI parallel architectures, first of which, a LISP machine is already commercially available. The second one is more serious, as it is conceptual: no amount of computational power can avoid problems caused by the *mixing of several distinct contexts*. Only a good well structured design of a Knowledge-Based System can provide a remedy.

With regard to the currently used rule based techniques, the number of the possible combinations of signs, symptoms, physical examinations, laboratory tests and diseases increases rapidly with each new body system. It is therefore not possible to represent such large amount of information with production rules and reach a conclusion by searching a tree with these rules in a normal diagnostic time scale, and by an on-line system.

Furthermore, the observations of a characteristic of a patient will often be more refined than merely 'present' or 'absent'. When we consider knowledge or information we are frequently not able to say that one piece of knowledge is, without doubt, true. We usually include some linguistic hedges such as, 'perhaps', 'frequently', 'rarely', etc., which restrict the degree of certainty of the knowledge. Although some Expert systems use "degrees of certainty," "probabilities" or "lower and upper probabilities" (i.e. Shefer-Dempster rules), they cannot deal properly with the linguistic hedges. That linguistic hedges are not just a fanciful invention of Lotfi Zadeh but are extensively used in medical practice can be seen from Chapter 16 of this volume.

In order to deal with all the problems outlined above, CLINAID uses fuzzy relational inference based on the triangle relational products, which were introduced in 1977 by Bandler and Kohout (cf. Bandler and Kohout 1987, Kohout and Bandler 1986). CLINAID chooses to use fuzzy relations to capture this large amount of clinical knowledge in a structured way, and to make it easier to deal with parallelism that is essential for a multi-centre approach.

As the foregoing discussion did suggest, from the point of view of system architecture, our approach is grounded on two essential features that are built into the system:

i) Plurality of control and inferential centres.
ii) Inference via triangular relational products.

The plurality of centres requires their *mutual co-operation*. Briefly, the plural centres co-operate as follows:
i) Each centre is adapted to dealing with a particular portion of the common task.
ii) Each centre filters out different aspects of data, according to to the context or to what its special competence.

The power of this way of organising things comes jointly from the *specialisation* of the former and the *simplification* of the latter. How the *common task* is *subdivided* and how the centres are co-ordinated are of course delicate and crucial questions, but assuming that they can be achieved successfully then the advantages of subdivision are evident:
i) Each centre deals only with a small portion of systemic knowledge.
ii) The centres can operate in parallel.

These provide a major weapon against combinatorial explosion, with the following desirable consequences:
i) Inference and meta-inference are both expressible as relations.
ii) Inference is computable in parallel.

This theme of parallel computation is one of the unifiers of the the plurality of centres and of relational inference.

When dealing with multiple contexts or multiple environments, the parallelism is essential, as in this situation the partial results concerning comparison and evaluation of several contexts or environments often arises.

10.6. FORMALIZATION OF CLINICAL MANAGEMENT ACTIVITIES

10.6.1. Introduction

In section 10.4 we have given the overall activity structure of the system showing that how its units interact. This was followed by a detailed description by the diagnostic unit, discussing not only its activity structures but also the construction of its substratum. In this section, we shall pay the attention to a more detailed description of the support of *clinical management activities*.

In our outline of the activity structures of the diagnostic unit we have put greater emphasis on the presentation of the dynamic descriptor structures as this captures the strategies of clinical inference. Semantic descriptor structures were mostly concerned with determining the meaning of the individual disease descriptors within the body systems, thus determining the medical content of the knowledge base defining the body systems.

In this section we shall present the semantic descriptors for activity structures concerned with patient management. We concentrate in this section on the semantic descriptors as these present the link between individual clinical contexts and environments. Our description is based on the material presented at 1986 AAMSI Congress in San Francisco (cf. Kohout, Anderson, Bandler and Behrooz 1986).

Patient management is concerned with overall organisation of the clinical process, integrating all the other clinical components and activities. It is the co-ordination and planning unit that performs the patient management activities as one of its essential tasks.

10.6.2. Definition of Semantic Descriptor Structures for Patient Management

By examining the clinical environmental activities involved in patient management we extracted several major activities that are described by means on informal, loose definitions, given in English. In the actual design specification, these are expressed formally by means of n-ary relations in their intensional form (Bandler and Kohout 1986, 1987).

The major activities of patient management have been divided into the major classes:

1. Working Diagnosis
2. Test choice
3. Therapy
4. Review process
5. Prognosis.

A brief definition of each class of activities follows.

Working diagnosis This usually is a list of relevant diagnostic hypotheses at a general level. These hypotheses are then explored by investigation and tested. If not proven, they are discarded. This may be called by some physicians the Provisional Diagnosis.

Test choice In exploring the working diagnoses, there are tests concerning the structure and function of each body system. Usually test choice is driven by doing early those tests which are convenient for the patient, easy to do and of low cost. As the diagnostic refinement proceeds, tests become more inconvenient for the patient, are often difficult to perform, and are more costly.

Therapy This is the attempt to remove the patient's symptoms and to treat the underlying cause or causes of disease, so that these are removed or in some way changed by adjustments by the patient, so that the patient can resume as normal a life as possible.

Review process This is a process of reviewing clinical care based on clinical data in relation to the objectives for care. It relates the clinical state to diagnosis, prognosis and therapy, and changes in each of these areas to other modalities. Clinical state is reflected by symptoms and signs (psychological and physical). The review process relates to clinical change by means of a review of clinical states (say daily or weekly) with therapy or investigation to determine if the parameters are changing.

Prognosis This has at least three components:

a) Prognosis of the disease the patient has, i.e. will he recover? How disabled is he likely to be?
b) Prognosis in relation to life expectancy, i.e. how will the disease reduce, if at all, his life expectancy?

c) Risk factors: these factors are determined by questioning and the investigation of certain basic data, which increase the risk of a poor or unsatisfactory outcome for the patient and so affect his overall state.

Each of these categories of activities described above, may operate in more than one environment. The set of environments for one category will be different from the set of environments of another. There will however be significant overlaps. Each overlap will induce an additional context dependency of a different kind.

The dynamics of expert knowledge and modes and strategies of inference are captured by the dynamic descriptor structures. These structures operate on semantic descriptor structures described in the previous section. The dynamics of the system are complicated further by time dependency of the therapy planning. Some aspects of this will be discussed in the following section.

10.7. TIME AND CONTEXT IN DECISION PLANNING

10.7.1. Planning in CLINAID Viewed as a Time and Context Dependent Inferential Process

The time dimension already discussed in section 10.5.2 has also to be taken into account in therapy planning. This involves decisions about time-indexed patient data and clinical activities in relation to clinical hypothesis about a patient held at that particular moment of time. This leads to distinguishing three different time entities: the past time t_p, the present time t_c, and the future time t_f. Formally, we have to define the boundaries of these three time parameters by specifying the three time intervals, namely

$t_p \in t_p = [t_i, t_c)$ ... past time interval
$t_c \in t_c = [t_{cl}, t_{cu})$ ... current time interval
$t_f \in t_f = (t_c, t_u]$ ... future (planning or prognosis) time interval.

In the above, t_i is the past time-value at which a patient's medical history has started; t_u is the future time value until which some future therapeutic activities or prognostication are to be considered at the time moment t_c. The bounds on t_c determine for how long all the structures that enter into the clinical inference can be kept constant in time. The decision inference is context dependent, where part of the context is time as defined above.

Thus the general decision scheme is set up by the following meta-logical construction:

1. From the current patient state and the family of acceptable clinical hypothesis, the current interpretation of results is determined (Kohout, Anderson, Bandler and Behrooz, 1986).
2. The acceptable interpretation obtained from (1) above is entered into the therapy planning relation TP and prognosis relation PROG.

3. The planning relation then generates a time dependent plan of clinical actions. Similarly, from the prognosis relation, the predictions about the future patient's state are made.

10.7.2. Formalization of the Planning Process by Means of Fuzzy Relations – Specification of Semantic Descriptors

The working diagnosis of a patient is a set of provisionally accepted hypotheses that enter into the planning process, determining part of the context of the planning inference. The time dependent description of the patient is provided by the family of the previous and current patient states. These two inferential components generate what we call the *interpretation* of the *patient medical situation*. Thus the interpretation is generated by the following meta-relation:

<accepted hypotheses, patient states> $\Longrightarrow$ INTERPRETATION

Formally, interpretation INT is an element of the lattice of all fuzzy relations defined by the following concept contrivance:

$$INT \in \mathcal{R}_F \left(PS \times Hyp \times Con \times T_p \times MVAL \right)$$

where

PS	...	the patient state-aggregate
HYP	...	the family of acceptable hypotheses
CON	...	context of interpretation descriptor
MVAL	...	valuation space of a Pinkava algebra
	...	(cf. Kohout 1974a, Pinkava 1988).

Medicine itself and physicians have not yet fully realised the importance of time in medical record system and its potential for planning of actions in the short term and for prognosis in the longer term.

10.8. REFERENCES

Anderson, J., Bandler, W. and Kohout, L.J. (1982):
Reports on CLINAID meetings September – December 1982. Dept. of Medicine, King's College Medical and Dental School, London.

Anderson, J., Kohout, L.J., Bandler, W. and Trayner, C. (1985):
A knowledge-based clinical decision support system using new techniques: CLINAID. In: *Proc. AAMSI Congeress 1985 (Amer. Assoc. for Medical Systems and Informatics*, San Francisco, Calif. May 20–22). Levy, A.H. and Williams, B.T. (eds.), 187–192.

Bandler, W. and Kohout, L.J. (1986):
On the general theory of relational morphisms. *Internat. Journal of General Systems*, **13**, 47–66.

Bandler, W. and Kohout, L.J. (1987):
Relations, Mathematical. In: *International Encyclopaedia of Systems and Control*, Pergamon Press, Oxford.

Behrooz, A. (1986):
A Description of Experimental Identification of Medical Knowledge. Ph.D. Thesis, Dept. of Computer Science, Brunel University, U.K.

Behrooz, A., Anderson, J., Kohout, L.J. (1982–85):
Transcripts and Reports on Knowledge Elicitation for Knowledge-Based System CLINAID. Dept. of Medicine, King's College Medical and Dental School, University of London, 1982–1985.

Gao, S. (1986):
Design and Implementation of Diagnostic Unit of Medical Knowledge Base System CLINAID. M.Phil. Thesis, Brunel University, U.K.

Gao, S., Kohout, L.J., Anderson, J., Bandler, W. (1987):
Questioning strategy in fuzzy knowledge-based systems. *Proc. of International Symposium on Fuzzy Systems and Knowledge Engineering*, (Guangzhou & Guiang, China, July, 1987), 1, 164–171.

Kohout, L.J. (1974a):
The Pinkava many-valued complete logic systems and their application in design of many-valued switching circuits. In: *Proc. 1974 Internat. Symposium on Multiple-valued Logic*, IEEE, New York (74CH0875-8C), 261–284.

Kohout, L.J. (1974b):
Algebraic models in computer-aided medical diagnosis. In: J. Anderson (ed.), *Proceedings of MEDINFO 74*, North Holland, Amsterdam, 575–579, addendum and list of typographical errors 1069–70.

Kohout, L.J. (1975):
A formal representation of functional hierrarchies of movement in the brain and its relation to cybernetics. Second Conference on Recent Topics in Cybernetics, Cybernetic Society, London.

Kohout, L.J. (1976a):
Representation of functional hierarchies of movement in the brain. *Internat. J. of Man-Machine Studies*, 8, 699–709.

Kohout, L.J. (1976b):
On functional structures. Presented as a companion paper to Kohout (1977) at NATO Internat. Conf. on Applied General Systems Research, Binghamton, August 1977. (Revised version reprinted in Kohout and Bandler (1986), 69–94).

Kohout, L.J. (1977):
Functional hierarchies in the brain. An invited paper for NATO Internat. Conf. on Applied General Systems Research (Binghamton, N.Y., U.S.A., 15–19 August, 1977). In: Klir, G.J. (ed.), *Applied General Systems Research: Recent Developments and Trends*, Plenum Press, New York, 1978, 531–544.

Kohout, L.J. (1978a):
Methodological Foundations of the Study of Action. Ph.D. Thesis, University of Essex, England, U.K., January 1978.

Kohout, L.J. (1978b):
Analysis of computer protection structures by means of multi-valued logics. In: *Proc. of Eight Internat. Symposium on Multiple-valued Logic*, IEEE, New York, 260–268.

Kohout, L.J. (1982):
Lecture notes on Activity Structures. Workshop of Man-Computer Studies Group, Brunel University, U.K.

Kohout, L.J. (1986):
On functional structures of behaviour. In: Kohout, L.J. and Bandler. W. (1986).

Kohout, L.J.(1987):
Activity structures: a general systems construct for design of technological artifacts. *System and Cybernetics: An International Journal*, **18**, 27–34.

Kohout, L.J.(1990):
A Perspective on Intelligent Systems: A Framework for Analysis and Design. Chapman and Hall, London; and Van Nostrand, New York.

Kohout, L.J., Anderson, J., Bandler, W., Behrooz, A. (1986):
Formalization of clinical management activities for a knowledge-based clinical system. *AAMSI Congress Proceedings*, American Association for Medical Systems and Informatics, Washington, D.C., 1986, 348–352.

Kohout, L.J. and Bandler, W. (1983):
Knowledge representation, clinical action and expert systems. Fuzzy Research Project Report FRP-31, Dept. of Mathematics, University of Essex, U.K., April 1983.

Kohout, L.J., and Bandler, W., eds. (1986):
Knowledge Representation in Medicine and Clinical Behavioural Science, An Abacus Book, Gordon and Breach Science Publishers, London and New York.

Kohout, L.J. and Bandler, W. (1986a):
Knowledge representation, clinical action and expert systems. In: Kohout, L.J., and Bandler, W., eds. (1986)

Kohout, L.J., Bandler, W., Anderson, J. and Trayner, C. (1985):
Knowledge-based decision support system for use in medicine. In: Mitra, G. (ed.), *Computer Models for Decision Making*, North-Holland, Amsterdam, 133–146.

Kohout, L.J., Behrooz, A., Anderson, J., Gao, S., Trayner, C. and Bandler, W. (1987):
Dynamics of localised inferrence and its embedding in activity structures architectures. An invited paper for Expert Systems Session at the Second

IFSA Congress, Tokyo, Japan, July, 20–25, 1987). Preprints of Second IFSA Congress, **2**, 740-743.

Kohout, L.J. and Gaines, B.R. (1975):
The logic of protection. *Lecture Notes in Computer Science*, **34**, Springer Verlag, Berlin, 736–751.

Kohout, L.J., Kallala, M. and Bandler, W. (1986):
Classification of spatio-temporal signatures of autonomous intelligent systems by means of fuzzy relational algorithms. *BUCEFAL* (France) **28** (Automme), 88–91.

Kohout, L.J., Keravnou, E., Bandler, W., Trayner, C. and Anderson, J. (1984) :
Construction of an expert therapy adviser as a special case of a general system protection design. In: Trappl (ed.), *Cybernetics and Systems Research 2*, North-Holland, Amsterdam, 97–104.

Pinkava, V. (1988):
Introduction to Logic for Systems Modelling, An Abacus Book, Gorodon and Breach, London and New York.

Trayner, C. (1983):
Demonstration of a Diagnostic Unit of CLINAID, Internat. Workshop on Fuzzy Sets and Knowledge-Based Systems, Queen Mary College, University of London, March 1983.

CHAPTER 11

DESIGN OF QUESTIONING STRATEGIES FOR KNOWLEDGE-BASED SYSTEMS

L.J. Kohout, S. Gao and H. Kalantar

Editorial Comment:

> The requirements for questioning strategies for Knowledge Based Systems are analysed and formalised. New proposals are made to expedite the KBS getting more and new information.

LIST OF CONTENTS

11.1 EXPERT SYSTEM NEEDS A QUESTIONING STRATEGY
11.2 THE BASIC CONCEPTS OF QUESTIONING STRATEGY
11.3 QUESTIONING STRATEGIES IN FUZZY KNOWLEDGE-BASED SYSTEMS
11.4 REALISATION OF A QUESTIONING STRATEGY IN CLINAID
11.5 EFFECTIVE QUESTIONING STRATEGIES FOR A MULTI-ENVIRONMENTAL SITUATION
11.6 CONCLUSION
11.7 REFERENCES

11.1. EXPERT SYSTEM NEEDS A QUESTIONING STRATEGY

In most medical expert systems dealing with diagnoses, the information which the users of the system have initially given to the system is not sufficient for the expert system to make the ultimate relevant conclusions. The expert systems therefore should be able to ask the user to give more information about the case being dealt with, so that the final conclusions can be expediently found.

For getting more relevant and useful information, an expert system has to ask the user appropriate questions, or requests or user directed actions, observations or investigations that may yield further information needed by the expert system.

It is obvious that what questions are asked or which requests are made, and how these are stated will strongly influence the quality of the system's performance. It will crucially depend on an appropriate questioning strategy, whether the system can find the conclusions that are correct and obtained fast and cheaply. The purpose of the questioning strategy is to ask the best questions and find the best inference path with respect to the previous information as early as possible during the expert system's reasoning cycle.

Questioning is defined as getting more information from the user, depending on the previous inference and for the use of further inference. Usually the previous inference generates a large set of questions to be asked. If the expert system asks the user to answer all of them without any choice and then makes further inferences from these answers, it will take a long time and the user will suffer an intolerable information overload. Later the user may find some questions which are not on the correct path to the final result and feels that answering these questions is just wasting time and money. Selecting questions to obtain further information for the expert system's reasoning process, therefore, is quite important.

In this situation, there are usually several questions that may be asked at the beginning, and some of them have a high cost. If the system leaves these expensive questions out and gets first as much of other cheaper information as possible, and then makes the inference from it, some of the expensive questions, while they can be asked about later, may be found to be no longer relevant to the final conclusion. For example, time and money can be saved in the process of medical diagnosis if the most expensive questions are not asked first. And in some time-dependent emergencies appropriate questioning strategy may save the patient's life. In the case of dealing with the industrial emergencies it may avert possible industrial catastrophes.

From the above statement we can conclude that an appropriate questioning strategy is indispensable for an expert system. If there is not a good questioning strategy, an expert system will be forced to ask too many questions during its reasoning cycle. This will overload the user, and it will also incur unnecessary costs in terms of time and money. This will also prevent the expert system from being widely accepted.

11.2. THE BASIC CONCEPTS OF THE QUESTIONING STRATEGY

There are two related problems the system has to deal with. The first is **how to determine the range of relevance** of the questions, so that these are not too *broad nor too specific*, and that they belong to the correct domain of relevance. For example, in the medical context, certain signs and symptoms indicate a number of distinct diseases which do not necessarily belong to the same body system (see Chapter 10 of this volume). This is further complicated by the fact that there are always too many candidate signs, symptoms, etc., to be selected from, and presented to the system user. This causes the second problem, the **information overload** of the user. For the above described reasons, the knowledge-based system has to have an appropriately defined questioning strategy.

Definition 11.2.1: *Questioning strategy*
A questioning strategy is defined as the *task* (Kohout, 1978a, b) of the system with the *aim* of reducing the information overload of the user.

Definition 11.2.2: *The means of the questioning strategy*
The aim is achieved by means of obtaining only the relevant information, depending on the *context of the previous inference* and for the use of the future inference. A different context is defined within each domain of relevance. Here the two concepts of *weight* and *cost* will be introduced into the design of the system, as being the criteria of choice for the best next questions that the users should ask.

Definition 11.2.3: *Weight*
Weight is a measure expressing how closely a question or a request for a particular feature of an investigative action is related to the facts that have been previously given.

Definition 11.2.4: *Cost*
Cost is a measure which values each item of the information obtained by the user as the result of a question or request provided by the system.

Let us take as an example the cost as defined in the medical context in CLINAID. When the user answers a question of the system seeking further information, he or she will ask the patient, make a physical examination, or undertake laboratory tests. *Cost* measures, in this context, how long it would take and how much money would be spent in general, to obtain the satisfactory answer.

11.3. QUESTIONING STRATEGIES IN FUZZY KNOWLEDGE-BASED SYSTEMS

Gao, Kohout, Anderson and Bandler (1987) outlined the basic concepts and algorithms for design of questioning strategies in multi-context fuzzy knowledge-based systems. Gao (1986) designed and implemented a successful questioning strategy for CLINAID. Because CLINAID is an expert system using fuzzy operations informing its inference methods, *weight* and *cost* play an important role in the guiding its strategies of inference. Indeed, arranging the questions in a weighted order is consistent with the basic idea of fuzzy inference.

In CLINAID, there are four levels of costs that have to be introduced.

a) **Cost 1**: *Direct observation or communication*
   The facts are obtained by directly asking or observing the patient. Most of the signs and symptoms in CLINAID's knowledge base have cost 1.

b) **Cost 2**: *Simple physical examinations*
   The observational facts are obtained by speedy and uncomplicated physical examinations.

c) **Cost 3**:
   Indicates the facts obtained by those questions which need a moderate physical examination or laboratory test.

d) **Cost 4**:
Indicates those questions which need a complicated physical examination or laboratory test. These usually cost a lot of money and take a long time.

Another concept which also plays an important role in the questioning strategy is *syndrome*, which is a combination of signs and symptoms indicative of some particular diseases.

11.4. REALISATION OF A QUESTIONING STRATEGY IN CLINAID

Crucial for the successful realisation of an appropriate questioning strategy are the following **design maxims** (for further details and other aspects see: Kohout 1974; Kohout, Anderson, Bandler and Trayner 1985; Anderson, Bandler, Kohout and Trayner 1985; Gao 1986; Anderson, Bandler, Kohout and Trayner 1987).

1) *Use syndromes.* The searching process is divided into two stages: In the first stage, inference and asking questions are to deal with the syndromes, and in the second stage inference and asking questions are about the diseases.
2) *Give preference* to those questions which relate to the current result with highest weight. This point is to make the search along the most appropriate and reasonably short path to the correct conclusion;
3) *Ask the least costly question* and leave the expensive questions for the later stages in the diagnosis. The system should ask as few expensive questions as possible so that the total cost of the diagnosis is low.

The activity structure describing broadly the interaction of the user and the system consists of the following eight **activity steps**.

Activity step 1: User enters the first facts.

Activity step 2: System selects the syndrome with the largest weight with respect to the previously given facts. This syndrome is used as a current result.

Usually the system does not select only the syndromes with largest weight, if there exist other syndromes whose weights are just slightly different from the former. The system will also include these as current results. The searching range of further inference consists of all these current results that fit into a predefined interval of the certainty values of results with the distance from the top value predetermined by an adjustable criterion called DTR. First the DTR is assigned a larger value, then it gets smaller and smaller during the progressing inference.

As a consequence of this, the searching range also gets smaller and smaller. The largest value of weights is called TOP, the weight of any other syndrome is called TR, if the difference between TOP and TR is less than DTR, the syndrome will also be selected, and put into searching range.

This strategy of the activity step 2 has been selected because of the following consideration:

At the beginning of a diagnosis the user sometimes gives very few facts so that the correct syndrome may not be selected, for the value of its weight is slightly smaller than the others. The system does not only select the syndrome with largest value of weight, but also selects the second, third,..., ones to avoid missing the correct syndrome.

DTR is a variable and, as more and more information is received, it becomes smaller and smaller so that the searching range is becoming smaller and smaller. When DTR becomes zero, only the syndromes with the largest weight can be selected.

Activity step 3: Pick up all the signs and symptoms which are related to the current result and arrange them into a collection (a family, a subset).

The selection criterion for doing this is to pick up all the signs and symptoms whose weights, related to at least one of the selected syndromes, are greater than zero. As the system will ask the user whether the patient has these signs and symptoms, a family constructed this way is called a collection of 'candidate questions'.

Each candidate question, that is, a sign or a symptom has a unique weight with respect to the current result.

If the sign or the symptom relates to only one syndrome out of the current results, the weight to this syndrome is also the weight of the current result. If the sign or symptom relates to more than one syndrome out of the current results, the largest weight selected from the collection of all weights with respect to these syndromes is the weight of the current result.

Activity step 4: Arrange all the candidate questions in the weight order.

Activity step 5: Ask the question with highest weight.

If the question with the highest weight is with cost 4, it means that the user has to spend a lot of time and money to answer it. Put this question aside unless the weight is much higher than others, that is, this question is quite important in the diagnosis. So not all the candidate questions picked up in step (3) will be asked, several questions which have lower weights and high cost will be left to the next loop.

Activity step 6: Go through from step (2) to step (5) again with all the given facts, both old and new, as if they had been received together.

In CLINAID, this procedure will usually loop two or three times.

Activity step 7: Start the second stage of the diagnosis, that is, inference for diseases. Go through from step (2) to step (6) but change the knowledge structure on which these steps are performed.

The knowledge structure used in this stage is not the relationship from signs and symptoms to syndromes, but the relationship from signs, symptoms, physical examinations and laboratory tests to diseases. The value of the variable DTR in this stage usually becomes even smaller than in the previous steps.

Activity step 8: The inference will loop two or three times to reduce the searching range.

When the system is approaching the final conclusion, we suggest that all the candidate questions should be asked, even those with high costs. In the case where variable DTR is zero, it means that only one specific disease is in the searching range.

Three samples of trial runs (Gao, 1986) are reproduced below, to show the magnitude of saving while using the syndromes in generating the questions. In the trial runs, two strategies of CLINAID for generating questions were compared:

1) a strategy based on signs/symptoms only;
2) a strategy based on additional structural information provided by the introduction of syndromes.

The number of questions in these samples are listed below:

number of questions	example1	example2	example3	total
strategy 1)	134	122	183	439
strategy 2)	67	59	60	186

It has been demonstrated that by introducing a questioning strategy using syndromes, the amount of facts (i.e. signs and symptoms in this case) decreases by 50% to 60% as compared with the strategy which is not using syndromes. It indicates that the strategy using the additional knowledge contained in syndromes eliminates from the inference effectively the facts that are not relevant in a particular context.

11.5. EFFECTIVE QUESTIONING STRATEGIES FOR A MULTI-ENVIRONMENTAL SITUATION

In a multi-environmental situation, we need effective two-way communication between the system and the users. The two ways of communicating between the system and the users are distinguished as follows.

a) The system must be able to formulate questions and queries that can be comprehended and dealt with by users of all the environments in which the system operates.

b) The system must respond in a meaningful way to questions and queries of the users of different environments.

Fig. 11.1 shows the general activity structure of a system presenting a query to a user. An activity structure evolved during an interaction in which the user presents a query to the system is given in Fig. 11-2. It can be seen that these two activity structures are significantly different.

A systematic questioning strategy can be developed only if attention is paid to the following problems.

1) When to ask an appropriate question?

Design of questioning strategies

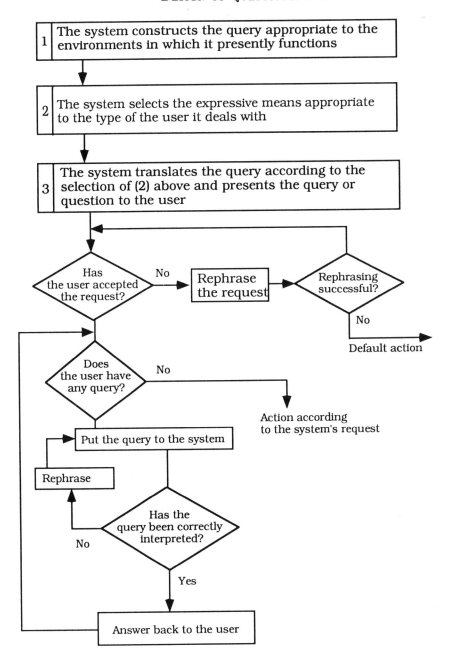

Figure 11.1. General activity structure of a system presenting questions or queries to a user

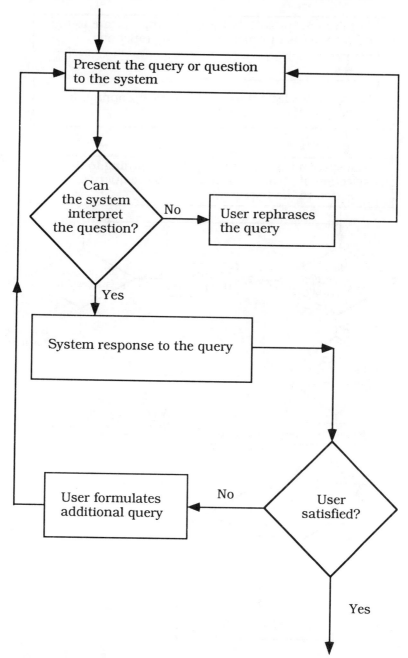

Figure 11.2. Activity structure specifying the interaction of a user with the system, when a user presents a query to the system

2) How to determine that a question is relevant to a particular context or environment?
3) How to construct a relevant question?
4) Finding a systematic way of asking the appropriate questions.
5) Classifying the questions into appropriate logical types in order to deal with their generating and processing in a way appropriate to the context in which these appear.

It should be realised that the sentences by means of which the two way communication between the users and system proceeds are not always perfect but may be deficient in various ways. We distinguish five types of sentence, according to the kind of possibilistic determinacy:

1) **Incomplete**: A part of the sentence is missing.
2) **Incorrect**: Not correct in sense of spelling, or its grammatic structure.
3) **Semantically meaningless**: The sentence cannot be interpreted, but it is not incorrect.
4) **Ambiguous**: The sentence can be interpreted in more than one way. The sentence can be assigned several meanings.
5) **Completely determinate**: The test for (1) to (4) above are negative.

Fig. 11.3 shows how CLINAID deals when the user enters an ambiguous non-standard term HEART INCREASED, meaning ENLARGEMENT OF HEART. CLINAID in return offers several alternative terms, each followed with the its corresponding degree of plausibility. The user rejects all of them and CLINAID suggests that the user should try the keyword *HEART* to trigger further action. The user accepts this suggestion and CLINAID offers as one of the new alternatives *ENLARGEMENT OF HEART* which is the term that the user meant. The user accepts this and CLINAID endorses the choice.

11.6. CONCLUSION

The initial information communicated by the user to an expert system is usually not sufficient for reaching the full conclusion concerning the problem, based only on the partial premises using this given initial information.

During the inference process, the expert system has to acquire some additional information from the user if, and when, it is required. To deal with this problem, an efficient strategy for generating *relevant questions* has to be built into the expert, or knowledge-based, system.

This chapter has described a new method of generating questions for knowledge-based systems dealing with multiple contexts. This has been accompanied by the description of the concrete design of a questioning strategy in the CLINAID knowledge-based system. Two strategies of CLINAID for generating questions were compared: one based on signs/symptoms only, and the other using the additional structural information provided by introducing *syndromes*.

"Heart-increased" is not a standard name.
Perhaps you will choose one of the following
standard names.

Select one of the following

1) Respiratory-rate-increased	0.999
2) Heart-rate-increased-70-to-80	0.999
3) Blood-pressure-raised	0.933
4) Dyspnea	0.749
5) Clubbing-of-fingers	0.749
6) Chest-jaws-arm-neck-radiate	0.749
7) Ascites	0.749

Enter the number
of the term you choose: ∅

Try to enter a key word: **heart**

The following are the alternatives:

1) No-heart-beat	0.999
2) Heart-sounds-normal	0.999
3) Heart-sounds-irregular	0.999
4) Heart-rate-increased-70-80	0.999
5) Heart failure	0.999
6) Faint-heart-sound	0.999
7) Enlargement-of-heart	0.999

Enter the number
of the term you choose: 7

The standard name is "Enlargement-of-heart"

Figure 11.3. CLINAID's response to a non-standard term

The last section was concerned with the examination of the problems involved while extending the described questioning strategies to multi-environment situations. Various types of indeterminacy, such as vagueness, incompleteness and ambiguity were discussed in some detail.

11.7. REFERENCES

Anderson, J., Bandler, W., Kohout, L.J. and Trayner, C. (1985):
The design of a fuzzy medical expert system. In: Gupta, M. M., Kandel, A., Bandler, W. and Kiszka, J. B. (eds.), *Approximate Reasoning in Expert Systems*. North-Holland, Amsterdam, 1985, 689–703.

Anderson, J., Bandler, W., Kohout, L.J. and Trayner, C. (1987):
A route-choosing medical diagnostic technique. *Fuzzy Sets and Systems* (Special issue on Fuzzy information processing in Artificial Intelligence and Operations Research, **23**(1):89–96.

Gao.S. (1986):
Design and Implementation of Diagnostic Unit of Medical Knowledge-Based System CLINAID. M. Phil. Thesis, Department of Computer Science, Brunel University, England, December 1986.

Gao, S., Kohout,L.J., Anderson,J. and Bandler, W. (1987):
Questioning strategies in fuzzy knowledge-based systems. In: Liu Xi Hui, Wang Pei Zhuang, Cheng Li Chun and Li Bao Wen (eds.), *Proceedings of International Symposium on Fuzzy Systems and Knowledge Engineering* (July 1987, Guangzhou and Guiyang, China). ISBN 7-5361-0030-2. Guandong Higher Education Publishing House, Guangzhou, China, 164–171.

Kohout, L.J. (1974):
Algebraic models in computer-aided medical diagnosis. In: Anderson, J. (ed.) *Proceedings of MEDINFO 74*, North-Holland, Amsterdam 1985, 575–9, addendum and list of typographical corrections, 1069–70.

Kohout, L.J. (1978a):
Methodological Foundation of the Study of Action. Ph.D. Thesis, Man-Machine Systems Laboratory, Department of Electrical Engineering Science, University of Essex, January.

Kohout, L.J. (1978b):
Analysis of computing protection structures by means of multiple-valued logic systems. In: *Proc. of the 8th Internat. Symposium on Multiple-Valued Logic*. IEEE, New York, 260–268.

Kohout, L.J. (1990):
A Perspective on Intelligent Systems: A Framework for Analysis and Design. Chapman and Hall, London; and Van Nostrand, New York.

Kohout, L.J., Bandler, W., Anderson, J. and Trayner, C. (1985):
CLINAID: Knowledge-based decision support system for the use in

medicine. In: Mitra, G.(ed.), *Computer Models for Decision Making*. North-Holland, Amsterdam, 1985, 133–146.

Kohout, L.J. and Bandler, W. (1986):
Knowledge representation, clinical action and expert systems. In: Kohout, L.J. and Bandler,W.(eds.), *Knowledge Representation in Medicine and Clinical Behavioural Science*. An Abacus Book, Godon and Breach, London and New York.

CHAPTER 12

CONCURRENCY IN CLINAID

G. MARSHALL AND L.J. KOHOUT

Editorial Comment:

> The operation of communicating knowledge sources is an important issue. The *whiteboard* is not just communication media but it has an implicit logical structure which acts as a relevance filter for incoming and outgoing messages.

LIST OF CONTENTS

12.1 REQUIREMENT FOR CONCURRENCY
12.2 BLACKBOARDS AND WHITEBOARDS
12.3 TWO SUBSTRATUM STRUCTURES TO SUPPORT CONCURRENCY
12.4 FUNCTIONAL STRUCTURES AND CONCURRENCY
    12.4.1 Diagnostic Unit
    12.4.2 Treatment Recommendation Unit
    12.4.3 Whiteboard
12.5 SUMMARY
12.9 REFERENCES

12.1. REQUIREMENT FOR CONCURRENCY

The CLINAID architecture was described in terms of Activity Structures in Chapter 10 of this volume. The general structure of CLINAID, as illustrated in Figure 10.1 of that chapter, allows its units to operate concurrently. Communication and cooperation are effected via the *whiteboard*, which forms a part of the coordinating and planning unit (Kohout, Bandler, Anderson and Trayner, 1985). This chapter investigates specific structures for supporting concurrent operations within CLINAID by examining means by which the whiteboard unit may fulfill its roles as coordinator and controller within different architectures. The requirement that the patient record unit should be able to update the contents of its database automatically is honoured by ensuring that all communications bearing the necessary information are passed to the coordinator unit. The information can then be extracted either at the coordinator or after that unit has passed the communications on to the patient record unit. The fidelity of an implementation based on a particular architecture can only be judged in the light of knowledge from the clinical environment. An analysis of the environment for its activities and the constraints imposed on them by the requirement of concurrency is presented. The results of this analysis are sufficient to permit the semantic match achieved by a particular implementation to be assessed.

12.2. BLACKBOARDS AND WHITEBOARDS

Blackboard systems have their origin in the Hearsay II system (Erman, Hayes-Roth, Lesser and Reddy, 1980) for understanding speech. The abstract model of a blackboard, illustrated in Figure 12.1, consists of three elements: the blackboard data structure, a number of knowledge sources and a control element. These elements operate as follows:

1. The blackboard is a global database that holds the data representing the current state of the problem being solved. The knowledge sources effect changes in the state of the blackboard that lead incrementally to the solution of the problem. Any communication and interaction between the knowledge sources occurs via the the blackboard.
2. The knowledge sources contain the knowledge necessary to solve the problem. The *overall knowledge* is partitioned between them, and they remain separate and independent.
3. The control strategy is to allow the knowledge sources to respond opportunistically to changes on the blackboard.

Nii (1986) offers the graphic example of doing a jigsaw puzzle by using a blackboard system. The blackboard is used to hold the jigsaw in its current state of completion, and the knowledge sources specialise in particular types of pieces of the jigsaw puzzle. Initially, the knowledge sources offer their most promising piece by placing it on the blackboard, and subsequently each knowledge source uses its expertise as it can to join one of its pieces to a piece already on the blackboard.

CLINAID's coordinator unit is not a blackboard in this precise sense. The solution to the problem CLINAID is tackling (in the form of finding recommendations for the treatment of a patient) are not built up on the coordinator unit but are inferred by the cooperation of the system's various units and are communicated to the user by the treatment recommendation unit. The requirement for extracting the information needed to update the patient record unit is also beyond that of a blackboard. For these reasons, CLINAID's coordinator unit is referred to as a *whiteboard*.

The whiteboard of CLINAID, then, is the *source of overall control* for the system and the means by which its units can communicate with each other. It may also serve as a *relevance filter*, gathering the local and global information necessary to perform centralised administrative tasks such as monitoring and auditing the operation of the system. These tasks are performed by the coordinating and planning unit.

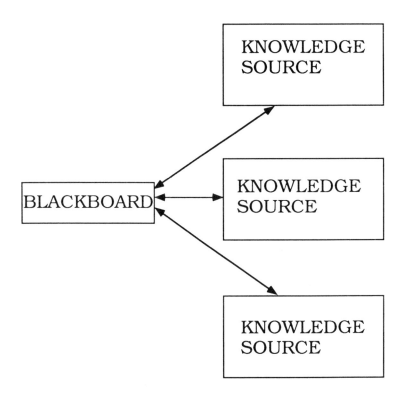

Figure 12.1. Blackboard

But, no matter what the unit is called, a description of the functional structures it is to support does not explain how to realise it as a computational artifact. This issue permeates the remainder of this chapter both for the whiteboard and for CLINAID as a whole.

12.3. TWO SUBSTRATUM STRUCTURES TO SUPPORT CONCURRENCY

In this particular section, two architectures for supporting concurrent operations as required by CLINAID are described and their associated merits and demerits discussed. It is assumed that the diagnostic unit, treatment recommendation unit, patient record unit and whiteboard are all supported by separate computers. In the first case all communication takes place through the whiteboard, but in the second signals are separated into those bearing information of concern to at least one of the units and those for control. Information-bearing signals are exchanged via the whiteboard, but control signals pass directly between units.

The centralised, or 'star,' arrangement illustrated in Figure 12.2 has obvious attractions as a model of concurrency if only on the grounds of simplicity. The illustration shows the signal paths between units, emphasising that all signals, whether for communication or control, are routed via the central coordinator unit. A unit with something to communicate sends it to the central whiteboard, while a unit that requires or expects a communication scans the whiteboard for it. The requirement that the patient record unit should be able to update its records automatically is taken care of by ensuring that the diagnostic unit and treatment recommendation unit post records of all their transitions on the whiteboard so that the patient record unit can examine them and extract any information needed to maintain its knowledge base.

Prolog has much to recommend it as the language for implementing such an arrangement. Most notably, its 'assert' and 'retract' commands provide direct mechanisms for managing the whiteboard. But it is of equal relevance that it has, in Parlog, a dialect suitable for parallel programming (Gregory, 1987).

Unfortunately, such a simple arrangement for concurrency has at least two major shortcomings. First, all the units must be implemented in such a way that they scan the whiteboard for messages intended for them in some consistent way. Simplicity might dictate that they scan the whiteboard only after they have completed an action, but there is no reason why scanning should not occur periodically, with the current process interrupted should the scan reveal a message awaiting attention. No matter how it may be implemented, such a passive policy will make it difficult to achieve an efficient system that can respond flexibly and, when required, rapidly to the appearance of messages on the whiteboard.

Second, and more important, this simple system will succumb to well known problems associated with any concurrent system that is not prevented from trying to write to the whiteboard at the same time to ensure that their messages do not 'collide' and so become lost. Indeed, while one process is writing on the whiteboard, all other processes must

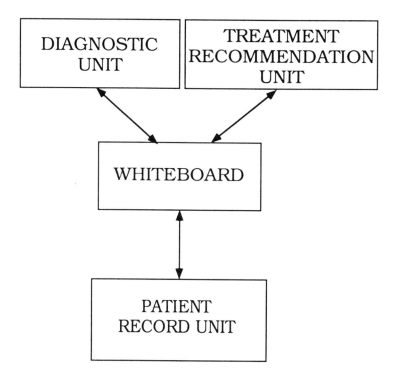

Figure 12.2. Star configuration for concurrent architecture

be prevented from doing so unless it is absolutely clear how much storage the first process requires, so as to ensure that part of one message does not overwrite another, thereby destroying it. This need to avoid collisions is suggestive of the requirements of the slotted and carrier-sense multiple-access (CSMA) protocols used by local area networks (LANs) and a protocol for this concurrent architecture could be organised along the same lines.

In principle, two processes can read their messages from the whiteboard simultaneously. Two successfully posted messages will occupy disjoint parts of the storage allocated to the whiteboard, and there is no objection to different processes accessing completely separate memory segments at the same time. When reading from the whiteboard, it is only necessary to ensure that a process does not begin to read a message before it has been completely written so as to be sure that no part of a message will be lost. Such an action can be prevented by not marking a message with its destination until it has been completely written on the whiteboard.

Thus, examination of this simple model of concurrency reveals that, although it provides a possible architecture, a rather more complex model may be needed to overcome the shortcoming associated with it.

Figure 12.3 shows a second architecture, again indicating all the signal paths, which is more highly connected than that of Figure 12.2. This architecture could be realised either by simply adding the direct connections indicated in the figure to the star arrangement or as a 'wheel'; that is, as the star within a ring that can provide the extra signalling paths. With this architecture, the units can still all read from and write to the whiteboard, but the additional paths allow the units to signal directly to each other. The purpose of the extra paths is to allow one unit to signal to another that it has posted a message for it on the whiteboard. When in receipt of such a signal, a unit can either interrupt its currently active process to deal with the message on the whiteboard or it can store a reminder and examine the whiteboard when its current task is completed. In contrast to the passive policy of the 'star' architecture, this active policy gives the system the capability to respond much more rapidly to events should that be necessary.

In fact, it may be appropriate for units to adopt different strategies for responding to the 'message posted' signals. The treatment recommendation unit will, in general, receive only one such signal, from the diagnostic unit, during a session. Ideally, it ought to respond to it at the earliest possible opportunity. By contrast, much of the activity of the patient record unit in response to its messages will be to sift them in order to make the appropriate updates to its database. Although important, this need not be done with rapidity and could wait until the unit had no other tasks to fulfill.

If the communication protocols suitable for the 'star' arrangement resemble those of a LAN, the appropriate protocol for this architecture resembles that of an operating system that can support concurrency (see Atwood, 1976). The possible pitfalls of the architecture that result from concurrency include all those of the star arrangement plus the possibility, should they arrive simultaneously, of the collision of the control signals giving notification of a posted message. In fact, since these signals are not

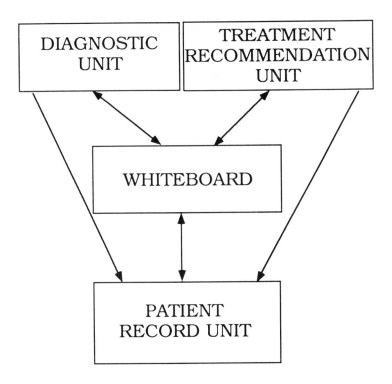

Figure 12.3. Second configuration for concurrent architecture

sent and received by all the units, the patient record unit is the only one at which such a collision can occur.

This observation throws some light on the way in which the architecture should be realised. If direct connections between units are employed for the control signalling, they can be wired directly between the signalling ports of the computers housing the units. The control signals on the links from the diagnostic unit to the patient record unit and the treatment recommendation unit to the diagnostic unit can be caused to set different bits at the treatment recommendation unit's input port. By always scanning the bits at its input port in a particular order, the treatment recommendation unit can cope with the receipt of simultaneous signals from the two units that can send signals to it. What is much harder to cope with, whether or not the unit can receive signals from more than one other unit, is the situation in which a control signal is received before the previous one has been dealt with. For this reason, it seems preferable to provide the control signal paths in the form of a ring. Then a unit can launch a control signal into the ring when it needs to and the ring will store it until the recipient is in a position to extract it and deal with it.

By providing primitive operations for interrupting servicing; for putting processes to sleep and for waking them; and for scheduling and running processes, distributed system software can allow the support of an efficient interrupt system. If semaphores are also supported, actions such as reading from and writing on the whiteboard can be made indivisible, so curing most of the problems that are caused by concurrency. However, the problem of ensuring that interrupt signals do not arrive simultaneously at the patient record unit will not be solved like this. But, with the control signal paths provided by a ring, one way of preventing this occurrence is to insist that interrupt signals are sent in synchronism with a centrally maintained clock. The clock can be maintained by the central coordinator unit which can also mediate contention between the units for transmission in any clock period. With a policy for deciding precedence between the competing units, the coordinator unit can ensure that no more than one of them transmits an interrupt signal in any clock period. If the clock period is short, no unit will be unduly delayed in transmitting its interrupt signal when it loses out in a bout of contention.

To make the choice between the two substratum structures described in this section, and in effect to decide on whether to separate information-bearing signals and control signals, requires knowledge from the clinical environment. This can be acquired by analysing the environment for its environmental activity structures and the constraints on them due to concurrency. These activity structures and constraints lead to the functional structures to be embedded in the information processing machine. In this way, a basis for examining the suitability of an architecture for supporting concurrency can be obtained. To this end, the next section presents an analysis of the clinical information with particular regard to the requirement for concurrency.

12.4. FUNCTIONAL STRUCTURES AND CONCURRENCY

Turning to an examination of concurrency from the point of view of its constraints on functional structures, rather than on substratum structures, one can discern the following requirements:

12.4.1. Diagnostic Unit

1. The diagnostic unit supports a number of body systems. Their diagnostic activities should take place concurrently to ensure that the working diagnosis for a patient suffering from multiple diseases is determined as quickly as possible, and to ensure that the working diagnosis is complete with respect to signs, symptoms and syndrome, prior to sending the patient for the diagnostic tests.
2. As a consultation with a patient proceeds, the corresponding patient record must be updated and consulted. For these reasons, a consultation with a new patient requires the creation of a new patient record, while with any other patient it is necessary to open the existing patient record. The activities of the diagnostic unit and the patient record unit therefore are essentially concurrent.
3. The treatment recommendation unit must produce its recommendations for treatment at the earliest possible stage during a consultation. Consequently, the activities of the diagnostic unit and the treatment recommendation unit are also essentially concurrent.

12.4.2. Treatment Recommendation Unit

The treatment recommendation unit must generate recommendations for any emergency treatment that a patient may require, quite apart from producing its recommendations for the appropriate treatment of any underlying disease. Any failure in this respect could leave the patient dead before being able to benefit from even the best treatment that it is possible to recommend, or even prior to completion of the working diagnosis.

Although the problem of how to trigger this activity immediately arises, it is not one that falls within the realm of the treatment recommendation unit, which is required simply to perform the activity of producing its recommendation when notified of an emergency via the whiteboard. Clearly, in such circumstances any current activity of the treatment recommendation unit will be interrupted to allow the emergency to be handled as quickly as is possible. Further, this activity will be concurrent with any that may be in progress in the other units.

12.4.3. Whiteboard

The whiteboard holds a list of **emergencies**, together with a specification of their **priorities**. Since, for each body system, the system contains a distinct set of **relevant** signs, symptoms, syndromes, diseases and tests, one way in which to recognise an emergency is by the occurrence of an associated interaction between diseases and syndromes. Thus, tests carried out across subsets of body systems could detect that emergency treatment action is required. Alternatively, interaction between the current treatment and the new patient state could be used as a trigger. Again, this activity may be concurrent with others at the coordinator unit, and certainly takes place concurrently with the activities of other units.

Both types of interaction are formed over elements drawn from the diagnostic set, DS, consisting of signs, symptoms, syndromes, disease and tests. For each patient, it is necessary to distinguish possible emergencies, PE, from actual emergencies, AE. This is done in terms of relevancy formulas, which are Many-Valued Logic (MVL) expressions involving any elements of DS, and actual relevancies, AR, thus:

$$PE \in \mathcal{R}_F(\text{Relevancy formulas} \longrightarrow \text{Emergency Action})$$
$$AR \in \mathcal{R}_F(\text{DS} \longrightarrow \text{Relevancy formulas})$$

The set of actual emergencies is then computed as the square product:

$$AE = AR \square PE$$

In this way, for each patient an actual emergency can be recognised so that the treatment recommendation unit can be triggered to produce the necessary recommendation.

Relevancy formulas used as the elements of PE and AR relations are formed by means of the Pinkava many-valued complete logical algebras (Pinkava, 1988; Kohout, 1974).

Because of the purpose of the whiteboard is to deal with concurrency, the dynamic protection of substratum modules and knowledge structures is essential. Efficient systems of many-valued logics for protection of architectures based on Activity Structures have been generated from the Pinkava algebras (c.f. Kohout, 1978, 1976, 1990).

12.5. SUMMARY

First, two substratum structures that are capable of supporting concurrent operations are proposed for CLINAID. They differ in that with one all communication takes place via the whiteboard, whereas with the other only information-bearing signals are sent to the whiteboard while control signals are routed directly between units. To assess the suitability of a substratum structure, it is necessary to appeal to knowledge from the clinical environment. For this reason, an analysis of the clinical environment to determine which of the clinicians' activities are truly concurrent is presented next. The environmental activity structures and the constrains on them due to concurrency as revealed by this analysis lead to the functional structures to be embedded in the information processing machine. From this position, the degree of semantic matching achieved by an embedding of the functional structures in a substratum structure can be assessed. This provides the tools necessary to assess the semantic gap associated with an implementation supporting concurrency that is based on a particular architecture, and to compare the gaps associated with two architectures.

12.6. REFERENCES

Atwood, J.W. (1976):
Concurrency in operating systems. *IEEE Computer*, **9**, 18–26.

Erman, D.J., Hayes-roth, F., Lesser, V.L. and Reddy, D.R. (1980):
The Hearsay II speech understanding system. *ACM Computing Surveys*, **12**, 213–253.

Gregory, S. (1987):
Parallel Logic Programming in Parlog. Addison-Wesley, Reading, Mass.

Kohout, L.J. (1974):
The Pinkava many-valued complete logic systems and their applications in the design of many-valued switching circuits. *Proc. Fourth International Symposium on Multiple-Valued Logic*, 261–284.

Kohout, L.J. (1976):
Application of multi-valued logics to the study of human movement control and of movement disorders. *Proc. Sixth International Symposium on Multiple-Valued Logic*, 224–231.

Kohout, L.J. (1978):
Analysis of computing protection structures by means of multi-valued logic systems. *Proc. Eighth International Symposium on Multiple-Valued Logic*, 260–268.

Kohout, L.J. (1990):
A Perspective on Intelligent Systems. Chapman and Hall, London and Van Nostrand Reinhold International, New York.

Kohout, L.J., Bandler, W., Anderson, J. and Trayner, C. (1985):
CLINAID: a knowledge-based decision support system for use in medicine. In: Mitra, G.(ed) *Computer-based models for decision making.*, North-Holland, Amsterdam, 133-146.

Nii, H.P. (1986):
Blackboard systems. *A.I. Magazine*, **7**, Summer, 38–53.

Pinkava, V. (1988):
Introduction to Logic for Systems Modelling, An Abacus Book, Gorodon and Breach, London and New York.

CHAPTER 13

DISTRIBUTED ARCHITECTURES FOR COMPUTER AIDED MANUFACTURING (CAM) AND OTHER EMBEDDED ROBOTIC SYSTEMS

L.J. KOHOUT

Editorial Comment:

> Activity Structures methodology enables dynamic multi-environment structures to be incorporated into knowledge based systems shells. It makes possible the transfer of generalised information handling functional structures (cf. Chapter 5) between different knowledge domains.

LIST OF CONTENTS

13.1 INTRODUCTION
13.2 THE STRUCTURE OF THE RECONFIGURABLE ARCHITECTURAL MODULES OF A MULTI-ENVIRONMENTAL SYSTEM SHELL
13.3 METHODS FOR EMBEDDING KNOWLEDGE INTO THE EMPTY SHELLS OF ACTIVE MULTI-ENVIRONMENTAL SYSTEMS
    13.3.1 Introductory Remarks
    13.3.2 Functional Refinements of Activity Structures
    13.3.3 Embedding Knowledge into a Reconfigurable Shell by Means of Functional Refinements
13.4 SKELETON KNOWLEDGE STRUCTURES OF A KNOWLEDGE-BASED SYSTEM EMPLOYING DEEP KNOWLEDGE
13.5 A MULTI-ENVIRONMENTAL ROBOTIC SYSTEM
13.6 BASIC CHARACTERISTICS OF FUNCTIONAL ENVIRONMENTAL ACTIVITY STRUCTURES FOR DIRECTING A COMPUTER-ASSISTED MANUFACTURING PROCESS
    13.6.1 Transfer of the Necessary Core of Knowledge Structures by Means of General Systems Constructs
    13.6.2 The Shift of Meaning of the Necessary Core Structure After the Transfer to the Manufacturing Knowledge Domain
    13.6.3 Some New Methodological Problems Concerning the Quality of Knowledge Structures
13.7 REFERENCES

Knowledge-Based Systems for Multiple Environments

13.1. INTRODUCTION

The aim of this chapter is to outline a new approach to design of architectures based on Activity Structures methodology. The main feature that distinguishes the Knowledge-based system modules described here is their ability to support hardware that performs direct action on its environments. This is the case for example in robotics or when the knowledge-based techniques are used in construction of integrated manufacturing systems. The basic elements of the construction method and a prototype of a generic architecture based on Activity Structures methodology (Kohout 1990, 1987, 1978) are presented in this chapter. The generic prototype modules described in section 13.2 form an empty shell that can be filled by the knowledge structures that are specific to a particular application. Section 13.3 of this chapter presents a general method that has to be applied in order to construct such environment specific knowledge structures. This is followed by a description of the knowledge structures needed for adaptive robots. The chapter is concluded by a presentation of knowledge structures needed in an active system for Computer Assisted Manufacturing.

The Activity Structures approach can be briefly characterised as one which starts by examining the activities, their purposes and goals, both within the system to be designed, and its environment (Kohout, 1987). It is assumed here that the reader is familiar with the exposition of my Activity Structures methodology that is presented in Chapter 5 of this volume.

In sections 13.3 and 13.4 we shall look in some detail at the type of knowledge that has resulted from application of the method of functional refinements that produced general purpose FEAS to be put into an empty shell. Two applications are considered here, namely, a robotic system (section 13.5) and a distributed system for computer assisted manufacturing (section 13.6).

13.2. THE STRUCTURE OF THE RECONFIGURABLE ARCHITECTURAL MODULES OF A MULTI-ENVIRONMENTAL SYSTEM SHELL

A complex multi-environmental system may include a mixture of automatic systems and of human elements. If this is the case, such a system will not be only advisory, but will also directly act upon the environment. Such a system is what Roberts (1991) classifies as an *active* Activity Structures based system. Hence, our generic structure (empty shell) has to have the basic capabilities to represent knowledge that is necessary for executing *multi-context* and *multitask* activities in the environments and can incorporate the theoretical knowledge and symbolic communication. In other words it has to have all the attributes of an *active robot*. The structure satisfying these requirements has previously been described in connection with knowledge representation for multilevel adaptive systems for movement control (Kohout 1976, 1976a, 1978a, 1981).

The architectural shell of the multi-environmental system (so called skeleton structure) is formed of a collection of mutually linked substratum modules (Fig. 13.1). Each module in its most general form is represented by a generalised virtual machine module as described in section 5.6, Chapter 5 of this volume and previously in Kohout (1978, 1990).

The interconnections of the modules are of a dynamic nature and change during the operation of the system. Each virtual module has a variable structure, which can be changed by the tuning input, that comes from a higher level. Each module operates on a dynamic stream of information that comes from the perceptual input. Each module has an efferent output which can be linked either to a perceptual input or a tuning input of another module.

The mutual interconnections of the individual modules are formed by a generator of bindings. It consists of

a) an interaction controller and
b) activity selector.

The interaction controller binds dynamically the virtual modules. The activity selector chooses the appropriate activities. Each activity is composed of some functions selected from the repertory of teleological functions by the activity selector.

Dynamic information the generator of bindings must provide consists of the following:

1) information specifying which VMs are to be bound;
2) what to bind, namely:
   2.1) what to accept from the environment of each module,
   2.2) what to affect in the environment.

Substituting a many-valued (fuzzy) logic for the conventional crisp valuations of truth or falsity in individual operations in each Virtual Machine we can achieve an information-flow triggered binding of the individual modules. This leads in most cases to the elimination of procedural (explicit) generators of bindings, or at least reduces its complexity. The structure of the binding effected by the information-flow triggering can also be modified. This is done by the dynamic changes of the alpha-cuts on the valuations of those expressions in each virtual module that effect decision making or activation of other Virtual Machines.

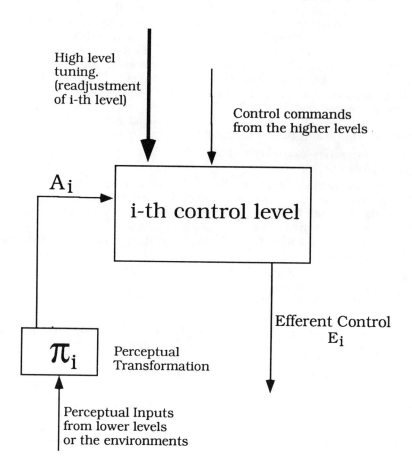

Figure 13.1. i^{th} level substratum module of the architectural shell for robot control

13.3. METHODS FOR EMBEDDING KNOWLEDGE INTO THE EMPTY SHELLS OF ACTIVE MULTI-ENVIRONMENTAL SYSTEMS

13.3.1. Introductory Remarks

The basic structure of the shell of an active multi-environmental system has to be capable of embedding the Environmental Activity Structures (EAS) of all the external environments. From this are generated all the functional activity structures that are necessary to perform the required activities of the system to be designed. Generalising from a particular environment or a family of environments generates the constraint functional environmental structures that are *common* to all the environments, the system will be concerned with. The superposition of these shared functional structures restricts appropriately the activities of the basic shell. This leads to the minimal functional structure of the basic shell which has to consist of information handling structures (IHS) and of protection functional structure (CP); see Kohout 1990 and Chapter 5 of this volume. This quadruple of functional structures (IHS, IHD, IHI, CP) then embeds the EAS structures of the system to be constructed (see Chapter 5 for details of this procedure).

The conceptual structure of a knowledge domain in which the system will operate is more complex in this case than that of an expert system. An expert system usually relates observables ("findings") to some explanations or recommendations for actions, to be taken in the environment. Here we deal with a more general knowledge system that has to incorporate some conceptual qualitative or quantitative models capturing some theoretical knowledge sources in addition to the empirical ones. This is the case even in CAD (computer-aided design) where we need the knowledge (models) of the underlying theories (i.e. the circuit theory in electronic design). This is usually called "deep knowledge" in the expert systems literature. We also need to incorporate in our knowledge structures algorithmic procedures, be it pertinent just to the activities of CAD or more complex real-time control.

In order to facilitate the maintainability of knowledge in such a system, the structure of the basic shell has to reflect in its partitioning the decomposition of the dynamics of the corresponding EAS. This EAS which comprises the effective encoding of the chosen *activity domain*, has to reflect the decomposition of this activity domain into the individual knowledge domains it utilises.

To satisfy these additional requirements that the activity domain of the system (EAS) has to fulfill, we need to have some methodological tools for the design of purpose-oriented EAS. It is clear that such a purpose-oriented EAS is a functional structure itself, where its functionality is determined by its purpose (cf. Chapter 5 on functional structure in Kohout (1990), for a detailed explanation and formal justification of this).

Such a method that provides *functional refinements* has been developed previously in connection with the design of knowledge structures for a knowledge-based system containing deep knowledge about neuro-psychological control of human movement. The reader is referred to Kohout

(1981, 1978a) for a detailed exposition and to Kohout (1990) for the explanation of its relevance to robotics. Only some basic notions of this method will be presented here, which will be needed in the sequel.

13.3.2. Functional Refinements of Activity Structures

As stressed above, (cf. Chapter 5 section 5.2.2), the Functional Activity Structures are the structures of the behaviour of a system, which do not coincide with the structure of its substratum, i.e. the software, firmware or software modules. From this it follows, that the decomposition of behaviour in terms of subfunctions does not coincide with the decomposition of a physical structure which generates this behaviour, into its substructures.

In an attempt to determine the subfunctions of a functionally described behaviour, we have to deal with two related problems: (Kohout 1978)

a) the problem of *segmentation* and of *identification of meaningful units* of behaviour,
b) the problem as to how to link the individual functional levels with the semantics of functional hierarchies.

Thus we can see that the problem of identification of the basic units of behaviour relevant to a particular purpose of the activity sequence plays the crucial role in any attempt to perform functional decomposition of any activity structure. Useful devices helping us to carry out this aim are the **task descriptors** and the procedures are available that are using the task descriptors in the analysis and synthesis of activities.

An activity leading to a certain aim or having a particular purpose can be characterised by a task descriptor $\bar{T}$ (cf. Kohout, 1978a, b).

Definition 13.3.2-1: *Task descriptor*

A task descriptor $\bar{T}$, associated with an activity g, performing a set of tasks T, is a partition of T into two disjoint subsets

$$\bar{T} = (T_p, T_f)$$

where T_p is the subset of permitted tasks and T_f the subset of forbidden tasks, of T.

Postulate 13.3.2-2: *Completion of an aim*

An activity *completes* its aim if all associated T_p are *achieved*. It completes it *correctly* if none of the associated tasks T_f have been performed during this act of completion.

In the process of performing a set of tasks T, some processes are active and some inactive. Each activity is completed by the activation or disactivation of some processes from X. Generally, there is no unique way of completion of an aim. The same completion can be achieved by many distinct patterns of activating or disactivating processes.

From the above principles, a general form of Activity Structures based shell follows. The shell consists of:

a) a family of virtual substratum modules
b) a family of potential links

c) a binding pattern, which determines which links are activated at a particular time instance.

The forms (a), (b), (c) above embed homomorphically the functional refinements of EAS into the virtual substratum. Further details are not provided here, as several examples of these structures can be found in (Kohout, 1978a, 1990). Because each process is embedded into some kind of a virtual substratum module and the activation pattern of individual processes is time dependent, it is necessary to provide dynamic binding of individual modules in an appropriate concurrent time-sequence. Thus we have an architecture with dynamically reconfigurable structure (Kohout 1981, 1978a, Chapter 9). It is essential to note that the dynamic protection against wrong reconfiguration of such a system is necessary (Kohout 1978a, 1990).

13.3.3. Embedding Knowledge into a Reconfigurable Shell by Means of Functional Refinements

One application of the method of functional refinements is for determining the transformation sequence of Environmental Activity Structure (EAS) capturing the domain knowledge that is to be inserted in the empty reconfigurable shell described in the previous section. The general sequence of transformation of activity structures involved in the design of the knowledge structures to be inserted can be particularised as follows (cf. section 10.3.3, Chapter 10, in this volume):

$$EAS \longrightarrow AEAS \longrightarrow FEAS \longrightarrow IHD, IHI, CP$$

By this sequence, the Environmental Activity Structure (EAS) is transformed to an Aims Environmental Activity Structure (AEAS), which is then further transformed (by means of the method of functional refinement) to a Functional Environmental Activity Structure (FEAS). Adding constraints and applying a further transformation yields the Functional Activity Structure of the Knowledge-Based System or Robotic System shell.

In the transformation, the task descriptors are dependent on the *general contents* and the *general and specific purpose* of the activities in the chosen activity domain. In the case of a usual advisory knowledge-based system the general purpose is to perform problem solving tasks, for a robot action-tasks directly acting on the external environment have to be added as well. The first step is therefore more complex for the active systems than for purely advisory systems.

In the next section we shall look at a particular example, a teleological (body) system that should provide the advice about the norm and pathology of movement. This was the original architecture from which other generalised shells have evolved. This will be followed by a section describing its generalisation in the domain of robotics and Computer aided Manufacturing (CAM).

13.4. SKELETON KNOWLEDGE STRUCTURES OF A KNOWLEDGE-BASED SYSTEM EMPLOYING DEEP KNOWLEDGE

A knowledge-based system concerned with the simulation of the norm and pathology of neuro-psychological control of movement is a particularly interesting example of KBS architectures. It is concerned not only with functioning of a system that deals with a multi-environmental situation involving the multiplicity of contexts, but it also importantly has to capture its dynamic and adaptive aspects. It is therefore an archetype for the construction of a proper multi-environmental robotic system.

Table 13.1 describes that part of Functional Environmental Activity Structure (FEAS) that has to be contained in the knowledge structure that is needed in this particular knowledge domain.

This Functional Environmental Activity Structure (FEAS) is the neuro-psychological description of the brain system for control of movement, the knowledge about which is to be embedded into the KBS in construction. We can see that it is itself based on a complex theory, in this case of Bernštejn (cf. Kohout, 1981) about the neuropsychology of movement. The Bernštejn system includes, however, also significant notions and concepts of (cybernetic) adaptive multilevel theory of dynamic control which are essential to robotics. It can be seen that the complexity of the "deep" knowledge to be embedded into this knowledge-based system is considerable.

Deep knowledge concerning the control of movement, and the multilevel structure of which is summarised in Table 13.1 can however be used in a variety of ways. The way in which this knowledge is used will determine the purpose for which the knowledge-based system, utilising this knowledge, will be used. In more general terms, the use of this knowledge in the environment determines the Aim Structure which is a Functional Refinement, determined by the tasks of the system. The EAS is used in a particular environment for a particular purpose. The particular purpose we are concerned with in this section is to build a neurological diagnostic system. This EAS can however be used (with slight generalisations) for an entirely different purpose, e.g., as the deep knowledge for building an intelligent robot with multilevel control (cf. Kohout 1990). The way in which this EAS has to be generalised for the latter purpose will be briefly touched upon in the next section. In each case, the designer of the system has to determine what the purpose is, and what are the available means necessary for realising this purpose.

The deep knowledge (a model of brain functions) based on the system of Table 13.1 contains just deep neuro-psychological knowledge. In order to build a diagnostic knowledge-based system, we also need to add the knowledge concerned with the aims of diagnosis into the Knowledge structure of the constructed system. These aims can be stated as follows (Kohout 1971):

1. The system should provide "repeated simulation of once observed movement behaviour".
2. The system "should give a description of movement in both normal and *pathological* states".

Table 13.1. Functional environmental activity structure to be used as the knowledge structure in a knowledge-based Active system for control of movement

FEAS	Purpose of the activity	Main characteristics, directing parameters
Level A Kinetic regulations (servo)	to maintain steady position of individual segments of the "skeleton."	tonus of effectors (e.g., muscles)
Level B Synergies	to co-ordinate the activation of individual effectors in a correct concurrent time-sequence	co-ordinates of mutual position of "skeleton" segments, relative positions & velocities
Level C Spatial field	maintaining correct spatial trajectory, where the exact mutual position of individual segments of the "skeleton" is irrelevant	control framed in terms of position of skeleton segments with respect to external (environmental) co-ordinates
Level D Object-directed actions	reaching the end point of a trajectory, distinguished by the type of the endpoint or the object to be reached; geometric plans for action	topological relations in space, representation of abstract percepts corresponding to objects in environment
Level E Symbolic co-ordination	similar to object-directed, but symbolic, the goal is directed by a symbol denoting an object or situation; symbolic plans for movement	representation and manipulation of symbolic concepts, names, semiotic aspects

A Source for the construction of IHD functional activity structure.

Knowledge Contents:
Model of Bernštejn's levels of movement control (cf. Kohout 1978a, 1981 for further detailed explanation of the significance of individual levels).

3. "The objective... is not only to describe pathological behaviour, but also state possible cases of that behaviour".

It is interesting to analyse the above stated aims further, as these yield the insight into the way the minimal knowledge structure grows when more objectives are added.

Thus to achieve the objective (1), provision of the dynamic trajectory of human movement, we need an input-output "black box" model of movement behaviour. To achieve (1) and (2) together, some additional knowledge has to be added. This addition consists of the following:

(a) the definition of what is the norm and what is pathological;

(b) the specification of how the class of possible behaviours produced by the KBS has to be partitioned into some equivalence classes, indexed by the names of all possible types of movement disorder.

To achieve all the objectives, (1), (2) and (3), we have to provide an adequate specification of meaning of the term "cause" that is used in (3) above. If for example the causes include possible brain damage, then some knowledge about anatomical structure of the brain has to be added, together with the list of possible impairments of these anatomical structures. The general rule is: the more deep expertise is required, the more deep knowledge has to be added.

The knowledge structures of Table 13.1 above only satisfy the objectives given (1) and (2). Linking this knowledge to some anatomical knowledge, such as that of Fig. 9-6 of Kohout (1978a) would yield the minimal knowledge structure required in order to deal with all the objectives. The specification of the way the structures of behaviour and the neuroanatomical structures are to be linked is also necessary. The link would consist in this case of the conceptual and inferential (meta-) relations as outlined in detail in (Kohout, 1978).

As we are concerned with the basic shell of a Knowledge-Based System, containing the essential knowledge necessary for achieving a particular purpose, we have to determine what is the minimal knowledge structure needed to support the achievement of this purpose. This in turn will determine the minimal structure of the supporting shell, in which the knowledge is to be encapsulated. The concrete example discussed in this section demonstrated how this can be done for an advisory system for neurological diagnosis of movement disorders which utilises deep neuroanatomical knowledge, the knowledge about the brain behaviour and the knowledge of the aims of diagnostics.

A Knowledge-Based System concerned just with a correct simulation of movement behaviour can also be modified in the above described manner. This modification will be discussed in the next section.

13.5. A MULTI-ENVIRONMENTAL ROBOTIC SYSTEM

If the purpose of the knowledge-based system is to control, e.g., some robot hardware, then the system needs to conform just to objective (1) of the above list. A system that has to distinguish the norm from pathology of the robot behaviour, i.e. to provide self-diagnostics, has to satisfy (1) and (2). The kind of information that Table 13.1 contains is sufficient for building the knowledge structures of such a system, if suitably modified. The robotic system that is to advise on the possible causes of its malfunctions has however to satisfy all three conditions (1), (2) and (3). Such a system needs the knowledge of its "anatomy" (i.e. a description of its hardware) to be embedded in its knowledge structure. In this latter case, the knowledge structures, the general content of which is given by Table 13.1, have to be supplemented by some additional information similar to that provided in Fig. 9–6 of (Kohout 1990) as well as with a link to the functional levels of Table 13.1 by suitable relational structures (Kohout 1978).

The general kind of architecture for a robotic system, the functional refinements of which are given by the information of the type similar to that of Table 13.1 can provide the following functions:

1. Support knowledge structures required for dynamic simulation of movement, which can be also used to drive some robot hardware.
2. Capture the knowledge concerning not only the norm but the possible malfunctions of its behaviour.
3. Provide the knowledge about their internal substratum (e.g., hardware) structure.
4. Use this information (cf. 3) for restructuring its behaviour, when the part of its structure is impaired, is malfunctioning, and has not yet been repaired.
5. Support the knowledge needed for object-oriented actions.
6. Support the knowledge structures needed for symbolic co-ordination and planning.

It is not difficult to see that all these functions may be needed in a well co-ordinated manufacturing process. Then of course, much more is required from the system than just providing all the "robotic" functions. This is the reason why more knowledge has to be added to the scheme discussed here so far. The remaining part of this chapter will be concerned with the analysis and a general outline of such a multi-environmental system for Computer Assisted Manufacturing (CAM).

The technical design of the minimal knowledge structure shell (cf. Kohout 1978a, 1990) is directly transferable to and could be used as a shell for a KBS for the support of manufacturing activities. The conceptual general contents of such a shell has to be, however, specified anew for the manufacturing problem. This means that the conceptual contents of the levels described in Table 13.1 have to be changed. What changes are required will be described in the following section.

13.6. BASIC CHARACTERISTICS OF FUNCTIONAL ENVIRONMENTAL ACTIVITY STRUCTURES FOR DIRECTING A COMPUTER-ASSISTED MANUFACTURING PROCESS

The aim of this section is to derive the basic characteristics of the environmental activity structures of the computer assisted manufacturing process.

13.6.1. Transfer of the Necessary Core of Knowledge Structures by means of General Systems Constructs

The technical design of the minimal knowledge structures (what shall be called *the necessary core*) presented in the last two sections is directly transferable to the design of a shell of a KBS for support of manufacturing activities. This is so because these structures satisfy the conditions of transferability between two domains and therefore form *General Systems Constructs* (cf. Chapter 5). The conceptual general contents (deep knowledge) of such a shell has to be, however, further extended in order to satisfy the necessary requirements for control of manufacturing processes.

Some additional activities have to be incorporated to this end. This extension is determined by the following aims:

1. Evaluation of performance.
2. Scheduling of emergency activities which preserve at least partially the function of the manufacturing system.
3. Diagnostics and scheduling of repairs.

These are the basic activities to be incorporated into a manufacturing system and have to fulfill the above aims. We can see that the design of an adequate Manufacturing Knowledge-Based System or a Computer Aided Manufacturing (CAM) System is not only the problem of the design of a bare architecture of that system, but also the problem of the control software design and the design of the activities of the whole manufacturing process.

13.6.2. The Shift of Meaning of the Necessary Core Structure after the Transfer to the Manufacturing Knowledge Domain

The nature of the activities of the manufacturing process is reflected in the shift of the conceptual meaning of the knowledge structures reflecting the deep knowledge. This means that the conceptual contents of the levels described in Table 13.1 have to be changed. What changes are required are briefly but comprehensively summarised below.

The levels of functionalities are again denoted from A to E. It should be noted that the levels form again a functional hierarchy. This functional hierarchy is expressed behaviourally, in terms of functional abstraction with respect to a control time-sequence. Each functional level can be embedded in a hierarchy or heterarchy of substratum modules (e.g., virtual machines).

A-level functionally describes: inter-communication or interaction of centres in terms of the description of individual variables defined over the family of centres. We describe here both, the statics and dynamics of direct interaction.

B-level provides the functional specification of the degree and pattern of co-operation of individual centres. These may be called Synergies by analogy with the brain movement control system.

C-level is functionally concerned with the evaluation of co-operation and competition in terms of some performance measures.

D-level provides functional task description. Also global and local teleological description of goals, that are to be achieved by the interaction of centres. There can be a goal for a centre, or for a group of centres (individuals, participants).

E-level provides a higher level symbolic description. This is the purpose of each task in a different symbolic setting or a perspective. "Ideology" of the co-operative system.

In order to link properly the individual functional levels, it is essential to look at the characteristics of a manufacturing system 'as a whole'. An analysis in such a holistic way yields some typical features that can be enshrined in the following *postulates:*

1. A manufacturing system consists of distributed centres that co-operate and possibly compete for the **means** by which they achieve their goals.
2. To insure that such a distributed system functions well, the activities of individual centres have to be coordinated.
3. In this approach, we assume that for co-ordination, a model of **relevant** features containing relevant knowledge about the manufacturing system is contained in the Knowledge-Based System.

13.6.3. Some New Methodological Problems Concerning the Quality of Knowledge Structures

The above postulates however pose new methodological problems to the designers of knowledge-based systems that have to be resolved. For example, at the object level (i.e. the level D in the above classificational scheme of levels), attention has to be paid to the qualities of the conceptual model that embeds the knowledge base.

In expert systems which incorporate the knowledge of the domain in the knowledge concerning the expert's problem solving process, the conceptual model of the knowledge usually is subordinated to the structural organisation of the knowledge base and the expert system tool. This may lead to distortion of the knowledge represented in the Expert System. In the systems with deep knowledge, where the conceptual and logical structure of the knowledge domain, may be present in the form independent of any particular problem solving strategy of a particular group of experts, the situation is even more complicated than for a traditional expert system case. Attention has to be paid to the problem of adequacy of the knowledge models which cannot be fully discussed here. The reader is however referred to Chapter 18 of this volume where we discussed the four essential conditions imposed on the knowledge structures, that a Knowledge-Based System should satisfy. These are:

1. Correctness.
2. Faithfulness of representation.
3. Maintainability.

4. Admissibility.

Formal conditions for correctness and faithfulness were presented (employing category theory) in Kohout (1978a, 1990).

13.7. REFERENCES

Bandler, W. and Kohout, L.J. (1979a):
The use of new relational products in clinical modelling. In: Gaines, B.R. (ed.) General Systems Research: A Science, *a Methodology, a Technology* (Proc. 1979 North American Meeting of the Society for General Systems Research), SGSR, Louisville, Kentucky, U.S.A., 240–246.

Bandler, W. and Kohout, L.J. (1979b):
Application of fuzzy logic to computer protection structures, In *Proceedings of the 9th. Int. Symposium on Multiple-valued Logics*, Bath, England, May 1979, IEEE New York, 200–207.

Bandler, W. and Kohout, L.J. (1980a):
Semantics of implication operators and fuzzy relational products. *International Journal of Man-Machine Studies*, **12**, 89–116.

Bandler, W. and Kohout, L.J. (1980b):
Fuzzy relational products as a tool for analysis and synthesis of complex artificial and natural systems. In: Wang, P.P. and Chang, S.K. (eds.). *Fuzzy Sets: Theory and Applications to Policy Analysis and Information Systems*. Plenum Press, New York, 341–367.

Bandler,W., and Kohout,L.J. (1981):
The identification of hierarchies in symptoms and patients through computation of fuzzy triangular products and closures. In: Parslow, R. D. (ed.), *BCS '81: Information Technology for the Eighties*, Heyden & Son, London, 191–194.

Bandler, W. and Kohout, L.J. (1982):
Fast fuzzy relational algorithms. In: Ballester, A., Cardus, D. and Trillas, E. (eds.), *Proc. Second Internat. Conference on Mathematics at the Service of Man* (Las Palmas, Canary Islands, Spain, 28 June - 3 July 1982). Universidad Politechnica de las Palmas, 123–131.

Bandler, W. and Kohout, L.J. (1986):
A survey of fuzzy relational products in their applicability to medicine and clinical psychology. In: Kohout, L.J., and Bandler, W. (eds.) *Knowledge Representation in Medicine and Clinical Behavioural Science*, An Abacus Book, Gordon and Breach, London.

Bandler, W. and Kohout, L.J. (1988):
Special properties, closures and interiors of crisp and fuzzy relations. *Fuzzy Sets and Systems*, **26**, No. 3, 317–331.

Bernštejn, N.A. (1947):
O Postrojenii Dviženij. (On the construction of movement). In Russian. Nauka, Moscow.

Gaines, B.R. and Kohout, L.J. (1975):
Possible automata. In: *Proc. of the 1975 Internat. Symposium on Multiple-valued Logic*, IEEE, New York, 183–196.

Gaines, B.R. and Kohout, L.J. (1976):
The logic of automata. *Internat. Journal of General Systems*, 2, 191–208.

Kohout, L.J. (1971):
Computer assisted system for merging of knowledge sources in Brain Sciences: A blueprint for design using many-valued logics and generalised topologies. Internal report EES-MMS-MOV71. Man-Machine Systems Laboratory, University of Essex, U.K.

Kohout, L.J. (1974):
The Pinkava many-valued complete logic systems and their application in design of many-valued switching circuits. In: *Proc. 1974 Internat. Symposium on Multiple-valued Logic*, IEEE, New York (74CH0875-8C), 261–284.

Kohout, L.J. (1974b):
Algebraic models in computer-aided medical diagnosis. In: J. Anderson (ed.), *Proceedings of MEDINFO 74*, North Holland, Amsterdam, 575–579, addendum and list of typographical errors 1069–70.

Kohout, L.J. (1976):
Application of multi-valued logic to the study of human movement control and of movement disorder, *Proceedings of Internat. Symposium on Multiple-valued Logics*, (Utah State University, May 1976) IEEE (76CH1111-4C), New York, 224–231.

Kohout, L.J. (1976a):
Representation of functional hierarchies of movement in the brain. *Internat. J. of Man-Machine Studies*, 8, 699–709.

Kohout, L.J. (1976b):
Automata and topology. In: Mamdani. E. and Gaines, B.R. (eds.), *Discrete Systems and Fuzzy Reasoning* (Proceedings of a Workshop, Queen Mary College, London, January 1976). Publ. by University of Essex (EES-MMS-DSFR-76), Colchester U.K., 88–110.

Kohout, L.J. (1976c):
Methodological Foundations of the Study of Action, EES-MMS-ACT-76, Man-Machine Systems Laboratory, Department of Electrical Engineering, University of Essex, U.K., December 1976.

Kohout, L.J. (1976d):
On functional structures. Chapter 5 of Kohout (1976c). Presented as a companion paper to Kohout (1977) at NATO Internat. Conf. on Applied

General Systems Research, Binghamton, August 1977. (Revised version reprinted in Kohout and Bandler (1986), 69–94).

Kohout, L.J. (1978):
The functional hierarchies of the brain, In Klir, G. (ed.), *Applied General System Research: Recent Development and Trends*. Plenum Press, New York, 531–544.

Kohout, L.J. (1978a):
Methodological Foundations of the Study of Action. Ph.D. Thesis, University of Essex, England, U.K., January 1978.

Kohout, L.J. (1978b):
Analysis of computer protection structures by means of multi-valued logics. In: Proc. of Eight Internat. Symposium on Multiple-valued Logic, IEEE, New York, 260–268.

Kohout, L.J., and Bandler, W. (1981):
Approximate reasoning in intellignt relational database. In: Parslow, R.D.,(ed.), *BCS'81: Infomation Technologies for the Eighties*. Heyden & Son, London, 483–486.

Kohout, L.J. (1982):
Lecture notes on Activity Structures. Workshop of Man-Computer Studies Group, Brunel University, U.K.

Kohout, L.J.(1987):
Activity structures: a general systems construct for design of technological artifacts. *System and Cybernetics: An International Journal*, **18**, 27–34.

Kohout, L.J. (1988):
Theories of possibility: Meta-axiomatics and semantics. An invited article for a special isuue on Interpretations of Grades of Membership. *Fuzzy Sets and Systems*, **25**, No.3 (March), 357–367.

Kohout, L.J.(1990):
A Perspective on Intelligent Systems: A Framework for Analysis and Design. Chapman and Hall, London and Van Nostrand Reinhold International, New York.

Kohout, L.J., and Bandler, W. (1982):
Fuzzy expert system: theory and practice of knowledge based system. In: *Expert Systems '82* (Seconed Technical Conference of the British Computer Society, Expert Systems Specialist Group), September 1982, 33–36.

Kohout, L.J. and Bandler, W. (1982):
Axioms for conditional inference: probabilistic and possibilistic. In: Ballester, A., Cardus, D. and Trillas, E. (eds.), *Proc. Second Internat. Conference on Mathematics at the Service of Man* (Las Palmas, Canary Islands, Spain, 28 June – 3 July 1982). Universidad Politechnica de las Palmas, 413–414.

Kohout, L.J. and Bandler, W. (1985):
Relational-product architectures for information processing. *Information Science*, **37**, 25–37.

Kohout, L.J., and Bandler, W., eds. (1986):
Knowledge Representation in Medicine and Clinical Behavioural Science, An Abacus Book, Gorodn and Breach, London.

Kohout, L.J. and Bandler, W. (1986a):
Knowledge representation, clinical action and expert systems. In: Kohout, L.J., and Bandler, W., eds. (1986)

Kohout, L.J. and Gaines, B.R. (1975):
The logic of protection. Lecture Notes in Computer Science, **34**, Springer Verlag, Berlin, 736–751.

Kohout, L.J. and Gaines, B.R. (1976):
Protection as a general systems problem. *Internat. Journal of General Systems*, **3**, 3–23.

Kohout, L.J., Keravnou, E., Bandler, W., Trayner, C. and Anderson, J. (1984):
Construction of an expert therapy advisor as a special case of general system protection design. In Trappl, R. (ed.), *Cybernatics and Systems Research 2*, North-Holland, Amesterdam, 97–104.

Mamdani, E.H. and Gaines, B. R. eds. (1981):
Fuzzy Reasoning and Its Applications. Academic Press, London.

Roberts, Z. (1985):
The functional structure of control in expert systems. In: *Proceedings NAFIPS 85 Workshop on Fuzzy Expert Systems and Decision Support*, (October 1985, Georgia State University, Atlanta, GA, USA).

Roberts, Z. (1991):
The Functional Structure of Control in Expert Systems, Gordon and Breach, London, in press.

CHAPTER 14

TOWARDS A DESIGN OF A REAL-TIME ADAPTIVE ROBOT FOR MULTIPLE ENVIRONMENTS: PART I - BASIC DESIGN AND THE FIRST EXPERIMENTS

C.S. JOHNSON AND L.J. KOHOUT

Editorial Comment:

> The robotic system that adapts to an environment faces challenges similar to a Knowledge-Based System in a static non-adaptive situation but in a multiplicity of environments. When it is placed in a multiplicity of environments, the situation becomes even more complex and intricate.

LIST OF CONTENTS

14.1 INTRODUCTION
14.2 A BLUEPRINT FOR THE DESIGN OF AN ADAPTIVE REAL-TIME MOBILE SYSTEM FOR A MULTI-ENVIRONMENTAL SITUATION
    14.2.1 Awareness of a Robot Viewed as an Identification Process
    14.2.2 Functional Decomposition of the Architecture of a Multi-Environment Adaptive Robot
14.3 INITIAL SELECTION CRITERIA FOR THE ROBOT HARDWARE
14.4 THE FIRST SET OF EXPERIMENTS
    14.4.1 The Purpose of the Experiments
    14.4.2 Equivalence and Non-Equivalence of Strategies for Achieving Various Aims
    14.4.3 Description of the First Set of Experiments, the Results of their Evaluation
    14.4.4 Multi-Environment Induced Deficiencies in Hardware
14.5 THE SECOND SET OF EXPERIMENTS
    14.5.1 An Overview and Justification of the Set-up
    14.5.2 Details of the Second Set of Experiments and their Results
14.6 CONSEQUENCES OF THE EXPERIMENTS FOR THE DESIGN BLUEPRINT OF A MULTI-ENVIRONMENTAL ROBOT
    14.6.1 An Overview
    14.6.2 Environment Interpretation

14.6.3 Control Restrictions
14.7 COMPUTER SIMULATION OF REAL ENVIRONMENTS
  14.7.1 The Choice: To Simulate – Or Not To Simulate!
  14.7.2 Problems with Simulation of Environments for Robots
14.8 APPENDIX
  14.8.1 The Basic Skeleton Algorithm Specifying the Overall Activity of the Hero Robot Used in the First Set of Experiments
  14.8.2 A Brief Characterisation of the Control Program Used in the Second Set of Experiments
14.9 REFERENCES

14.1. INTRODUCTION

In this chapter we describe some of the investigations that were undertaken into the suitability of certain types of robot hardware, which could be used for the purpose of exploring various implementation strategies of adaptive robots in multi-environmental situations. The robot hardware aspects involved the design of a robotic device, which has been subjected to some multi-environmental experiments in real-time. This shed light on the limitation of the simulation of robots and their environments, and led us to believe that real-time experiments with real (non-simulated) environments are essential in the multi-environmental situation. The experiments also led to further understanding of the control of the effectors and of the performance of sensors in various environments.

In the next section we describe the general principles that were chosen for the construction of a real-time learning mobile system (robot) that would be capable of performing in multiple environments or in a continuously changing environment. The purpose of this introduction is to provide a suitable framework for the discussion of rather interesting real-time experiments in a multi-environmental situation.

14.2. A BLUEPRINT FOR THE DESIGN OF AN ADAPTIVE REAL-TIME MOBILE SYSTEM FOR A MULTI-ENVIRONMENTAL SITUATION

14.2.1. Awareness of a Robot Viewed as an Identification Process

This section briefly describes one of the key concepts in the approach of Christopher S. Johnson (Johnson, 1981), and discusses its connection with the mainstream of possibilistic identification of adaptive systems as developed by Zadeh and further extended by Gaines. The consequent development of C. S. Johnson's work and its further details can be found in (Johnson 1984, 1986).

C. S. Johnson's approach was influenced by Kohout (1978), and both these authors are strongly indebted to Brian Gaines for the ideas concerning adaptivity of behaviour of dynamic biological and artificial systems. Gaines' "Axioms of adaptive behaviour" are crucial in this context (cf. Gaines 1972a, b). Kohout (1978) was also strongly influenced by N. A. Bernštejn's work on the control and the dynamics of human movement control. A wealth of detail on Bernštejn's work can be found in Kohout (1978a, 1981 and 1986). It should also be noted that Zadeh was the first to point out that adaptivity of a system is a relative notion and that it depends on the context which is dictated by the purpose of the system and the nature of the environment of the system (Zadeh 1963).

The now traditional approach to expert systems or robotics splits such a system into two functional parts:

1. control of the system,
2. knowledge of the system,

which are closely interrelated.

Most commonly, the control is programmed in by the designer and the knowledge is restricted to a small subset which allows for it being conceptually programmed into the system. The designer then can formulate the complete data organisation by a judicious use of constants.

In the conventional expert systems approach, both the control and knowledge parts are preprogrammed and fixed. In knowledge-based systems with learning, the control part is fixed. In now classical adaptive control systems (cf. Gaines 1968) the control part is variable. In the majority of Artificial Intelligence based approaches to learning, no clear distinction is made between learning of control and learning of knowledge (cf. Forsyth and Rada 1986, for a good survey). The systemic brain studies concerned with the dynamics of control of human movement on the other hand, display some distinction between adaptivity of knowledge and adaptivity of dynamic control (Bernštejn 1947, 1961; Laufberger 1947; cf. Kohout 1978a, 1986 for an account Bernštejn's and Laufberger's approach). This is a very important distinction, not fully appreciated yet.

According to C. S. Johnson (1981), learning of knowledge is the prime consideration, and from this the adaptive control follows, the control increasing its dominance as the system becomes more established. The internal and external controls have to be distinguished. The *external adaptive control* is a fairly extensive set of rules, either imposed at the design stage or loaded into the system by an external agent, utilising a control mode set up in the design stage. Internal adaptive control on the other hand, has its generating source within the system.

If the system possesses the internal adaptive control, it must have what C.S. Johnson calls "awareness." This awareness he defines as a the knowledge of:

a) What the system has done.
b) What it is currently doing.
c) What it will be doing.
d) Why it will be doing it.

Awareness as C. S. Johnson defines it is a teleological, functional, dynamic description (Kohout, 1976c, d; 1986) of the system's behaviour. In terms of systemic epistemology it is in fact an intensional meta-description. The reader unfamiliar with the issues of intensional description of system behaviour and the related notion of cybernetic equivalence of systems, is referred to Gaines (1972) and the discussion of Gaines' work in (Kohout 1976a).

Within a concrete realisation of a robot, it is not sufficient to have a meta-description or a meta-definition of awareness just in its intensional form. It is required that what is defined intensionally is also embedded "in extenso" into some concrete model representation of goals in the robot artifact. Thus we define the **awareness goal structure** as:

Definition 14.2.1-1: awareness goal structure consists of a quadruple of structures:

<PROBLEM, PLAN, PERFORMANCE, REASON>, where the meaning of the individual components is as follows:

PROBLEM ... a problem to be solved.

PLAN ... the plan for activity formulated (or just the method).

PERFORMANCE ... abstract characterisation of a result, with a fuzzy weighting grading of its success or failure.

REASON ... a reason why it should be done in this manner possibly distinguishing the past, present and future cases.

The *Awareness Goal Structure* (AGS) as defined above is a possibilistic model structure in Zadeh's sense. When the robot is put into an environment and starts interacting, the AGS models embedded in its substratum (i.e. hardware, firmware or software) will have to initiate the activity that Zadeh calls an identification process (Zadeh 1956). In our case, the class of possible identification models is determined by AGS, and the identification process is performed by the robot by means of some **monitoring procedures**. In a multi-environmental situation, which is rather complex, all the problems that are usually encountered in so called General System Identification (cf. Gaines 1977) may also appear. It should also be noted that there exists an interesting parallel between the Awareness Identification Process (AIP) and Bernštejn's plans for actions that ought to be further explored (cf. Kohout 1978a).

14.2.2. Functional Decomposition of the Architecture of a Multi-Environment Adaptive Robot

The Awareness Identification Process (AIP) is the essential activity in C. S. Johnson's approach. Its purpose is to *identify and update* the CONTENTS of the Awareness Goal Structure (AGS). As the essential feature of a Multi-Environmental Adaptive Robot (MEAR) appears to be its *internal control*, a number of the robot's *internal* activities have to be monitored. This is in addition to the robot's surveillance of the activities in the external environments. The most efficient way of monitoring internal activities, is to break them down into a discrete number of sub-processes (i.e. tasks in sense of Kohout 1978 a, b; cf. also Chapter 5.7 of this volume), and then to monitor these sub-processes individually.

Because of the need for efficient monitoring of the sub-processes of the adaptive robot, C. S. Johnson (1981) structured, what he called then **"adaptive expert system,"** into *"... functionally discrete and complete units, all of which ran independently, and provided monitoring processes (e.g. demons) and a meta-level control structure"* (Johnson 1981).

In terms of the Activity Structures approach, C. S. Johnson localises each functional decomposition (task descriptor – Kohout 1978 a, b) of activities in a separate substratum module of the robot. The functional structure which localises (Kohout 1977) each function in a substratum module has to satisfy the completeness requirement of a knowledge structure as defined by the abstract condition of completeness of the inductive family of functional refinements (Kohout 1976a, 1978a) of the task descriptor structure.

In concrete terms, the functional decomposition of the robot system's processes into a family of sub-processes is performed according to their function within the total context of the robot's interaction with the family of all possible multi-environments, with which the robot may interact during its life-cycle.

The architecture (substratum structure) of the robot that resulted from the application of the method described above is depicted in Fig. 14.1, which is reproduced from Johnson (1981). During the subsequent development of the robot, the structure was further refined (cf. Johnson 1984).

Each substratum module contains embedded in itself appropriate sub-process activities. Thus, for example, the substratum module called INPUT is functionally decomposed as indicated in Fig. 14.2. It can be seen that this decomposition is a functional decomposition into a family of perceptual modalities. The substratum module called MOTIVATION TABLE is decomposed into several functional substructures as displayed in Fig. 14.3. It consists of a number of important sub-processes, namely, those dealing with IMPORTANCE, PRIORITY, RESOURCES_USED, context (CURRENT_ASSOCIATED_KNOWLEDGE). Again, all these examples are reproduced from the original report of C. S. Johnson (1981). Further development of these ideas is reported in the subsequent reports (Johnson 1984, 1986).

The high level processes of the robot have to be supplied with the appropriate relevant information and the relevant lower level knowledge concerning the state of the environments, with which the robot interacts. The question as to what is or is not relevant when dealing with a whole family of environments or a continuously changing single environment is a nontrivial research and design issue.

After the first exploratory steps with these new approaches it has become obvious that more systematic ways of selecting the low level processes and of evaluating their utility in the overall framework of this design, were needed. Hence a series of multi-environmental experiments was performed in real time, with a real family of multiple environments. The role and efficacy of a human observer in judging what is or is not relevant of the low level robot's precepts has also been investigated. The results of these preliminary explorations are described in the sequel. Selection of

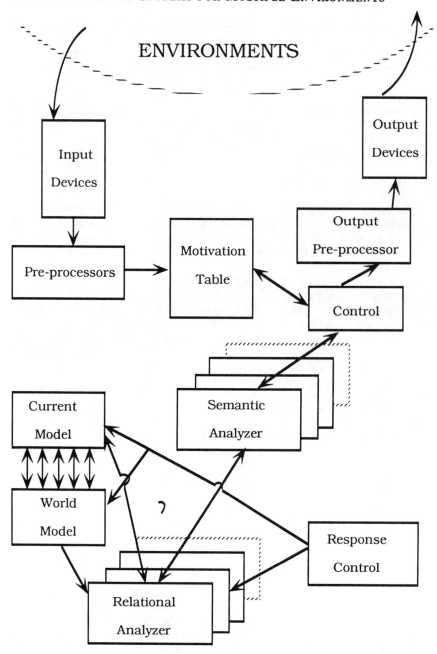

Figure 14.1. The overall architecture of a multi-environmental robot

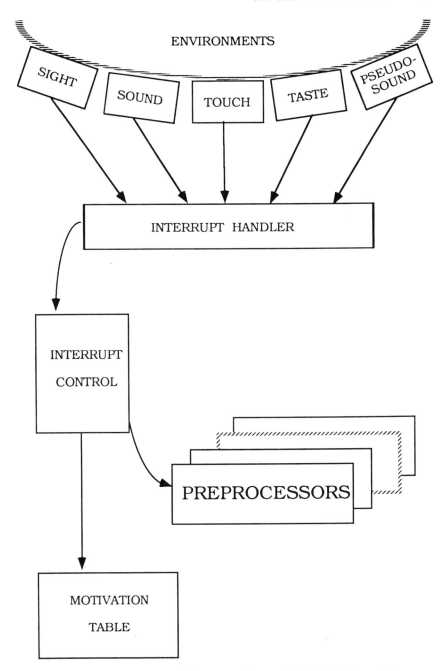

Figure 14.2. Functional decomposition of the INPUT module

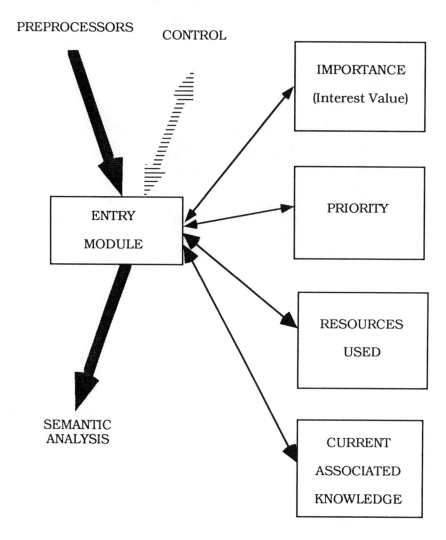

Figure 14.3. Structure of functional module called 'importance table'

hardware is discussed in the next section, followed by the description of the real-time experiments presented in sections 14.4 and 14.5.

14.3. INITIAL SELECTION CRITERIA FOR THE ROBOT HARDWARE

In order to commence with the implementation of a robot mobile system within the blueprint specification of the previous section, it was necessary to determine the basic criteria for selecting an adequate hardware system, that would allow the exploration of a number of environments. The following criteria were provisionally adopted:
1) The robot should have the ability to move freely in the environment. This behavioural feature of the robot requires the following means for its realisation:
    a) Some feedback sensors on the motors for steering and travel providing the robot with an appropriate proprioception for exploring diverse environments.
    b) The means for extracting the pertinent features of each environment. These should include adequate sensors on the hardware.
    c) The means for sensing from a distance.

The axiomatic benefit (i.e. *a priori* inbuilt) of a distance sensor rests on the fact that the robot can detect moving objects in the environment and thus form one of the signals triggering the process maintaining the robot's security.

There is a tradeoff between the number of sensors and the overall complexity of the system. On the one hand, the increase in the number of the types of sensors allows for checking the functioning of other sensors and also provides the additional means for enhancing the interaction of the robot with the environment. On the other hand this leads to an increase of the complexity of the overall system.

A device that has met the initial selection criteria was the Heathkit HERO 1 Robot. This is self-contained, in that it contains the energy source, control, sensors and effectors, all in a device approximately 60 centimetres high and 30 centimetres in width and depth. The robot travels on three wheels, the single wheel at the front providing both steering and motion power. The robot also possesses a head about 5 centimetres in depth which can rotate approximately 355 degrees. Apart from the drive wheel sensor, all other sensors are mounted in the head. The batteries on board give the robot an hour of continuous running between charges.

The robot is equipped with the following sensors:

S1. *Light sensors* (resolution graduation 0–255)
S2. *Sound sensor* (resolution graduation 0–255).
S3. *Sonar sensor* (graduation 0–255, resolution approximately 0–255 centimetres).
S4. *Movement sensor* (Boolean), (travel distance (sensed optionally from the rotation of the drive wheel, graduation 0-1023, resolution approximately 1 centimetre).

S5. *Low battery charge* sensors.

S6. *Time sensor* in the form of a clock showing years, months, days, hours, minutes and seconds.

The effectors consists of:

D1. *A drive motor* which can be driven forward or backward.

D2. *Steering motor* (angular range 180 degrees, graduation of control 0-232).

D3. *Head motor* (angular range 355 degrees, graduation of control 0-190).

D4. *Sleep control* which when activated only provides power to refresh RAM and powers the systems up every ten seconds to check if the sleeptime counter is zero, otherwise one is subtracted from the sleeptime counter.

The controller consists of a Motorola 6808 microprocessor with 4k bytes of RAM and ROM interpreter that uses the unallocated machine instructions of the 6808 processor to control the sensors and effectors. The level of control provided by the interpreter for the control of the sensors and effectors allows the motor to be switched on and off for fixed amounts of movement and sensor readings to be taken. The light, sound, sonar and movement sensors can also be turned on and off.

14.4. THE FIRST SET OF EXPERIMENTS

Two qualitatively different sets of experiments were performed with the robot. The first set, concerned with the robot's performance in various environments, is described in the present section.

The second set of experiments were designed to investigate the environment as detected through a robot's sensors. This filtered image of the environment was used for controlling the robot by human operators unfamiliar with the actual physical environments, in order to enhance the understanding of what is the relevant low level information needed for higher levels of control of the robot in real-time operation. The second set is described in section 14.5.

14.4.1. The Purpose of the Experiments

A number of experiments were performed in order to understand better what is involved in exploring the multi-environmental situation.

The robot moved in various environments, and the way it performed in each environment was evaluated. For the *evaluation criterion*, the *lengths of the survival* of the robot's function are chosen.

From the designer's point of view, the experiments were aimed at:

1) exploring the behaviour of the software for data acquisition, data representation, and controlling the hardware of the HERO 1 robot, both relatively unknown areas;

2) using the results from these experiments to derive an integrated design that would take into consideration the features of multi-environments or, more generally, of a continuously and substantially changing environment.

In more specific terms, the experiments were to aid the construction of a framework for the integration of the robot body, with its map-making and routing system. In order to do this, the characteristics of the robot have to be determined as well, because the control program acts as an interface between the robot and the map-maker and router.

14.4.2. Equivalence and Non-Equivalence of Strategies for Achieving Various Aims

A human, in learning and performing motor skills, explores a number of strategies, to achieve a certain predetermined movement goal. Although some strategies may be equivalent in some situations, it would be erroneous to assume that they will have the same final effect in all environments. Thus, two strategies, or movement plans, while executed in one environment yield equivalent effects, but may yield two vastly different effects in another environment. Also, if the brain structures controlling the movement are partially impaired, two different movement control policies, executed in two different contexts, yield two vastly different effects, although these would yield the equivalent effect under normal conditions (cf. Kohout 1978a, b).

We may conjecture that this will be also the case with a real-time, truly adaptive mobile robot. In order to test experimentally the equivalence or difference of seemingly identical or equivalent actions, various modifications of the basic program were explored. For example, for relative movement of the head against the robot's body the following movement actions were tried:

1. The body turned as a unit to the left or right instead of the head.
2. The head scanned approximately 10 degrees left and right as the robot moved forward.
3. On stopping the head looked approximately 45 degrees left and right the body turned in the direction of the longer of the two until it found a sonar distance greater than half of the maximum range.

From what has been said about human movement, it should be the case that while these movement actions are equivalent from the point of view of an external observer, these may not be always equivalent in their effect in different environments. Also, if the impairment of a part of the robotic structure is considered as possible, the resulting impaired structure may have different residual capabilities (cf.. Kohout, 1977).

14.4.3. Description of the First Set of Experiments, the Results and their Evaluation

In the first set of experiments, the aim of the robot was to move around the environment continually without immobilising itself, e.g. by attempting to move through an object. The algorithm to attain this goal just utilised the distance sensor, the travel motor and sensor, the head motor and the steering motor. The basic skeleton of the algorithm specifying the overall activity for the multi-environmental experiments is given in the Appendix, section 14.8.

The programs based on this skeleton algorithm were run in a number of environments:

Knowledge-Based Systems for Multiple Environments

(a) in a home with many soft obstacles,
(b) in a pen constructed of tables turned on their sides with various obstacles inside the pen,
(c) in a foyer with few obstacles and a number of people,
(d) in a corridor,
(e) in an office with a door and connecting passage way.

The results of the first set of experiments confirmed the conjecture of non-equivalence of some actions in different environments. The results were illuminating to say the least. It was discovered that a program version which worked well in one environment (e.g.: the robot moving around in the environment without running into an obstacle and being unable to continue) would not necessarily work at all in another, seemingly not very different environment.

In the home the programs worked often surprisingly well, while in the pen, the corridor and the office the success of the program depended on the initial orientation of the robot and the types of surface of the obstacles.

The types of problem encountered were:

(a) The robot running obliquely into an object, not detecting it and becoming jammed.
(b) Low or high objects outside of the sonar range causing jamming.
(c) The head jamming itself against an obstacle when looking left and right.
(d) The robot not running perfectly straight, although this was often an advantage in that it prevented the robot oscillating backwards and forwards, and in the case of the corridor environment where the radius of the turn was less than the width of the corridor, the robot proceeded successfully along the corridor in a series of semicircles.
(e) The head or the wheel catching on some obstacle in the environment. As the robot had no feedback for the head or the wheel this caused the actual position not to agree with the program position; e.g., move head right 90 degrees and the head stops against an obstacle at 45 degrees which is not detected by the robot so the program assumes the head is 90 degrees right. Consequently all future movements are incorrect with respect to the environment.

The first set of experiments demonstrated that the HERO 1 robot is still deficient in its hardware, when used in a not fully predictable environment, or in a multiplicity of environments. This in turn suggested some additional features were required for it to successfully perform in the more difficult environments. Below some such necessary enhancements are listed for illustration:

(a) The light sensor should be mounted at the front of the head.
(b) The sound sensor should be similarly mounted at the front or, following the human model, mounted on both sides. This is probably the better solution.
(c) The robot needs to know when it is charging the batteries, and preferably, it should be given a sensor with the ability to recognise charging points (hardware feature).

(d) Some form of touch, e.g. bumpers should be incorporated although this facility could be driven using software.
(e) The sensor needs to be able to measure small distances. At the moment the minimum resolution of the sensor is the distance between the transmitter and the receiver beam tubes, 20 angular degrees on the sonar scale of 255.

14.4.4. Multi-Environment Induced Deficiencies in Hardware

When the HERO 1 robot was selected for the experiments it was thought that the capabilities (viz. the sensors and effectors) of the robot were more than adequate for the proposed tasks and that where the hardware failed to meet expectations, the problem could be overcome with software.

The main lesson learned from the experiments has been that sophisticated hardware is a handicap in the multi-environment situation. In constructing an intelligent system, there are two areas where the intelligence can reside: in the hardware or in the software. Hardware intelligence is *a priori* knowledge and as such can be neither derived from the basic programmable assumptions nor subsequently modified either by adaptation or by the act of the designer. In other words, we can say that the *axioms of the operations* are *below the threshold of modifiability* of the system.

This can be illustrated by a practical example. At one stage of the development, consideration was given to incorporating an automatic cut-out of the travel motor in the actual robot, instead of having it programmed in the controller, when the robot ran into an obstacle. Doing this however would have as the consequence an *undesirable change* of the robots actions. Namely, at no stage could the system push an object aside because the robot would have automatically cut the power to the travel motor. This is an example of an undesirable action being introduced as the *side-effect* of introducing a desirable one (cf. Chapter 5).

We can see from the above example again that the actions that are equivalent from the positive point of view may carry different secondary associated undesirable effects with them. Thus, while considering the equivalence of actions we have to take into account the equivalences of both classes: of the desirable as well as of the undesirable consequences (Kohout 1978a).

14.5. THE SECOND SET OF EXPERIMENTS

14.5.1. An Overview and the Justification of the Set-up

For the higher level control of the robot, it is necessary to look at various abstractions and interpretations of the environments. For this reason, a second set of experiments was conducted. This set was concerned with a navigation and map keeping experiment, which involved human interpreters of robot's perceptions.

In the navigation and map-making experiment, an environment was constructed unknown to the experimenters, and the robot was placed in this environment. The experimenters consisted of teams of two people, one controlling the robot and one constructing the map. They worked in unison in the decision making.

To give a better understanding of the interpretation of the environment through the sensors and to facilitate programming of the robot, the robot was connected to a microcomputer, using an RS232C serial asynchronous 1200-bits-per-second link along a wire.

To allow all decision making to be made by the team of human interpreters via a microcomputer in the second set of experiments, the robot was programmed to be a passive device, which would respond to command issues on the link and to report the status of all sensors. The only control the robot possessed was provided with the following emergency situation, namely, in the event of a communication failure longer than 3 seconds the robot would abort what it was doing and await the re-establishment of the communication link.

Polling of the robot occurred every second, and the message was sent in both directions. The polling frequency was chosen so as to allow the controlling program the time needed to perform any processing which might be required.

The greatest benefit of the controlling program was that it displayed the sensor readings and the current active robot command continuously (or at least on updating every second), which led to a greater understanding of each particular environment as seen through the robot's sensors.

14.5.2. Details of the Second Set of Experiments and their Results

Two types of experiment were conducted using the controlling program:

1. The original program from the first experiment was reprogrammed and run remotely.
2. Navigation of the robot in an unknown environment was conducted by humans guided by the robot's sensors. In addition the human users attempted to construct a map of the environment.

The navigation experiment with human interpreters of the robot's perceptions revealed the deficiencies of the strategy of the map-makers to recognise the environment by constructing a detailed map as soon as possible.

There were problems with the human interpretation of data for the human high level controller, namely, some relevant data were not picked up, and some data picked up were irrelevant.

Another problem with the use of humans as the high level interpreters in the evolutionary design was the strong coupling between the changes of the control programs and the way the humans interpreted the robot's low level perceptions in the second set of experiments. It is difficult to test the effect of the changes of the man-machine program on the quality of performance without changing the performance of the low level system itself. That makes it difficult to explore this approach fully, without introducing unnecessary changes in the low level system program design which are not relevant to the robot's performance, but just induced by the instability of human pattern perception.

This difficulty of changing the behaviour of the robot consistently by the second method stems in general from the fact that the human interpreters are part of the experiment and the evaluation of the data by them may not be in consistent agreement with the factors relevant to the evaluation of the quality of robot's performance. This leads to the conclusion that the structure of the robot allowing for *adaptivity and learning* is to a certain extent necessary in the multi-environmental situation, especially when the real-time environments are so complex that they cannot be faithfully simulated with ease.

14.6. CONSEQUENCES OF THE EXPERIMENTS FOR THE DESIGN BLUEPRINT OF A MULTI-ENVIRONMENTAL ROBOT

14.6.1. An Overview

The difficulties can be categorised into:
1. Inadequacies of the hardware.
2. Problems with adequate interpretation of the environment.
3. Specification of what is correct control being dependent on a particular environment.

As the inadequacies of hardware were discussed above, we shall proceed directly with the discussion of the problems of interpretation and control.

14.6.2. Environment Interpretation

To produce a system to control the robot, the designers have to have a full approximation of the interpretation of the environment as detected through the sensors. When designing systems around robots, designers tend to decompose backwards from their interpretation of the environment. This is not a simple task in view of the wealth of information the robot's sensors provide. It is extremely difficult to remove all the additional sensor input beyond that which the robot can utilise. The alternative to this method is to have the robot in an unknown environment, where the designers use the robot's sensors and effectors to explore the environment via robot, and to construct a model of that environment using as their input the low level percepts of the robot.

14.6.3. Control Restrictions

Any control function of the robotic system that is *a priori* at any level in the system, and cannot be modified by the system, becomes *axiomatic* (i.e. given *a priori*) and will place a restriction on the robot system in some form. For this reason, a prototype robotic system should be designed in a flexible way, so that as many functions as possible can be monitored and modified when required. This is essential particularly in the case when the robotic systems is to display some form of adaptation or intelligence.

14.7. COMPUTER SIMULATION OF REAL ENVIRONMENTS

14.7.1. The Choice: To Simulate – Or Not To Simulate!

While in the process of constructing an artifact that interacts with a natural environment, the designers need to input the relevant data concerning the environment into their design procedure. If the artifact also actively acts upon the environment (e.g. the case of a robot), either the real environment or its simulated version has to interact with the a prototype (or the simulation) of the artifact that is being designed. Similarly, in the case of large mainframe multiprogramming interactive systems with thousands of terminals and powerful pipelined central processors, we need either a good model of the dynamics of users' behaviour or real-time experiments during the design stage, which may be costly, difficult or impossible to achieve.

When creating new designs in new application domains where computers or other artifacts interact with the real world in a feedback situation, or when the environment changes rapidly during the life cycle of the artifact, the designers generally have two options:

1. To simulate the relevant domains of the environment on a computer first, and use it in the design process and test in a real environment only at later stages.
2. To build the actual real world interface to the basic system and then to extend the system in an evolutionary manner, by exploring the real world during the construction of the complete artifact.

As it is generally cheaper, easier and more time efficient, the simulation approach is usually taken. The benefit of this method is that the modifications of the environment can be induced easily by the designer. Hence the control and a finer adjustment of the properties of the simulated domains are possible. The degree of relevance of the individual variables can be measured by varying their values easily in the simulated environment. On the other hand, as every real environment is complex, any simulation of it is its simplified version of it: metaphorically speaking, a picture of the real landscape, which may or may not contain in it all the features relevant to the design problem. The second set of experiments described above indicates that there may be problems with the simulation of real environments when used for robots with multilevel control centres containing knowledge of various degrees of abstraction.

14.7.2. Problems with Simulation of Environments for Robots

Any robotic system that does not acquire its internal model from *learning by interacting* with its *real* environment must have the knowledge (information and control) programmed into it, or be taught in a simulated environment. Unfortunately, the complexity of most simulations falls far short of that which is required even to model the environment of a classroom, namely light (natural and artificial), walls and ceiling (acoustic and electromagnetic reflection and absorption), carpet (coefficient of friction), furniture (mass, friction, placement to the nearest millimetre), students (movement, noise, communication, sweat, behaviour) teachers, blackboard (information thereon, noise, dust, cleaning), cleaning staff etc. It is far cheaper in these environments actually to use them rather than simulate them. It is in these environments that humans and animals learn the basics of 'common sense' which are then extended to the other environments that they are likely to encounter.

Thus exclusive simulation eliminating any real-world experiments with the real environments cannot in general be used successfully in the development of robots designed to be operating in a multi-environmental situation. Systems that are developed using simulations of environments and then placed in the real environments will possess blindspots corresponding to the deficiencies in the simulation.

As a simulation may not always capture all the relevant features of the real environment, the results of the experiments with the simulated environments are not identical with the experiments in the real environments. The necessary theoretical condition to be so is the existence of a partial homomorphism of the relevant features of the environments with respect to their simulation models. These homomorphisms may be generated by the factorisation of the necessary perceptual and effector survival abilities of the robot in the way described in Kohout (1976a; 1978a, Chapter 3). But this is an intricate theoretical issue that is outside the scope of this chapter, dealing with the description of some practical experiments and their design ramifications.

We shall conclude by saying that if robotic systems for multi-environments are to become successful they have to 'get out into the real world and experience it firsthand'! The multi- environment is too subtle to be modelled correctly in all its relevant features. Real experiments within it seem to be necessary.

KNOWLEDGE-BASED SYSTEMS FOR MULTIPLE ENVIRONMENTS

14.8. APPENDIX

14.8.1. The Basic Skeleton Algorithm Specifying the Overall Activity of the Hero Robot Used in the First Set of Experiments

```
begin
    if batteries have sufficient charge then
    begin
        initialise head and steering motor;
        turn on distance motor;
    end;
while batteries have sufficient charge do
begin
    get sonar-distance;
    if sonar-distance greater than buffer-distance then
    begin
        move forward (sonar-distance - buffer-distance);
    end.
else
begin
    turn sonar 90 degrees left:
    get left-sonar-distance;
    turn sonar 180-degrees right;
    get right-sonar-distance;
    turn sonar 90 degrees left;
    if right-sonar-distance less than buffer-distance and
        left-sonar-distance less than buffer-distance then
    begin
        turn 180 degrees;
        move forward buffer-distance;
    end
    else
        if left-sonar-distance greater than
        right-sonar-distance then
    begin
        turn 90 degrees left;
    end
    else
        begin
            turn 90 degrees right;
        end
end {if};
end {while};
end {program}.
```

14.8.2. A Brief Characterisation of the Control Program Used in the Second Set of Experiments

The controlling program was approximately 70 pages of Pascal code which compiled down to 50K of 8086 machine code. The program went through approximately 3 months of development and enhancement. Another program was written to convert the robot language to an interpreted form quickly executable by the robot controlling program. This program performed some elementary syntax checking. The program for the HERO 1 was about 2K of 6808 machine code. As an exercise, a simulator was constructed for the robot and included in the original controlling program. The modular nature of the system is illustrated by the fact that the addition of the simulator module took 3 days and was subsequently ported to a VAX where it provided the basis for a map generating program written in PROLOG (Johnson and Briggs 1985).

A command language that could be entered in real-time in the computer was devised. This language consisted of command to turn the sensors on and off and to issue the commands to move the motors to change the direction of the robot at present distance (i.e. turn the head or wheel 90 degrees left or right) or to move the motors an arbitrary distance. Added to this system was an interpreter that could run the robot according to a higher level program. The programming language consisted of the command language plus control statements, including conditionals and 52 variables for storing the sense data. At a later stage some procedures and subprograms were added.

14.9. REFERENCES

Bernštejn, N.A. (1947):
  O Postrojenii Dviženij, (On the construction of movement), In Russian. Nauka, Moscow.

Bernštejn, N.A. (1961):
  Current problems in the theoretical physiology of activity (In Russian). *Problemy Kibernetiki*, **6**.

Forsyth, R. and Rada, R. (1986):
  MACHINE LEARNING: Applications in Expert Systems and Information Retrieval. Ellis Horwood, Chichester and John Wiley, New York.

Gaines, B.R. (1968):
  Adaptive control theory. In: *Encyclopedia of Information, Linguistics and Control*, Pergamon Press, Oxford.

Gaines, B.R. (1972a):
  The Human Adaptive Controller. Ph.D. Thesis, Cambridge University, England, U.K.

Gaines, B.R. (1972b):
  Axioms for adaptive behaviour. *Internat. J. of Man-Machine Studies*, **4**, 169–199.

Gaines, B.R. (1977):
General system identification – Fundamentals and results. In: Klir, G. (1978).

Johnson, C.S. (1981):
Background to The Design of an Adaptive Expert System. Technical Report, Man-Computer Studies Group, Brunel University. Part 1 – October 1981. Part 2 – December 1981.

Johnson, C.S. (1984):
Adaptivity and Learning in Intelligent Systems I. Technical Report, School of Information Sciences. The New South Wales Institute of Technology, Australia, September 1984.

Johnson, C.S. (1986):
Adaptivity and Learning in Intelligent Systems II. Technical Report, School of Information Sciences. The New South Wales Institute of Technology, Australia, August 1986.

Johnson, L.A.S. and Briggs, B.G. (1985):
Myrtales and myrtaceae - a phylogenetic analysis. Annals of the Missouri Botanical Garden, 1985.

Klir, G. ed. (1978):
Applied General Systems Research: Recent Developments and Trends. (Proc. of the NATO Internat. Conference, Binghamton, N.Y., August 15–19 1977). Plenum Press, New York, 531–544.

Kohout, L.J. (1976a):
Representation of functional hierarchies of movement in the brain. *Internat. J. of Man-Machine Studies*, **8**, 699-709.

Kohout, L.J. (1976b):
Automata and topology. In: Mamdani. E. and Gaines, B.R. (eds.), *Discrete Systems and Fuzzy Reasoning* (Proceedings of a Workshop, Queen Mary College, London, January 1976). Publ. by University of Essex (EES-MMS-DSFR-76), Colchester U.K., 88–110.

Kohout, L.J. (1976c):
Methodological Foundations of the Study of Action, EES-MMS-ACT-76, Man-Machine Systems Laboratory, Department of Electrical Engineering, University of Essex, U.K., December 1976.

Kohout, L.J. (1976d):
On functional structures. Chapter 5 of Kohout (1976c). Presented as a companion paper to Kohout (1977) at NATO Internat. Conf. on Applied General Systems Research, Binghamton, August 1977. (Revised version reprinted in Kohout and Bandler (1986), 69-94).

Kohout, L.J. (1977):
Functional hierarchies in the brain. In: Klir, G. (1978).

Kohout, L.J. (1978a):
Methodological Foundations of the Study of Action. Ph.D. Thesis, University of Essex, England, U.K., January 1978.

Kohout, L.J. (1978b):
Analysis of computer protection structures by means of multi-valued logics. In: *Proc. of Eight Internat. Symposium on Multiple-valued Logic*, IEEE, New York, 260–268.

Kohout, L.J. (1981):
Control of movement and protection structures. *Internat. J. of Man-Machine Studies*, 14, 397–422.

Kohout, L.J. (1986):
On functional structures. In: Kohout and Bandler, eds. (1986), 69–94.

Kohout, L.J. and Bandler, W. eds. (1986):
Knowledge Representation in Medicine and Clinical Behavioural Science. An Abacus Book, Gordon an Breach, London.

Laufberger, V. (1947):
Vzruchová Theorie (A Theory of Activation, in Czech), Prague.

Zadeh, L.A. (1956):
On the identification problem. *IRE Transactions on Circuit Theory*, **CT-3**, December 1956, 277–281.

Zadeh, L.A. (1963):
On the definition of adaptivity. *Proc. IEEE*, 469–470.

CHAPTER 15

THE DESIGN OF THE HOUSE AS A SYSTEM IN MULTI-ENVIRONMENTAL SPACE

V. Mancini

Editorial Comment:

> Not only in medicine, business and finance but also in high quality architectural computer-aided design, the issue of multi-environments is important. In this chapter, an expert architect outlines the most pertinent multi-environmental features of house design that must be adequately accommodated by the knowledge structures incorporated into a knowledge-based system.

LIST OF CONTENTS

15.1 INTRODUCTION

15.2 THE IDEA OF THE HOUSE

15.3 THE "ASPATIAL STRUCTURE"

15.4 ENVIRONMENT AND MEANING

15.5 CONTEXT AND MEANING

15.6 MULTI-ENVIRONMENTS

15.7 THE ENSEMBLE: IS SYMBOLIC DESIGN POSSIBLE?

15.8 REFERENCES

KNOWLEDGE-BASED SYSTEMS FOR MULTIPLE ENVIRONMENTS

15.1. INTRODUCTION

Conceptually, the design of an object to interact with human beings in multiple environments requires the recognition of an invariant bundle of structural characteristics over the function of the object, and a variety of alternative local specifications to allow the object to perform in various modes, corresponding to changing environmental input. This chapter will deal with this problem in connection with the individual human habitation, the house. Fundamental though the house is to all cultures, it is a system of extraordinary complexity, providing as it must a whole gamut of functions, so that designing the core of a house for multi-environmental adaptation requires very wide and deep considerations.

In order to provide an appropriate Computer Aided Design (CAD) support for this activity, the problem of multi-environments also has to be handled appropriately by any knowledge-based system accommodating the architectural knowledge needed in the architectural design process. Unfortunately, current CAD systems pay virtually no attention to such issues.

The purpose of this chapter is to extract the most important aspects of the design of *the house* viewed as a system in multi-environmental space. This will provide the essential basis for a detailed structuring of architectural knowledge that ought to be incorporated in a knowledge-based system capable of dealing adequately with the multi-environmental issues in house design.

It is to be hoped that this inquiry will consequently throw light on the design problems of the house as such, for at the present moment in Western architecture even this is experiencing formidable difficulties. Indeed it can be said that architectural design is failing to meet the challenge of this most human of building tasks. The reason, to put it bluntly, is the failure of architecture to supply symbolic forms whose roots reach deep enough into contemporary human experience. We may be, at best, capable of envisaging the morphology of significance, the practicality of function and its repetitive phenomenology, but as Langer (1942) reminds us, "The meanings which are capable of indefinite growth are symbolic meanings: connotations not significations."

It was not in the programmatic goals of the Modern Movement in Architecture, at least not in Europe, to pursue 'nature-symbols' or 'life-symbols'. It did provide new forms for living, and a remarkable synthesis of the aspirations of that time coming from the various arts' fields, notably abstraction, centrifugal space, dynamic asymmetrical balance and a kinetic expression of time. But the visual imagery was derived from the poetical perception of abstract mechanical forms and industrial materials, the symbols of science and technology.

Langer, writing forty-five years ago, wondered whether our technological forms were too new, yet to "have acquired that rich, confused historic accretion of meanings that makes familiar things 'charged' symbols to which we seem to respond instinctively." (Langer, 1942).

But the nature of science and technology, its internal logic of growth – its endlessness – is not allowing architecture the time to turn technological processes into cultural symbols. The speed of these processes is best illuminated by the development of environmental engineering. The result of mechanically managed environments is "... the liberation of performance from form." Banham (1969) goes on to conclude, "This leaves behind a building that is perfectly honest about its functioning but offers no clues to what that functioning may be."

In this perspective the natural physical environment as a form-giver is receding fast, taking away significance and meaning. Banham, writing in 1969, seems even more pessimistic than Langer. " It is probably true that only when the architecture of the well-tempered environment disposes of a language of symbolic forms as entrenched in our culture as are those of the older dispensation, will it be able to hope for equal conviction and monumental authority but that possibility seems to be excluded ..." Are the pathological expressions of disorientation, apathy, alienation, induced by some of our urban environments the result of the loss of 'life-symbols' and 'nature-symbols'? Whitehead said that the essence of freedom is the practicability of purpose. Are architects responsible for the frustration of one of mankind's most prevalent purposes, namely 'to dwell'?

15.2. THE IDEA OF THE HOUSE

There is a factual description of Kublai Khan's Palace and Garden Pavilion by Marco Polo and there is the poetic statement of the building task in Coleridge's poem. Although the one requirement "measureless to man" would paralyse a present-day designer's mind, is it not such content that generates a building program?

Curtiss (1982) declares, "... when one investigates an artist of any depth one discovers a sort of mythical content which pervades the forms. Ultimately we have to do with the ways in which fantasies and ideas are translated into a vocabulary."

The difference between the two descriptions is one of 'distance' only. Distance is a tool for investigation and ought to provide an overall description of the significant properties of the object (Klir 1985). Let's use another distance. Norberg-Schulz (1985) in *The Concept of Dwelling* investigates the existential meaning of man's being-in-the-world. He points out that the common denominators of the four modes of dwelling (settlement, urban space, institution and house) are identification and orientation. "In general to dwell implies the establishment of a meaningful relationship between man and a given environment ... to relate meaningfully to a world of things and to apprehend spatial order." He quotes from Merlaut-Ponty's *Phenomenology of Perception* : "The life-world does not consist of sensations but is immediately given as a world of characteristic, meaningful things which do not have to be 'construed' through individual experience." And from Heidegger's *The Thing* Norberg-Schulz (1985) goes on to quote: "... expression is the language of the thing and springs from its configuration ... the things are a 'gathering of the world' and the world they gather is a 'four-fold' of earth, sky, mortals and divinities which belong together in a mirror-play where each of the four mirrors is in its own way the essence of the others."

The yearning for the complement, for the opposite, and the potential for acquiring it is a fundamental concept. "The intangible being of a thing, therefore, may be interpreted as that which is the obvious complement to the thing, giving it interrelated and reversible oneness and full reality." (Chang 1956). In the making of physical space, the immaterial, the void, preserves the desirable potential for unforeseen service. Chang (1956) quotes from the philosopher Laotzu's *Tao-te-ching* :

> *Moulding clay into a vessel, we find the*
>   *utility in its hollowness;*
> *Cutting doors and windows for a house, we*
>   *find the utility in its empty space.*
> *Therefore the being of things is profitable,*
>   *the non-being of things is serviceable.*

Norberg-Schulz (1985) relates Heidegger's expressions to the field of architecture and says, "in relating the concept of 'thing' to the problem of dwelling, we may say that the dwelling primarily consists in the appropriation of a world of things, not in the material sense, but as an ability to interpret the meaning the things gather." "While identification involves the quality of things, orientation grasps their spatial interrelationships ..." therefore "works of architecture are objects of human identification because they embody existential meaning."

In architectural terms, identification and orientation correspond to the functions of embodiment and admittance.

Our awareness of built form and meaning is a many-distanced one. But inspite of the fact that we continually change from one mode to another in our urban environment, our experience remains fragmented and patchy. Sometimes it is still possible to be aware of wholeness and multi-layered meaning in old buildings. An old farmhouse, nested in the landscape, in harmony with its natural environment, is one of those archetypal images that strongly manifest a sense of identity and purpose. The rhythm of life as lived there as well as the rhythms of nature have come together to give form to the building. The form manifests both, having drawn from both. "Form is communication, the presentation of meaning." (McHarg 1969).

In the presence of a strong tradition, the presentation of meaning is the result of a spontaneous, unselfconscious process, within which the 'idea' of the object is shared, implicitly, by the designer and the user. Symbolism spills over from the object to the very act of making it; legends and myths are recalled. Forms are not discarded lightly; local adjustments are enough to redress eventual local misfits. (Alexander 1964). In our fractured, complex and differentiated society this is no longer possible; the only way is through an explicit effort.

We can distinguish, basically, three modes of designing: for the individual client who provides the relevant content; for the building industry and property developer for whom a prototype is more useful; for no one in particular when the architect simply makes a proposal, a general reinterpretation of the task. Each mode establishes a different rapport with the environment (physical), with the context (physical and socio-cultural) and with the ensemble (context and form together).

To 'see' the house from all relevant distances requires placing it at the center of a relational network that reaches out to other modes of dwelling; the envisagement of the house presupposes the others; each mode integrates the others and compensates for their shortcomings. The user cannot escape this reality; the designer needs to gauge it and make it explicit. "The pattern of social relations is far and away the prime determinant of the quality of life." (Lynch 1975). Conventionally we capture a total picture by saying (Brett 1970), "... buildings have three uses: functional – they shelter our activities; environmental – they create the scene on which we act out our lives; symbolic – they represent to us larger than life certain ideas current in our societies at the time they are built." This comprehensive and yet vague picture does not capture the synthesis of the individual concrete case. Nor does a conventional brief. We need a much wider tale, in which vision and ideology are scaled down to the task and become instrumental tools. I shall call this wider tale the 'aspatial structure'.

15.3. THE "ASPATIAL STRUCTURE"

The *house world* is one of intimate relationships, of refuge, of harmony not competition, of caring not strife, of personal development, the acquisition of skills and knowledge, of feelings and a language to express them, of the first orientation to other people and to the world. These and many others are all 'functions' around which we build the house. To travel along the course of personal development demands spiritual and theoretical discipline and informed dedication, exercised in freedom. All the great expressions of domestic architecture imply this discipline; so did Le Corbusier's early masterpieces. The aspatial structure is in effect the human context of the house-form but as yet it does not reveal its potential for spatial organization. The potential for spatial organization is best expressed by typical actions, events, occasions, situations and activities.

Discreet events, that persist in space and repeat in time, unfolding through recognizable parts, are repositories of the potential for spatial organization. The activity 'to eat' manifest itself as a meal, a snack, a breakfast, a formal dinner, a feast, and so on. We soon learn to associate with each event a psychological 'climate', a social and cultural significance. Activities gather other activities, they mingle, they attract or repel one another, exploring always new relationships, setting up rhythms. Some rhythms seem to express qualities of proportion, balance, universal order. When rhythm is achieved, time seems neither short nor long; rhythm is timeless.

To a trained and imaginative mind, the clear perception or image of an event effortlessly conjures up a corresponding spatial structure. This faculty of man-the-maker is seen by Alexander, et al., (1975) as a spontaneous, universal and timeless language. Yet the context-form cannot be described uniquely. It is the designer's task to be aware of the adaptation and fit between context and form within a variety of boundaries. The ability to hold simultaneously different levels must be complemented by the intuitive grasp of spatial organization. (Alexander 1964).

When the designer has a clear model of how activities interact with one another we can say he has grasped the functional structure of the building task, in the teleological sense of Kohout (1990). This is best thought of as a system with a finite number of subsystems, and their relationships. It is the potential for spatial organization of the functional subsystems that the designer is interested in, and in my view this is the main principle for dealing with complexity. It is important in the general case, and indispensable in multi-environmental space.

Artifact design is complex in inverse proportion to its specificity, that is, the part of the task which can be put into propositional form. Order and complexity are antagonistic. To order, one needs a principle, and the principle tends to eliminate that which cannot fit into the order, yet the organization which maintains a high level of complexity is by its very richness capable of higher tasks. (Arnheim 1969).

Now if the designer relies on his skill to stretch the context-form boundary while remaining aware of various levels of form-context adaptation at once, if "... we ought always really to design with a number of nested, overlapped form-context boundaries in mind" (Alexander 1964), it can only mean that the designer is intuitively searching for the whole form and for its parts at the same time. There is a push from below as well as an order from above.

We can now rephrase the functional structure as a system of finite, hierarchically organized subsystems (that is, of various degrees of organized complexity), working together towards a goal, within which each subsystem performs a specified task. The functional structure is matched to a three-dimensional spatial structure which mirrors the other in its organization, that is, shows structural correspondence, which answers the question 'how?' as well as 'what?', and whose recognizable spatial qualities echo the intangible components of living: the 'being' as well as the 'doing'. The concretization of this structure gives us the object, the house.

The spatial structure answers the functional subsystems with clearly recognizable spatial *Gestalten* and pulls them together into a particular configuration. Hence the spatial structure and the aspatial one showing correspondence can be said to be *congruent*. Congruence is the quality that manifests the degree of matching of the two structures, a systemic quality. "There is relative freedom in the way subsystems adjust to subsystems in the pursuit of their goal. What remains invariant is their function." (Laszlo 1972).

Congruence must respect the functional program of the building task while the freedom it allows generates individual and unique forms. The same functional structure generates a family of forms, giving rise to the typology of the house. Architecturally we can say that the invariant elements of the subsystem give character to the building, while the variant ones provide individuality. The human life-situations and the concretized form constitute a hypersystem in purposeful action. Like a natural one it is a self-repairing and self-maintaining one. And in mirroring the hierarchical order of nature it is a whole in respect to its parts and a part with respect to higher-level wholes (neighbourhood, town).

15.4. ENVIRONMENT AND MEANING

The physical environment is form-maker. Light, rain, heat, wind, sound, humidity are all manipulated toward achieving interior comfort and at the same time are used to achieve the figural quality that responds to the function of embodiment.

In traditional technical systems, this manipulation was expressed through characteristic shapes of roofs and bounding walls, whose supporting task already provided considerable thickness.

Exceptional cunning and wisdom are the hallmarks of the igloo house of the Eskimos, the adobe house of the American Indian, which uses the building section as well as roofs and terraces to regulate the absorption and retention of heat according to the season (Knowles 1975), the Japanese house, and so on. As an example of form-giving by environmental forces, let us consider the traditional type of house developed in the Southeastern parts of the United States, where hot and humid conditions prevail. The house-form responds to environmental input by acquiring the following features (from James Marston Fitch, *The Uses of History*, quoted in Banham (1969)):

1. Elevated living floors ... offering maximum exposure to prevailing breezes.
2. Huge, light-mass, parasol-type roofs to shed the subtropic sun and rain.
3. Continuous porches to protect walls from slanting sun and blowing rain.
4. Large, wall-to-ceiling doors and windows for maximum ventilation.
5. Tall ceiling, central halls, ventilated attics for warm-weather comfort.
6. The louvred jalousie, providing any combination of ventilation and privacy.

The resulting building is immediately and effortlessly 'readable'. A remarkable symmetry is achieved between indoor spaces and outdoor ones, a subtle variable arrangement which accomodates the changing moods of the weather into the changing rhythms of daily life. Indoor and outdoor spaces are differentiated appropriately to private and public occasions, to work and rest, to display and withdrawal, to intimacy and gregariousness.

The history of the progressive reliance on technology, energy and power to regulate the internal environment of the house and the effect of all this on form is interestingly told by Banham (1969). Traditional houses had always relied, of course, on burning wood or coal for heat, and exhibited that characteristic sign-symbol, the chimney stack. The hearth moves first of all to the center of the house and becomes part of a unified central core of services. As a most natural outcome, the house can now open up and acquire an open plan.

The centrifugal space of the modern movement and the new openness of plan in modern architecture depended on a unified management of the domestic environment but two major attitudes were at work, exemplified by Wright and Le Corbusier. Wright was absorbing the new techniques into the working together of the parts of the building.

> *Here for the first time was an architecture in which environmental technology was not called in as a desperate remedy nor had dictated the form of the structure, but was finally and naturally subsumed into the normal working method of the architect, and contributed to his freedom of design. (Banham 1969)*

Le Corbusier, having obliterated, as a matter of programmatic principle, the load-bearing wall in favor of the reinforced concrete frame, was having a harder time. The all-glass-fronted skyscrapers, the dream of Mies and Le Corbusier, could only be concretized when the modern air-conditioning plant made the sealed environment a workable proposition. Even so, the housing of the power-plant components and ducting remained a difficult problem, and as the size of sealed environments has kept steadily increasing, the volume of service ducts and power installation has become such that they had to burst out of the envelope. The internal logic and consistencey of scientific and technological development and its continual experimentation is inescapable. The sealed, ideal environment can be no more than a thin boundary-skin, continuous and undifferentiated, which is either hung from the power-plant components or kept inflated by the very air we breathe.

15.5. CONTEXT AND MEANING

The traditional Japanese house is a perfect example of a functional system seen through a cultural one, and of a universal concept, the house, acquiring highly individualistic and subtle forms because of the way 'function' is understood. In Western eyes environment and function are strongly bonded together. Every word, gesture or situation gathers a discrete environment around itself. Buildings explicitly offer a multiplicity of environments.

The Japanese house does not tie function to a finely differentiated space, which instead remains multi-functional or multi-purpose. In conditions of humidity similar to the ones affecting the American house described earlier, the degree of openness of the Japanese house is extreme; and yet, only with respect to the garden walls which are its private shell and where the real entrance door is. The sliding panels, almost uniform whether inner or outer, are meant to divide or merge spaces rather than rooms. The very concept of 'room' is unknown; one refers to the 'front-realm' or 'middle-realm' or the 'furthest-in-from-the-street-realm'. A sense of secrecy and drama follows the opening and closing of panels, revealing a continually changing spatial flow. (Nishihara 1968).

The simplicity of the Japanese house can be easily misinterpreted by Western observers. Its wooden frame construction, its modular planning, lack of symmetry, the high degree of standardization, have only a superficial resemblance to our mass-produced modular systems, whose rigidity breeds an atomized simplicity if not poverty. The simplicity of the Japanese house, like that of a bonsai tree, is a holistic aesthetic goal, a cultural ideal that permeates every act of its growth and constitutes that overall invariance that ensures the form's validity. This form withholds the local fitness, between the aspatial and spatial structure, preventing it from becoming too tight, too precise and trivial. The episodic differentiation of space is achieved by portable and easily removed objects.

The vagueness of spatial organization has a psychological and social complement. As if to compensate for the impermanency of the 'relevant environment', the house's life-situations tend to acquire the character of ritual.

15.6. MULTI-ENVIRONMENTS

As buildings are equated in the West with market products, the question arises about the impact of the dissemination of prototypes across geographical and cultural frontiers. (I am using the term 'multi-environment' to refer to both environment and context together.) The great variety of geographical, climatic and cultural conditions might conjure up in one's mind a correspondingly rich variety of forms, but the ever-expanding environment leaves the technological form unaffected, assuming of course that energy and power are available as well as the money to pay for them.

The exportation of industrialized buildings raises major interrelated issues, the more so the greater the technological gap. Broadly speaking, two parallel processes are at work: the transformation of the prototypes into cliché imitations (devaluation) and the breaking-down of the local context (relevance). Both processes are especially visible in developing countries, where in a single generation we may witness the change from an agricultural to an industrial society. The ponderous 'image' of multinational corporations, mass tourism, the needs of the foreign-educated elites, property developers and local bureaucracies, all combine to devalue modern forms. At the same time, the devalued model acquires elitist status: it is meant to reflect a progressive intellectual outlook as well as a superior standard of living. Function as a cultural 'datum' is lost.

The observed impact of technological forms upon vernacular ones is one of confusion and decay; the congruence between traditional solutions and the social structure is dislodged. The promises of instant liberation are to be won, in effect, over a long period of adjustment, requiring imagination, a firm hold on reality and an appreciation of continuity as well as change. The adjustment has to come from the inside. Expertise is necessary rather than ready-made solutions. The high degree of congruence of the vernacular form ought not to be thrown away lightly, but analysed for meaningful adaptation. "There is an inherent tension as well as circularity between continuity and development – between the stabilities and connections needed for coherence and the ability to change and grow." (Lynch 1981).

At some important level, the concept of house is universal, its purpose capable of general expression, its subsystems interdependent and yet free, their function specific and yet multivalent. It is possible that a new interpretation of the 'function' of the house will come from a dialectical process of mutual accommodation rather than one of confrontation. It requires that traditional means and technological ones work as a system.

To design a prototype for a multi-environmental space requires first of all a model of the common, invariant elements of the physical environment and the socio-cultural context relevant to the artifact. This represents the core of a shared functional structure. The general character and regional variations of the Mediterranean house may be of help in envisaging such a process. The shared core is responsible for the general character of the house. From here on, the variant elements of the subsystems come into play; each subculture provides a different input to specify the form into more detailed definition. We confront, therefore, the task of modelling a common core and various 'packages'.

15.7. THE ENSEMBLE: IS SYMBOLIC DESIGN POSSIBLE?

There is an ongoing debate in the architectural profession nowadays about the role of high technology in the building industry as it spills over from scope-complex, function-specific, machine-housing environments down to more purpose-complex, humane environments like residential forms. (Venturi 1966). The debate is fuelled by new sensitivities and values related to ecological concerns, the complex relationships between peoples, the man-nature relationship. It articulates a great variety of stances around two main themes: who controls scientific and technological processes and how the need for personal autonomy asserts itself. Christopher Alexander's experience has shown that in order to break the 'product' monopoly view of built form, one needs to change political, legislative, economic and fiscal structures as well. Here we see not only the influence of multiple environments upon the artifact, but the reciprocal influence of the artifact upon the multiple environments.

A 'cultured' view of science and technology in architecture by a master of both, Renzo Piano (as quoted by Farrelly (1987)) places them at the service of the humanities, including ethics and politics; their role "being valuable at a much more intimate scale: as a language of communion between each individual and his universe..." Piano rejects High-Tech as a style, "... wholly inimical to true creativity, contradicting everything that architecture – and at its best the twentieth century – ought to be about." (Farrelly 1987).

The level of technological use will stem from inside the building task itself as in Wright's prairie houses: a holistic vision of building-shell, technical equipment, site and climatic conditions. The architect will determine where the particular building task falls in the continuous line between minimum and maximum use of technology.

We can begin to envisage the expression of personal autonomy and the purpose of 'dwelling' at the level 'house'. It will be a teleological model in which the 'aspatial structure' attempts the representation of the individual's 'universe' and is the point of departure for a learning process of personal development and understanding of the world which will determine the overall objective of the building task. The model depends on computer technology; it requires a great deal of analysis and cognitive restructuring to work out ones bearings in the larger network of community and society. No one can really construct a personal 'aspatial structure' but the person in question. But the architect can help here if his mind is open and his emotions involved. Nor does it promise a happy tale for all: for a lot of people, it will make a mockery of the 'quality of life'.

The aspatial structure will generate a strategy and associated goals. Recognizable future situations will generate a cascade of subgoals and determine the activities as a goal-seeking adaptive system which predicts the necessary achievements but leaves open the means to achieve them.

The interaction with an expert system will be especially strong in the analysis and restructuring phases as well as in goal development and the setting up of requirements. As far as creativity is concerned, it remains a human prerogative.

"Current expert systems encode the expertise of people and make it more widely available. Access to this expertise may encourage users to be more creative, but the system itself has no direct role to play in the creative process." (Gaines and Shaw 1986).

Langer (1942) notes that 'the symbolic function of the mind', the 'symbolific transformation of experience' is an ongoing activity which asserts itself whether we are aware of it or not. Le Corbusier himself became with time more and more receptive to the instinctive element of the design process, going back to primitive biomorphic forms and mythical content. The storeroom of symbols is the mind, as far as it can be opened. To make symbols available to the design process requires no more, perhaps, than a particular state of mind, a way of being, the engagement of the whole personality, the structure of intellect and feeling.

Meanwhile the greatest symbolic expression of science and technology in architecture is working out its tremendous power to impress. Surrounded by a depleted and unsafe urban environment, the high-atrium tower turns inwards. Sealed off and self-sufficient, it allows a pale presence of the lost landscape inside its glass-topped atrium shell, like a faded memory of things lost. In the central void, forty or fifty storeys high, with exposed elevators silently gliding along vertical shafts, in the hushed artificial climate amid subdued voices, walking along stacked continuous balconies to identical doors, looking out from a sealed windowpane over an unfriendly perceived landscape ... is this not a most exalted symbol of the space-ship, a training and a rehearsal?

15.8. REFERENCES

Alexander, Christopher (1964):
Notes on the Synthesis of Form. Harvard University Press, Cambridge MA.

Alexander, Christopher; Ishikawa, Sara and Silverstein, Murray (1975):
A Pattern Language: Towns, Buildings, Construction. Oxford University Press, New York.

Arnheim Rudolph (1969):
Visual Thinking. University of California Press, Berkeley CA.

Banham, Reyner (1969):
The Architecture of the Well-Tempered Environment. Architectural Press, London, 2nd ed.

Brett, Lionel (1970):
Parameters and Images. Weidenfeld and Nicholson, London.

Chang, Amos Ih Tiao (1956):
Intangible Content in Architectonic Form. Princeton University Press, Princeton NJ.

Curtiss, William, Jr. (1982):
Modern Architecture Since 1900. Phaidon Press, Oxford.

Farrelly, E. M. (1987):
"Technica, The Quiet Game." *Architectural Review*, **1007**, page 70.

Gaines, B.R. and Shaw, M.L.G. (1986):
"The changing technologies underlying computer-aided design." *Environment and Planning B: Planning and Design*, **13**(4), 377–384.

Klir, George J. (1985):
Architecture of Systems Problem Solving. Plenum Press, New York and London.

Knowles, Ralph (1975):
Energy and Form. M.I.T. Press, Cambridge MA.

Kohout, Ladislav J. (1990):
A Perspective on Intelligent Systems. Chapman and Hall, London.

Langer, Susanne (1942):
Philosophy in a New Key. Harvard University Press, Cambridge MA.

Laszlo, Ervin (1972):
The Systems View of the World. Basil Blackwood, Oxford.

Lynch, Kevin (1975):
"Grounds for Utopia." In Honikman, Basil, editor, *Responding to Social Change.* Dowden, Hutchinson and Ross, Stroudsburg PA, 27–46.

Lynch, Kevin (1981):
Good City Form. M.I.T. Press, Cambridge MA.

McHarg, Ian L. (1969):
Design with Nature. Doubleday, Garden City NY.

Moholy Nagy, Laszlo (1939):
The New Vision. Norton, New York.

Nishihara, Kiyoyuki (1968):
Japanese Houses. Japan Publications, Tokyo.

Norberg-Schulz, Christian (1985):
The Concept of Dwelling: On the Way to Figurative Architecture. Electa and Rizzoli, Milan and New York.

Rapoport, Amos (1969):
House Form and Culture. Prentice-Hall, Englewood Cliffs NJ.

Venturi, Robert (1966):
Complexity and Contradiction in Architecture. Museum of Modern Art, New York.

PART IV

METHOD FOR DESIGN VALIDATION OF MULTI-ENVIRONMENTAL KNOWLEDGE-BASED SYSTEMS

Editorial Comments:

Validation of correctness is important in multi-environmental situation not only after the completion of a design but at every stage of its construction. Thus we need to compare structures which superficially appear to be identical but need not be as they may have originated from different environments or contexts. The correctness of interaction of a multi-environmental system needs to be tested by simulation multi-environments before the completion of the system. Fuzzy logics and relational products play an important role.

CHAPTER 16

THE USE OF FUZZY RELATIONAL PRODUCTS IN COMPARISON AND VERIFICATION OF CORRECTNESS OF KNOWLEDGE STRUCTURES

M. BEN-AHMEIDA, L.J. KOHOUT AND W. BANDLER

Editorial Comment:

> A formal methodology for structural comparison of knowledge sources based on the triangular products of fuzzy relations is used here to compare two diagnostic structures, yielding surprising and rather unexpected results.

LIST OF CONTENTS

16.1 INTRODUCTION
16.2 SOURCES OF ENDOCRINE MEDICAL KNOWLEDGE
    16.2.1 The CMIT Source
    16.2.2 WTE Source
    16.2.3 Comparison of CMIT and WTE Sources
16.3 TRISYS - THE AUTOMATIC PROCESSING PACKAGE
16.4 SEMANTIC MEANING OF RELATIONAL PRODUCTS
16.5 CRITERIA FOR SELECTING THE APPROPRIATE IMPLICATION OPERATORS
    16.5.1 Results of Analysis of Symptom–Symptom Relations of the CMIT
    16.5.2 Results of Analysis of Symptom–Symptom Relations of the WTE
    16.5.3 Results of Analysis of Sign–Sign Relations of the CMIT
    16.5.4 Results of Analysis of Sign–Sign Relations of the WTE
16.6 THE COMPARISON AND EVALUATION OF THE ENDOCRINE KNOWLEDGE STRUCTURES BY MEANS OF APPROPRIATE IMPLICATION OPERATORS
    16.6.1 Comparison of the Symptom–Symptom Relational Products
    16.6.2 Comparison of the Sign–Sign Relational Products
    16.6.3 Evaluation of Partitions of the Hasse Diagrams of Both Structures

16.6.4 Summary of the Results
16.7 SUBSTRATUM CLASSIFICATION OF ENDOCRINE KNOWLEDGE STRUCTURES
16.8 ACKNOWLEDGMENT
16.9 REFERENCES

16.1. INTRODUCTION

The aim of this chapter is to investigate the medical knowledge structures of two sources which are taken as representing various medical environments.

Our selected medical knowledge consists of two distinctive endocrine diagnostic knowledge structures which we extracted from two major medical sources; the Current Medical Information and Terminology (CMIT), and the Textbook of Endocrinology (WTE). Both these structures relate the selected sets of signs, symptoms, and diseases as well as the linguistic modifiers and equivalent terms. These sources were chosen after consulting a medical expert in the field.

16.2. SOURCES OF ENDOCRINE MEDICAL KNOWLEDGE

The first task was to select the medical diagnostic knowledge as it is documented in the medical textbooks and other medical literature* from the available sources of medical environments. Medical endocrine diagnostic knowledge has been chosen as an experimental area of expertise.

The next stage was to find reliable written sources which are used by the medical professions. Two well known medical endocrine sources were selected by consulting a medical expert in the field. The first source is the Current Medical Information and Terminology (CMIT) fifth edition, edited by Finkel et. al. (1980).

The second source is the Textbook of Endocrinology, fifth edition, edited by R. H. Williams (1974) with contributors by thirty-eight authorities and published by W. B. Saunders Company in 1974. In the next two sections we will review both sources respectively.

The information on the endocrine system is presented in different ways in both sources. The knowledge structures are introduced in a classified way in the CMIT and in an essay form in the WTE. The first source gives usually very brief description for each entity, while the second source provides a detaied description.

The CMIT source is presented by the American Medical Association. The goal of this edition (as the Association claims) is referred to as to be a system for naming and describing diseases. In other words they state that CMIT functions both, as a reference and as "distillate of a vast amount of medical knowledge." The American Medical Association refers to this edition as a trustful and reliable source in identifying, describing, clinical

---

* The medical literature: Definition: For each linguistic environment we have a literature.

recording and reporting of disease entities and their diagnosis. It will be also of value in computerization of medical information.

The Textbook of Endocrinology is the fifth edition 1974; the first edition was published in 1950. This textbook has been translated, into several languages. For example, the third edition has been translated into the Polish language and the fourth edition has been translated into Spanish, French, Italian, Japanese, and Serbo-Croatian.

16.2.1. The CMIT Source

Current Medical Information and Terminology (CMIT) contains names and disease descriptions for eleven body systems in more than 700 pages, which are:

1) body as a whole including Psychology.
2) integumentary system,
3) musculoskeletal system,
4) respiratory system,
5) cardiovascular system,
6) hemic and lymphatic systems,
7) digestive system,
8) urogenital system,
9) endocrine system,
10) nervous systems, and
11) organs of special sense.

In the main body of this book, preferred terms for diseases and appropriate crossreferences appear in the alphabetical order. The preferred term is immediately followed by one or two digit numbers that places the entry into one or two system(s) classification listings. The complete list of the eleven systems appear at the end of the book. The 2-digit system designation is followed by a randomly selected 4-digit identification number that also appears on the first line of each entry.

Disease descriptors are presented systematically in paragraphs with divisions or levels. Abbreviations designate parts of the definition as follows: [at] additional term(s) including synonyms and aponyms, [et] etiology(ies) designating or suggesting cause [s] of the disease, [sm] symptoms or complaints of the patient, [sg] physical signs, including mental status findings observed on examination or during history taking, [lb] laboratory data including special tests and examinations such as EEG, ECG, opthalmoscopy, [xr] patients radiology findings, [cr] disease course and prognosis including complications and results of treatment when known, and [pa] pathological findings including gross and microscopic changes. The following is quotation of Goiter, simple, nonendemic disease, page 273.

GOITER, SIMPLE, NONENDEMIC 08 1257
  see also Cretinism,
  goitrous, sporadic.
  at Goiter, colloid; Goiter, adolescent; Goiter, nodules,
    nontoxic; Goiter euthyroid.
  et Impairment of thyroid, secreting insufficient qualities of
    physiologically active hormone; enhancement of TSH

secretion stimulating glandular growth, activity for intrathyroidal reactions involved in synthesis of thyroid hormone; compensating responses possibly inadequate.
sm Asymptomatic; rarely, sensation of pressures.
sg Most common in adolescent females; in pregnancy, location, following menopause; progressive enlargement of thyroid; entity of simple goiter poorly differentiated from goiterous hypo-thyroidism.

In many instances not all parts of the above definition appear for every entry, and the final entry for a described disease consists of a reference to one or more recent comprehensive reviews as an introduction to the literature.

16.2.2. WTE Source

The textbook of endocrinology contains medical knowledge about disease descriptions of the endocrine system only, which are documented in more than 600 pages. In the main body of this textbook, organs of endocrine system and their diseases appear in chapters with long and detailed descriptions. Each chapter contains several sections, and each section deals with a variety of disorders and abnormalities. These descriptions appear in detailed essays which are not very easy to understand for readers who are not familiar with medical knowledge.

Most sections usually start with a short introduction about the association of one disease to the other. Pathogenesis, physiopathology, and histopathology are in many instances provided. Symptoms and signs usually appear together with a detailed description. The following is a quotation of the clinical picture of the same disease which was quoted in the previous section from CMIT.

This disease is Simple Nontoxic goiter, diffuse and multinodular from textbook of endocrinology, page 212.

The clinical features of Nontoxic Goiter are those that result from thyroid enlargement. Most commonly, the effect either is merely disfiguring or is felt as a tightening of garments worn about the neck. With larger goiter, displacement or compression of the esophagus or trachea may occur, leading to dysphagia, a choking sensation, and inspiratory stridor. Narrowing of the thoracic inlet may compromise the venous return from the head, neck and upper limbs sufficiently to produce venous engagement. This obstruction is accentuated when the patient's arms are raised (Pemberton's sign); dizziness and even syncope may result. Compression of the recurrent laryngeal nerve leading to hoarseness suggest carcinoma rather than nontoxic goiter. Hemorrhage into a module or cyst produces acute, painful enlargement locally and, if crucially situated, can enhance or induce obstructive symptoms. Nontoxic goiter seems to occur more commonly during adolescence, pregnancy, and at the time of the menses. The pathogenetic relationship of these events to the development of goiter is unknown.

In the Textbook of Endocrinology, laboratory tests are usually described in separate sections with each disease. Furthermore, differential diagnosis are provided on many occasions. In this source, in addition, many tables and photographs are provided to show pictures about the effect of some symptoms or signs on the patients. For example, one figure shows a photograph of outer and cut surface of Nontoxic Nodular Goiter observed in patients for 15 years to display variations in size of structure of the modules.

16.2.3. Comparison of CMIT and WTE Sources

As the results of analysis of the CMIT and WTE knowledge structures, we found that there are significant differences between the total number of symptoms and signs in both sources. The first significant finding is that the amount of symptoms and signs available in the WTE exceed in their number that which is available in CMIT. This is significant because the samples taken from both sources range over the same set of diseases.

Figure 16.1 shows the differences between the number of symptoms related to each disease in both sources. It is apparent from this figure, that the number of symptoms of the majority of the diseases from the WTE is greater than the number of symptoms related to the diseases extracted from the CMIT. Furthermore, we can see clearly from the Figure 16.2 that there are significant differences in some diseases, such as the diseases number 1, 4, 8, 15 and 22, which are Thyrotoxicosis, Hypothyroidism, primary Hyperparathyroidism, Andrenal cortex Hyperpliasia and Hyperglycemia, respectively.

Figure 16.2 shows the overall signs of each disease according to the presence of these signs in both sources. We can see in this figure that in most of the number of signs related to diseases in the WTE are more than the number of the signs related to the diseases of the CMIT source.

By looking at both Figures 16.1 and 16.2, we can conclude that from quantitative point of view, that the amount of medical endocrine knowledge available in the WTE is larger in the number of its components than the knowledge available in the CMIT source. It is also worth to note that the differences between the total number of *symptoms* attached to the majority of the diseases of both sources is much bigger than the differences between the total number of signs attached to the same diseases, as is clear in Figures 16.1 and 16.2.

These results show clearly that there is a significant similarities between the structure of the descriptors from both sources. This means that patients from different medical environments report or complain in a similar way and use almost the same descriptors in reporting the same diseases of the same body system.

These results show clearly that there is a significant similarity between the structure of the descriptors from both sources. This means that patients from different medical environments report or complain in a similar way and use almost the same descriptors in reporting the same diseases of the same body system.

In the case of signs, however, there are larger differences between the both sources than in the symptoms case, and in particular when the

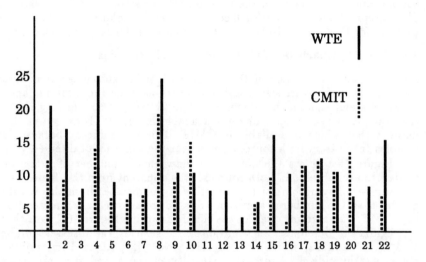

Figure 16.1. Availability of symptoms for each disease in both sources

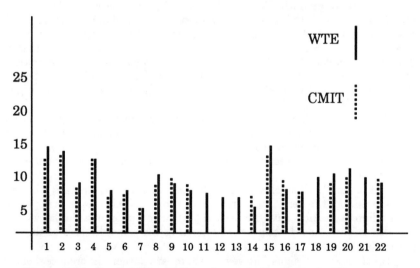

Figure 16.2. Availability of signs for each disease in both sources

Table 16.1 Shows the comparison of descriptors' structure of both sources

Descriptor	CMIT				WTE			
Structure	# sy.	.% sy.	# sy.	.% sy.	# sy.	.% sy.	# sy.	.% sy.
One word	32	40	20	19	47	40	19	17
Two word	37	44	50	46	49	44	41	36
More than two words	12	15	37	35	19	17	53	47

signs consist of more than one word. This indicates that different medical professionals use different descriptor structures in describing the signs, see Table 16.1 for more detail.

From the above findings, we can say that there are more symptoms that are similar to each other, for the similarity comparison made between both sources. This agrees with the conclusion above, in which we stated that there are more similarities between patient's complaints (symptoms) than between what medical professions observations (signs) on the patients.

In later sections we shall see the use of relational products to analyse the knowledge contained in CMIT and WTE leads to a deeper understanding of the differences between the structures of the knowledge in the two sources.

16.3. TRISYS – THE AUTOMATIC PROCESSING PACKAGE

TRISYS is a software package which is described in detail by Bandler and Kohout, (1981). It is used here to calculate the fuzzy matrix of dependencies among symptoms and diseases, and signs and diseases for all the operators. This package also analyses the fuzzy matrix at four different alpha-cuts, which are cut at height, half-upper cut, cut at mean and half-lower cut. At each alpha-cut, the properties of the relation are computed and a Hasse matrix is printed and a corresponding diagram is produced. The input data to this package is in the form of a matrix R, to which we apply different implication operators to form the triangle product. First way to apply is $(s,d) \triangleright (d,s)$, and the result is $\mathcal{R}_F(S,S)$ for the symptoms. The second way is the product $(d,s) \triangleright (s,d)$ and the result is represented by the matrix $\mathcal{R}_F(d,d)$ for the diseases.

To formulate our system that can be implemented by TRISYS, we started by specifying a set of medical endocrine knowledge components (a new set of components will be produced as a result of computation on the sets). A defined set of S of the states of endocrine knowledge from the selected sources is given. A structure R of relation is defined, and this relation involves a set of diseases d, with disease identifiers d_i and a set of manifestations (symptoms or signs) which the set of properties which are identified as symptoms or signs $s_i \ldots s_n$. From this $R(d, s)$ is defined within the cartesian product of the set of d and s which is the set of possible ordered pairs from d and s. Each pair is represented by "0" or "1" in crisp logic or a fuzzy degree in intervals [0,1] inclusive in fuzzy logic. The implementation of these systems will be discussed further in the sequel.

Results of using TRISYS for our sample of medical endocrine knowledge from two medical written sources are given in sections 16.6 and 16.7. The next section starts by providing the basic information for the unfamiliar reader, about how to study the Hasse diagrams which are subsequently used throughout the chapter.

16.4. SEMANTIC MEANING OF RELATIONAL PRODUCTS

The representation and semantic meaning of relations using our actual sample of endocrine knowledge from both sources as well as the semantic meaning of triangular relational products are described in this section. The relations are represented by matrices, which contain our example of endocrine knowledge. The TRISYS software package has the capability to depict the Hasse matrices and Hasse diagrams in a graphical representation of the results. The following is a brief description for the understanding of "symptom-symptom" interelationship by means of Hasse diagrams:

a) The Hasse diagram is depicted by a hierarchy of levels of the "symptom-symptom" relations, which are linked to each other according to their interrelationship.
b) The symptoms at the low levels are implied by the symptoms at the higher level if they are linked.
c) The symptoms which are not linked to other symptoms at a higher level are regarded as independent symptoms.
d) The symptoms at the bottom level of the diagram are mostly implied by many of the symptoms of the higher levels. Therefore the symptoms of the lower level are to be considered the most specific symptoms to the diseases.
e) The symptoms at the top level of the diagram are considered the most independent symptoms and the broadest symptoms for diseases of a body system.

After the computation of the appropriate fuzzy transitive closure of the product of endocrine data, the output values are crispified by means of alpha-cuts at the following levels:

1) Alpha-cut at height
2) Alpha-cut at half-upper
3) Alpha-cut at mean
4) Alpha cut at half-lower

Each cut is a crisp relation, which tend to be an order, (that is a partial order) antisymmetric, reflexive, and transitive, etc. Equivalence classes which can be extracted from the Hasse diagram show that the same symptoms are attached to specific diseases.

The formal application of the triangle product to the endocrine diagnostic data proceeds as follows: The input sets to the TRISYS system are (d,s,g):

$D = d1, d2......dm$ set of diseases
$S = s1, s2......sn$ set of symptoms
$G = g1, g2,.....gp$ set of signs

Where $m = 22$, $n = 48$, $p = 49$ for our selected samples. Using the triangle product new relations are produced utilizing all the implication operators available in TRISYS. The following relations are selected to compute our data by means of the triangle product:

1) R (s,d) represents the relations of symptoms-disease in which (R_{ij}) is the entry to indicate the degree of possessing a symptom i by a disease j.

2) R(g,d) represents the relation of signs-disease in which (R_{ij}) is the entry to indicate the possessing of a sign i by a disease j.

In this stage, the relation over the same 22 diseases from both sources, and their descriptors (48 symptoms, and 49 signs of the elicited samples of endocrine knowledge system were selected from both sources described as depicted in Table 16.2 for the name of the diseases, Table 16.3 for symptom names, and Table 16.4 for sign names).

The entries of the first matrix show the degree to which the sample of diseases possess their symptoms and the entries of the second matrix indicates the degree to which the same sample of diseases posses their signs. The actual knowledge structures were represented in the entries by means of crisp or fuzzy values. These values were estimated by means of degrees of membership corresponding to the linguistic modifiers attached to symptoms and signs.

As a result of executing the 10 operators which were described in using TRISYS, four other tables for each matrix of each operator are automatically displayed. These new tables are products of alpha-cuts described in section ealier.

The original relations produce new composed relations, by means of fuzzy relational products. The new relations have semantic meanings according to the type of the product, the domain semantic meaning, and the range of the original relations.

The products of the above relations are many, and the following are of our concern. They deal with diseases, symptoms, and signs classifications (Figure 16.3).

Any fuzzy relational product of the set $\{\circ, \triangleleft, \triangleright, \square\}$ can replace the asterisk * in the four fuzzy compositions displayed in Figure 16.3.

The analysis and evaluation are performed in two stages which presuppose the following:

I) TRISYS input:

Table 16.2 Selected diseases for the experiment

Organs	Disease No.	Disease Name
Thyroid	1	Thyrotoxicosis
	2	Goiter Toxic Adenoma
	3	Toxic Adenoma
	4	Hypothyroidism
	5	Goiter Adolescent
	6	Thyroditis
	7	Thyroid Carcinoma Anaplastic
Parathyroid	8	Primary Hyperparathyroidism
	9	Hypoparathyroidism
	10	Pseudohypoparathyroidism
	11	Osteopetrosis
	12	Rickets (Vitamin D Deficiency)
	13	Pseudo-deficiency Rickets
	14	Primary Hypercalcetenomea
Adrenal	15	Adrenal Cortex, Hyperplasia
	16	Virilism
	17	Hyperaldosteronism
	18	Primary Adrenal Failure
	19	Pheochromocytoma
Pancreas	20	Diabetes Mellitus Syndrome
	21	Hypo-Osmolar Coma
	22	Hypoglycemia

Table 16.3 The symptoms possessed by the selected 22 diseases

No.	Symptoms	No.	Symptoms
1	Apathy	25	Nocturia
2	Abdominal pain	26	Pressure in neck
3	Anorexia	27	Palpitation
4	Anxiety	28	Polydipsia
5	Bone pain	29	Polyuria
6	Backaches	30	Paraesthesia
7	Blurred vision	31	Restlessness
8	Cramps of muscles	32	Round face
9	Carpopedal spasm	33	Sweating
10	Difficulty in standing	34	Short stature
11	Dyspnea	35	Stiffness
12	Depression	36	Short finger
13	Diarrhoea	37	Shock
14	Fatigue	38	Thirst
15	Hoarseness	39	Trembling of head
16	Hunger	40	Weakness of muscles
17	Headaches	41	Dysphagia
18	Heat intolerance	42	Vomiting
19	Irritability	43	Appetite increased
20	Loss of weight	44	Pain in neck
21	Lethargy	45	Sensitivity to cold
22	Numbness	46	Dry skin
23	Nervousness	47	Thick tongue
24	Nausa	48	Slow speech

Table 16.4 The signs possessed by the selected 22 diseases

No.	Signs	No.	Signs
1	Pigmentation of skin	26	Middle age group
2	Exophthalmos	27	Tiredness in joints
3	Lid lag	28	Hypertension
4	Tachycardia	29	Hypotonia
5	Weight loss	30	Calcified keratitis
6	Pallor	31	Chvostek sign positive
7	30–40 years old	32	Trousseau sign positive
8	Elderly pateints > 50 years	33	Polyuria
9	In females	34	Carpopedal spasm
10	Weakness of muscles	35	Mental retardation
11	Tremor	36	Round face
12	Young age group	37	Thin skin
13	Pain in neck	38	Stiffness
14	Dry skin	39	Growth of facial hair in female
15	Cool skin	40	Increased body hair
16	Cardiac enlargement	41	Wasting muscles
17	Hoarseness of voice	42	Bruising
18	Syncope	43	Dehydration
19	Coma	44	Pigmentation of mucosa
20	Thinning eyebrows	45	Sweating
21	Blood pressure decreased	46	Tumor
22	Adolescent and pregnant women	47	Obesity
23	Slow speech	48	Trembling
24	Enlarged Thyroid	49	Thirst
25	Middle aged women		

1) ds * ds^T

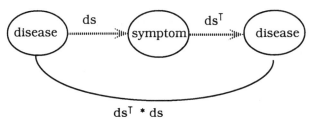

2) ds^T * ds

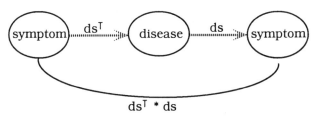

3) dg * dg^T

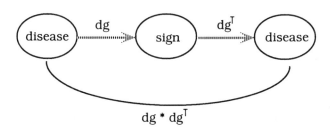

4) dg^T * dg

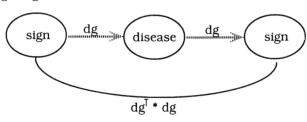

Figure 16.3. Compositions of diagnostic relations

1) Data as described above.
2) Products and meaning as discussed above.
3) Understanding of Hasse diagrams.

II) Evaluation of TRISYS output:
   1) Selection of the most appropriate operators which analyse the medical endocrine knowledge structures that could give good results for diseases classification by symptoms and sign interrelationships.
   2) Comparison of the results of the selected operators by analysing the results of Hasse diagrams of both medical knowledge structures to find out the degree of differences and similarities between both of them.

In the next section we shall address the first step in the second stage by studying the results of using the implication operators to the symptom-disease and sign-disease relations of our medical knowledge structures of both sources.

16.5. CRITERIA FOR SELECTING THE APPROPRIATE IMPLICATION OPERATORS

The representation of the results of the symptom-symptom, sign-sign and disease-disease interrelationships will be represented by Hasse diagrams at various levels of alpha-cut as we pointed out in the previous section. All these were constructed by relational products from symptom-disease, and sign-diseases of both knowledge structures as described before. The composition consists of the following steps:

i) Each set of Hasse diagrams is computed using all logical implication operators in order to decide which are the best operators for the evaluation

ii) Each computation yields a different set of diagrams. As we have 10 distict implication operators, we have 10 different sets for each type of composition to mutually compare. This comparison decides, which Hasse diagrams reflect most faithfully (with least irregularity) the ordering of the symptoms and signs.

The following are the criteria by which the appropriate implication operators were chosen. These criteria were applied to the intermediate results as well as to the end results which were subsequently used for the analysis and comparison of the CMIT and VTE (see the diagrammatic representation in Figure 16.4 for the evaluation sequence, to which the criteria were applied):

1) The *basic assumption* was that the Hasse diagrams that were selected had the maximum number of symptoms or signs *possessed by a single disease* classified in the bottom level (level-O). This is because if we choose the Hasse diagrams with smaller number of symptoms or signs classified, some symptoms or signs disappear. Therefore, we lose some of the information which is needed for the analysis, and evaluation.

2) Then the basic assumption of number 1, was applied to all the Hasse diagrams that satisfy criterion 1. The examination of the selected Hasse diagrams yields the intermediate result: higher number of independent symptoms or signs that are not connected to other symptoms or signs in the higher levels indicates better classification and lesser irregularity. (See figure 16.5). This was accepted as an *additional criterion*.

3) In the Hasse diagrams satisfying the criteria 1 and 2, note the appearance of a higher number of symptoms or signs at all levels than in those diagrams that do not satisfy 1 and 2.

4) Also notice that the diagrams satisfying 1 and 2 contain more partition blocks than the other.

5) As a result of examining the yield of number 3, some "jumping" links were found between the symptoms or signs of various levels in these Hasse diagrams. A link from one level to another not immediatly adjacent, without linking also the level in between, is called a "jumping" link.

6) Another result shows that a fewer number of levels of the hierarchies indicates good structural interrelationships and gives better classification.

16.5.1. Results of Analysis of Symptom–Symptom Relations of CMIT

The symptom-symptom relation used in the analysis of this section was obtained by the composition over the domain of diseases as described in detail in section 4. Let us discuss the results obtained from the first operator 1, and the alpha-cut at the height and half-upper. The Hasse diagram of the Figure 16.6 shows that the symptoms are rather scattered with only one disease appearing at the bottom level. One extra level appears in the diagrams of Figure 16.7 (operator 7), which shows unstructured interrelationship as well as 9 independent symptoms in the upper levels. This clearly indicates the inportance of the choice of adequate implication operators.

The diagrams at mean at alpha-cut and half-lower alpha-cut, show that just one disease has been classified and very few partition blocks are displayed.

In operators 2, 3, 4, 4', 5, 5.5 and 6, tables and diagrams give better results at alpha-cut = 1 for which the index of transitivity = 1. In these diagrams, 10 diseases are classified and 35 partition blocks are represented, but the diagram as still in an irregular state. There are many direct links from the higher levels to the bottom level without going through the middle level and 11 independent symptoms in the upper levels. At half-upper alpha-cut, less diseases are classified and less symptoms are displayed and the diagrams are more scattered than at alpha-cut at height. At alpha-cut = .94 for which the index of transitivity =.81, only 14 symptoms are displayed and one disease is classfied. At half-lower alpha-cut, the diagrams shows just two symptoms.

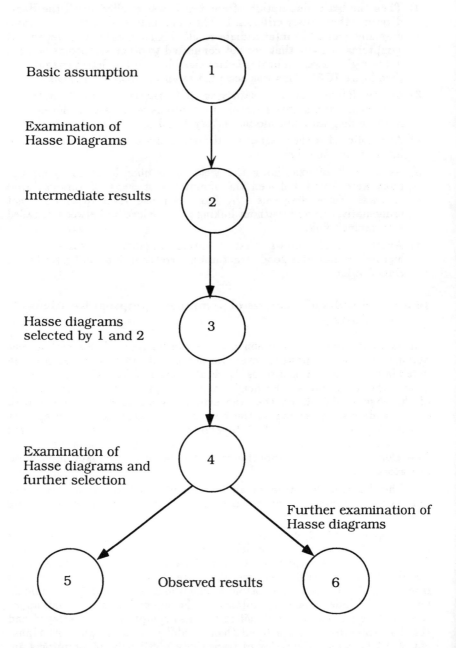

Figure 16.4. The evaluation sequence for the selection of suitable implication operators

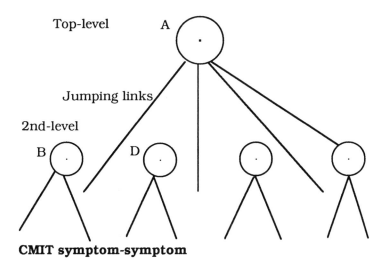

CMIT symptom-symptom

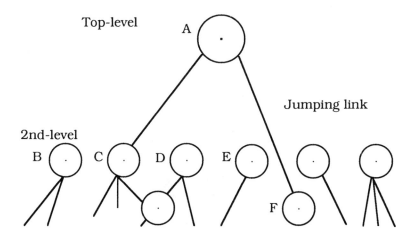

WTE symptom-symptom.

- A, B, and D are independent symptoms.
- C and F are not independent as they have connection with upper levels.

Figure 16.5. The independent symptoms in the higher levels

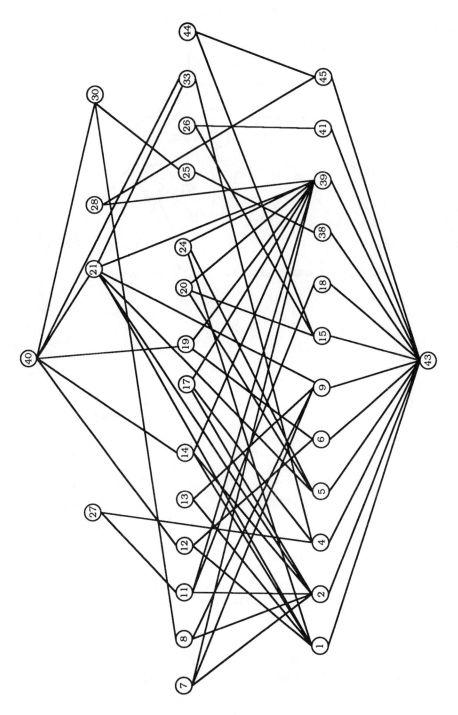

Symptom	Disease indiscernibility class	Organ	Symptom	Disease indiscernibility class	Organ
1	18	A	21	8,10	PT
2	10	PT	24	1,8,18,19	T, PT, A,
4	22	P	25	17,20	A, P
5	8	PT	26	3,5,6,7,14	T, PT
6	15	A	27	1,2,10,18,22	T, PT, A, P
7	9,10,19	PT, A	28	17,19,20	A, P
8	9,10,17	PT, A	30	9,10,17,20	PT, A, P
9	9	PT	33	18,22	A, P
11	1,10,19	T, PT, A	35	19	A
12	9,15,18	PT, A	38	20	P
13	1,14,18,20	T, PT, A, P	40	2,4,8,9,10,15, 18,19,20,22	T, PT, A, P
14	10,18	PT, A	41	3,6	T
15	7	T	43	1	T
17	10,17,19,22	PT, A, P	44	4,6,7,14	T, PT
18	1	T	45	4	T
19	15,18,20	A, P			
20	2,7,8,20	T, PT, P			

T = Thyroid organ; PT = Parathyroid organ; A = Adrenal gland; P = Pancreas gland

Figure 16.6. Symptom-symptom relation of CMIT, using implication operator 1 at height and half-upper

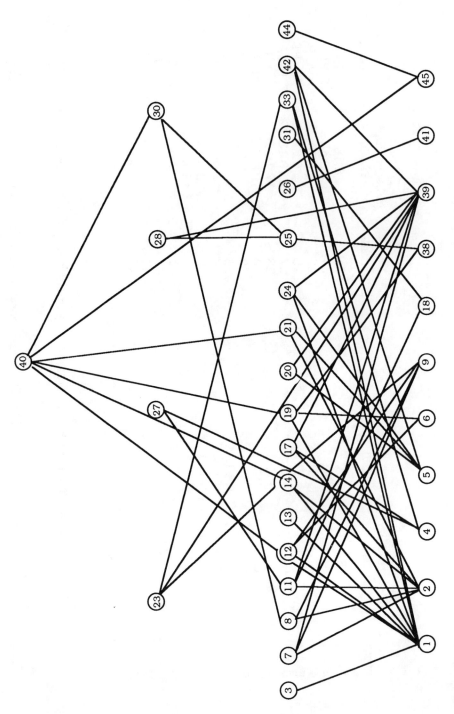

Symptom	Disease indiscernibility class	Organ	Symptom	Disease indiscernibility class	Organ
1	18	A	21	8,10	PT
2	10	PT	23	2,9,18,19,22	T, PT, A, P
3	1,22	T, P	24	1,8,18,19	T, PT, A
4	22	P	25	17,20	A, P
5	8	PT	26	3,5,6,7,14	T, PT
6	15	A	27	1,2,10,18,22	T, PT, A, P
7	1,10,19	PT, A	28	17,19,20	A, P
8	9,10,17	PT, A	30	9,10,17,20	PT, A, P
9	9	PT	31	1,2	T
11	1,10,19	T, PT, A	33	18,22	A, P
12	9,15,18	PT, A	38	20	P
13	1,14,18,20	T, PT, A, P	39	19	A
14	10,18	PT, A	40	2,4,8,9,10,15	T, PT, A, P
17	10,17,19,22	PT, A, P		18,19,20,22	
19	15,18,20	A, T	41	3,6	T
20	2,7,8,20	T, PT, P	42	1,8,18,19	T, PT, A
			44	4,6,7,14	T, PT
			45	4	T

T = Thyroid organ; PT = Parathyroid organ; A = Adrenal gland; P = Pancreas gland

Figure 16.7. Symptom-symptom relation of CMIT, using operator 7 at alpha-cut 1

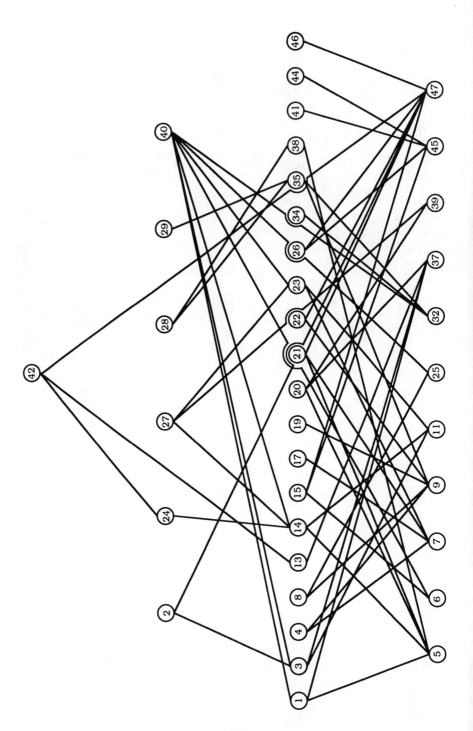

Symptom	Disease indiscernibility class	Organ	Symptom	Disease indiscernibility class	Organ
1	8,12,18	PT, A	25	17	A
2	1,4,12,18	T, PT, A	26	4,5,14	T, PT
3	1,18	T, A	27	1,8,9,19,22	T, PT, A, P
4	19,22	PT, P	28	8,14,20,21	PT, P
5	8	PT	29	8,9,14,20,21	PT, P
6	15	A	32	10	PT
7	22	P	34	10,12	PT
8	9,17	PT, A	35	9,10	PT
9	9	PT	37	18	A
11	1	T	38	14,20	PT,P
13	17,21	A, P	39	19	A
14	1,8	T, PT, A	40	1,2,8,12,15, 16,17,18,22	T, PT, A, P
15	4,5,6,15	T, A	41	5,6,21	T, P
17	19,20,22	A, P	42	1,4,8,16, 18,19,21	T, PT, A, P
19	9,12	P, T			
20	8,18,19,20	PT,A,T	44	5,6,7	T
21	4,8,22	T, PT, P	45	5	T
22	4,9,20	T,PT, P	46	4	T
23	1,22	T, P	47	4	T
24	1,8,16,18,19	T, PT, A			

T = Thyroid organ; PT = Parathyroid organ; A = Adrenal gland; P = Pancreas gland

Figure 16.8. Symptom-symptom relation of WTE, using operator 7 at alpha-cut at height

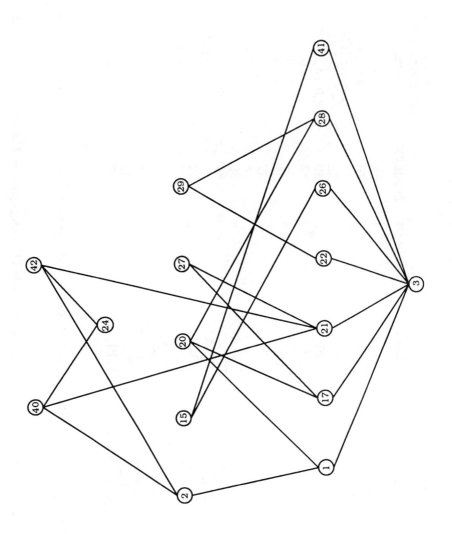

306

Symptom	Disease Indiscernibility Class	Organ	Symptom	Disease Indiscernibility Class	Organ
1	8,12	PT	24	1, 8,16,18	T,PT,A
2	1,4,12,18	T,PT,A	26	4,5,14	T,PT
3	1, 18	T,A	27	1,8,9,19,22	T, PT, A, P
15	4,5,6,15	T, A	28	8,14,20,21	PT,P
17	19,20,22	A,P	40	1,2,7,8,10,12,15 16,17,18,22	T,PT,A,P
20	8,18,19,20	PT,A,P			
21	4,8,22	T,PT,P	41	5,6,21	T,P
22	4,9,20	T,PT,P	42	1,4,8,16,18,19,21	T,PT,A,P

T = Thyroid organ; PT = Parathyroid organ; A = Adrenal gland; P = Pancreas gland

Figure 16.9. Symptom-symptom relation of WTE, using operator 5 at alpha-cut at mean

Diagram of operator 7 provides rather consistent results at alpha-cut at height. At alpha-cut = 1 (see Figure 16.7) and the index of transitivity =.97, the number of the disease classified is 10 , the number of the partition blocks is 33 and the number of the independent symptoms that appeared in the higher levels is equal to 14. The diagrams more regular and there is smaller number of the direct lines from lower levels to higher levels. This means that the interrelationship between symptoms is more structured in this situation. At half-upper alpha-cut, the diagram gives results similar to the previous one.

Operators 2, 3, 4, 5, 5.5 at alpha-cut = 1, give slight differences in symptoms distribution on the hierarchy levels. At the mean and half-lower alpha-cuts, the results are exactly the same as the previous operators at the same mean and half-lower alpha-cuts.

In the case of the operator 8, the diagrams give the same results as the results of operators 7 in the case of alpha-cut=1, and the index of transitivity is 1. By this diagram, 10 diseases are classified and it is quite consistent diagram at alpha-cut = 1 but there are just 26 partition blocks. This is much less than the 33 partition blocks produced by operator 7 and only 7 independent symptoms in the upper levels.

From the above analysis of the results of the operators 1, 2, 3, 4, 4, 5, 5.5, 6, 7 and 8, we can see that operator 8 at alpha-cut at height provides a better classification in general, but operator 7 is the best at alpha-cut = 1 with the the index of transitivity = .97, In this case diseases 1, 4, 8, 9, 10, 15, 18, 19, 20 and 22 are completely classified with 33 partition blocks.

16.5.2. Results of Analysis of Symptom–Symptom Relations of WTE

The symptom-symptom relation of WTE, discussed in this section was obtained by the composition over the domain of diseases as described earlier. All the symptoms elicited from William's Textbook of Endocrinology (WTE) are represented by crisp relations according to the actual data and therefore all the implication operators give the same results. Operator 7 is used and the diagrams give better classifications at alpha-cut = .97 (height), where the index of transitivity is 1 (see Figure 16.8).

From the twenty two diseases processed, 11 diseases are classified and 37 partition blocks are produced and 18 independent symptoms have appeared in the upper level of the diagram. At half-upper alpha-cut, the diagram shows the same result as alpha-cut at height, but at mean alpha-cut (see Fig. 16.9) diagrams give scattered results, and also without any classification for any disease at half-lower alpha-cut, where one disease only is classified.

Diagram of operator 7, at alpha-cut at height with the index of transitivity = 1, or diagrams at alpha-cut = .97, with the index of transitivity = 1 give the best results to the classification of diseases of WTE. Diseases classified by this diagrams are 1, 4, 5, 8, 9, 10, 15, 17, 18, 19, and 22. From the analysis of the results (of the previous sections) of symptom-symptom relations composed over the disease of CMIT and WTE, (see Table 16.4), using all the implication operators mentioned earlier we found out the following:

Table 16.4. Classification results of those symptom-symptom relations of CMIT and WTE that satisfy criteria 1, 2 and 3

Alpha-cut at	Operator	CMIT	WTE
Height	1	very poor	very good
Half-upper	1	very poor	very good
Height	2,3,4,4',5,5.5,6	poor	very good
Half-upper	5,5.5,6,8	good	very good
Half-upper	3,4,4'	poor	very good
Mean	1,2,3,4.4',5,5.5,6,7,8	very poor	very poor
Height	7	very good	very good
Half-upper	7	good	very good
Height	8	good	very good
Half-upper	8	good	very good

1   Very good   Maximum number of diseases classified satisfying all the criteria of section 16.5
2   Good   High number of diseases classified but not satisfying all the criteria.
3   Poor   Less than half of the number of diseases classified by number 1.
4   Very poor   Just a few of diseases classified.

Knowledge-Based Systems for Multiple Environments

a) For the analysis of the endocrine knowledge of the CMIT, *operator 7* at alpha-cut *at height* and the index of transvitivity = .97 gives the best results in which 10 diseases are classified, 33 partition blocks are displayed and 14 independent symptoms appeared.

b) For the analysis of the endocrine knowledge of the WTE, *operator 7* is the best at alpha-cut at *height* and the index of transitivity = 1, in which 11 diseases are classified, 37 partition blocks are produced and 18 independent symtoms are presented in the upper levels.

16.5.3. Results of Analysis of Sign - Sign Relations of the CMIT

The sign-sign relation discussed in this section was obtained by the composition over the domain of diseases as described in detail ealier. The results of the diagram of operator 1 give scattered results at the alpha-cut at height and the index of transitivity = 1 where 5 levels are shown and many direct links between the top levels and the second levels to the bottom level have appeared. Only one disease is classified at the bottom level, 37 partition blocks are displayed from the diagram and 12 independent signs appear in the higher levels of the diagrams (see Figure 16.10).

At the half upper alpha-cut, the diagrams show the same results as those for the previous operator 1, at the same alpha-cut. For alpha-cut =.95 with the index of transitivity =.55, no diseases are classified and just 9 signs are displayed. At the half-lower alpha-cut, very few partition blocks are shown in the diagrams, without disease classification. Operator 1 therefore is not of suitable for evaluation of the CMIT symptom-disease relation, since it does not produce structural results.

Operators 2, 3, 4, 4', 5, 5.5 and 6 (diagrams at alpha-cut =1 with the index of transitivity =1), and operators 2, 3, 4, and 4' (diagrams at alpha-cut at half-upper with the index of transitivity = 1) give almost the same results. They show better results than the diagrams of the operator 1 from the point of view of disease classifications and the appearance of independent signs, but the diagrams remain scattered with more direct links from top levels to lower levels than the previous operator 1.

Operators 2 and 4 (diagrams at alpha-cut .94 and the index of transitivity = .54) do not display a wide range of partition blocks (13 partitions from 49 sign) and no diseases are classified. Operators 3 and 4 (diagrams at mean alpha-cut) give the same results as operators 2 and 4 diagrams with different distribution. Operators 5, 5.5, and 6 (diagrams at alpha-cut = .97 and the index of transitivity = .95), give almost the same diagrams as operators 1 with diagrams at alpha-cut at height. The differences between both diagrams are the appearance of more partition blocks in the diagrams of operators 5, 5.5 and 6, they are rather more scattered, one sign are displayed in the bottom levels and 12 sign appeared in the higher levels. At mean alpha-cut diagram displays only 13 signs and they do not classify any disease.

For operator 7, diagrams give rather regular results as the previous operators except for the value of alpha-cut equal to 1 and the index of transitivity equal to 0.96, in which 9 diseases are completely classified with

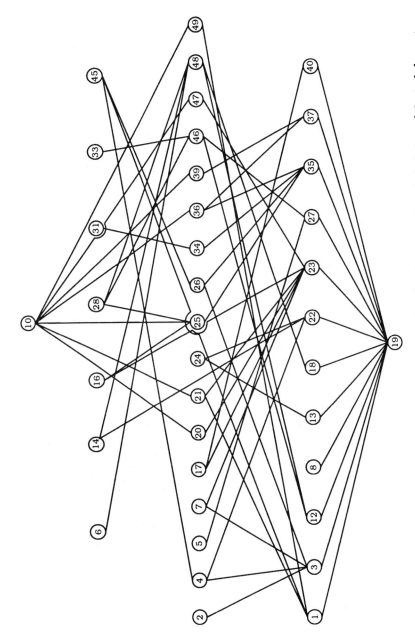

Figure 16.10. Sign-sign relation product of CMIT, using implication operators 1, 5, 5.5, and 6 at alpha-cut at height

311

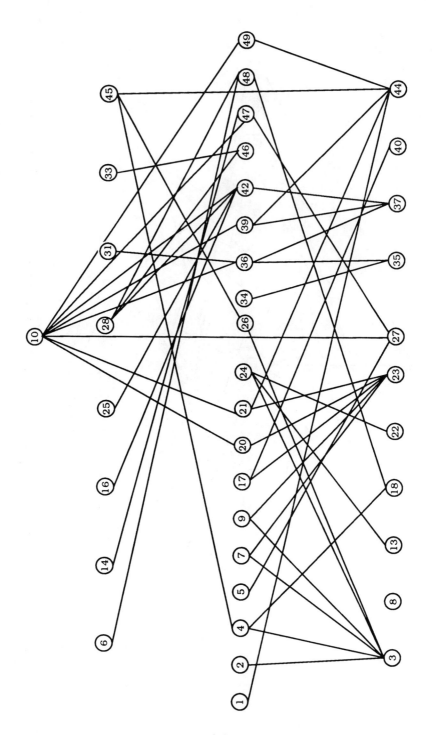

Sign	Disease Indiscernibility Class	Organ	Sign	Disease Indiscernibility Class	Organ
1	16,18	A	24	3,5,6,7,14	T,PT
2	1,2	T	25	6,8,15,17	T,PT,A
3	1	T	26	6,8,15,17	T,PT,A
4	1,22	T,A	27	8	PT
5	2,7,8,20	T,PT,P	28	14,15,17,19,22	PT,A,P
6	19,20,22	A,P	31	9,10,17	PT,A
7	1,4,6,13,17	T,PT,A	33	8,14,17,19,20	PT,A,P
8	2,9	T,PT	34	9,10	PT
9	1,2,4,6,14,15,17	T,PT,A	35	10	PT
10	2,4,8,9,10,15	T,PT,A,P	36	10,15	PT,A
13	17,18,20,22	T,PT	37	15	A
14	7,14	T,P	39	15,20	A,P
16	4,5,20	T,A	40	16	A
17	3,4,15,17	T,A	42	17,19	A
18	3,4,16	P	44	18	A
20	22	T,PT	45	1,7,18	T,A
21	4,9	T,A	46	8,14,19	PT,A
22	4,18	T	47	4,20	T,P
	5		48	19,22	A,P
			49	18,20	A,P

T = Thyroid organ; PT = Parathyroid organ; A = Adrenal gland; P = Pancreas gland

Figure 16.11. Sign-sign relation product of CMIT, using operator 7 at alpha-cut at height

a range of 39 partition blocks. These diagrams are quite consistent and 15 independent signs appeared in the upper levels (see Figure 16.11). At half upper alpha-cut the results are the same as the diagrams of operators 5 at the same alpha-cut. At means alpha-cut, diagrams are more scattered than the mean alpha-cut diagrams of the other operators, and no diseases are classified. Operator 7 at alpha-cut 1 and the index of transitivity = .96 is the best candidate so far for classification of diseases of the CMIT.

Operator 8 (diagrams at alpha-cut at height and index of transitivity = 1) shows better results than all the previous operators except operator 7 at alpha-cut=1 and the index of transitivity = .96. In the diagrams of operator 8 at alpha-cut 1 and the index of transitivity = 1, 9 diseases are classified with a range of 32 partition blocks represented in the diagrams and 13 independent signs appearing in the higher levels.

At alpha-cut = .94 and the index of transitivity = .49 diagrams are more irregular than any other operators diagrams at the same alpha cut, with two more signs represented in the diagram. Diagrams at half-lower alpha-cut of all operators from 1 to 8 are not of much use for CMIT endocrine knowledge, since they provide bad classification with limited range of partition blocks (see Figure 16.12).

From the above discussion and analysis of the results of operators 1, 2, 3, 4, 4', 5, 5.5, 6, 7, and 8, the diagrams at mean, and half-lower alpha-cuts are not suitable for endocrine disease classification of the CMIT. All implication operators at height and half-upper alpha-cuts other than operators 7 and 8, are also not of much use. In the next section, data from Williams Textbook of Endocrinology (WTE) will be analysed and the structures of the diagrams will be described.

16.5.4. Results of Analysis of Sign–Sign Relations of the WTE

The sign-sign relation used in the analysis of this section was obtained by the composition over the diseases of WTE as described in the above sections. The results of the diagrams of operator 1 at alpha-cut height and the index of transitivity = 1 give the same structures as diagrams at alpha-cut at half-upper=.97, and the index of transitivity = 1. These diagrams show quite scattered results, 10 diseases are classified with 39 partition blocks and 11 independent signs appear at the higher levels. At the alpha-cut at mean, the number of partition blocks that are displayed is 11 and no diseases classified.

All operators diagrams at half-lower alpha-cut give the same results. Just one partition block is involved in the diagram, and two signs.

Operators 2, 3, 4, 4', 5, 5.5, and 6 diagrams at alpha-cut at height and the index of transitivity = 1, and operators 2 and 4 diagrams at half-upper alpha-cut and the value of the index of transitivity equal to 0.97 offer the same results. These diagrams have a mesh interrelations with jumping links between the signs of all levels and the involvement of 40 partition blocks. At the means alpha-cut diagrams, 15 partition blocks are displayed and no diseases are classified.

Operators 3, 4, 5, 5.5 and 6 diagrams at alpha-cut .97 and the index of transitivity = 1 give the same results as operator 1 diagrams at alpha-cut

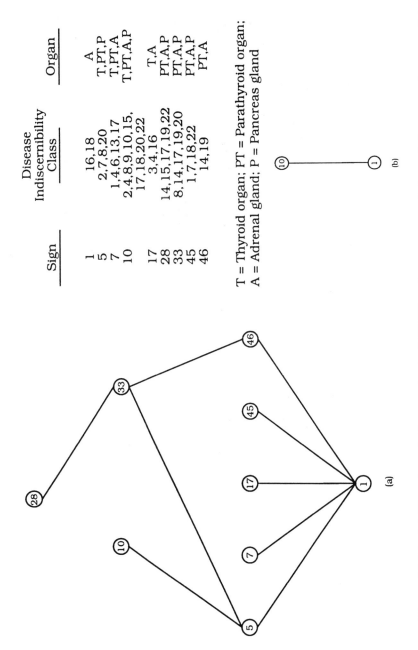

Figure 16.12. (a) Sign-sign relation product of CMIT, using operators 1-8 at alpha-cut and mean. (b) Sign-sign relation product of CMIT, using operators 1-8 at alpha-cut at half-lower

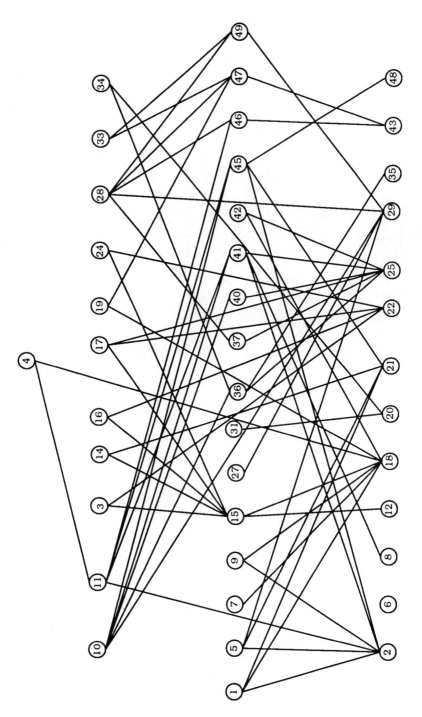

316

Sign	Disease Indiscernibility Class	Organ	Sign	Disease Indiscernibility Class	Organ
1	18	A	24	3,4,5,6,7	T
2	1	T	25	15	A
4	1,3,4,19,21,22	T,A,P	27	7,13,18,19	T,PT,A
5	1,8,18,19,20	T,PT,A,P	28	8,14,15,17,19,21	PT,A,P
6	11,20,22	PT,A	29	8	PT
7	3,4	T	31	9,17	PT,A
8	2	T	33	8,18,20,21	PT,A,T
9	1,2,16	T,A	34	9,10,15,22	PT,A,P
10	1,2,8,12,16,17,18	T,PT,A	35	10	PT
11	1,19	T,A	36	10,15	PT,A
12	3	T	37	15,19	A
13	3,4,5,6	T	40	14,15	PT,A
14	3,4,18	T,A	41	1,2,14,17	T,PT,A
15	4	A	42	4,8,11,13,15,18,20	T,PT,A,T
16	3,4,5,17	T,A	43	21	P
17	4	T	45	1,18,22	T,A,P
18	4	T	46	19,21	A,P
19	4,20,21,22	T,P	47	20,21	P
20	9	PT	48	19,22	A,P
21	18	A	49	8,13,20	PT,P
22	5	T			

T = Thyroid organ; PT = Parathyroid organ; A = Adrenal gland; P = Pancreas gland

Figure 16.13. Sign-sign relation product of WTE, using operator 7 at alpha-cut at height

at height, 10 diseases are classified, 39 partition blocks are displayed and 13 independent signs are presented in the higher levels.

Operators 7 diagrams give rather irregular results except at alpha-cut $= 1$ with the index of transitivity $= .98$ where 11 diseases were classified with a range of 40 partition blocks in the diagrams and 18 independent signs in the higher levels. The diagram in this case seem to be less scattered with less direct links between sign of the upper levels and lower level than any diagram of the previous operators so far (see Figure 16.13). At half-upper alpha-cut, diagrams give the same results as diagrams of operator 3 with the same alpha-cut and index of transitivity where 14 partition blocks are displayed.

For operator 8, diagram at alpha-cut 1 and the index of transitivity $= 1$ gives quite similar results as the diagrams of operators 7 at the height alpha-cut, with the appearance of smaller number of partition blocks than operator 7 and less independent signs, but the same number of diseases are classified.

At half-upper alpha-cut results of the diagrams are the same as results of the diagrams of operator 8 at the same alpha-cut. At the mean alpha-cut the diagrams are similar to the diagrams of operator 7 with a different distribution of symptoms. In this diagram 15 signs only are displayed.

From the foregoing discussion and the analysis of the results of the above sections, (see Table 16.5) we can see that the appropriate operators for the diseases classification are:

i) For the *WTE sign-sign* relation, both operator 7 and operator 8 are good, but *operator 7* is the best at alpha-cut $= 1$ with the index of transitivity $= .98$.

ii) Using operator 7, 11 diseases are classified with 40 partition blocks. The diagrams are less scattered than those at any other operator and leave a higher number of independent signs than any diagram before. The classified diseases are 1, 2, 3, 4, 8, 9, 10, 15, 16, 18 and 22.

iii) By looking at the results of operators 7 and 8 diagrams of *CMIT* we can see that operator 8 at height alpha-cut provides a better solution for diseases classification in general, but *operator 7* is considered the best operator at alpha-cut at height, and the index of transitivity $= .96$, where more partition blocks are represented and less scattered diagram have appeared than operators 8.

iv) Using operator 7 diagrams at alpha cut at height the following diseases are classified: 1, 4, 5, 8, 10, 15, 16, 18 and 22 from the total of 22 diseases, and 39 partition blocks are represented in the diagrams and 15 independent signs appeared in the upper levels.

Table 16.5. Classification results of those sign-sign relations of CMIT and WTE that satisfy criteria 1, 2 and 3

Alpha-cut at	Operator	CMIT	WTE
Height	1	very poor	good
Half-upper	1	very poor	good
Height	2,3,4,4′,5,5.5,6	good	good
Half-upper	,3,4,4′	good	good
Half-upper	5,5.5	very poor	good
Height	7	very good	very good
Height	8	good	good
Half-upper	7,8	very poor	good
Mean	1,2,3,4,4′,5,5.5,6,7,8	very poor	very poor
Half-lower	1,2,3,4,4′,5,5.5,6,7,8	very poor	very poor

1 Very good Maximum number of diseases classified satisfying all the criteria of section 16.5
2 Good Higher number of diseases classified but not satisfying all the criteria.
3 Poor Less than half of the number of diseases classified by number 1.
4 Very poor Just a few of diseases classified.

16.6. THE COMPARISON AND EVALUATION OF THE ENDOCRINE KNOWLEDGE STRUCTURES BY MEANS OF THE APPROPRIATE IMPLICATION OPERATORS

In this section we compare the Hasse diagrams computed by means of implication operator 7 for both, CMIT and WTE endocrine sources. The results of applying this operator in both knowledge structures are evaluated by analysing and comparing the results of the new relational products represented diagrammatically in the Hasse diagrams using the same criteria.

16.6.1. Comparison and Evaluation of the Symptom–Symptom Relational Products

Having decided on the appropriate operators, and starting from the diagram of Figure 16.7 of the CMIT knowledge structures and the diagram of Figure 16.8 of the WTE, we can see that in Figure 16.8 there are more direct links between the higher level and the lower level without the middle levels being linked, while in the WTE results Figure 16.7, there are not so many of these links.

The diagram of the CMIT results is represented by 11 symptoms in level-0, 18 symptoms in level-1, 4 symptoms in level-2 and 1 symptom in level-3 (the highest level), but the symptoms of the WTE are represented by 11 symptoms in level-0, 20 symptoms in level-1, 6 symptoms in level-2 and 1 symptom in level-3.

Looking at the links between symptoms and the distribution of these symptoms and the individual level, we can see that symptoms in the WTE are more structured into levels and that the interrelations between the diseases are not the same in both sources. Furthermore, by examining the diseases having the symptoms classified in the bottom level (level-0) of the Hasse diagrams, we find that 10 diseases are completely classfied by the results of the CMIT knowledge structures while 11 disease are completely classified in the WTE (see Table 16.6). From the symptoms that are displayed in the bottom level of both diagrams only 5 are the same. In the next level (level-1), only 10 symptoms are the same, from about 20 symptoms in both diagrams, and only 2 diseases are the same at level-2.

By looking at the independent symptoms in the diagrams of the results of both structures, we find that 14 symptoms appeared in the CMIT and 18 in the WTE.

Examining the attachment of these symptoms to the syndromes we note that in the CMIT diagram, 1 symptom in the upper level is attached to 1 syndrome, 3 symptoms in the middle level attached to 5 syndromes, and 4 symptoms in the bottom level attached to 5 syndromes, while in the WTE 2 symptoms from the upper level are attached to 3 syndromes, 6 synptoms are attached to 9 syndromes at the middle level, and 3 symptoms to 3 syndromes in the bottom level. This will be highlighted in the next chapter.

Table 16.6. Diseases classified by symptom-symptom relation displayed by Hasse diagrams in the bottom levels

	CLASSIFIED DISEASES	
Organs	CMIT	WTE
Thyroid	Thyrotoxicosis	Thyrotoxicosis
	Hypothyroidism	Hypothyroidism
		Goiter adolescent
Parathyroid	Primary hypoparathyroidism	Primary hypoparathyroidism
	Hypoparathyroidism	Hypoparathyroidsm
	Pseudohypoparathyroidism	Pseudohypoparathyroidism
Adrenal	Adrenal cortex hyperplasia	Adrenal cortex hyperplasia
	Primary adrenal failure	Hyperaldosteronism
	Pheochromocytoma	Pheochromocytoma
		Primary adrenal failure
Pancreas	Diabetes mellitus syndrome	
	Hyperglycemia	Hyperglycemia

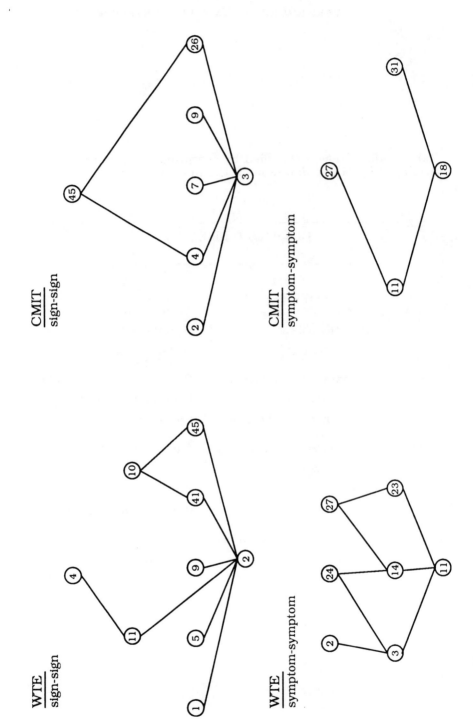

WTE

Sign	Disease Indiscernibility Class	Organ
1	1,4,18	T,A
2	1	T
4	1,3,4,19,21,22	T,A,P
5	1,8,18,19,20	T,A,P
9	1,2,4,14,15	T,PT,A
10	1,2,7,8,12,16,17,18,20,22	T,PT,A,P
11	1	T
41	1,2,14,17	T,PT,A
45	1,18,22	T,A,P

Symptom	Disease Indiscernibility Class	Organ
2	1,4,12,18	T,PT,A
3	1,18	T,A
11	1	T
14	1,8	T,PT
23	1,22	T,P
24	1,8,16,18,19	T,PT,A
27	1,8,9,18,22	T,PT,A,P

CMIT

Sign	Disease Indiscernibility Class	Organ
2	1,2	T
3	1	T
4	1,22	T,P
7	1,4,6,13,17	T,PT,A
9	1,2,4,6,14,15,17	T,PT,A
26	6,8,15,17	T,PT,A
45	1,7,18,22	T,A,P

Symptom	Disease Indiscernibility Class	Organ
11	1,10,19	T,PT,A
18	1	T
27	1,2,10,18,22	T,PT,A,P
31	1,2	T

T = Thyroid organ; PT = Parathyroid organ; A = Adrenal gland; P = Pancreas gland

Figure 16.14. Diagnostic trees of thyrotoxicosis disease of both sources

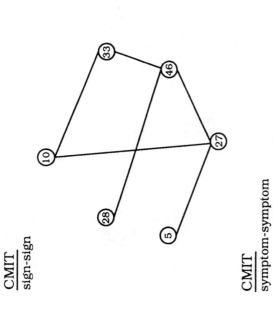

WTE
sign-sign

CMIT
sign-sign

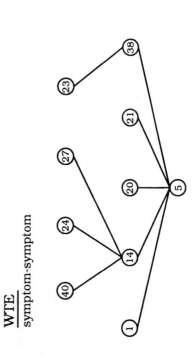

WTE
symptom-symptom

CMIT
symptom-symptom

WTE			CMIT		
Sign	Disease Indiscernibility Class	Organ	Sign	Disease Indiscernibility Class	Organ
5	1,8,18,19,20	T,PT,A,P	5	2,7,8,20	T,PT,P
10	1,2,8,12,16,17,18	T,PT,A	10	2,4,8,9,10,15, 17,18,20,22	T,PT,A,P
27	7,13,17,18	T,PT,A	27	8	PT
28	8,14,15,17,19,21	PT,A,P	28	14,15,17,19,22	PT,A,P
29	8	PT	33	8,14,17,19,20	PT,A,P
33	8,18,20,21	PT,A,P	46	8,14,19	PT,A
42	4,8,11,13,15,18,20	T,PT,A,P			
49	8,13,20	PT,P			

Symptom	Disease Indiscernibility Class	Organ	Symptom	Disease Indiscernibility Class	Organ
1	8,12,18	PT,A	5	8	PT
5	8	PT	20	2,7,8,20	T,PT,P
14	1,8	T,PT	21	8,10	PT
20	8,18,19,20	PT,A,P	24	1,8,18,19	T,PT,A
21	4,8,22	T,PT,P	40	2,4,8,9,10,15, 18,19,20,22	T,PT,A,P
23	1,22	T,P	42	1,8,18,19	T,PT,A
24	1,8,16,18,19	T,PT,A			
27	1,8,9,19,22	T,PT,A,P			
38	8,14,20	PT,P			

T = Thyroid organ; PT = Parathyroid organ; A = Adrenal gland; P = Pancreas gland

Figure 16.15. Diagnostic trees of primary hyperparathyroidism of both sources

From the above discussed analysis of the results of both structures of CMIT and WTE, we can confirm that *symptom-disease structure of CMIT* endocrine knowledge *differs from the symptom-disease structures of the WTE*. The dissimilarity of their knowledge is not only due to quantitative reasons but also because the *interrelations* of symptoms are different.

16.6.2. Comparison and Evaluation of Sign–Sign Relational Products

We start from diagram Figure 16.11 of the sign-sign relation of the CMIT source at the alpha-cut $= 1$ and the index of transitivity $= .96$.

We can see from these results that there are several links from the top level to the lower level directly, without going through the middle level. This is not the case with the results of the diagram (Figure 16.13) of the WTE. In addition, connection lines from the signs in level-2 in the diagram of the CMIT are linked to small group of signs in level-1 which is not the case in the WTE results. The above points to the irregularities in the signs interrelations of the knowledge structures of CMIT source.

Having discussed the links between the signs, we now examine the position of the signs on the levels of the Hasse diagrams where both diagrams in Figure 16.11 and Figure 16.13 have four levels and the number of signs from the top level to the bottom level are 1,8,19 and 11, while in the other diagram of the WTE, the signs are 1,11,16 and 13 from the top to the bottom level.

This distribution of the signs between levels of Hasse diagram shows that signs are more structured in the WTE case than for the CMIT. Furthermore, the diseases that are classified in the bottom level of the CMIT diagram are 9 and 11 diseases are classified in the level-0 of the diagram of the WTE (see Table 16.7). At the bottom levels of both diagrams, only three signs are the same, and 7 diseases are the same; and in level-1 about half of the symptoms are the same. Furthermore, there are 15 independent signs in the CMIT structure and 18 in the WTE structure.

From the results of the above analysis of the sign-sign relations of the knowledge structures of both CMIT and WTE sources, we find that *sign-disease structure of WTE differs from the sign-disease structure of CMIT*. This also confirms the results of the previous section in which the differences of both knowledge structures are not because of statistical reasons but it is because of the differences in the interrelations of signs.

16.6.3. Evaluation of Partitions of the Hasse Diagrams of Both Structures

In this section we examine samples of parts of the results of Hasse diagrams of both knowledge structures, CMIT and WTE. These parts are selected randomly and represent trees that classify the same disease in both sources. By analysing the results from the symptoms and sign structures of both sources of the partitions of these diagrams in view of the classified diseases, we can **extract diagnostic strategies** from both sources.

As an example, two classified diseases are selected randomly from level-0 which represent 2 different organs to compare the levels of diseases

Table 16.7. Diseases classified by sign-sign relations as they are displayed by Hasse diagrams

	CLASSIFIED DISEASES	
Organs	CMIT	WTE
Thyroid	Thyrotoxicosis Hypothyroidism Goiter adolescent	Thyrotoxicosis Hypothyroidism Goiter toxic modular Toxic adenoma
Parathyroid	Primary Hyperparathyroidism Pseudohypoparathyroidism	Primary Hyperparathyroidsm Pseudohypoparathyroidism Hypoparathyroidism
Adrenal	Adrenal cortex hyperplasia Primary adrenal failure Virilism	Adrenal cortex hyperplasia Primary adrenal failure
Pancreas	Hyperglycemia	Hyperglycemia Hyposmolar

diagnosis obtained from the the available information of each source. The same diseases are selected from both sources.

In Figure 16.14, we can see that the symptoms are not completely the same in diagnosing the same diseases of both sources. The same disease appears at the bottom of the trees but not the same symptoms. The number of symptoms and signs participating in the diagnosis process in this disease in the WTE is larger than in the CMIT. Two symptoms in both trees and four signs are exactly the same and the others are different in the case of "Thyrotoxicosis" disease.

By studying one of the Parathyroid diseases "Primary Hyperparathyroidism" (see Figure 16.15), we find that there is no complete similiarity betwen the symptoms of both trees, but the symptoms of the lower levels are attached to the same disease. In addition to that, the total number of symptoms in both trees differ, but all symptoms are attached to disease 8, at all levels of the tree.

From the above analysis we can see clearly that the symptom and sign-disease structures for the same individual diseases of both sources differ. It is very obvious also that there is more information in the WTE than CMIT.

16.6.4. Summary of the Results

The results of the foregoing analysis can be summarized as follows:

1) The symptom-disease structures of CMIT and WTE sources differ from each other.
2) The sign-disease structures of both sources are also different.
3) The differences between the sign-disease structures of both sources are greater than the differences between the symptom-disease structures of both sources.
4) There is more information contained in the WTE than the CMIT.
5) The differences between the interrelations of the symptoms of both sources seem to be smaller than the differences between the sign interrelations of both sources.
6) The dissimilarity between the knowledge structures of both sources is not caused only by the statistical reasons but primarily also because the internal relational structure of symptoms is different from the relational structure of signs.

16.7. SUBSTRATUM CLASSIFICATION OF ENDOCRINE KNOWLEDGE STRUCTURES

With regard to the availability of partitions of the endocrine diseases with respect to organs, the endocrine data gives the opportunity to examine the relation of descriptors of diseases (i.e. symptoms, signs, syndromes) to the corresponding body systems. In the terminology of Activity Structures this means the attachment of functional structures (descriptor of disorder) to the substratum structures (body organs), cf. Kohout (1978).

In this section, we shall examine the relationship between the symptoms and body organs, and signs and body organs from the relational products of both knowledge structures, in order to determine whether the findings of the previous sections, concerning the differences between the functional structures of medical endocrine knowledge are also valid for substratum structures (i.e. endocrine body organs).

From these relations, by a relational composition, new relations, involving susbstratum elements only were obtained, which have their semantic meaning formed according to the types of products, the domain semantic meaning and the range meaning of the original relations (cf. Bandler and Kohout 1979, 1986). The form and semantics of these relations is given below.

From the above results we can see that the knowledge structures of both sources differ not only from the symptoms and signs interrelationships point of view, but also the combination of both gives different structures which indicate that there are significant differences between the structures of the diagnostic knowledge of both sources (see Figure 16.17). From the foregoing discussion we can conclude that the dissimilarity between medical endocrine knowledge of both sources CMIT and WTE, is not only from the functional structure point of view but also the relations between the functional and substratum structures of both sources are different.

Apart from the above, other interesting results can be extracted from the analysis of functional and substratum structures (cf. Ben-Ahmeida 1987) of the appropriate results of the Hasse diagrams. It is obvious when we examine the levels of symptoms and signs and their attachment to diseases, syndromes and body organs, diagnostic levels can be detected. These diagnostic levels appear more clearly in the results of WTE than CMIT. In the upper levels of the diagram, most of symptoms and signs are attached to the whole body system. When we go down, in the middle levels most of the symptoms and signs are attached to syndromes and if we go down further, the attachment of most of symptoms and signs appears to be to specific diseases.

In summary if we start in the diagrams with the selection of higher level symptoms and signs first and continue descending, this diagnostic path can be represented as:

Body system $\longrightarrow$ syndromes $\longrightarrow$ specific diseases.

16.8. ACKNOWLEDGMENT

The authors are indebted to Professor John Anderson of Kings College Medical School, London for extracting the signs/symptoms vs. diseases relations from the textual description of endocrine diseases in WTE. To extract the relational information from a plain medical text is by no means trivial but arduous task. Without his kind help the comparison results presented in this chapter would not have materialised.

The research has been partially supported by the National Science Foundation (U.S.A.) grant IST-8604575.

KNOWLEDGE-BASED SYSTEMS FOR MULTIPLE ENVIRONMENTS

1) sd o do

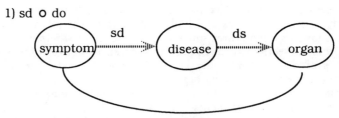

sd o do
Symptom s is related to an organ o, if s and o have at least one disease d in common

2) gd o do

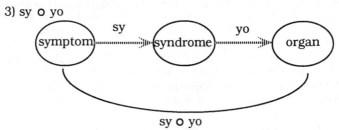

gd o gd
Sign g is related to an organ o, if g and o have at least one disease d in comon.

3) sy o yo

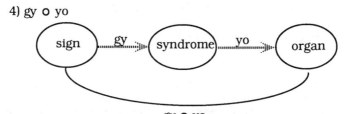

sy o yo
Symptom s is related to an organ, o, if s and o have at least one syndrome y in common.

4) gy o yo

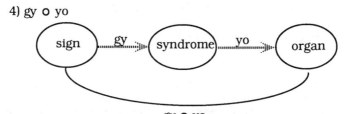

gy o yo
Sign g is related to an organ o, if g and o have at least one syndrome y in common.

Figure 16.16. Composition of diagnostic relations

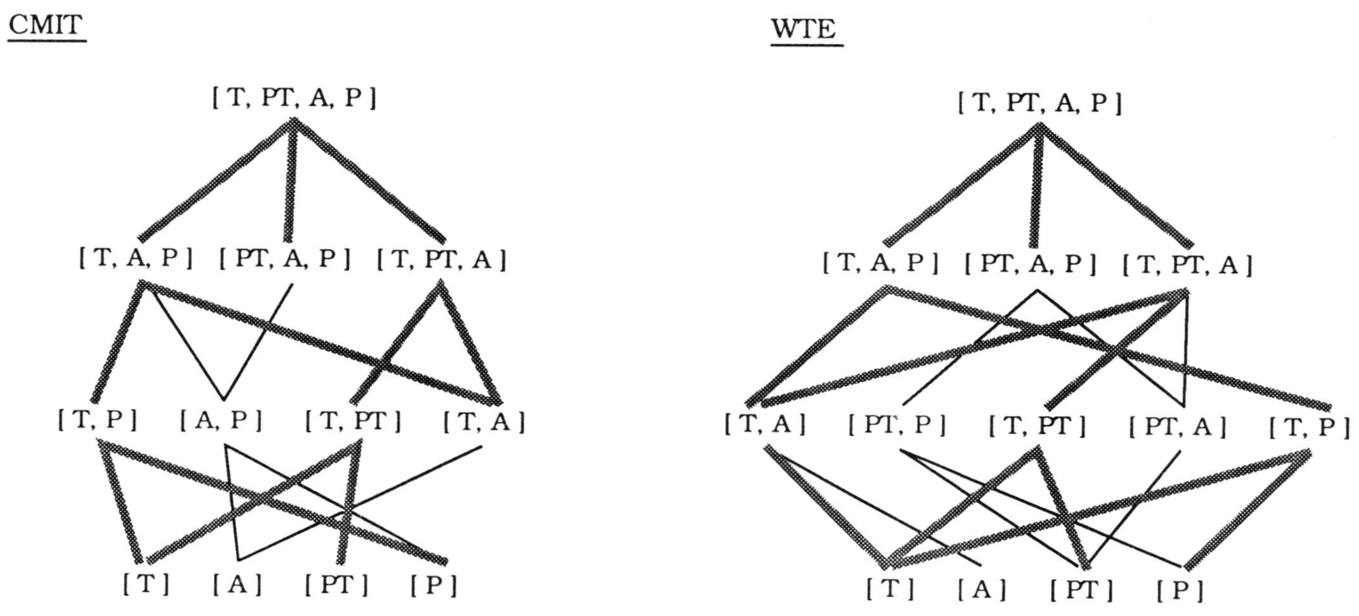

Figure 16.17. Symptom-organ and sign-organ product

16.9. REFERENCES

Bandler, W. and Kohout, L.J. (1979):
The use of new relational products in clinical modelling. In: Gaines, B.R. (ed.) General Systems Research: A Science, a Methodology, a Technology (Proc. 1979 North American Meeting of the Society for General Systems Research), SGSR, Louisville, Kentucky, U.S.A., 240–246.

Bandler, W. and Kohout, L.J. (1980a):
Semantics of implication operators and fuzzy relational products. *International Journal of Man-Machine Studies*, **12**, 89–116. Reprinted in Mamdani, E. H. and Gaines B. R. (1981).

Bandler, W. and Kohout, L.J. (1980b):
Fuzzy relational products as a tool for analysis and synthesis of the behaviour of complex artificial and natural systems. In: Wang, P.P. and Chang, S.K. (eds.). *Fuzzy Sets: Theory and Applications to Policy Analysis and Information Systems*. Plenum Press, New York, 341–367.

Bandler,W., and Kohout,L.J. (1981):
The identification of hierarchies in symptoms and patients through computation of fuzzy triangular products and closures. In: Parslow, R. D. (ed.), *BCS '81: Information Technology for the Eighties*, Heyden & Son, London, 191–194.

Bandler, W. and Kohout, L.J. (1982):
Fast fuzzy relational algorithms. In: Ballester, A., Cardus, D. and Trillas, E. (eds.), *Proc. Second Internat. Conference on Mathematics at the Service of Man* (Las Palmas, Canary Islands, Spain, 28 June - 3 July 1982). Universidad Politechnica de las Palmas, 123–131.

Bandler, W. and Kohout, L.J. (1986):
A survey of fuzzy relational products in their applicability to medicine and clinical psychology. In: Kohout, L.J., and Bandler, W. (1986), 107–118.

Bandler, W. and Kohout, L.J. (1988):
Special properties, closures and interiors of crisp and fuzzy relations. *Fuzzy Sets and Systems*, **26**, 317–331.

Ben-Ahmeida, M.,M. (1987):
A Study of the Design, Reliability and Knowledge Structures of a Multi-environmental Medical Expert System, Ph.D thesis, Department of Computer Science, Brunel University of West London, April 1987.

Finkel, A. S., Gordon, B. L., Baker, M. R. and Fanta. C. M. eds. (1980):
Current Medical Information and Technology, (CMIT) American Medical Assocciation, 5th edition.

Kohout, L.J. (1974):
Algebraic models in computer-aided medical diagnosis. In: J. Anderson

(ed.), *Proceedings of MEDINFO 74*, North Holland, Amsterdam, 575–579, addendum and list of typographical errors 1069–70.

Kohout, L.J. (1978):
The functional hierarchies of the brain, In Klir, G. (ed.), *Applied General System Research: Recent Development and Trends.* Plenum Press, New York, 531–544.

Kohout, L.J.,and Bandler,W.(1986):
Knowledge Representation in Medicine and Clinical Behavioural Science, An Abacus Book, Gordon and Breach, London and New York.

Mamdani, E.H. and Gaines, B. R. eds. (1981):
Fuzzy Reasoning and Its Applications. Academic Press, London.

Williams, R. H. (1974):
Textbook of Endocrinology., Fifth edition, W. B. Saunders Company, London.

CHAPTER 17

DEVELOPMENT OF THE SUPPORT TOOLS AND METHODOLOGY FOR DESIGN AND VALIDATION OF MULTI-ENVIRONMENTAL COMPUTER ARCHITECTURES

L.J. KOHOUT AND S.M.A. MOHAMAD

Editorial Comment:

The dynamics of interaction of a Multi-environmental system with a multiplicity of environments is very complex and has to be tested early during the construction of the system architecture. The authors present a novel approach to possibilistic simulation.

LIST OF CONTENTS

17.1 THE ROLE OF ACTIVITY STRUCTURES IN THE DESIGN AND PERFORMANCE EVALUATION OF MULTI-ENVIRONMENTAL ARCHITECTURES

17.2 THE OBJECTIVES OF OUR APPROACH

17.3 POSSIBILISTIC DESIGN PROCESS

17.4 A TOOL FOR POSSIBILISTIC DESIGN OF MULTI-ENVIRONMENTAL WELL-PROTECTED COMPUTER ARCHITECTURES

    17.4.1 The Substratum Structure of the Possibilistic Simulator and Its Use in the Design Process

    17.4.2 Concepts and Model Structures Employed in the Possibilistic Simulator

    17.4.3 Validation of the Possibilistic Simulator

17.5 DESCRIBING THE ACTIVITIES OF THE POSSIBILISTIC SIMULATOR BY MEANS OF ACTIVITY STRUCTURES

17.6 REFERENCES

KNOWLEDGE-BASED SYSTEMS FOR MULTIPLE ENVIRONMENTS

17.1. THE ROLE OF ACTIVITY STRUCTURES IN THE DESIGN AND PERFORMANCE EVALUATION OF MULTI-ENVIRONMENTAL ARCHITECTURES

Here, we present a basic outline of the methodology that is suitable for design of multi-environmental computing architectures. We shall attempt to characterise the design of a system as a process of building a representation of a composite object that is to be constructed according to some requirement specification. Since software is not a physical object, the role of representation is especially important.

The human – computer interface is becoming the major component causing the success or failure of a computer system. This extends also to the design of multi-environmental systems. Environments and the Information Processing Machine (IPM) in mutual dynamic interaction have to enter into the paradigm for design of the architectures for multi-environmental situation.

Our design paradigm consists of the following fundamental description of the design situation:

```
DESIGN_PARADIGM ::= <SYSTEM_MODEL, DESIGN_PROBLEM, DESIGNER>.
SYSTEM_MODEL ::= <MULTI-ENVIRONMENT, IPM, ME-IPM_INTERACTION>
```

Multi-Environmental SYSTEM MODEL, the DESIGN PROBLEM and the DESIGNER's activities strongly interact. The specification (stated above) of the elements of the SYSTEM MODEL used in the design of the architecture (i.e. Substratum Structure) that could support multi-environmental activities indicates that some kind of Functional Environmental Activity Structures have to be included in the design sequence.

Thus, in terms of Activity Structures Methodology described in Chapter 5 we have the following sequence:

```
FEAS ==> FAS --> SUB --> IPM-AS,
```

where the meaning of the abbreviations (explained in detail in Chapter 5) is as follows:

FEAS... Functional Environmental Activity Structure
FAS ... Functional Activity Structure of IPM
SUB ... Substratum structure of the architecture (IPM) to be designed.
IPM-AS ... Overall activity structure of the SUB.

In the design process, the DESIGNER acts iteratively on the whole Activity Structures sequence given above. This implies that the designer is involved not only in the design sequence proper, but also (at least)in a part of the knowledge-representation sequence. We recall from Chapter 5:

```
AEAS --> FEAS (knowledge representation)
FEAS == >FAS--> SUB --> IPM-AS (design)
```

If the designer is also involved in the evaluation of the effect of dynamic changes of the environmental activities (e.g. user demand as the function of time) on the performance of the architecture, the Environmental Activity Structures (EAS) have to be included as well. That means that the whole Activity Structures construction sequence

EAS --> AEAS --> FEAS ==> FAS -->SUB --> IPM-AS
enters into the design paradigm.

It has been shown previously (Kohout 1987, and Chapter 5 of this volume), that Activity Structures represent kinds of relevance models. What is relevant to a designer of a multi-environmental architecture *may be different* to what was considered to be relevant by a knowledge elicitor (cf. Part 2 of this book). Both may be involved in the exploration of an Environmental Activity Structure or the whole Activity Structures construction sequence. It should be understood, however, that an EAS used by a knowledge elicitor may be different from that to be used by the designer of the architecture, even if both are involved in the construction process of the same IPM. This is an obvious consequence of the fact that each may apply a different criterion of relevance. This of course does not exclude the possibility that the Activity Structures used by a knowledge elicitor and a designer do not under some circumstances interact.

If the designer is concerned with prediction of performance of some architecture that has not yet been implemented (projection process), simulation plays a crucial role. A simulator that would be effective the in evaluation of multi-environmental architectures has to capture the dynamics of changes within the set of all environments entering into the projection process. This implies that the whole Activity Structures construction sequence has to enter into the consideration both, in the actual process of simulation, and when designing a simulator and methodology suitable for the use in a multi-environmental situation. A new approach to this problem was initiated by Mohamad (1986), Kohout, Mohamad and Bandler (1989).

17.2. THE OBJECTIVES OF OUR APPROACH

Our aim is to provide the means for dealing with the following objectives:
1. To provide a multi-environmental and multi-context system model which can serve as a basis for building a variety of well-protected Knowledge-Based Systems for a variety of environments. This model forms the core of a tool for computer-aided design.
2. The tool has to be accompanied by a well-formed construction methodology, with adequate prescriptive methods for representation and design of total systems. An adequate representation of a total system should include relevant aspects of hardware, software and of environments of a family of systems that is being constructed.
3. The representation methodology ought to contain adequate means for expressing the user requirements, and also for representing the system constraints (reflecting relevant features of both, the hardware and software). It should also contain a method for evaluating the protected system before it is actually implemented.

The reasons for studying design representation may well be known to the reader, we shall nevertheless recapitulate those aspects that are particularly relevant to a multi-environment situation. In this context the following points are particularly pertinent:

Knowledge-Based Systems for Multiple Environments

1. Efficient representations of designs are needed for communicating with others and across environments.
2. The limited capacity of the human mind for technical detail needs augumenting, in particular in a multi-context, multi-environmental situation.
3. The form of representation may greatly affect the performance of various design tasks.
4. The representation of information at a particular resolution level may greatly affect the success or failure in producing more refined representations, that are closer to the desired completed design.

Only by externalising our methodological representation can we hope to deal efficiently and fully with the above outlined design objectives for the design of multi-environmental architectures. The goal of our methodology is to provide tools for solving the following problems:

(a) Protected multi-environmental system model which can serve as a basis for the construction of protected Knowledge-Based Systems for a variety of environments.
(b) Representation and design methodology which can create a variety of protected Multi-Evironmental Architectures with ease.
(c) A way of expressing the user requirements of each environment.
(d) A way of expressing the hardware constraints imposed upon the multi-environmental designs.
(e) A method of evaluating the protected system while in the design stage before commencing its implementation.

Our approach is possibilistic (cf. Kohout 1988) because of the complexity of concepts, involvement of dynamics of protection and multiplicity of environments, and because of the need to involve uncertainty and approximation. That designing a total system taking into account its dynamic interaction and further evolvment during its life-cycle is considerably more intricate than designing algorithms, is clear. The following quotation from Lampson however highlights this point.

> *Designing a computer system is very different from designing an algorithm: the external interface is – that is the requirement – is less precisely defined, more complex, and more subject to change. The system has much more internal structure – hence many internal interfaces; and the measure of success is less clear. The designer usually finds himself floundering in the sea of possibilities, unclear about how one choice will limit his freedom to make other choices or affect the size and the performance of the entire system.*
> *(Lampson, 1984).*

In the field of machine architecture design, The design approaches divide into four distinct categories:

1) Dedicated language – dedicated architecture approach.
2) Non-dedicated language – dedicated architecture approach.
3) Dedicated language – non-dedicated architecture approach.
4) Non-dedicated language – non-dedicated architecture approach.

Our approach belongs to the fourth category.

17.3. POSSIBILISTIC DESIGN PROCESS

The core part of the design process based on the Activity Structures methodology is generating the Substratum structure from the family of Functional Activity Structures (FAS) that capture the design description in a functional way. In Chapter 5.4, a creative design transformation starting from Information Handling Structures (IHS) and Constraint Structures (CS) was described in some detail. The reader will recall that these are two subfamilies of FAS.

Validation of the design, i.e. of the resulting Substratum structure (SUB) is performed then by examining the total IPM-AS that represents the behavioural description of the SUB. The possibilistic nature of the transformation FAS $\longrightarrow$ SUB is manifested by the fact that the individual components of the FAS family (i.e. the IHS and CS subfamilies) can be recombined and modified in a variety of ways.

To be able to validate the architecture fully, requires the completion the whole process of construction. As the design is of an iterative nature, we need to compare the effect of various design primitives or substructures on the quality of the resulting architecture, or indeed of the whole multi-environmental system. This is so even in the case of single environment. For example, the combined effect of using heavily certain protection features, while the user demand on the system strongly fluctuates, may be detrimental to the performance of a certain type of architecture, and may be an important design feature to optimise. To explore fully the possibilities of optimisation without fully completing some non-optimal design first, calls for using dynamic simulation of machine - environment interaction.

The projection process, which involves approximate simulation of the Substratum structure (SUB) before the actual SUB is completely designed, forms an important part of the design process. This allows the designer to evaluate the effects of various design decisions on performance, dynamic protectability, as well as the influence of changes of various environments not only on the performance of the architectures but on the overall quality of the total Multi-Environment System.

Evaluation of various design possibilities and experimenting with various alternatives *during* the design process is sometimes called the *exploration phase* of the design process. Figure 17.1 depicts a typical multi-environmental exploratory phase. The aim of the designer is to evaluate the effect of various environmental changes on the performance of a prototype of the architecture being designed. The modifications of the previously considered environment or selection of some new environments are made by the designer, and the effect on the change of the dynamics of the substratum structure (SUB) are observed. In this exploratory process, the changes induced into the Environmental Activity Structure (EAS) filter through the Activity Structures design sequence to the SUB. The performance of the SUB is measured by inserting probes into it, which monitor the segments of its behaviour (i.e. parts of its IPM-AS).

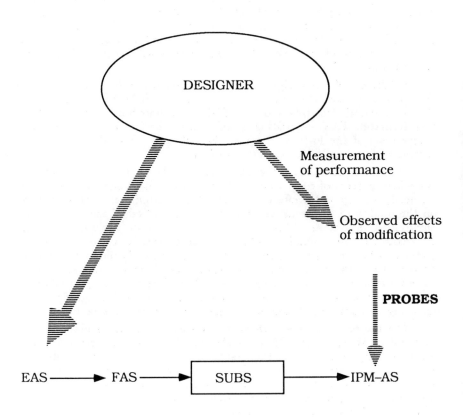

Figure 17.1. Typical exploration phase of a design process

The first problem that a designer faces is how to provide the environments for the performance evaluation. These can be either real or simulated. Even if the SUB is an actual physical prototype not a simulation and the family of environments provided is a real one, not simulated, the designer faces the problem of having suitable software to be put onto the SUB hardware in order to interface the SUB to the tested environment. Thus it may be advantageous to use simulators even in the exploratory phase dealing with a single environment.

In the exploratory phase of the design of a multi-environmental system we face the problem of combinatorial explosion that we have to deal with by exploring an adequate methodology. A typical example of multi-environmental exploration that faces this problem and is depicted in Fig. 17.2. Here, the designer after making some changes in the functional features changes the SUB by modification of Functional Activity Structure (FAS) of the designed architecture. This may be for example the modification of some protection features or even some changes in the SUB hardware primitives. After these changes are made, the designer proceeds with the investigation of the effect of various environments on the modified architecture. The changes again migrate through the design sequence and their effect is monitored by the probes. Because the modification of the FAS or of the SUB primitives may be repeated many times and each change has to be tested with a whole family of environments, we have a complexity problem.

Thus it becomes obvious that the design of well-protected multi-environmental architectures that would have a near optimal performance in more than one environment may be prohibitively costly. This necessitates the use of an appropriate simulation tool to be employed during the exploratory phase of the design process.

The remainder of this chapter is devoted to the description of a design decision support tool, that includes a possibilistic Activity Structures based simulator. This tool has been designed to be used in the exploratory phase of design of multi-environmental architectures. Our approach has evolved from a fruitful combination of the work of Mohamad concerned with the design and evaluation of the performance of well-protected computer architectures (Mohamad 1981, 1982, 1983; Mohamad and Cavouras 1982, 1984; Mohamad and Ohiorenoya 1983; Ohiorenoya and Mohamad 1983) and the Activity Structures design methodology of Kohout (Kohout 1987, 1990, Kohout and Gaines 1975, 1976; Kohout and Bandler 1987, 1982a; Bandler and Kohout 1980).

17.4. A TOOL FOR POSSIBILISTIC DESIGN OF MULTI-ENVIRONMENTAL WELL-PROTECTED COMPUTER ARCHITECTURES

17.4.1. The Substratum Structure of the Possibilistic Simulator and Its Use in the Design Process

Because of the problem of combinatorial explosion we are facing in the exploratory phase of the multi-environmental design process, the

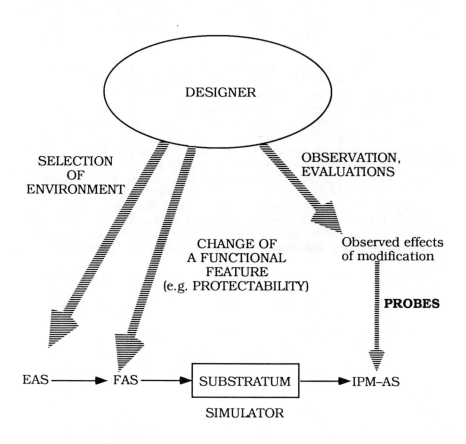

Figure 17.2. Modification of the functional structure of a multi-environmental substratum

construction of the simulator must be compatible with the design methodology that would admit the use of *possibilistic methods* in order to reduce the complexity of design decisions choices, which are increased due to combination of the multiplicity of functional and substratum architectural features with the multiplicity of environments. As the Activity Structures methodology evolved from research into possibilistic systems (Kohout 1988, 1990, 1974a, 1976, 1978a) and in turn was influenced and motivated fuzzy theories of possibility (Gaines and Kohout 1975, Zadeh 1978), it forms a natural base for the possibilistic design. It should be noted that probabilistic and possibilistic modelling techniques are necessary to express adequately the relevant features of the dynamics of, and the uncertainties involved in, the simulation of real live computer environments.

Application of the possibilistic methods of the Activity Structures approach yields as a result a possibilistic generator of various architectures and environments. This is embedded in a complete shell of the support tool. The shell design captures an Activity Structures based conceptual model, from which a variety of computer systems can be built. The shell also contains the supporting structures necessary for investigating the dynamic interaction of various architectures and environments. The postulates, on which the conceptual model is based, are stated below, in section 17.5. In the present section we outline the modular structure of the tool and the basic categories of design activities in which the possibilistic simulator can be used.

The form of the substratum structure of the simulator is dictated by nature of the (possibilistic) family of the architectures to be simulated, as well as by the design methodology employed by the designer during the construction stage of a multi-environmental system architecture.

The design cycle, in which the possibilistic simulator is used, is a particularisation of the general Activity Structures based construction process as described by Kohout in Chapter 5 of this volume. A metatheory of the Activity Structures based design process given in section 5.3.3, is internalised by a creative transformation, yielding the five classes of activities of the designer utilising the possibilistic simulator. These classes are determined by the purpose of the activities and are defined by *intension*. If described formally, the above mentioned internalisation is an internalisation in the category theoretical sense, as used for example by Ulrich Höhle for categorical investigation of fuzzy logics.

The new design definitions for the identification and control of Activity Structures based artifacts (Kohout 1978a, 1976, 1974b) are defined in terms of realisations (cf. Mohamad 1986). The classes covered in the possibilistic simulator supported design process consist of:

1. The identification of the designer activities.
2. The identification and control of the machine's distributed structures of behaviour.
3. The identification and control of the conversational environment activities (i.e. randomised/adaptive activities and interactions of both the user and the machine multi-environment).

4. The identification and control of the substrata needed for the realisation of the machine.
5. The identification of the admissible design data, both user-oriented and machine oriented, that can force the conversational environment to act in a self-regulating manner.

The complete shell consists of two separate simulation shells mutually coupled. Into the inner shell we embed the machine simulation environment, whereas the user interaction environment is embedded in the outer shell. The Activity Structures based shell programs are written to handle both the possible behaviours generated by the user stimuli, and then by the functional strategies and possibilistic constraints of simulated computer system architectures.

The software tool itself consists of the following modules:

1. Preprocessor for eliciting the design information from the designers wishing to construct Activity Structures based computer architectures.
2. Subsystem simulating the user intentions and learning capabilities for the purpose of generating the user interaction environment.
3. A subsystem simulating the machine activities and learning, for the purpose of generating the machine environment.
4. A highly parametrised shell which provides the designer with the essential design and functionality constraint modules (called the functional structures). These modules are linked in a distributed fashion (i.e. message-passing) and consist of:

4.1 *Design Modules:*

These represent the essential Functional Activity Structures (FAS) that are needed for producing the *primary activities* of the computer system (Kohout 1982) and were called in section 5.2.4 of chapter 5 Information Handling Structures (IHS). These are:

    i) Knowledge Representation Structures.
    ii) Inferential Structures.
    iii) Control Structures.

4.2 *Constraint Modules:*

These represent the *secondary activities* imposed on the primary activities (Kohout 1982).These consist of the following Functional Activity Structures (FAS):

    i) Protection Structures.
    ii) Communication Structures.
    iii) Interpretive Structures.

The flexibility provided by structuring the design tool into the modules described above, and the use of Activity Structures functional decompositions of the design system activities allows the designer to explore the variations of any chosen design by direct dynamic experimentation. This allows the designer to force it to behave in an *interesting way*. Interestingness is a class of design criteria specifying what is relevant with respect to the requirement specification of the system to be designed. In the case of work described by Mohamad (1986) the system was

VALIDATION OF MULTI-ENVIRONMENT KBS   17

deemed as interesting if it satisfied the criteria of high performance and well-protectedness, specified by quantitative and consistency measures, respectively.

17.4.2. Concepts and Model Structures Employed in the Possibilistic Simulator

This section contains the exposition of the essential concepts and modelling structures employed in the multi-environmental simulation process embedded in the possibilistic simulator. These are needed for discussion of the validation procedure of the possibilistic simulator presented in section 17.4.3 as well as for a fuller comprehension of section 17.5, which is concerned with the description of the possibilistic simulator by means of Activity Structures based postulates.

The **COMPLETE SHELL** is an Activity Structures based simulation model of a computer system (or more generally of an Information Processing Machine). It is a total model, which incorporates the use and the machine environments. In the current implementation of the Complete Shell, the interaction between the user environments and the machine environments is *maximally constrained*.

MAXIMALLY CONSTRAINED BEHAVIOUR is the co-operative behaviour between a user environment and the machine environment which is restricted to one degree of freedom of interaction.

CO-OPERATIVE BEHAVIOUR is the interaction which reaches the stable condition of satisfactoriness.

The **USER ENVIRONMENT** is represented by what is called, a *user oriented possibilistic automaton*, which updates its demand stochastic measures on the basis of the resulting machine environment *performance*, so that it chooses asymptotically the optimal demand. The implementation of this environment is called the OUTER SHELL.

The **MACHINE ENVIRONMENT** is a machine oriented possibilistic automaton that controls its performance on the basis of the required user environment demand, so that it asymptotically reaches the optimal performance. Its implementation is called the INNER SHELL. The control criterion in this context is referred to as the machine environment self-regulation.

The **USER POSSIBILISTIC AUTOMATON** is a highly-parametrised user model stochastic automaton which generates the user demand and is connected in a feedback loop with the machine environment.

The **MACHINE POSSIBILISTIC AUTOMATON** is a highly-parametrised and extensible computer system model stochastic automaton which is connected in a feedback loop with the user environment.

The **STOCHASTIC AUTOMATON** is a realisation of a possible automaton (cf. Gaines and Kohout 1975, 1976) which uses in its algebraic structure a membership function that has imposed upon it a stochastic restriction.

STOCHASTIC RESTRICTION is a constraint that is imposed on the valuation membership function of a many-valued logic based set or relation by restricting it by some General Stochastic Logic.

GENERALISED STOCHASTIC LOGIC is a many-valued logic (MVL), the valuation of which goes into a *stochastic uncertainty measure*. It can be for example a stochastic measure in the Gaines sense (Gaines 1976), special cases of which are either conventional probabilistic logic, or the MVL that forms the base of Zadeh's standard fuzzy set (Zadeh 1965). Or it can be almost-probabilistic logic, such as the one described by Kohout and Bandler (1982), which satisfies all but one of the Popper axioms of probability.

STOCHASTIC UNCERTAINTY MEASURE is the term that denotes a general uncertainty measure that satisfies some basic *possibilistic observational requirements* (cf. Kohout 1988). For example probability, possibility measure, entropy, U-uncertainty measure (Klir and Folger 1988).

The **USER MODEL** is a stochastic model that represents a quadruple $< r, \alpha, p, T >$, where

r	...	total number of user demands;
$\alpha = \{\alpha_1 \ldots, \alpha_r\}$	...	set of demands of the user environment;
$Q = \{q_1, \ldots, q_r\}$	...	demand stochastic uncertainty measure vector of the user environment;
T	...	an updating operator.

If $\alpha(t)$ represents the demands chosen by the user environment at time t, then $q_i(t)$ =STOCH$[\alpha(t) = \alpha_i]$. This means that q represents the the value of the stochastic uncertainty measure such that it satisfies the condition(s) in [...]. Specified by a recursion we have $Q(t + 1) = T[Q(t), \alpha(t), \beta(t)]$, where $\beta(t) \in \{0, 1\}$ is the binary set of performance reactions from the machine environment that is input into the user environment. $\beta(t) = 1$ is called the penalty performance input and $\beta(t) = 0$ the reward performance input. The penalty stochastic uncertainty measure vector

$C = [c_1, \ldots, c_r]$ has the the values given by
$c_i =$ STOCH $[\beta(t) = 1 \quad |\alpha(t) = \alpha_i]$.

The operator T represents an algorithm called the updating (or user adaptive) algorithm.

COMPUTER SYSTEM MODEL: This is a simulation model which is partly driven by itself and partly driven by the outer shell. This model represents a quadruple <FS, ST, UD, PCR>, where

FS ... Functional Structures;
ST ... Substratum Structures;
UD ... User Demand;
PCR ... Performance and Changes Requirements.

FS and ST were listed in section 17.4.1. UD and PCR will be defined below.

USER DEMAND: This is the average user demand, expressed by the number of concurrent tasks or processes placed by the user environment. This measure implicitly identifies the user environment average penalty.

PERFORMANCE AND CHANGE REQUIREMENTS: These are the measures used to monitor the performance of the modelled computer system activities via the software probes. There are two types of measures that can be used to assess the average penalty of the machine environment. These are the average response time for an interactive system, and the average system throughput for the general system. These change requirements include the designer changes on the computer system model, introduced in order to achieve a target computer system. The change that involves the algorithmic nonparametric changes on the original computer system model produce a possibilistic CONSTELLATION. This is a collection of types of system families. The changes that involve *parametric* (i.e. non-algorithmic) changes on a constellation produce a general SYSTEM FAMILY. The repeated changes on the general system family produce the ADMISSIBLE DATA. These are used to tune the general system to reach the stable state. This tuning procedure is called the PERFORMOACT modelling (cf. Mohamad 1986).

17.4.3. Validation of the Possibilistic Simulator

The implementation of the tool represents the effort of three man-years. The simulator software is available in C version running under UNIX on IBM PC/XT. It is an established fact that a validation of a complex software system such as the possibilistic generator is a complicated process. That is in addition to the fact that the Activity Structures based possibilistic simulation is not meant to simulate existing computer architectures but rather to help in the projection validation of the yet not realised prototypes. For this reason we need rigorous validation proofs. Validation of the implementation of our possibilistic simulator mainly depends upon the verification of the logical structure of the simulator program implementations in the C language.

Three kinds of validation process were applied to the implemented shell. Namely,

a) Validation of the simulator results by comparison with two theoretical models: Boyse and Warn (1975) and a model based on operational laws of Buzen (1979).

b) Validation by comparison of our simulation with real computer system data.

c) Validation of performance of the simulator software by the direct comparison of performance of some components of the possibilistic generator with the real performance data concerning selected components of some existing computer systems.

Typical results of the (a) above are depicted in Fig.17.3. The comparisons show a close agreement between the possibilistic simulator model and the theoretical models. Correlation with Boyse and Warn response times is 0.9090 and with operational analysis response times is 0.9357, indicating that our possibilistic simulator can be trusted for modelling conventional computer architectures.

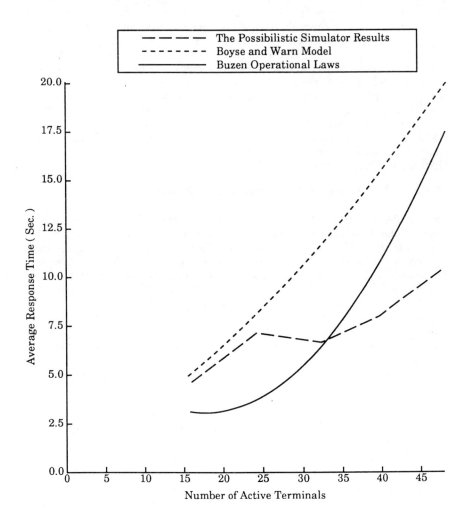

Figure 17.3. Validation of the possibilistic simulator by comparison with the theoretical models of Boyse and Warn, and of Buzen

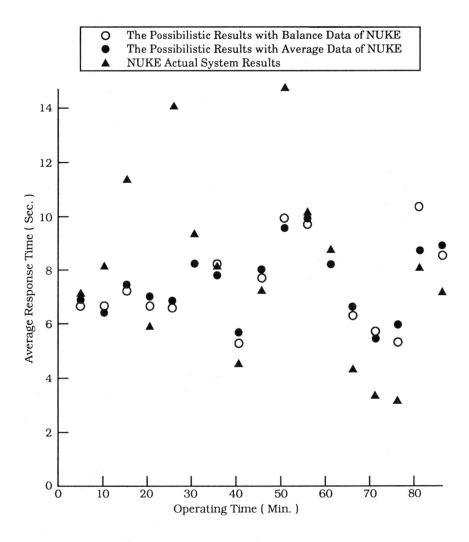

Figure 17.4. Comparison of the results of possibilistic simulator with the actual NUKE response

Fig. 17.4 displays the comparison of a simulation with real system result (DEC NUKE-oriented system as reported by Penny and Sheedy). The correlation between the actual system response times and our possibilistic simulator balance-tuning response times was 0.5933, and for our average-response the tuning time was 0.5319. This is relatively high, considering that our possibilistic simulator possesses the self-regulating behaviour due to the learning mechanism that the actual system does not implicitly have.

For (c) above we selected simulated performance data from the activity of the memory system concerned with disk utilisation that were available from the simulation, and compared them with disk utilisation data of CAP computer (Wilkes and Needham 1979) and also of a HYDRA computer (Cohen et. al. 1974). Fig. 17.5 shows the results. The correlation coefficients 0.5215 and 0.5404 with CAP and HYDRA data respectively, indicate that our possibilistic simulator modelled disk is overutilised compared with two notable computer systems. This again may strengthen our confidence in the possibilistic simulator results. All the validation studies were performed on VAX 11-750 under UNIX (Mohamad 1986).

17.5. DESCRIBING THE ACTIVITIES OF THE POSSIBILISTIC SIMULATOR BY MEANS OF ACTIVITY STRUCTURES

In this section we shall briefly outline an Activity Structures based meta-description of the possibilistic simulator. By *meta-description* we mean the intensional prescription of the Activity Structures of the shell of the possibilistic simulator that has to be enforced at any level of abstraction. The necessary substrata structures satisfying the basic postulates stated below can be found in Mohamad (1986).

The basic meta-principles that are of major interest for further development of a construction process of any multi-environmental possibilistic family of architectures, are stated below in the form of sixteen postulates. These postulates are the result of the analysis of an implementation of our support tool after the tool was validated. Hence we believe that our basic principles provide practical advice for the success of activity structures based computer system designs and implementations.

POSTULATE 1: *Essential functionality*

Activity Structures based shell achieves its required goals by the co-operation of both the external (user) and the IPM environments, as well as by the co-operation of the functional structures of the inner (i.e. within an IPM-system) environments.

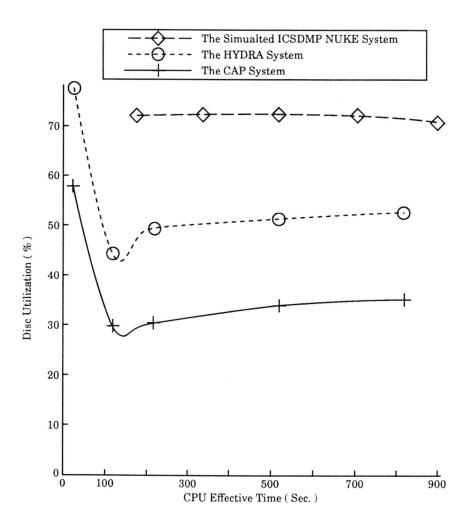

Figure 17.5. Possibilistic simulation of disk utilization in the NUKE operating system and its comparison with the literature data on HYDRA and CAP

POSTULATE 2: *Functionality uniqueness*
Each functional structure is characterised by a specific type of behaviour which is different from the others.

POSTULATE 3: *Syntactical decomposition*
Activity Structures based shell realisation syntactically decomposes into functional substructures.

POSTULATE 4: *Representing functional structures – Structural statics*
Each functional structure is statically represented by a state determined system. This system is modelled by a manager. The manager's responsibilities and duties can be changed via changing the information deposited in the resource descriptor of the managed object.

POSTULATE 5: *Representing functional structures – Dynamics of variation*
The change of each functional structure can be represented dynamically by a process which acts as an active entity that is mainly issuing requests to the other processes and resources in order to accomplish this goal.

POSTULATE 6: *Distribution criterion*
The Activity Structures based architecture is called functionally distributed, if its functional structures or their components communicate via a message passing technique.

POSTULATE 7: *Essential substrata simulation*
Two extensible primitive substrata structures are required to realise the simulation of the activity structures based shell. These are the coroutines and the interpretive descriptors, corresponding to the simulated managers and resource descriptors, respectively.

POSTULATE 8: *Concurrency control*
Concurrency in any activity structures based shell has, as its functional realisation, a system of objects composed from managers and resource descriptors. These objects are in mutual co-operation and synchronisation.

POSTULATE 9: *Behaviour – substratum structure match*
The shell has maximal match in a substratum structure if the semantic gap between the behaviour of functional structures and the behaviour of their corresponding substrata in which the functional structures are realised, is minimal.

POSTULATE 10: *Communication styles*
The communication style of the shell in execution depends upon whether the time factor has been used. It can be synchronous or asynchronous

POSTULATE 11: *Computer model*
A computer model description represents an interconnection of co-operating processes. In this co-operation some of the processes can receive information from the user or the designer environments, and some processes can produce and pass information for these environments.

POSTULATE 12: *Measurement probes*
Statistics can be collected via the insertion of performance probes at various places of the shell simulation.

POSTULATE 13: *Multi-environmental nature of the total shell*

The realisation of the activity structures based shell should include both the behavioural modelling of the machine and the user interaction environments.

POSTULATE 14: *Stable shell*

The activity Structures based shell behaviour is stable relative to a multi-environment, if there exists a set of admissible design data of that multi-environment concerning the user environments and machine environments, within which the conversational environment can behave in a self-regulating manner.

POSTULATE 15: *The nature of an Activity Structures based Computer System (ASCS) produced by the total shell.*

An ASCS model can be produced by the total shell, and its interaction between the user environment and the machine environment is maximally constrained.

POSTULATE 16: *Shell soundness*

Any Activity Structures based shell is said to possess a sound design if a compromise can be reached, between the intended conceptual model of the problem environment and the actual shell model of the designer environment. In an effective design the shell soundness can be reached by tuning the shell (i.e. finding the admissible data for a particular multi-environment).

17.6. REFERENCES

Bandler, W. and Kohout, L.J. (1980):
Fuzzy relational products as a tool for analysis and synthesis of complex artificial and natural systems. In: Wang, P.P. and Chang, S.K. (eds.). *Fuzzy Sets: Theory and Applications to Policy Analysis and Information Systems.* Plenum Press, New York, 341–367.

Boyse, J.W. and Warn, R.D. (1975):
A straightforward model for computer performance prediction. *ACM Computing Surveys*, vol.7, No.2., 73–93.

Buzen, J.P. (1979):
The predictable problem. *ACM Computing Surveys*, vol. 11, No.1., 70–72.

Gaines, B.R. (1976):
Fuzzy reasoning and logics of uncertainty. In: *Proc. of 6th Internat. Symposium on Multiple-Valued Logics*, IEEE, New York (76CH1111-4C), 178–188.

Gaines, B.R. and Kohout, L.J. (1975):
Possible automata. In: *Proc. of the 1975 Internat. Symposium on Multiple-Valued Logic*, IEEE, New York, 183–196.

Gaines, B.R. and Kohout, L.J. (1976):
The logic of automata. *Internat. Journal of General Systems*, vol. **2**, 191–208.

Klir, G.J. and Folger, T.A. (1988):
Fuzzy Sets, Uncertainty, and Information. Prentice Hall, Englewood Cliffs, N.J.

Kohout, L.J. (1974a):
The Pinkava many-valued complete logic systems and their application in design of many-valued switching circuits. In: *Proc. 1974 Internat. Symposium on Multiple-Valued Logic*, IEEE, New York (74CH0875-8C), 261–284.

Kohout, L.J. (1974b):
Algebraic models in computer-aided medical diagnosis. In: J. Anderson (ed.), *Proceedings of MEDINFO 74*, North Holland, Amsterdam, 575–579, addendum and list of typographical errors 1069–70.

Kohout, L.J. (1976):
Representation of functional hierarchies of movement in the brain. *Internat. J. of Man-Machine Studies*, vol. **8**, 699–709.

Kohout, L.J. (1978a):
Methodological Foundations of the Study of Action. Ph.D. Thesis, University of Essex, England, U.K., January 1978.

Kohout, L.J. (1978b):
Analysis of computer protection structures by means of multi-valued logics. In: Proc. of Eight Internat. Symposium on Multiple-valued Logic, IEEE, New York, 260–268.

Kohout, L.J. (1982):
Lecture notes on Activity Structures. Workshop of Man-Computer Studies Group, Brunel University, U.K.

Kohout, L.J.(1987):
Activity structures: a general systems construct for design of technological artifacts. *System and Cybernetics: An International Journal*, vol.**18**, 27–34.

Kohout, L.J. (1988):
Theories of possibility: Meta-axiomatics and semantics. An invited article for a special isuue on Interpretations of Grades of Membership. *Fuzzy Sets and Systems*, vol. **25**, No.3 (March), 357–367.

Kohout, L.J.(1990):
A Perspective on Intelligent Systems: A Framework for Analysis and Design. Chapman and Hall, London; Van Nostrand, New York.

Kohout, L.J. and Bandler, W. (1975):
Relational-product architectures for information processing. *Information Science*, vol. **37**, 25–37.

Kohout, L.J. and Bandler, W. (1976):
Knowledge representation, clinical action and expert systems. In: Kohout, L.J., and Bandler, W., eds. (1986) *Knowledge Representation in Medicine and Clinical Behavioural Science*, Abacus Books, Gordon and Breach Science Publishers, London and New York.

Kohout, L.J., and Bandler, W. (1982a):
Fuzzy expert system: theory and practice of knowledge based system. (Second Technical Conference of the British Computer Society, Expert Systems Specialist Group), September 1982, 33–36.

Kohout, L.J. and Bandler, W. (1982b):
Axioms for conditional inference: probabilistic and possibilistic. In: Ballester, A., Cardus, D. and Trillas, E. (eds.), *Proc. Second Internat. Conference on Mathematics at the Service of Man* (Las Palmas, Canary Islands, Spain, 28 June – 3 July 1982). Universidad Politechnica de las Palmas, 413–414.

Kohout, L.J. and Bandler, W. (1987):
Computer security systems: Fuzzy logics. In: *International Encyclopedia of Systems and Control*, Singh, M., et al., (eds.), Pergamon Press, Oxford, 741–743.

Kohout, L.J. and Gaines, B.R. (1975):
The logic of protection. *Lecture Notes in Computer Science*, vol. **34**, Springer Verlag, Berlin, 736–751.

Kohout, L.J. and Gaines, B.R. (1976):
Protection as a general systems problem. *Internat. Journal of General Systems*, vol. **3**, 3–23.

Kohout, L.J., Mohamad, S.M.A. and Bandler, W. (1989):
A support tool for evaluation of knowledge engineering structures. In: *Proc. of 2nd Florida Artificial Intelligence Research Symposium*. Fishman, M.B. (ed.) The Florida AI Res. Symp. P.O. Box 12560, St. Petersburg, Florida 32733 (ISBN 0-9620-1731-O, U.S.A.)

Lampson, B.W. (1984):
Hints for computer system design. *IEEE Software*, vol. **1**, No. 1, 11–28.

Mohamad, S.M.A. (1981):
A Comparison of Some Performance Evaluation Techniques. M.Sc. Thesis, Glasgow University, Scotland, U.K.

Mohamad, S.M.A. (1982):
A gudeline to the problem of designing well-protected computer systems. Man-Computer Studies Group Technical Report MCSG/TR19, Dept. of Computer Science, Brunel University, U.K.

Mohamad, S.M.A. (1983):
Descriptor-oriented system. MCSG/TR28, Dept. of Computer Science, Brunel University, U.K.

Mohamad, S.M.A. (1986):
Construction of a Support Tool for the Design of the Activity Structures Based Computer System Architectures. Ph.D. Thesis, Department of Computer Science, Brunel University, U.K.

Mohamad, S.M.A. and Cavouras, J.C. (1982):
Performance models of computer systems. MCSG/TR18, Dept. of Computer Science, Brunel University, U.K.

Mohamad, S.M.A. and Cavouras, J.C. (1984):
Performance study of descriptor oriented architectures, *Computer Performance Journal*, vol. **5**, No.1, 14–22.

Mohamad, S.M.A. and Ohiorenoya, M. (1983):
Design criteria for expert systems. *NAFIP II Conference*, New York, June 29 – July 1.

Ohiorenoya M. and Mohamad, S.M.A. (1983):
Software tools for decision support systems: Review and Proposals. *IUCC Conference*, Glasgow University, 13–16 September.

Zadeh, L.A. (1965):
Fuzzy sets. *Information and Control*, vol. **8**, 338–353.

Zadeh, L.A. (1978):
Fuzzy sets as a basis for a theory of possibility. *Fuzy Sets and Systems*, vol. **1**, 3–28.

PART V

EPILOGUE

Editorial Comments:

The authors of this postscript, a computer scientist and a sociologist look in their highly speculative paper at the impact of restricting the selfregulatory mechanism of scientific criticism which may be result of excessive comercialisation of the sources of basic scientific knowledge. They discuss the possible influence of these negative trends on the quality of the advice provided by knowledge-based systems.

CHAPTER 18

KNOWLEDGE AS A CONFIDENTIAL MARKETABLE COMMODITY: CULTURAL DANGER OR ECONOMIC BLESSING?

L.J. KOHOUT AND S. WIESBAUER

Editorial Comment:

> It was seen in the first chapters of this book that in a multi-enironmental situations the semantics of the knowledge structures used in the KB systems strongly depends on the cultural context, which manifests itself most permanently in the use of these systems. The results provided by KBS have to be interpreted in this cultural context and the correctness of the interpretation of the results crucially depends on the correctness of this interpretation.

LIST OF CONTENTS

18.1 INTRODUCTION
18.2 KNOWLEDGE AS A MARKETABLE COMMODITY
18.3 STRUCTURE OF THE KNOWLEDGE-BASED SYSTEM
18.4 THE DISTINCTION BETWEEN SURFACE KNOWLEDGE AND DEEP KNOWLEDGE
18.5 THE DISTINCTION BETWEEN BASIC AND PURPOSE-ORIENTED KNOWLEDGE
18.6 CONSEQUENCES OF THE WITHDRAWAL OF KNOWLEDGE FROM OPEN CIRCULATION
    18.6.1 Impairment of the Regulating Mechanism for Maintaining the Correctness of Basic Knowledge by Withdrawal of some Purpose-Oriented Knowledge
    18.6.2 Uses of the Basic Knowledge Within the Context of Knowledge Engineering
    18.6.3 Consequences of the Withdrawal of Purpose-Oriented Knowledge
18.7 KNOWLEDGE STRUCTURES WITHIN THE CONTEXT OF A CULTURE
    18.7.1 Interactions of Distinct Contexts and the Loss of Correctness of Knowledge Structures
    18.7.2 Dynamic Evolution of Knowledge Structures and the Change of their Meaning

Knowledge-Based Systems for Multiple Environments

18.8 CONCLUSION: THE NEED FOR TECHNOLOGICAL ARTEFACTS CAPABLE OF ADAPTING TO THE DYNAMIC CHANGES OF THE ENVIRONMENT
18.9 REFERENCES

18.1. INTRODUCTION

> ...the essence of *'myth'* is found in man's complete self-surrender to the object, in his explanation of the world and of himself by analogies, and by hasty analogies. Contrasted with this is...critical thought and conduct. By the critical mind, things are deduced from other things as a result of careful observation and comparison.
>
> Thomas Garrigue Masaryk

Since the Renaissance, European culture, and indeed the whole of European civilisation, has been based on the principle of the freedom of dissemination of knowledge and the freedom of its public discussion. The mechanics of self-regulation of correctness of scientific knowledge has been dependent on that paradigm. Is this basic principle under the attack from the newly emerging "Advanced Information Technology"? That is the question that we intend to ask. The aim of this chapter is to present a critical scrutiny of the following scenario:

> *Knowledge extracted from the expert by means of some knowledge elicitation techniques is encapsulated into a powerful computer system and used consequently for some form of decision making. The manufacturers and owners of these systems tend to view the knowledge contained in the system as a marketable commodity and may extend considerable effort to make confidential the contents of the knowledge base and the exact way of system functioning.*

If the knowledge contained in the expert system concerns just special expertise pertinent to some special manufacturing process etc., then the above described view is usually acceptable. However, in the context of intelligent knowledge based systems of a more general nature, where the domain of knowledge contained in the system is broader, concerning a particular scientific, medical, or engineering field, or a part of it, the situation may be different. In this case treating knowledge as a marketable commodity, with imposed confidentiality of the contents, may have serious technological and social consequences.

We shall analyse the possible consequences of this view. In particular, the question of correctness, maintainability, faithfulness of representation and extendability of knowledge sources will be discussed. We also adumbrate the possible consequences of such "technological" censorship on the evolvement of of new scientific knowledge and its verifiability.

The key issue in dispute is the following: can the confidentiality consistently imposed on the knowledge sources of powerful knowledge based information processing and expert systems threaten the correctness of scientific and technological knowledge and the freedom of dissemination of knowledge and education, on which the proper functioning of our current western civilisation is based?

After discussing the concept of a marketable commodity in section 18.2, and the basic structure of a knowledge-based system in section 18.3, we outline the distinction between the surface knowledge and deep knowledge in sections 18.4 and 18.5, respectively. The analysis of the consequences of the withdrawal of knowledge of various kinds follows.

It will become apparent from the ensuing argument that the notions of context, environment, dynamics and stability play the central role in our speculative analysis.

18.2. KNOWLEDGE AS A MARKETABLE COMMODITY

> Truth is a judgement which has survived the probing fire of criticism. ...But not only of our criticism. Every field of scientific knowledge is subject to continuous scrutiny and criticism of many individuals.
>
> T.G.Masaryk. (In: Čapek, 1935)

Two kinds of commodities are distinguished by economists: reproducible and irreproducible. We shall exclude the irreproducible ones from what follows, as we suppose that computer programs are usually reproducible, at least in theory.

Reproducible goods can be traded on open markets or closed markets. We define an open market as one with increasing demand or increasing supply, or both. Contracting markets should not be entirely disregarded in this definition but these do not apply to newly introduced commodities, hence are not relevant to the issue of expert systems at present.

When a closed market reaches stable equilibrium, development is possible in quality, but not in quantity of supply and demand. Such a market does not expand in terms of quantity of commodities, and the money equivalent for the commodities allows for a stable calculation of the input and output, on the producer's side. On the consumer's side, the time factor of how long the goods will be used, when these will be replaced or repaired, is equally calculable. These calculations serve as one of the regulating processes of the exchange of goods.

For an expanding market, the rules are different, as is the case of every system that is far from the equilibrium (see Prigogine 1980). Such a system does not obey unique functional rules, but also some historical rules. The survival in such an environment is a question of all or nothing, depending on speculation about further developments, based on historical experience and correct interpretation of the situation.

Knowledge-Based Systems for Multiple Environments

What kind of markets might be the ones in which expert systems, or knowledge based systems, will be placed ? We suppose, these will be of the second kind. This implies that several dangers have to be dealt with.

First of all, there is the possibility of failure, even for very good products. This is not because these are lacking in quality, or have exaggerated prices, but due to some market conditions at the very special moment when the product is placed there. Then the product will disappear from the market and the knowledge stored in it may disappear as well.

Secondly, there is an implicit risk of success. If a good program is sold well, the consumers get adapted to it and will not buy another quickly enough to allow a continuous production process. Or the program may get mal-adapted after some time to the enterprise using it, which will then be faced by an increasing danger of lack of correct function. A human co-operator, interested in the future of an enterprise, may ask unpleasant, but necessary questions, founded on his own experience and reflections, may develop initiative and creativity. This part of "the good will" cannot be replaced by the use of computers, and can became neglected when a computer program is used instead. Then the fault is usually ascribed to the computer program which is being used inappropriately, instead of looking at the underlying deeper causes.

The impact of mass selling of a special program might exclude anything else from the market, perhaps better adapted for the concrete purpose, but not competitive at the price and implementation level. Therefore, the introduction of newly developed products would bear an increasingly incalculable risk. Known products may be sold to customers for whom they are unnecessary, preventing the customers from buying more appropriate products that are available from another supplier and even leading them to believe that the whole technology is useless for them.

The state of the market, its characteristic features and possible undesirable consequences of aggressively introducing a new product are summarised in Table 18.1 that follows.

It can be seen from that table that two characteristics of the market in non-equilibrium could lead to the restriction in the range of products on the market. This restriction imposed on the variety of other products may lead to limitations of various kinds:

1. elimination of products of better quality,
2. limitation of variety of products.

The limitation of variety may have the following effects:

    2.1 Limitation of performance (e.g.: affects the price of the product or of the service it provides).

    2.2 Elimination of the products that have greater performance or better quality in different circumstances or environments.

    2.3 Restriction of the diversity of new developments, as different types of systems may have different potential for future developments. The (2.2) above is related to the issue of relevance of the product in a particular context or environment. If the product operates in a dynamic and changing environment, this issues is very important. It will be shown in section 18.6 that it has a direct impact on the

Table 18.1. Possible undesirable consequences of introducing aggressively a new product to a market in non-equilibrium state

State of the market	Characteristic features of the market	Undesirable consequences that may appear
Market in equilibrium	No quantitative expansion	
Market in non-equilibrium	(i) Bad conditions for introducing new products and the consequent suppression of good products	• Bad influence on the evolution of the field • Bad service to the users of the product
	(ii) Success of a product	• No adaptation to dynamic changes of the conditions under which the products operate • Exclusion of other, perhaps better products, resulting in decrease of quality and variety

acceptability of a knowledge-based system. It may also affect the correctness of the purpose oriented knowledge which the knowledge based system contains.

It can be shown that the availability of a variety of products stabilises the (economic) system which operates under some dynamic fluctuations, and leads therefore to a kind of *distributed* optimisation. The product A which is perhaps worse than the product B in some context, may be better than B in a different context or under different conditions. If the contexts or the conditions dynamically change with time within a certain scope or region, this variety is essential to ensure the operation of the system over the whole region of change, and to stabilise and globally optimise the parameters over this region.

KNOWLEDGE-BASED SYSTEMS FOR MULTIPLE ENVIRONMENTS

18.3. STRUCTURE OF THE KNOWLEDGE-BASED SYSTEM

> Acquiring knowledge is activity, thinking and knowing is activity, extremely energetic creative activity. ...One speaks of the technological age, one assumes that the contemporary man is a technologist, not a thinker. But where the technology would be without the wast theoretical scientific work that always precedes it?
>
> T.G.Masaryk. (In: Čapek, 1935)

It is common to divide the development of an expert system into several stages where some stages depend directly on the domain of expertise in which the knowledge-based system is intended to operate.

In a commercial development, the manufacturers usually provide some kind of expert system or knowledge based system shell, a software tool, which is then filled by some knowledge pertaining to a chosen knowledge domain. This knowledge is contained in a knowledge-base, the contents of which are obtained by the knowledge elicitation process of some kind, either directly from experts, or from the expert literature of the field. As knowledge of the field changes with time, it may be essential to update the knowledge base regularly, in order to maintain the expertise of the knowledge-based system at an acceptable level or standard.

Each particular kind of the shell may be suitable only for a certain purpose or for encapsulating only certain forms of knowledge. It is therefore essential to distinguish in the process of the construction and maintenance of the system three different aspects of it:

1. How to construct the shell of the artifact itself, disregarding particular concrete knowledge contents of the knowledge-base.
2. How to produce and maintain a knowledge base of the system for a particular domain of expertise.
3. How to keep the compatibility of the shell with the knowledge base that is continuously changing due to updating and maintenance.

These construction problems lead to some more general problems of acceptability of a knowledge-based system, namely to the following questions.

4. What are the criteria of acceptability of the system ?
5. Who is to be responsible for providing the standards of acceptability?

It is essential to clarify at this point what the term *acceptability* means in the context of our discussion. This can be done best by defining the conditions of our knowledge-based system in terms of the necessary conditions that the knowledge encapsulated in it ought to satisfy.

If the system is acceptable, then it has to satisfy at least the following conditions:

1. Correctness

The elicited knowledge used for constructing the knowledge base should be *correct*.

2. Faithfulness of representation

The knowledge contained in the knowledge base should faithfully represent the knowledge relevant to the problem the knowledge-based system purports to deal with.

3. Maintainability

It should be possible to update and change the knowledge base without impairing the correctness of knowledge that is represented in it.

4. Admissibility

The knowledge contained in the system should not generate undesirable consequences as side-effects to a correct action of the system, when used in a particular context, or environment.

In the context of our discussion, the conditions (1) and (4) have the most exorbitant consequences. Although all the conditions of acceptability may appear obvious when stated explicitly, they are often violated by the implementations of currently existing expert systems.

A knowledge-based system can be portrayed as an actor interacting with, and having effect upon, its environment (cf. Kohout, 1990, Chapter 3). As the effect of the system is enacted either by the system giving advice or, in the case of a robot by a physical action, the **local correctness** and **relative consistency** are crucial for explicitly and formally defining the **standards of acceptability** of knowledge-based systems. A rigorous meta-logical formulation of the necessary conditions that such a standard of knowledge representation should satisfy can be stated (Kohout, 1975). This is essential in the design of knowledge-based systems (Kohout, 1987), but we shall not dwell on it here. In the present context it suffices to say that if a knowledge-based system is placed in a changing environment, as is usually the case, the satisfaction of condition (3), *maintainability*, is essential. From this it follows, that *any incremental update* of the knowledge structure of the knowledge-based system *must also satisfy* the conditions (1), (2) and (4), i.e. *correctness, faithfulness of representation* and *admissibility*, otherwise an incorrect activity of the knowledge-based system ensues.

18.4. THE DISTINCTION BETWEEN SURFACE KNOWLEDGE AND DEEP KNOWLEDGE

The majority of existing expert systems have been concerned with capturing the knowledge of experts in a problem solving situation. This usually consists of the heuristic knowledge that is obtained by a knowledge engineer during the knowledge elicitation process. During this process, the knowledge engineer and an expert interact in a meaningful dialogue, the purpose of which is to capture a part of expertise of a specialist expert in a particular knowledge domain.

The expert systems of the second generation in particular, and the knowledge-based systems in general, may also contain some knowledge that is formulated as a formalization of a theory or model of a specific scientific field. This may be in part scientific knowledge that has belonged traditionally to the public domain, which has formed what is considered to be the content of a particular science. It will be shown in the sequel that the distinction we made between basic and purpose-oriented knowledge is important here.

In particular, the knowledge of this kind, if withdrawn, may cause the breakdown of the regulating feedback during the process leading to scientific discoveries, and may cause substantial distortions in the contents and the interrelationship of some knowledge domains, or even of whole scientific fields.

18.5. THE DISTINCTION BETWEEN BASIC AND PURPOSE-ORIENTED KNOWLEDGE

To analyse the plausibility of our argument, and to demonstrate how this distortion could happen, we have to examine in greater detail how the knowledge in general can be classified according to its use.

We have to distinguish *basic* and *purpose-oriented* knowledge. Basic knowledge includes scientific knowledge. On the other hand, purpose-oriented knowledge includes technological knowledge, medical knowledge, legal knowledge, clinical-psychological knowledge, etc. These fields may, under certain limiting conditions, be called purpose-oriented.

Let us concentrate here on the technological knowledge, and explain how and why the concept of directed knowledge, that is, **directed** *towards a particular purpose,* is indistinguishable in the discussion of technological as well as other purpose-oriented knowledge.

There are certain basic characteristics by which purpose-oriented knowledge can be distinguished from basic knowledge. Basic knowledge is concerned solely with its domain: that is with the logical consistency and validity of the concepts and facts within this domain, and also with their explanatory and predictive power.

Purpose-oriented knowledge, on the other hand, is concerned with the combination of the relevant facts of various basic knowledge domains together with some other additional facts and concepts. This is done in order to provide an adequate knowledge domain for supporting and directing activities that result in achieving certain *a priori* prescribed goals. These goals, which are specified by the purpose of this activity, in turn determine what is to be selected as the ingredients forming a particular purpose-oriented knowledge field.

The relevant parts of basic knowledge which come into this selection, we call *directed* knowledge. It is called directed because its selection, forming a particular basic knowledge field, is guided by its relevance to the purpose for which it will be used. The *intended* use of this specifically selected basic knowledge will then partially determine the way in which the goals, of the activities of the knowledge-based system in which it is used, will be achieved.

Let us look at a particular example that will illustrate the distinction between the basic and directed knowledge within a particular knowledge-field.

Entomology is that part of zoology concerned with the scientific study of insects. The research by which the basic knowledge of this field is acquired is solely (or primarily) determined by the cognitive aims of basic natural sciences. If, on the other hand, the aim of the insect study is to determine primarily those facts that are pertinent to the effects of pesticides, it will be, what we call *directed knowledge*. One of the uses of this knowledge may be its application to the development of some new pesticides, or to the explanation of the effects of some extant pesticides.

It is essential to realise, that the contents of a knowledge structure containing directed knowledge will also be (directly) determined by some other factors, which may be economical, ecological, political, etc. Focusing on some issues only, makes it directed. So we can say that the directed knowledge is generated by two kinds of forming factors:

(a) those that determine how it will be used
(b) those that determine what basic knowledge of the field it will initially contain.

18.6. CONSEQUENCES OF THE WITHDRAWAL OF KNOWLEDGE FROM OPEN CIRCULATION

> Scientists and Philosophers are honoured by the society not because of their talent, but for their grandiose effort to come closer to the truth. That is an act of moral and ethics. ...and for this reason we percieve any misuse of science as a sin, a sin against God.
>
> T.G.Masaryk. (In: Čapek, 1935)

As the main paradigm of this work, we assume that basic scientific knowledge belongs to the public domain, and that the basic regulating mechanism which maintains the correctness of this type of knowledge is provided by means of it being tested openly by the scientific community. It is well known and accepted that the progress of basic scientific knowledge has been maintained since the Renaissance by its open and free accessibility.

On the other hand, there may be strong commercial reasons to withdraw some purpose-oriented knowledge. This however, may have under some conditions very unfortunate consequences.

The purpose-oriented knowledge ought not to be withheld in the following circumstances:

1. If the regulating mechanism for maintaining the correctness of basic knowledge is likely to be impaired.
2. When the confindentiality enforced could affect acceptability of the constructed or marketed knowledge-based system.

The consequences of violating the above maxims would affect the quality of the basic sciences, or of the environment in which the artifact is to be used.

18.6.1. Impairment of the Regulating Mechanism for Maintaining the Correctness of Basic Knowledge by Withdrawal of some Purpose-Oriented Knowledge

There is an interaction between the individual fields of basic knowledge as well as mutual interaction between basic and purpose-oriented knowledge. It is the interaction between purpose-oriented knowledge and basic knowledge that primarily interests us here, as this interaction may unduly influence the regulating mechanism by which the correctness of the basic knowledge is maintained.

In order to demonstrate how the dependence between the purpose-oriented knowledge and the basic knowledge operates, we have to examine the mechanism for maintaining the correctness of the basic knowledge, the conditions under which it normally operates, as well as the consequences caused by the withdrawal of purpose-oriented knowledge

In fairly general terms, the correctness of the basic scientific knowledge is maintained by testing the hypothesis and scientific theories against some empirical data and also by evaluation and criticism of the method and the procedures or meta-procedures by which the theories are built.

The basic scientific knowledge of a particular field does not remain static but *develops dynamically*. Because of this dynamic change, testing and criticism have to be applied repeatedly to maintain the correctness of the newly generated part of the scientific field. It is not, however, sufficient to scrutinise only new, previously untested parts of a basic knowledge field.

Each knowledge structure has its *context of validity*, and this context of validity may also change. This change is due to the fact, that various parts of the knowledge structures interact in different ways and new interactions and dependencies can emerge during this dynamic development. Such changes affect the context in which the knowledge interacts.

It should also be noted that the context of validity has dynamic features as well. These factors lead to the need for re-testing also of those older parts of the knowledge structure that were tested previously, not only those that have newly developed.

In order to perform this testing adequately, we have to pay constant attention to the following factors:

1. the factors that act as the agents of change;
2. the factors that have a stabilising effect;
3. the factors that influence and change the context of validity of knowledge;
4. the relative importance of individual contributing factors.

Also the scope of the applicability of the methodology used in a particular research process has to be carefully documented. If this is not done, a particular methodology might be applied unintentionally outside the context of its validity, with consequent ensuing distortion of the outcome of its application.

18.6.2. Uses of the Basic Knowledge Within the Context of Knowledge Engineering

In the previous section we briefly outlined the regulating mechanism and the dynamics of the process by which the correctness of the basic scientific knowledge is maintained. In this section, we shall examine reasons, some producers-owners of knowledge-based systems may have for withdrawing the basic knowledge from the open circulation.

There are at least two distinct ways in which the basic scientific knowledge directly interacts with the purpose-oriented knowledge used in the construction of knowledge-based systems.

Firstly, the basic knowledge may provide theoretical support for some purpose-oriented knowledge domains. The attempts to keep that basic knowledge confidential would be made in this case in order to prevent competitors from developing further the essential purpose-oriented knowledge. That might happen as the result of the insight provided by the basic theoretical support.

Secondly, the supporting basic knowledge may be used directly in forming some purpose-oriented knowledge which is inbuilt into the artifact itself. The supporting basic knowledge in this case *legitimises* the production of the artifact. The basic knowledge which is used this way might be openly questioned and in some instances proved to be deficient. This situation may, viewed from the point of view of the producer of the artifact, endanger the legitimisation of the artifact, and the artifact may become also deficient as the consequence.

Producers may therefore have a strong tendency, either to stop the criticism of the basic support knowledge, or to make this basic knowledge confidential. It is obvious from the argument of the previous section that in both instances this may lead to a significant impairment of the mechanism for preserving the correctness of knowledge that is available to an open society.

What has been described above we shall call the inner factors of impairment. These are formulated in terms of the epistemology of knowledge, exemplifying what can go wrong. To answer the question *as to how* this may happen, we may have to look at the economic or social factors. We shall call these *external* factors.

For example, one of these external factors might be the *marketing strategy* of a big firm. In these terms, anything that leads to the criticism of the basic knowledge that legitimises the big investments in purpose-oriented knowledge fields may be interpreted by such a firm as endangering its marketing strategy. This may be the case unless the decreased quality of the knowledge inbuilt in the marketed artifact endangers the viability of the artifact itself, so that at the end nothing remains to be marketed.

18.6.3. Consequences of the Withdrawal of Purpose-Oriented Knowledge

Withdrawal of purpose-oriented knowledge has two different kinds of consequences which should be clearly distinguished. It has significant impact

KNOWLEDGE-BASED SYSTEMS FOR MULTIPLE ENVIRONMENTS

1. on the quality of the knowledge-based systems, and
2. on the quality of basic knowledge.

We shall deal with the latter only, as it is the main objective of this chapter.

In order to explain what seems to be a paradox, namely, that the withdrawal of purpose-oriented knowledge may influence the quality of the basic knowledge, the evolutionary dynamics of the interaction of empirical facts with basic scientific theories will be briefly touched upon, for the creation of a new further reaching theory requires certain special conditions to be fulfilled. Also certain ranges of empirical experience have to be available to those involved in this process. The juxtaposition of the empirical evidence into a new framework, in a new and perhaps unusual context, may originate a significant breakthrough in the advancement of the knowledge available to the workers in a particular scientific field, hence this new construct is deemed a "new, significant, far reaching,..." etc., scientific theory.

It may be argued that such an advance can be made not only by those who are operating in an open scientific community, but also by those who are privileged to possess the confidential information concerning the knowledge-based system that generated *the new significant empirical evidence* necessary for a new breakthrough and witnessed its **emergence**. This secretly kept empirical evidence, however, might be only a necessary, but not the sufficient condition for such a new breakthrough. Those in its secret posession might not be capable, or competent enough, to make that basic breakthrough.

We learn from the history of science that in the long run an interaction of many new concepts is required; that is significantly different from the one that can appear in a closed environment, operating without broad enough and deep enough tests. In a closed environment without critical interaction with other environments and contexts, scientific knowledge usually degenerates, or its reliability strongly decreases.

Let us take a specific example, in order to demonstrate how a new, "further reaching" theory is created by the juxtaposition of a new context to the new empirical facts. Consider the famous Michelson experiment concerning the measurement of the velocity of light. Without certain basic assumptions that Einstein conjectured before he had became familiar with the Michelson experiment, the theory of relativity would not have been developed that time. This presupposition of Einstein, however, was not available to Michelson. On the other hand, without the result of the Michelson experiment Einstein would had not possessed the crucial empirical fact which was so essential for validating his theory. Some may argue that Einstein would have had to arrange the experiment himself, but this might or might not have been the case.

We can conclude that when a knowledge-based system which interacts with the environment is used, the new empirical data essential for the further advancement of the basic scientific theories and knowledge may emerge. This *emergence*, however, is possible only if we can interpret correctly the empirical data on which this phenomenon is based. To provide for a correct interpretation in an appropriate context, it is necessary to know the conditions and theoretical assumptions under which the empirical knowledge has been acquired. If the inner contents (i.e. the Domain-Dependent Knowledge Structure of the knowledge-based system, cf. Chapter 5 of this volume) are not publicly available in such a situation, the above emergence cannot occur. To make the Domain-Dependent Knowledge Structure available publicly may not always be possible, but what is essential here is the extent to which the total amount of knowledge available to mankind is stored by means of "Advanced Information Technology" under the condition of restricted availability and with restricted circulation. If it is an insignificant proportion, retardartion of new theories may or may not occur. If, however, the situation that most of the new empirical knowledge is generated and stored under these conditions prevails, the outcome may be different.

This might be the case if the number of knowledge-based systems with confidential knowledge structures participating in generating this new evidence were significant in proportion. This would have far-reaching effects not only on the further advancement of the scientific knowledge but also on the objectivity of any abstract knowledge reflecting our place in the universe. Thus this may become significant and shatteringly disastrous. Let us hope that it may never happen but be aware of this slowly emerging possibility. Free availability of knowledge, the possibility of its public scrutiny and of its criticism in an **informed open discussion**, are essential to prevent the full emergence of such a possibility.

18.7. KNOWLEDGE STRUCTURES WITHIN THE CONTEXT OF A CULTURE

18.7.1. Interactions of Distinct Contexts and the Loss of Correctness of Knowledge Structures

Every theory capturing a particular field of human knowledge is interpreted within a particular broad, albeit specific cultural context. Hence the cultural aspects that would "make or break" the conceptual validity of particular interpretation of a knowledge structure cannot be brushed aside. From the previous discussion it follows that by preventing interaction and regulatory feedback between the individual parts of a knowledge structure capturing basic or directed knowledge one might invalidate the structure in question.

This loss of correctness of a knowledge structure may be caused either

(a) by evolutionary changes of the real world system which is modelled by this structure, or

(b) by the changes of the modelled knowledge structure or some of the related knowledge structures, or of the context of their interpretation.

To understand what undesirable effect the dynamic changes of the involved structures may have, we shall look at the aspect of modelling in the greater depth. A particular knowledge structure, including structure capturing a "portion" of basic knowledge is a model depicting some aspects of the real-world situation. As such, this model captures just the relevant aspects, leaving the irrelevant ones aside.

If the real world exhibits some evolutionary dynamics, those attributes that are depicted by a particular "basic knowledge" structure may change as well, rendering the previous model incorrect, thus generating the demand for its updating.

On the human time-scale, the evolutionary dynamics pertain to the biological and social attributes of a real world system. The basic knowledge structures which utilise these attributes therefore require continuous revision.

A basic knowledge structure, say A, related to a particular knowledge based system or a family of systems, is only a part of a bigger "distributed" structure consisting of other parts, say B,C,D,... etc. This distributed structure captures a whole field of knowledge which has many interacting knowledge domains. If some parts of this collection, say C, D, evolve, the new elements of each of C, D may interact with other structures, necessitating some kind of revision of these other structures. If the structure A is isolated from this interaction, *inconsistencies* may arise, which *invalidate joint use* of any of the parts of the collection.

Each owner of a knowledge structure that is withdrawn from the public domain is inevitably a participant in a common cultural domain. Within this domain his "private" knowledge structure exists, and within the same domain this owner participates whether he likes it or not.

If the regulatory interaction of the type discussed in the preceding sections is prevented, each structure of the knowledge domain would develop in isolation. Each participant (owner) would consequently develop his/her own peculiar internal standpoint. The scenario outlined by Rosen in the context of his discussion of "Complexity and error in social dynamics" gives a lucid characterisation of such a situation:

> *The members of the culture will, from the internal standpoint, make their own models..., and that the more differentiated the culture is, the more differentiated these internal models will be from each other.*
>
> Rosen (1975, p.147)

The consequences of this differentiation of internal models are also outlined by Rosen in the same paper. He describes the situation in which the conditions change, under which a culture operates, outlining the inadequacy of the individual internal models in coping with these changes:

> *We can see...how inadequate the internal models of the culture can be in deciding the erroneousness of cultural responses to external stress. The converse is also true... namely a particular cultural behaviour can look erroneous to all of the members of the culture on the basis of their own internal models, but that behaviour can be perfectly appropriate from the standpoint of an external observer.*
>
> Rosen (1975, p. 147)

18.7.2. Dynamic Evolution of Knowledge Structures and the Change of their Meaning

Rosen's theory of internal models adumbrated in the previous section deals with the *statics* of interpretation and meaning of knowledge structures, the view that linguists would call synchronic. This could deal adequately only with the distortions of meaning of knowledge structures caused by different internal partial models of the situation, that are owned synchronously by different participants. The concurrently contributing factors forcing the distortion are:
1. Partiality of the knowledge structures, at time t_i, of each participant-owner.
2. Dynamic changes of the knowledge domain not captured adequately. This is because the boundaries of relevance of each partial knowledge structure (i.e. internal models of participants) are not redrawn adequately, and therefore the shifts of the meaning or context due to the dynamic changes are not attended to.

In order to capture adequately the shifts of meaning and context that are required for redrawing the boundaries of relevance of the concepts of the knowledge structures changing with time, attention has to be paid to the **historicity** of knowledge. This involves diachronic knowledge structures as well as the dynamics of their history (cf. Masaryk, 1885, 1969). According to Masaryk, a distinction has to be made between a **metadescription** of a particular knowledge field (including its ontological and epistemological aspects), and the **object description** of the facts of the field. The former he calls "the philosophy" of a particular knowledge field.

Important observations concerning evaluation and interpretation of the knowledge of the field of history is pertinent to diachronic (i.e. historical) evaluation of the knowledge of any field.

> *The difference between the philosophy of history and concrete history is precisely that in the latter we deal with concrete historical events while in the former we are looking at the meaning of these events...On one side there is a description of facts, on the other side there is an attempt at understanding their meaning.*
> Masaryk (1932), quoted from Čapek and Hrubý (1981, p. 272)

Understanding this meaning is however more complicated and problematic, if the user of the knowledge belongs to a different time period than the original knowledge structure that is being interpreted.

> *... such a theory of historical 'detachment' is incorrect. The historian* de facto *evaluates the past in the light of the present; the present is nothing but a less remote past and both cannot be separated from each other.*
> Masaryk (1932), quoted from Čapek and Hrubý (1981, p. 275).

This clearly applies also to our diachronic - historical interpretation of the knowledge structures used in the context of knowledge-based systems. With the only difference that a "fossilised" knowledge of the past, which has not been revised adequately due to its removal from the public domain is being interpreted in the present context of the whole public domain, at any instant when it is used. But such an interpretation may be incorrect, owing to historical discrepancy caused by the isolation of the structure caused by the attempts to enforce confidentiality.

18.8. CONCLUSION: THE NEED FOR TECHNOLOGICAL ARTEFACTS CAPABLE OF ADAPTING TO THE DYNAMIC CHANGES OF THE ENVIRONMENT

We have argued that isolating some components of knowledge from the mainstream of the continuously evolving public domain knowledge can lead to retardation and degeneration of both the public and private knowledge sources. Ignoring the dynamic changes of the knowledge shared by mankind and ignoring the changes of its interpretation which capture the historicity of the evolvement of the human culture may lead to the deterioration of the basic knowledge. The other side of this coin, namely, the consequences of the application of knowledge and of the use of technological artefacts in order to support this application should not be ignored either. To take this properly into account necessitates continuous matching of the dynamic changes of the cultural environment to appropriate changes of the knowledge engineering structures. This is called maintenance in computing terminology. To maintain big commercial conventional software packages is a perennial and costly problem. This may be even a bigger problem where large and complex knowledge structures are involved.

The maintenance should at least consist of updating and revising the knowledge bases contained in expert and knowledge-based systems currently in use. This, of course, must be matched by the revision and maintenance of the other parts of the knowledge-based systems, in order to prevent the mismatch of these other parts with the knowledge bases. It is possible that the rate of change in each environment and context may be different. On the one hand this points to the difficulties of maintaining adequately a multi-environmental system. Pretending that this problem does not exist however does not help the situation. Using a system designed rigidly for a single environment in a multi-environmental or multi-context situation would be even more dangerous, as it would also hide the proper formulation or even identification of the existence of this problem.

From the above argument we can conclude that the structure of the knowledge bases and of the knowledge-based systems has to adapt continuously to the environments in which these are used. In order to do this effectively, we need a methodological framework that would contain

1. a framework for dealing with adaptivity of behaviour of systems;
2. a framework that can link the changes of the behaviour of systems to the changes in the structures capturing the description of their functions (so called functional structures);
3. a framework that can link the behaviour and the functional structures of systems to their hardware (i.e. substratum) structures.

A suitable theoretical framework for (1) above is provided by theory of adaptive behaviour of Gaines (1969, 1972). The framework that can deal with (2) and (3) above is provided by the Activity Structures methodology developed by Kohout (1990, 1987, and Chapter 5 of this volume). The first steps in combining these were taken by Zofia Roberts (1991), in order to design Activity Structures based architectures of "active expert systems with intelligent control."

In this volume, various authors provide the foundations for, and applications of, a new generation of knowledge-based systems. We would like to remind them that in order to preserve and strengthen the "human face" of our world, "Information technology" based artefacts have to be incorporated into the world of human-based activities and decision making carefully and with due caution. The Dreyfus brothers point out a very realistic danger that a commercial firm or a government may face, if they place an excessive reliance on uncritically used expert or knowledge-based systems:

> *To the extent that junior employees using expert systems come to see expertise as a function of large knowledge bases and masses of inferential rules, they will fail to progress beyond the competent level of their machines. With leap beyond competence to proficiency and expertise thus inhibited, investors in expert systems may ultimately discover that their wells of true human expertise and wisdom have gone dry.*
>
> (Dreyfus and Dreyfus, 1986, p.121).

In addition to the issue of the quality of expertise, elaborated in some detail in Dreyfus (1986), we can point out another equally pertinent one. That is the question of interpretability of linguistic statements and descriptions. When making personal, implicit knowledge communicable while using natural language, only part of it can be transformed; when leaving the natural language context, in order to computerize this knowledge the inherent properties of natural language are lost – at least its multivalence within a given text and the historically established path of meaning. These processes – obvious to those working within these transofrmation-interpretation procedures – might not be readily and easily accessible to those *just using the outcome*. But, when knowledge is to be applied in a concrete human context, this very nature and history of knowledge has to be taken into account to use it properly. Being able to retrace this path of knowledge development and abstraction allows for shared understanding and mutual trust and might be a fundamental feedback process between eliciting and applying knowledge.

18.9. REFERENCES

Čapek, K. (1935):
Hovory s T. G. Masarykem. Vol. **3**. Borový Publ., Prague.

Čapek, K. (1938):
Masaryk on Thought and Life, Conversations with Karel Čapek. Allen & Unwin Publ., London, 1938.

Čapek, M. and Hrubý, K. eds., (1981):
T. G. Masaryk in Perspective, Comments and Criticism. (ISBN 0-936570-04-0). SVU Press, (Czechoslovak Society of Arts and Sciences Inc.), Washigton, D.C.

Dreyfus, H. L. and Dreyfus, S. E. (1986):
Mind over Machine, Basil Blackwell, Oxford.

Gaines, B. R. (1969):
Adaptive control theory. In: Meetham, A R. (ed.) *Encyclopaedia of Linguistics, Information and Control.* Pergamon Press: Oxford.

Gaines, B. R, (1972):
Axioms of adaptive behaviour. *Internat. J. of Man-Machine Studies*, vol. **4**, 169-199.

Kohout, L. J. (1975):
Representation of functional hierarchies of movement in the brain. *Internat. J. of Man-Machine Studies*, vol. **8**, 699-709.

Kohout, L. J. and Bandler, W. (1986):
Knowledge representation, clinical action and expert systems. In: Kohout, L. J. and Bandler, W. (eds.), *Knowledge Representation in Medicine and Clinical Behavioural Science*, Abcus Press: Cambridge, Mass., U.S.A. and Tunbridge Wells, U.K.

Kohout, L. J. (1987):
Activity structures: a general systems construct for design of technological artifacts, *Cybernetics and Systems. An International Journal*, vol. **18**, 1–8.

Kohout, L. J. (1990):
A Perspective on Intelligent Systems: A Framework for Analysis and Design. Chapman and Hall, London and Van Nostrand Reinhold International, New York.

Kovtun, G. J. ed., (1981):
T.G. Masaryk 1850–1937. A Selective List of Readings in English. U.S. Library of Congress (European Division), Washington D.C. (Libr. of Congress Card Catal. No. 80-600139).

Masaryk, T. G. (1885):
Základové Konkrétné Logiky, Bursík & Kohout Publ., Prague. German edition Versuch einer concreten Logik, Konegen, Wien, 1887. Reprinted 1969. English translation in preparation.

Masryk, T.G. (1932):
On the periodization of Czech history (In Czech, under the initial Č.P.). *Česká Mysl*, 1932, Spring issue. English translation in Čapek and Hrubý (1981) 262–275.

Prigogine, I. (1980):
From Being to Becoming. Time and complexity in physical sciences, W. H. Freeman, San Francisco.

Roberts, Z. A. (1991):
The Functional Structure of Control in Expert Systems, Gordon and Breach, London, in press.

Rosen, R. (1975): Complexity and error in social dynamics, *Internat. J. of General Systems*, **2**, 145–148.

SUBJECT INDEX

Acceptability: 11, 364
Action(s): 59, 84, 183, 248
Activity: 25, 48, 68, 78, 84, 93, 127, 177, 179, 181, 206, 207, 231, 248, 344
 undesirable: 62
Activity Structures (AS): 7, 12, 54, 72, 73, 199, 101, 166, 175, 179, 183, 195, 208–210, 215, 222, 328, 343, 350, 353
 Constraint Structures (CS):
  Environment-IPM interface and interaction constraint (CEM): 60
  Protection Constraints (CP): 60, 71
  Technology-Dependent Implementation Constraints (CT): 60, 71
 Environment Activity Structure (EAS): 56, 57, 66, 72, 179–185, 191, 231, 233, 339
 Information Handling Structures (IHS): 55, 57, 67, 191, 231, 344
  Control Structure (IHC): 60, 71
  Domain-of-Expertise-Dependent Knowledge Structure (IHD): 60, 71, 231, 233
  Inferential structure (IHI): 60, 71, 194, 231, 233
 Information Processing Machine Activity Structure (IPM-AS): 63, 66, 180
 Knowledge Elicitation AS see Knowledge:
Adaptive: 228, 234, 247
Adaptivity: 374
Admissibility: 240, 365
Agreement: 69
Aim: 232
Algorithm: 59
Alpha-cuts: 289–329
Analysis: 145
Architecture: 7, 55, 175, 177, 221, 222, 233, 267, 335, 336, 338
Argument: 124, 127, 132, 134, 137–139, 148, 150, 152, 160
Artificial Intelligence: 3, 8, 158, 174
Awareness: 247–248

Banking: 49
Behaviour: 12, 77, 232, 259, 343, 352, 372, 374

Blackboard: 216, 217
Brain: 234, 236, 247
Business: 48, 49, 92, 94, 168, 267

CLINAID: 39, 173–198, 215–224
Clinical record: 178
Communication: 24, 68, 69, 93, 97, 114, 178, 205, 211, 220, 352
Computer:
 aided: 7
 manufacturing: 7
Computing: 195
Concepts: 96, 107
Concurrency: 79, 113, 215–224, 233, 352
Constraint see also Structures: 25, 338
Construction: 56, 59
Constructs:
 general system: 31, 36, 82, 238
Context: 4, 7, 8, 9, 46, 73, 94, 96, 167, 168, 192–195, 197, 211, 228, 249, 281, 361, 368
Control: 231
Conversation: 69
Correctness: 190, 240, 365, 367, 369, 371
Culture: 8, 22, 24, 31, 42, 275, 372, 374

Decision:
 -making: 8, 9, 124, 126, 143, 155, 161, 165, 174, 175, 181
Deontic: 147
Design: 63, 124, 125, 127, 132, 145, 152, 155, 159, 169, 179, 190, 281, 338, 343, 353
 house: 267, 268
 process: 146
Developing country: 17
Diagnosis: 3, 9, 27, 40, 43, 100, 112, 114, 175, 179, 181, 187–196, 206, 207, 236
Diagnostic: 222, 238
Disease: 4, 8, 18, 43, 107, 109, 113, 114, 117, 177, 190, 196, 206, 223, 281–329
Dynamic: 55, 74, 96, 191, 229, 234, 237, 247, 368
Dynamics (of): 197, 231, 361, 373
 actions/activities: 62, 83
 behaviour: 179

Elements: 59, 109, 117, 118, 127
Entities: 81

379

KNOWLEDGE-BASED SYSTEMS FOR MULTIPLE ENVIRONMENTS

Environment see also Structures,
Environmental Activity (EAS): 56, 57, 72, 179–185
Equilibrium: 361, 363
Evaluation procedures: 125, 145, 148
Experiment: 254
Expert systems: 3, 4, 8, 9, 10, 13, 17, 18, 20, 21, 25, 34, 41, 46–48, 50, 70, 76, 92, 96, 99, 102, 107, 118, 169, 174, 203, 211, 239, 249, 277, 360, 365, 366, 375

Faithfulness: 239, 365
Finance: 92, 167, 170, 267
Form: 275
Formalisation: 95, 98, 101, 112, 166, 198
Function: 7, 42, 84, 159, 178
  (teleological): 7
Functional structure see Structure: 7, 58, 71, 80, 191
Functional: 12
  constraint: 56
  Fuzzy: 13, 27, 35, 99, 125, 178, 191, 194, 198, 205, 229, 281–329, 343

Goal: 109, 239, 248

Hardware: 67, 253, 257, 337, 338, 375
Hasse diagrams: 290–329
Hyper-processes (see Process): 184

Identification: 7, 74, 78, 232, 248, 270, 343
Implication operators: 296, 320
Inconsistencies: 372
Industry: 94
Inference: 192, 204
Information processing see Machine, Information Processing:
Insurance: 5, 165, 167
Interaction: 62, 81, 101, 117, 372

Knowledge: 4, 9, 13, 32, 44, 49, 83, 93, 96, 109, 113, 117, 158, 165, 179, 190, 195, 207, 231, 237, 245, 247, 284, 357, 360, 365, 366, 368, 373
  base: 96, 158, 177
  elicitation: 10, 67, 68, 72, 74, 92, 94, 97, 105, 106, 108, 112, 114, 117, 118, 166, 167, 168, 337, 365

engineering: 8, 33, 55, 92, 102, 105, 107, 165, 166, 369
identification: 72
purpose oriented: 366, 370
representation: 68, 72, 181
sources: 216, 360
Knowledge-based system (KBS): 4, 5, 7, 10, 11, 67–71, 106, 178, 192, 205, 211, 228, 234, 236, 238, 239, 338, 357, 360, 361, 364, 370, 374

Learning: 97, 247
Locality: 192
Logic(s): 81, 94, 101, 134, 138, 140, 170, 224, 229, 239, 269, 290, 343, 346

Machine:
  Information Processing (IPM): 32, 55, 57, 60, 62, 68, 72, 79, 179, 180, 183, 186, 222, 336, 337
  virtual: 75, 76, 229, 238
Maintainability: 239, 365
Manufacturing, computer-aided (CAM): 7, 227–239
Market: 361, 362, 363, 369
Measurement probes: 352
Medical/medicine: 3, 4, 8, 11, 13, 17, 18, 20, 21, 24, 25, 40–42, 44, 47, 50, 55, 62, 92, 94, 96, 113, 118, 174, 183, 191, 197, 263, 284, 360
Model: 48, 101, 336, 346, 352, 372
Movement:
  human: 247
Multi-centre: 76
see also Control:
Multi-context: 338
Multi-environment: 18, 20, 21, 23, 25, 46, 80, 255, 275,
Multi-environmental: 5, 67, 165, 192, 208, 231, 234, 246, 249, 257, 267, 268, 335, 336, 353

Object: 59, 81, 83

Parallel: 195, 218
Participants: 24, 25, 27, 59, 239, 372
see also Acceptor, Object, Subject:
Patient record: 112, 220
Performance: 107, 204, 238, 248, 347, 362

Subject Index

Planning: 124, 155, 197, 198, 237
Plausibility: 153
Political: 123, 125, 126, 276
Possibilistic: 246, 335, 341, 344, 345, 347, 349
Probability: 125, 194
Process: 73, 113, 123, 127, 132
  hyper-process: 184
Prognosis: 43, 196
Programming:
  parallel: 218
Properties: 59, 81
Protectability: 11
Protection: 12, 46, 50, 62, 94, 99, 101, 102, 106 191, 233
  dynamic: 233
  constraints: 193
Protocols: 220
Purpose: 55, 78, 233

Question(s): 143, 166, 184, 204–206, 208, 211
Questioning: 118, 168, 193, 203, 204, 205, 211

Receiver: 59
Relation: 55, 134, 236
  Fuzzy: 13, 27, 35, 99, 125, 178, 191, 194, 198, 205, 229, 281–329, 343
Relational products: 13, 281–329
  triangle: 191, 194
Relevance: 59, 60, 204, 211, 216, 239, 249, 260, 275
Reliability: 11, 102
Review process: 196
Robot: 228, 237, 246, 249
Robotics: 5, 7, 58, 247

Semantic descriptor: 191, 195, 198
Semiotic(s): 74
Sender: 59
Sign: 8, 18, 107, 109, 117, 177, 187, 190, 192, 206, 208, 211, 228, 281–329
Simulator: 337, 341, 345, 347, 349
Software: 344
Statistics: 155
Stochastic: 345
Strategy: 108, 168, 193, 203, 211, 369
Structure(s): 7, 43, 110

AIM Environmental Activity Structure (AEAS): 56, 57, 66, 72, 183, 191, 193, 233
  aspatial: 271
  constraint: 55, 60, 339
  distributed: 343
  environmental activity (EAS) see Activity
  Structures: 56, 57, 66, 72, 180–185, 191, 231, 23, 339
  functional (FS): 58, 71, 809, 191, 224, 328, 346, 375
  functional activity (FAS): 7, 56, 57, 66, 72, 179, 180, 191, 194, 235, 272, 336, 337, 339, 344
  Functional Environmental Activity Structure (FEAS): 58, 66, 179, 180, 191, 228, 233, 234, 336, 337
  Information Handling (IHS): 55, 57, 67, 191, 231, 344
  Information Handling Control (IHC): 60, 71
  Information Handling Domain (IHD): 60, 71, 231, 233
  Information Handling Inferential (IHI): 60, 71, 193, 231, 233
  potentiality: 67
  substratum (SUB): 7, 12, 56–58, 66, 70, 72, 77, 79, 179, 180, 183, 184, 194, 195, 222, 224, 237, 238, 249, 328, 336, 337, 339, 341, 346, 350
SUB see Structures – substratum:
Subject: 81, 84
Substratum structures (SUB) see Structures – substratum:
Symbol: 277
Symptom: 8, 18, 24, 25, 107, 109, 112, 113, 117, 177, 187, 190, 193, 206, 208, 217, 221, 223, 281, 329
Syndrome: 113, 187, 206, 207, 208, 211, 223
Synergies: 239

Task: 3
  descriptor: 78, 232
Teleological: 58, 63, 74, 84, 179, 239, 248, 272
Therapy: 196
Treatment: 178, 223

Knowledge-Based Systems for Multiple Environments

TRISYS: 289–296

Users: 211, 338, 346

Validation: 108, 275, 347
Verification: 281–329

Virtual - see Machines, virtual: 75, 76, 229, 238
Voting: 126, 143, 155

Whiteboard: 216